One Day Too Long

One Day Too Long

TOP SECRET SITE 85
AND THE BOMBING OF NORTH VIETNAM

Timothy N. Castle

COLUMBIA UNIVERSITY PRESS

NEW YORK

Columbia University Press
Publishers Since 1893
New York   Chichester, West Sussex
Copyright © 1999 Columbia University Press

Library of Congress Cataloging-in-Publication Data
Castle, Timothy N. (Timothy Neil)
One day too long : top secret site 85 and the bombing of
North Vietnam / Timothy N. Castle.
p.   cm.
Includes bibliographical references (p. 333) and index.
ISBN 978-0-231-10316-9 (cloth : alk. paper)—ISBN 978-0-231-10317-6 (pbk. : alk. paper)
1. Vietnamese Conflict, 1961–1975—Laos.
2. Vietnamese Conflict, 1961–1975—Secret service—United States.
3. Vietnamese Conflict, 1961–1975—Aerial operations, American.
4. United States. Central Intelligence Agency. I. Title.
DS559.73.L28C37   1999
959.704'348—dc21   98–43117
                                              CIP

Casebound editions of Columbia University Press books are
printed on permanent and durable acid-free paper.
Printed in the United States of America
c 10 9 8 7 6 5 4 3 2 1
p 10 9 8 7 6 5 4 3

For the men of Project Heavy Green
and the families of those who did not return from Site 85

CONTENTS

ACKNOWLEDGMENTS

The 1968 catastrophe on the cliffs of Pha Thi mountain in northeastern Laos remains an especially agonizing event for many families and
participants who, despite three decades of U.S. government obfuscation, continue to hope for a complete and truthful explanation of the
losses at Site 85. Much of this book is about their lives and, as the notes
and bibliography convey, many have shared their recollections with
me. Although my questions probed matters long past and often highly
sensitive, nearly all were very kind and helpful. Although Ann Holland
would have you believe that she is not special among the waiting family members, this book could not have been written without her assistance. Indeed, if not for her extraordinary inner strength and indefati-
gable determination, this entire incident might well have remained
hidden in classified government documents. One must respect and
admire her commitment to a man who loved his family and his country. Colonel Jerry Clayton has lived every day with the horror of the
communist assault on Site 85 on March 11, 1968; as we walked among
the ruins of the site in 1994, I hoped the visit would bring him to closure. He has been an invaluable source and his dedication to a thorough examination, no matter the personal consequences, has allowed
me to write a full account of the events at Site 85. While this book cannot bring peace to Ann Holland or Jerry Clayton, I hope it has done
justice to their sacrifices.

Colleagues in academia, government, and the private sector have
also been very generous, often providing otherwise unavailable insights
and material. The thoughtful suggestions of Robert Schulzinger, John

Prados, and Joe Guilmartin have been especially valuable. Richard Immerman has been a longstanding and unsurpassed source of encouragement and support. It is my great fortune to be a part of the Immerman circle. Kate Wittenberg, my editor at Columbia University Press, accepted delays with good humor and always provided valuable guidance. For much appreciated help at various points along the way, I must thank Leslie Bialler, Joe Caver, Mark Clodfelter, Howard Freeman, Warren Gray, Ann Mills Griffiths, Mary Hall, Joe Harvey, Budd Jones, Tony Litvinas, Tom McKay, Dave Rosenau, Deth Soulatha, Woody Spence, Geoff Stephens, William Sullivan, JoAnne Travis, and Jay Veith. A special debt is owed to George Scearce and Richard Arant, who have taught me a great deal about honor. I am, of course, responsible for any errors and the views expressed herein are mine alone and do not necessarily represent the views of Air University, the Department of the Air Force, or the Department of Defense.

It is difficult to adequately express my appreciation to a number of very special anchors in my life. Michael Elliott is the consummate soldier-scholar and, for nearly thirty years, I have profited from his keen insights and sage advice. My father also answered our country's call and served several dangerous tours in Vietnam, all the while completely confident my mother would skillfully deal with the myriad issues she faced in raising four children. Because I have experienced the dedication and strength of Will and Eunice Castle I am better able to understand the Hollands' courage.

Since beginning this book four years ago I have moved from an academic position in a civilian institution to government service as an analyst and researcher, and then to a senior academic position at the U.S. Air Force Air University. Whether working in Southeast Asia or closeted in my home office with books and notes, I have spent far too little time with my family. At one point my daughter Jamie even resorted to placing screen saver messages on my computer—strongly suggesting an end to my writing. In my absence, Parinya, whose patience as partner and wife has endured over twenty-six years, has managed to hold everything together. My karma has been very good.

TIMOTHY N. CASTLE
September 1998

LIST OF ABBREVIATIONS AND TERMS

AMEMBASSY: American Embassy

A1E/H: U.S. propellor aircraft used for rescue, strike, and special operations missions

AN-2 Colt: Soviet-built, propeller biplane used by the North Vietnamese to attack Site 85

BARREL ROLL: Code name for U.S. bombing operations in northern Laos

CEVG: Combat Evaluation Group

CHECO: Contemporary Historical Evaluation of Combat Operations; later modified to Contemporary Historical Examination of Current Operations. Reports written under this U.S. Air Force program have provided unique information on American activities in Southeast Asia

CINCPAC: Commander in Chief, Pacific

CINCPACAF: Commander in Chief, Pacific Air Forces

CINCPACFLT: Commander in Chief, Pacific Fleet

COMBAT SKYSPOT: Code name for ground-directed radar bombing operations. The majority of these missions were flown by B-52 aircraft. Missions controlled from Site 85 involved F-105 aircraft. Two earlier nicknames were "Skyspot" and "Combat Proof"

COMMANDO CLUB: Code name for air strikes flown under the control of the radar equipment at Site 85

COMUSMACV: Commander, United States Military Assistance Command Vietnam

CORONA HARVEST: A program established by the Chief of Staff of the Air Force in mid-1968 to evaluate the effectiveness of American air power in Southeast Asia

DAC CONG: North Vietnamese special forces, also known as sappers

DAO: Defense Attaché Office

DCM: Deputy Chief of Mission

DDRS: Declassified Documents Reference System

DIA: Defense Intelligence Agency

DPMO: Defense Prisoner of War/Missing in Action Office

FAR: Forces Armées du Royaume (Royal Lao Army)

FIREFLY: Nickname for A1E/H aircraft involved in strike missions

FOIA: Freedom of Information Act

HEAVY GREEN: Code name for the top secret program established in Laos to allow U.S. Air Force personnel to covertly operate a ground-directed radar system from Site 85. Tactical air navigation (TACAN) operations in Laos were also placed under this program

HUEY: Nickname for UH-1 helicopter

HMONG: Highland peoples living throughout southern China and mainland Southeast Asia. During the war in Laos Hmong clans loyal to General Vang Pao became the basis for the CIA-directed secret army in Laos

JANAF: Joint Army-Navy-Air Force

JCRC: Joint Casualty Resolution Center. Established in January 1973 under the command of CINCPAC. JCRC was assimilated into JTF-FA in January 1992

JCS: Joint Chiefs of Staff

JTF-FA: Joint Task Force-Fullest Accounting. Established in January 1992 under the command of CINCPAC

LADC: Local Area Defense Commander

LIMA SITE: Air America designation for aircraft landing sites in Laos

MIA: Missing in Action

MR II: Military Region Two, as designated by the Royal Lao government. Located in the northeastern province of Houa Phan along the border with North Vietnam

MSQ-77: Technical designation for ground-directed radar bombing systems established in South Vietnam and Thailand. The success of the MSQ-77 operations prompted the development of Project Heavy Green

PACAF: Pacific Air Forces

PACFLT: Pacific Fleet

PARU: Police Aerial Resupply Unit. These Thai teams were trained by the CIA and served at Site 85

PAVN: People's Army of Vietnam

PC6: Pilatus Porter. Small fixed wing, STOL aircraft used by Air America

PHA THI: The Lao name for the mountain in northeastern Laos where the U.S. Air Force established a ground-directed radar bombing system

POW: Prisoner of War

RCC: Rescue Coordination Center

ROLLING THUNDER: Code name for U.S. bombing operations against North Vietnam, begun in March 1965

RPs: Route Packages. Under Rolling Thunder, the U.S. divided North Vietnam into various operations areas called Route Packages

SANDY: Nickname for A1E/H aircraft involved in rescue missions

SAC: Strategic Air Command

SECSTATE: Secretary of State

SITE 85: The code name for the location, in northeastern Laos, of the TSQ-81 ground-directed radar bombing system

7TH AIR FORCE: Headquarters for U.S. Air Force operations in Vietnam

7/13TH AIR FORCE: Headquarters for U.S. Air Force operations in Thailand and Laos

STEEL TIGER: Code name for U.S. bombing operations in southern Laos

STOL: Short Take-Off and Landing aircraft. See PC6

TACAN: Tactical Air Navigation. In late 1967 responsibility for the maintenance and operation of the Lao-based TACANs was placed under Heavy Green

TACC: Tactical Air Control Center

TSD: Technical Services Division of CIA

TSQ-81: Technical designation for the air transportable ground-directed radar system placed at Site 85

USAID: United States Agency for International Development

VNOSMP: Vietnamese Missing Persons Office

One Day Too Long

NORTH VIETNAM

Phong Saly

Yen Bai

Phuc Yen

Thai Nguyen

Hanoi

Nam Bac

Site 85+ Sam Neua

Na Khang Vieng Sai

Luang Prabang

Xiengkhoang

Plain of Jars

Long Tieng

LAOS

Vientiane

Udorn

Nakhon
Phanom

Muang Phalane

Savannakhet

Tchepone

THAILAND

Saravane

Pakse

*Bolovens
Plateau*

0   100 NM

INTRODUCTION

In March 1994 I stood on the edge of the windswept western cliffs of Phou[1] Pha Thi, a 5,800-foot karst located a scant twelve nautical miles south of the Laotian-Vietnamese border. Taken aback by the breathtaking vista of lush emerald valleys and the soft pillows of white clouds that covered the region's lesser peaks, I tried to envision the intense military activity that had occurred at what during the Vietnam war had been a critical U.S. outpost—the home to project "Heavy Green," one of the Vietnam war's most highly classified programs. Now the rugged and unforgiving land was eerily peaceful, except for the indifferent bleating of a few goats.

Over the past twenty years, I have regularly encountered oral and written accounts of a top secret, American-operated facility in Laos called "Lima Site 85." Perched on the southwestern aspect of Phou Pha Thi, the base had two distinct missions. Since at least 1962 the CIA had operated an intelligence collection program in northeastern Laos, supported by a crude 600 by 50-foot runway scratched out along the mountain's southeastern flank. The small landing strip was part of a Laos-wide aerial supply system operated by Air America, Inc., a supposedly private airline contracted by the U.S. government.[2] Although U.S. operations were conducted near Pha Thi's summit, more than a mile from the runway, "LS 85" or "Site 85," became the common terms for the American base at Pha Thi mountain.[3]

LS 85's other major role, which began in late October 1967 and ended catastrophically in early March 1968, involved the top-secret operation of a U.S. Air Force radar system that provided the United States with a heretofore unavailable all-weather bombing capability in Laos and North Vietnam. In particular, the Site 85-based radar enabled the Heavy Green technicians[4] to direct F-105 fighter-bombers against important targets in and around the North Vietnamese capital of Hanoi—125 nautical miles to the east. The facility was controversial. The U.S. ambassador to Laos was opposed to it, while CIA experts warned that the North Vietnamese would quickly move to destroy the site. The Joint Chiefs of Staff, however, convinced the White House that the military gain outweighed the personnel and political risks.

Indeed, the increased American presence evoked an unprecedented response from the North Vietnamese. On January 12, 1968, Hanoi launched four lumbering Soviet-built AN-2 Colt biplanes against the site in a midday bombing attack. Two of the aircraft fired rockets and dropped modified mortar rounds near radar and navigational equipment before they were driven off and crashed, likely due to the hot pursuit of an Air America helicopter. Although one of the Heavy Green personnel was wounded and the tactical air navigation system was temporarily knocked off-line, the men stayed at their posts and the radar system remained in service. The North Vietnamese began almost immediately to bring heavy weapons and thousands of troops to bear on the vexing American base.

Nonetheless, confident they could monitor the enemy movements and provide adequate warning for a controlled evacuation and destruction of the site, U.S. Air Force officials continued and even expanded the radar operations at Site 85. In early 1968, faced with exceptionally poor flying conditions, radar often provided the only means by which Air Force bombers could reach their targets in North Vietnam. More importantly perhaps in terms of inflicting casualties and damage, the site was controlling hundreds of air strikes against People's Army of Vietnam and Pathet Lao forces in northeastern Laos. Ironically, although the men were told they would be attacking Hanoi only a handful of their missions were directed at key targets near the capital city. Nevertheless, senior 7th Air Force officers in Saigon believed Heavy Green was a unique capability and, notwithstanding numerous CIA reports of an impending attack, demanded the site be kept open.

Unbeknownst to the Americans, the North Vietnamese had also ordered a special sapper unit, called *Dac Cong*, into action.[5] On March 11, 1968, in a well planned and orchestrated attack supported by a heavy artillery, mortar, and rocket bombardment, the sappers climbed the southwestern face of the mountain and under cover of darkness overran the radar and navigational facility. Sixteen Heavy Green technicians bore the brunt of the attack while, some 200 yards below them to the east, the shelling forced two CIA case officers and a U.S. Air Force combat controller to remain in their bunkers. Hmong and Thai security forces, variously located around the mountaintop, failed to detect or deter the sappers.

Surveying the ruins of Site 85 in 1994, I thought of the men who had secretly served their country at this lonely and harsh mile-high base. Brave Americans who, despite the certain knowledge that they were surrounded by communist forces, continued for weeks to operate their radar and navigation equipment: dedicated men, who believed their efforts provided U.S. Air Force pilots a critical measure of safety during difficult and dangerous "Rolling Thunder" bombing missions; men skilled in electronics, not the use of combat arms, who suddenly found themselves the object of a deadly North Vietnamese assault.

The clever PAVN tactics silenced Heavy Green and exacted a terrible human toll—the largest single ground combat loss of U.S. Air Force personnel in the history of the Vietnam war. Despite a daring and hurried rescue operation carried out by U.S. Air Force and Air America helicopters, just four of the technicians, the combat controller, and the two CIA officers escaped the mountain. As for the others, eleven have never been found, and another was killed by enemy gunfire shortly after being pulled aboard a helicopter. Two of the eleven technicians are known to have been killed outright, but many unanswered questions cloud the fate of the remaining men.

For the man standing at my side, gazing off into the distance that was now the Socialist Republic of Vietnam, this mountaintop evoked especially painful memories. Now fast approaching his seventieth birthday, Retired Air Force Colonel Gerald H. ("Jerry") Clayton, had been the Heavy Green commander. From the command post at Udorn Royal Thai Air Base, he monitored the final hours of a program he had guided since its inception. Colonel Clayton had approved the selection of each man; he knew their families and their dreams.

Nearly twenty-six years later, almost to the day of the attack, Colonel Clayton and I were technical advisers to an NBC News team investigating the loss of Site 85. Accompanied by the first U.S. government investigators to ever reach the mountain, we were allowed to briefly walk around and film the site. Jerry led the Defense Intelligence Agency (DIA) investigator on a hurried tour, pointing out the former locations of buildings, equipment, and key geographic features. Ultimately, the rocky mountain gave up no firm evidence with which to resolve the fate of the missing men. The whereabouts of more than 150 tons of equipment was also unexplained. However, the lack of bomb craters and other indications that the site was not destroyed by U.S. aircraft and U.S.-directed artillery fire (as had been reported in official accounts) presented the possibility of new explanations as to the fate of the facility and its men.

Seeking additional facts we interviewed local villagers, Lao soldiers present in the area during the attack, and key provincial officials. We gained rare permission to visit the normally off-limits town of Vieng Sai near the Vietnam border and spent a day surveying and filming the extensive cave system that served as the wartime headquarters of the communist Pathet Lao government.[6] In the Laotian capital of Vientiane we pressed to view communist wartime films at the government film archives and discovered footage related to the Phou Pha Thi battle. Our search extended to Vietnam and, in a Hanoi military museum, we located an extraordinary mock-up and a detailed description of the January 1968 air attack on Site 85. In less than a month we had learned more about the final hours of Heavy Green, especially from the communist perspective, than had been uncovered by the U.S. government in the past quarter century.

On our last night in Hanoi, Jerry Clayton and I sat in his room at the Metropole Hotel and discussed in depth the genesis, operation, and aftermath of the Heavy Green program. I became convinced the true story of Site 85 needed to be told. In the nearly three decades since the facility was lost, not a single accurate account had emerged. A detailed U.S. Air Force monograph "The Fall of Site 85" (originally classified top secret and officially declassified in 1988) contains numerous errors.[7] Other official Air Force histories of the war, one published as late as 1993, are likewise flawed.[8] Various popular accounts of Site 85 have also appeared in books dealing with the American war in Laos, mostly using a mixture of the inaccurate Air Force accounts and the sometimes self-indulgent recollections of U.S. Air Force, Air America, CIA, and State Department participants.[9] In fairness, none of these authors had personal access to the site and the vast amount of information gained as a result of the March 1994 investigations at Phou Pha Thi, Vientiane, and Hanoi. Nevertheless, many of these earlier accounts have confused and sometimes enraged those family members who continue to seek answers to the fate of their loved ones.

And one must wonder, given the substantial information available on Site 85 to military and civilian authorities, why have some U.S. government representatives deliberately obfuscated the facts? The deception began immediately after the fall of the site and continued for more than a decade. Some family members believe, and official actions and documents seem to support the charge, that the deception continues. This book will document these efforts to mislead the public and various Heavy Green family members and offers explanations for this behavior.

In 1996, while working as the Chief of Southeast Asia Archival Research, Defense POW/MIA office, I was asked by the director, Deputy Assistant Secretary of Defense James W. Wold, to prepare a written assessment of the facts surrounding the status of the U.S. government's investigation of the Site 85 losses. After reading the evaluation, which was critical of sloppy and inappropriate work by two senior people in the office, Secretary Wold ordered a full-scale reevaluation of the case. Regrettably, I then became part of the Site 85 story—caught up in trying to focus attention on the facts of the attack, especially Vietnamese knowledgeability, while others were embarrassed, angry, and intent on closing the case.

Because this controversy attracted Congressional scrutiny and resulted in the surfacing of important new information proving the Vietnamese have withheld access to witnesses and records pertinent to the Site 85 loss, I have included a documented review and my recollections of these events. Recognizing that this may cause some to question my academic objectivity, I would simply ask the reader to judge the book on its documentation and scholarship.

On the communist side, glaring falsehoods and inconsistencies in responses to family members and U.S. POW/MIA officials raise troubling questions about their often stated commitment to a full accounting of U.S. servicemen. Multiple requests over many years to the Vietnamese and Lao governments for information on the military campaign against Site 85 go unanswered, although there can be no doubt that current and former senior Vietnamese and Lao officials know, or could easily determine, precisely what happened at Phou Pha Thi. In this regard, I am especially guided by a 1997 conversation in Phnom Penh, Cambodia with a very senior Cambodian Communist Party historian who spent decades working in Hanoi with Vietnamese Communist Party historians. Comfortably retired and no longer constrained by any political agenda, he was quite open and unequivocal in his views. When asked about the completeness of North Vietnamese wartime record keeping he smiled and nodded. "They know," he said, "they know."

This book's goal, then, is to provide an authoritative account of the Heavy Green program. What emerges is a covert operation conducted within the framework of a duplicitous and unparalleled American foreign policy—the presidentially directed introduction of American military men into neutral Laos to improve the effectiveness of U.S. bombing in North Vietnam. When disaster struck Heavy Green, perhaps due to official negligence, U.S. representatives embarked on an immediate and decades long coverup. Senior Air Force officers with extensive knowledge of the Site 85 operation and loss have misrepresented the facts in official written accounts and during a lawsuit filed by a Heavy Green family. They accomplished much of their obfuscation by maintaining the secrecy of relevant documents. Indeed, had the families and attorneys been provided full access to those documents, the government could scarcely have claimed the attack was a surprise. Without the persistence of Heavy Green family members and POW/MIA activists in the face of the outrageous conduct in Hanoi, Vientiane, and Washington, none of this might ever have come to light.

Using heretofore unavailable and unpublished official documents and the oral accounts of American, Thai, Lao, and Vietnamese witnesses, I trace the evolution of Heavy Green from its inception, placement in Laos, operation, and destruction. I show its impact on the families, and the efforts (both positive and negative) undertaken by the United States and the governments of Vietnam and Laos to learn the fate of the eleven missing men.

Using these unique resources I address the following questions: Why and how was the Heavy Green program established? What were the roles and responsibilities of the U.S. ambassador to Laos and senior Air Force officials? What were the actual targets? Who was ultimately responsible for the decision to continue the operations in the face of certain communist attack? Was the U.S. embassy in Laos, specifically the CIA station there and the U.S. Air Force Attaché Office, conscientious in its oversight of the Heavy Green project? How was the communist assault at Site 85 carried out and why was it so successful? Why were the families of the Heavy Green participants not accurately informed of the known circumstances at Site 85? Faced with a lawsuit by a Heavy Green family in 1975, how was the U.S. government able to claim the attack on Site 85 was a surprise? Why did it take the U.S. government until 1981, eight years after hostilities ended, to place the eleven men on the official unaccounted for list? What actions have been undertaken by the Defense Department? Thirty years after the loss of Site 85, why is the U.S. government still reluctant to seek a complete review and explanation for what happened at Phou Pha Thi?

Despite the paucity of information from North Vietnamese and Pathet Lao sources, and less than complete access to all U.S. records, I am confident that this book is an accurate history of project Heavy Green, the loss of Site 85, and a three-decade-long U.S. government coverup. Perhaps it will serve as a case study for U.S. foreign policy decisionmakers, especially those empowered to send men and women into harm's way. Those who are prepared to forfeit their lives should have no doubt that in the event of their death or capture their families will be treated with compassion and respect. Most of all, I believe I have provided the American public and the surviving Heavy Green personnel and their families a clear and unbiased account of a little known, but critically important chapter in the Vietnam war.

Nothing, short of strong physical evidence, however, will replace the uncertainty and suspicion that continues to pervade the lives of many Heavy Green families. Surely their government owes them and all the other MIA families a meaningful accounting.

1

Sustained Reprisal

*The spring-summer of 1965 may be the most crucial single period in the
history of U.S. escalation of the war in Vietnam. During that time, the
United States mounted a sustained, regular bombing campaign against
North Vietnam, one that eventually reached enormous proportions.[1]*

Project Heavy Green and the decision to place a ground-directed
radar bombing facility at Site 85 evolved from a February 7, 1965, White
House staff memorandum, which urged President Lyndon B. Johnson
to undertake "a policy of *sustained reprisal* against North Vietnam—
in which air and naval action against the North is justified by and
related to the whole Viet Cong campaign of violence and terror in the
South."[2] The author, McGeorge Bundy, Johnson's special assistant for
national security, forecast, but dispassionately accepted, the certitude
of a bloody air campaign:

> While we believe that the risks of such a policy are acceptable, we empha-
> size that its costs are real. It implies significant U.S. air losses even if no
> full air war is joined, and it seems likely that it would eventually require an
> extensive and costly effort against the whole air defense system of North
> Vietnam. U.S. casualties would be higher—and more visible to American
> feelings—than those sustained in the struggle in South Vietnam. Yet mea-
> sured against the costs of defeat in Vietnam, this program seems cheap.

And even if it fails to turn the tide—as it may—the value of the effort seems to us to exceed its cost.[3]

A week later, President Johnson approved the inauguration of an air warfare campaign against North Vietnam. Code-named "Rolling Thunder," the first strike missions were scheduled for February 20, 1965. Typical of the obstacles inherent to a bombing campaign against North Vietnam, however, political and weather problems quickly forced a delay in the attacks. On February 19 South Vietnamese army Colonel Pham Ngoc Thao staged a coup, throwing the government into chaos. Concurrently, diplomats in London and Moscow began talks on reopening the 1954 Geneva Conference. Johnson, reluctant to have bombs falling on North Vietnam in the midst of Saigon's political instability and in the wake of the joint British-Soviet peace initiative, deferred the bombing. A week later, when what passed for normalcy returned to the South Vietnamese capital and the British and Soviet negotiators failed to reach a consensus on a conference format, the strike missions were rescheduled for February 26.[4] The airplanes remained grounded, however, as seasonal rains and cloud cover prevented safe and accurate air operations. Finally, on March 2 USAF bombers attacked an ammunition depot located some 35 miles north of the Demilitarized Zone, while South Vietnamese aircraft struck a small naval facility at Quang Khe.[5]

The policy of "sustained reprisal" had been inaugurated, but many military and civilian officials thought the initial target selection wrongheaded and ultimately ineffectual. Admiral U.S. Grant Sharp, Commander in Chief, Pacific (CINCPAC), an outspoken proponent of bombing North Vietnam, called the attacks "insignificant" and decried the unwillingness of the White House to follow up with additional air strikes. In Saigon, Maxwell D. Taylor, U.S. Ambassador to South Vietnam and a former chairman of the Joint Chiefs of Staff, exclaimed in a March 8 cable to Washington, "I fear that to date Rolling Thunder in their eyes [North Vietnamese] has merely been a few isolated thunder claps."[6] But this was to be a bombing campaign encumbered by extraordinary political constraints. According to General William C. Westmoreland, Commander, United States Military Assistance Command Vietnam from 1964 to 1968:

Interference from Washington seriously hampered the campaign. Washington had to approve all targets in North Vietnam, and even though the

Joint Chiefs submitted long-range programs, the State Department constantly interfered with individual missions. This or that target was not to be hit for this or that nebulous nonmilitary reason. President Johnson allegedly boasted on one occasion that "they can't even bomb an outhouse without my approval."[7]

Westmoreland was referring to a list of ninety-four strategic targets, including twelve railroad routes, developed by the Defense Intelligence Agency and approved by the Joint Chiefs.[8] Under a time-consuming and increasingly frustrating system, targets were initially recommended by in-theater Air Force and Navy Air commanders. These selections were passed up the chain of command for review by staff experts at CINCPAC, International Security Affairs (ISA), the State Department, and the Joint Chiefs of Staff (JCS). The Joint Chiefs then sent the list on to the White House for final target approval. The venue for this last step, a luncheon hosted by the President every Tuesday, was normally attended by Defense Secretary Robert S. McNamara, Secretary of State Dean Rusk, Special Assistant for National Security McGeorge Bundy, and White House press secretary Bill Moyers. Amazingly, no military representative regularly attended until October 1967, when General Earle G. Wheeler, Chairman of the JCS, was invited to participate.[9]

Aside from the Washington-based political considerations, the effective use of air power to counter North Vietnam's support of the Viet Cong was further complicated by an expanding U.S. bombing campaign in South Vietnam and Laos. Communist attacks in late 1964 and early 1965 against South Vietnamese forces and U.S. personnel and facilities, in which the "Viet Cong, bolstered by North Vietnamese regulars, were displaying new aggressiveness and tactics," caused General Westmoreland "to rely heavily on air power to turn the tide against the mounting enemy offensive."[10] On December 14, 1964 the United States initiated "Barrel Roll," an aerial bombing program intended to interdict communist infiltration and resupply activity in eastern Laos.[11] Two months later, American B-57 bombers attacked enemy forces east of Saigon; this was the first combat use of jets in South Vietnam.[12] In April, U.S. Navy carrier-based aircraft flying from the *Midway, Coral Sea,* and *Yorktown* began air support,[13] and, on June 18, 1965, B-52 bombers, one of the most powerful weapons in the U.S. arsenal, began dropping bombs for the first time on targets in South Vietnam. Called

"Arc Light" strikes, this initial effort involved 27 aircraft releasing ordnance on a 1-mile by 2-mile "target box." According to an official U.S.
Air Force history, "Within 30 minutes, 1,300 bombs fell, slightly more
than half of them in the target area."[14] While the results were mixed,
America's Southeast Asia air war was now underway.[15]

Although Admiral Sharp was technically responsible for managing
this effort, in practice he relied on his subordinates, the Commander,
Pacific Air Forces, (PACAF), and the Commander, Pacific Fleet,
(PACFLT), to direct their individual air units. This lack of a single air
commander, according to air power historian Mark Clodfelter, produced unnecessary layers of bureaucracy and fostered a counterpro-
ductive interservice rivalry between the Navy and Air Force.[16]

More pernicious, and directly related to the creation of Heavy
Green, was the encouragement of a policy that Clodfelter believes fostered "[a] dearth of inter-service cooperation . . . [whereby] Navy air
units vied with Air Force squadrons for higher sortie totals against the
North."[17] In a manner similar to how some ground force commanders
in South Vietnam measured success by the number of enemy bodies
counted after an engagement, the Navy and Air Force engaged in a
quest to determine which service could achieve the highest sortie rates,
and it appears that this attitude originated at a very senior level.
Advised in April 1966 that a lack of bombs might reduce the number
of sorties scheduled to be flown, Admiral Sharp said that because sortie rates were a "measure of effectiveness" he wanted "as many sorties
as were planned regardless of the size of their [bomb] loads."[18]

As with the often inflated body counts of the ground war,[19] the
number of sorties flown did not necessarily equate to effective bombing. An Air Force study concluded, "Reporting effectiveness based on
sortie rates favored Navy planes, which carried lighter loads from car-
riers, more than it did Air Force aircraft. The Air Force was against
sending its planes on missions with less than complete loads, for to do
so required more sorties and more pilots exposed to danger to drop
the same amount of ordnance."[20] Nonetheless, the situation did create a strong interservice rivalry and the consequences of this sortie
competition were not lost on the pilots who flew the missions. An Air
Force officer recalled, "There is nothing more demoralizing than the
sight of an F-4 taxiing out with nothing but a pair of bombs nestled
among its ejector racks. However, it looks much better for the commander and the service concerned to show 200 sorties on paper, even

when 40 or 50 would do the same job."[21] In his defense, Sharp has said, "The organization for air operations was criticized at times, usually by people who did not understand it, and occasionally by people who had a parochial axe to grind. The organization satisfied diverse operational requirements and performed to my satisfaction."[22]

Sharp's view notwithstanding, the competition increased in November 1965 when North Vietnam was divided by an Air Force-Navy Coordinating Committee into six target zones, called Route Packages, divided between the Navy and the Air Force.[23] In addition to the political and service-imposed restrictions, aircrews had to deal with severe weather problems and aircraft limitations.

During the northeast monsoon, usually September to mid-May, rain, fog, and cloud cover over North Vietnam obscured aerial detection of targets and created serious problems for accurate and safe bombing operations—factors not taken into account at President Johnson's Tuesday lunches—during which the decisionmakers ignored weather considerations, thus greatly increasing the difficulty and danger of the missions. In an effort to reduce collateral damage to civilian areas adjacent to approved military targets, American air crews were required to make a positive identification of their objectives. For the vast majority of attacking aircraft this meant visual acquisition. Meanwhile, the American planes had to contend with a deadly environment of more than 7,000 anti-aircraft artillery guns, some 200 possible surface-to-air missile (SAM) launching sites, and approximately 80 Soviet-built interceptor jets. Optimum accuracy and safe operations, therefore, dictated that the bombers have at least a 10,000-foot cloud ceiling with five miles of visibility and no more than 50 to 60 percent cloud coverage. This condition allowed the pilots time to see their targets, take into account the threat from anti-aircraft activity, and retain "sufficient visibility to see a SAM launch and adequate ceiling for maneuvering to avoid the SAM."[24] Under the best of conditions, however, only about 75 percent of the bombs hit within 400 feet of the intended target. In bad weather bombs often landed 1,500 to 2,000 feet from the target.[25]

Most Rolling Thunder missions were conducted by F-105, F-4, and A-4 aircraft; ill-suited "to the forbidding environment of North Vietnam." The single-seat F-105 Thunderchief, more often called the "Thud," was designed in the 1950s to carry a small nuclear weapon. Fully loaded with 14,000 pounds of conventional bombs the planes weighed more than twenty-five tons, making it difficult to control in combat operations. Nevertheless, the USAF-operated F-105 would fly more than 75 percent of the Rolling Thunder sorties. The two-seat F-4 Phantom, flown by both the Navy and Air Force, could carry some eight tons of bombs, but the engines emitted a heavy black smoke that made the planes vulnerable to detection by enemy aircraft and ground defense forces. The single-seat Navy A-4 Skyhawks saw considerable service, yet could carry a maximum bombload of only 8,200 pounds. All three aircraft shared a basic deficiency: the lack of a ground target acquisition radar. Without such a radar, the pilot relied on visual sightings, and therefore needed generally good weather to locate and attack his target.[26]

Two other in-theater aircraft, the Navy and Marine Corps A-6 Intruder and the Air Force B-52 Stratofortress, had the capability to undertake all-weather bombing. The two-seat A-6, with a bomb capacity of nearly eight tons and an on-board radar which allowed the crew to acquire their target in any weather, was ideally suited for Rolling Thunder. Unfortunately, only two squadrons, with less than three dozen aircraft were assigned—too few for an effective all-weather bombing campaign.[27]

The B-52s, designed especially for all-weather nuclear bombing and capable of carrying more than twenty-five tons of bombs, were not used because of political considerations. President Johnson believed the expanded use of the heavy bombers would be considered by the Soviets and Chinese communists as "too provocative." He also wanted to avoid any losses to America's premier fleet of nuclear strike aircraft. As a result, B-52s flew only 141 missions during Rolling Thunder, most near the demilitarized zone.[28]

Deeply concerned, the U.S. Air Force studied the effects of darkness and weather on air operations in Southeast Asia and concluded:

> The absence of accurate night and weather bombing capability required that strikes be confined to those days when they could be visually conducted; the tactics imposed by enemy defenses further limited strike opportunities to days when weather was suitable for countering these tactics.[29]

Thus in 1966, when there was growing pressure from senior military and political leaders to increase the tempo of the Rolling Thunder bombing campaign, the air components, and particularly the Air Force, were ill-equipped to carry out one of their principal missions.

Ironically, as Air Force leaders sought increased funds to build and operate the world's most technically sophisticated air weapons, the initial solution to the all-weather bombing conundrum in Southeast Asia was a basic radar bombing system first used during World War II.[30] The radar, modified in the 1950s and early 1960s, had become central to an extensive bombing evaluation program operated by the Strategic Air Command (SAC). By 1963 the world-wide testing of SAC aircrews was being conducted by the 1st Combat Evaluation Group headquartered at Barksdale Air Force Base, Louisiana. In addition to the headquarters, the group included fourteen detachments located throughout the United States and three railroad-car-mounted systems, called "Express" sites, which were moved at random to provide unfamiliar or "strange" target training. Using a ground-based radar/computer (MSQ-35), commonly called a Radar Bomb Scoring (RBS) system, SAC technicians could track and update an aircraft's position, direction, and rate of travel. Upon a signal from the aircraft indicating that simulated bomb release had occurred, the actual aircraft position and rates as determined by the ground radar computer could be compared to those computed by the aircrew. This information allowed the SAC technicians to calculate a predicted impact point for the bombs.

In early 1965 SAC engineers began to study the feasibility of reversing the RBS process by converting the equipment to a strike-directing system. They successfully determined that by using constantly updated ballistic solutions obtained by the tracking of an aircraft, the ground computer could determine the exact desired release point. Voice commands from the ground controller could then direct the aircraft to the required position and give the command for bomb release. Visual reference to the ground or the target was not required.

The result was the MSQ-77, a ground radar system which, when used in conjunction with an aircraft-installed transponder, had an effective range of about 200 nautical miles. The MSQ-77 was a stand-alone system, designed to function independently without any additional support. Large and complex, the system required eight technicians for operation. The components included a control and plotting van, two diesel generator vans, an administrative and supply van, and a communications and maintenance van. A computer supplied data to an instrument board, which displayed the aircraft's ground speed, true altitude, and heading. The computer also linked the radar to the plotting board, which created an ink trace of the aircraft's path. Technicians used this information to voice-direct a single flight to an exact target and bomb release point.[31]

Because radar signals cannot pass through obstructions, the system required an unimpeded line of sight to the aircraft. It was this need for an unobstructed path to incoming aircraft, together with a proximity of not more than two hundred nautical miles from any targets, that led to the selection of Phou Pha Thi in northeastern Laos as the site for Heavy Green.

In October 1965 SAC began testing the MSQ-77 with F-100 aircraft and live bombs at the Matagorda Island, Texas bombing range. After some seven hundred test flights the results were deemed "highly successful," and in March 1966 the technology was deployed in Southeast Asia.

Over the course of a year SAC established six fully operational CS sites: five in South Vietnam (Bien Hoa, Pleiku, Dong Ha, Dalat, and Binh Thuy), and one in Thailand (Nakhon Phanom). These radar sites were able to direct air strikes over all of South Vietnam, southern Laos, and a major portion of southern North Vietnam.[32] The new system was dubbed "Combat Skyspot" (CS).[33]

Success did not come without significant human cost. On June 5, 1966, six members of the 1 CEVG were killed by communist forces in an ambush carried out within sight of the Dong Ha air base. The men, four surveyors and two radar technicians, had ventured in a jeep outside the base security perimeter to complete their final calculations in preparation for site activation. Viet Cong soldiers concealed along the roadway sprayed the vehicle and its occupants with small arms and automatic weapons fire. The jeep was then set afire, burning many of the bodies. Despite the tragedy, seven days later the Dong Ha site became operational.[34]

By mid-August CS had directed some 350 missions against targets in Laos; by year's end total missions in all three countries reached 10,000. Although photo analysis showed that the bombs were falling an average of between 300 and 350 feet from their intended targets, Combat Skyspot was considered a success. According to an official USAF history, "Skyspot's greatest advantage was the intended one: to assure more bombing accuracy at night and in bad weather than previously. It thus complemented rather than replaced visual or other airborne bombing systems."[35]

Senior American military commanders were quick to grasp the potential impact of CS-directed missions against North Vietnam's most important military and industrial facilities. These included railroad yards, an iron and steel mill, a cement factory, and half a dozen electric power stations mostly located north of the 20th parallel and near the cities of Hanoi and Haiphong. If Combat Skyspot was to be used against these targets, however, geography and system requirements dictated that the equipment be placed in northeastern Laos.[36] Given the impressive charade of neutrality being played out by the United States, the communists, and the Royal Lao government, the operation of such a system in Laos seemed highly problematic at best.

Political appearances notwithstanding, by 1966 the United States was deeply involved in a major military struggle with the North Vietnamese army and their Pathet Lao allies for control of northeastern and southern Laos. Despite being a signatory to the July 1962 Geneva Accords, in which it pledged "not to impair the sovereignty, independence, neutrality, unity, or territorial integrity of Laos,"[37] a month later the U.S. moved to establish a major clandestine paramilitary operation there. This remarkable decision, to publicly support Lao neutrality while the Departments of State and Defense and the Central Intelligence Agency equipped and directed a major in-country war, is unparalleled in American history. Douglas S. Blaufarb, who served as CIA Chief of Station in Vientiane in the mid-1960s, has cogently summarized the difficulties associated with this strategy.

A major concern was to keep departures from the terms of the Accords to a minimum and as inconspicuous as possible. Thus, while U.S. military and paramilitary activities were to be undertaken, an obvious and undeniable U.S. military presence would clearly be an embarrassment and would be avoided. In effect, all the functions of a Military Assistance Advisory Group, some of the functions of a U.S. military command, and numerous unconventional activities in support of irregular troops, including a requirement for airborne logistics adapted to an area without airfields or navigational aids, would have to be effectively performed in circumstances which prohibited an avowed military presence of the type normally considered essential.[38]

The justification for this course of action was the continued presence in Laos, in clear violation of the Accords, of thousands of communist troops. Communist violations of Lao neutrality were countered by U.S. transgressions and, for the most part, the American public was oblivious to an increasingly bloody and expensive war. As the war in South Vietnam expanded, Washington's Lao policy focused on reducing the flow of communist combatants and materiel moving through Laos en route to South Vietnam and Cambodia via the so-called "Ho Chi Minh Trail."[39] Indeed, as mentioned above, the Combat Skyspot sites quickly played an active role in the bombing of communist targets in southern Laos. But northeastern Laos was the locus of a much more complex struggle between the communists and American-directed ground and air forces. It was also destined to be the site for project Heavy Green.

The provinces of Houa Phan and Xiengkhouang, designated Military Region Two (MR II), encompassed some of the country's most strategic real estate. Sam Neua, the provincial capital, is less than 25 miles from the North Vietnamese border. Not surprisingly, the Royal Lao government was never able to exert much military or political influence in this area and as early as 1953 the communist Pathet Lao and their Vietnamese allies maintained de facto control of this critical gateway into Laos. Sam Neua and the nearby cave complexes at Vieng Sai would serve as the Pathet Lao headquarters until 1975.[40] Xiengkhouang, located southwest of Houa Phan, included key access routes to Thailand, Cambodia, and South Vietnam, as well as the strategic Plain of Jars. Named for the presence of prehistoric stone mortuary jars, this limestone plateau, between 3,500 and 4,500 feet above sea level, is approximately 10 miles across and surrounded by some of the highest and most spectacular mountains in Southeast Asia.[41] For centuries armies had crossed through the area en route to wars to the north and south. This pattern continued during the Second Indochina War. By the time the bombing finally ended in 1973 several million tons of munitions had rained down on this remote locale, making it one of the world's most heavily bombed areas. Moreover, the deadly legacy of unexploded ordnance to this day scars the lives of rural Laotians.[42]

In the late 1950s, CIA paramilitary officers and the U.S. military trainers began to arrive in Laos. They quickly recognized the military and political significance of the country's northeastern region.

Initially given the task of building a credible lowland Lao national army, known as the *Forces Armées du Royaume* (FAR), the Americans found considerable corruption, apathy, and a desire to avoid combat. Leadership and morale in the Royal Army were extremely poor; it was not unusual for the its general staff to send units into the field without proper training or equipment. Despite the expenditure of some $350 million in military assistance and being bolstered by American advisers, the army was clearly no match for the Vietnamese-assisted Pathet Lao forces.[43] What the Americans discovered in northeastern Laos was a fiercely independent hill tribe called the Hmong. These relatively recent migrants from southern China were quite able and willing to take up arms against any group that threatened their mountaintop homes and opium poppy fields.[44] Moreover, these innate guerrilla fighters had claimed the mountains of what was now MR II as their homelands. In short, they were culturally and geographically disposed to counter any intrusions into northeastern Laos.

There was another, only slightly less important, reason to believe that the Hmong could become an important factor in countering communist activity in northeastern Laos: Vang Pao, a young, brave, and charismatic Hmong soldier whose military experience began when he served as an interpreter for Free French forces in 1945. Graduated from the French-run officer training school in Dong Hene, he was the first Hmong to have received a FAR army commission.[45] First approached by CIA paramilitary officers in early 1961, Vang Pao was a lieutenant colonel and commander of Laotian forces on the Plain of Jars. "VP," as he became known to his CIA advisers, reported that Hmong villages located near the Plain were increasingly becoming the target of communist attacks and intimidation. The Pathet Lao and Vietnamese were seizing opium crops and villagers were being conscripted for use as porters and guides. Vang Pao feared that the plain would soon become a major battlefield.

Characteristically, he had a bold plan of action to go along with his concerns: move large numbers of Hmong into a series of fortified areas in the mountains surrounding the Plain of Jars. From there, he suggested, the Hmong would be safe and could be trained to fight the communist forces. Here was someone, the CIA officers agreed, who exhibited an American "can do" attitude.[46]

The CIA was soon using its proprietary airline, Air America, to ferry the Hmong to their new homes. To carry out its work in such a mountainous environment, the agency undertook the survey and establishment of small dirt or grass landing strips known as Lima Sites (LS). Air America pilots, flying helicopters and short takeoff and landing (STOL) aircraft, were soon expert at operating from these often dangerous fields. As the war expanded more sites were created and by 1970 there were some three hundred Lima Sites scattered throughout Laos. Many, as territory shifted sides, were lost to enemy control.[47]

Also assisting in the movement of the Hmong, as interpreters and trainers, were several dozen members of the elite, CIA-trained, Thai Police Aerial Reinforcement Unit (PARU). Established in 1958 by career CIA officer James W. "Bill" Lair, the PARU program was designed to provide the Thai government with a highly trained mobile force capable of responding to insurgent threats in remote areas along Thailand's lengthy borders.[48] The Thais, with advanced military training and a spoken language similar to Laotian, would be used by the CIA in Laos for a number of important projects. This would include manning CIA radios at Site 85, Phou Pha Thi. Bill Lair, operating mostly from Thailand, would become the principal CIA strategist for this Hmong-based plan to defend northeastern Laos. Using his extensive Thai military and police contacts, Lair would manage the creation of a covert, CIA-funded Thai organization, Headquarters 333, whereby Thai military volunteers were sent to Laos.[49] A small number of Thai forces served at Phou Pha Thi.

Vang Pao's plan also included the establishment of a military headquarters at Phadong, located some six miles south of the Plain. CIA, PARU, and U.S. Army Special Forces "White Star" military training teams were soon at work. The message was simple: "The Vietnamese will soon come to take your land. We [the U.S.] will give you the means to fight and defend your homes."[50] According to Ray Bowers,

> By May 1961 the CIA had equipped some five thousand Meo [Hmong] fighting men and had established a logistics pipeline entirely separate from that supporting other [Royal Lao] government forces. Vang Pao meanwhile cemented the loyalty of widespread Meo [Hmong] villages northeast of the plain, visiting them by light aircraft and arranging for air delivery of food and arms.[51]

Meanwhile, reacting to the total breakdown of the 1954 Geneva Agreements, Soviet and British diplomats arranged for a general ceasefire in Laos and announced a second Geneva Conference.[52] The cease-fire took effect on May 11, 1961 and five days later representatives from Cambodia, the People's Republic of China, France, Laos, the Soviet Union, the United Kingdom, the United States, South Vietnam, North Vietnam, India, Canada, Poland, Burma, and Thailand convened to discuss the fate of Laos. Despite the cease-fire, Pathet Lao and Vietnamese forces launched a massive mortar attack on Vang Pao's Phadong headquarters, forcing the Hmong and their CIA, PARU, and White Star advisers to abandon the site on June 6.[53] In protest the U.S. and other western delegations walked out of the talks, forcing a five-day suspension.[54]

Over the next eleven months there would be numerous violations of the cease-fire, some quite serious, as the communists and the Lao government forces jockeyed for territory.[55] Early in 1962 Vang Pao, with American assistance, established two new bases a few miles south of the Plain of Jars. Sam Thong became the civil headquarters for the northeastern Hmong. Long Tieng, the headquarters for Military Region II, was located just a mountain ridge away.[56] This installation would soon grow to become the CIA operations center for America's secret war in Laos and a major staging area for Air America and Lao air force operations. By the mid-1960s it would also serve as a refueling and forward staging area for USAF special operations and search and rescue helicopters destined for North Vietnam. Beginning in 1966 Air Force forward air controllers, called "Ravens," would call the base home.[57]

In mid-1962, however, there was still cautious hope for a neutral Laos free of all military entanglements. On July 23, 1962, in Geneva Prime Minister Souvanna Phouma was a witness as the foreign ministers of fourteen countries signed the Declaration and Protocol on the Neutrality of Laos. Major provisions of the agreements required the Lao government to disassociate itself from all military alliances and to bar the introduction of foreign military personnel and civilians performing quasi-military functions. The only exception was to be the continued presence of a small French military training mission. Additionally the agreements forbade the establishment of any foreign military installations in Laos and the use of Laotian territory to interfere in the affairs of another country.[58]

In accordance with the agreements, by October 6 the U.S. had withdrawn from Laos all military and civilian advisers.[59] Nonetheless, two CIA paramilitary officers remained in northern Laos "to monitor the situation and report." The two men remained with the specific approval of Ambassador W. Averell Harriman, who led the American delegation at Geneva, with the stipulation that they could not receive "any weapons or military supplies."[60] On October 7 the official North Vietnamese news agency reported that "the Vietnamese military personnel which were previously sent to Laos at the request of the Royal Lao Government have all been withdrawn from Laos."[61] According to William Colby, then chief of CIA clandestine operations in the Far East, "There had been some 7,000 North Vietnamese troops in Laos at the time of the Accord. But during the so-called count-out [conducted by the International Control Commission] only forty went through the formalities of leaving the country."[62]

The facade was in place. By mid-1963 the United States was actively involved in organizing and directing a clandestine army to counter the communist presence in Laos and the ever-expanding North Vietnamese infiltration through Laos of combatants and supplies destined for the war in South Vietnam. Support of this military force and their families was principally made possible through the combined efforts of the CIA, the United States Agency for International Development (USAID), and the Department of Defense.[63] All of these activities were conducted under the direction of the U.S. ambassador to Laos. Within two years the scope of the operation had become immense. And, lest there be any doubt about the true nature of this facade, William H. Sullivan, U.S. Ambassador to Laos, 1964–69, summed up his feelings in a May 14, 1965, cable to the State Department. With regard to the suggestion that the U.S. might want to convene another conference on Laos, Sullivan wrote:

> We now conduct an average of fifty combat air sorties daily by U.S. aircraft against targets on Laos territory; we maintain, encadre, and direct a [words deleted] guerrilla force of 20,000 men which inflicts daily casualties on the enemy. We operate a fleet of about fifty aircraft primarily engaged in paramilitary activity; and we conduct a clandestine military aid program here on a fifty million dollar a year scale. We get away with all this by elaborate precautions of dissimulation, tight discipline over loose talk, and a spritely collusion with our Lao hosts. However, the enemy is fully aware of what we are doing and would lose no opportunity in a conference to expose us. Once we became exposed, it would be inevitable that many of our activities would have to be suspended. Those of us who conduct these operations harbor the illusion that they are of some value to the United States and cause some annoyance to our enemies.[64]

As the Air Force strained to complete the installation of the Combat Skyspot radar sites, William Sullivan was beginning his third year of service as the U.S. Ambassador to Laos. Sullivan, who had served as Averell Harriman's deputy at Geneva, was determined to make the U.S. appear to adhere to the agreements. Moreover, by virtue of a May 1961 presidential directive sent to all U.S. Chiefs of Mission and the Geneva Accords-imposed absence of a U.S. military command structure in Laos, Sullivan had become the *de facto* military commander.[65] It was a role the ambassador, a U.S. Navy veteran of World War II, undertook with great confidence and enthusiasm. Sullivan has written, "Washington gave me a free hand to run it as best I could without interference. I can remember only two direct military instructions in the four-and-a-half years in Laos."[66] Both of these orders, described later, involved Site 85.

Understandably, this caused some strain in his relationships with senior military officers. General Westmoreland and Admiral Sharp have both confirmed that Sullivan wielded virtually unchallenged authority over U.S. military activity in Laos. Says Sharp, "Sullivan had presidential authority in Laos and that was OK with me. I was convinced the fight was in Vietnam."[67] Although Westmoreland was a bit more testy about the issue of control, claiming that "Sullivan was often involved in purely military matters," the general conceded the ambassador "had marching orders from the White House and made no secret of his clout."[68] Nonetheless, there was always a good deal of sparring by electrical message between Sullivan and senior military officers over the ambassador's control of the U.S. military in Laos.[69] Sullivan, well known for his often caustic comments, was at the top of his game in July 1967. On the 24th he cabled Sharp's headquarters, "If the CINCPAC staff officer who wrote REFTEL [the cable Sullivan was responding to] will kindly raise his right hand, he can have my job tomorrow . . . . I am disappointed that messages of this type are permitted to move in official channels and receive wide dissemination. It is the sort of thing which is giving marijuana a good name."[70]

Despite his considerable autonomy Ambassador Sullivan did not eschew military advice. Important decisions were normally made following the embassy's daily operations meeting, where senior embassy officials reported to Sullivan in detail on their ongoing projects. According to a senior CIA participant the meetings "reiterated daily that the war in Laos was a joint effort, that the Ambassador had wide authority over all the agencies participating, and that he expected all participants to be open and accommodating toward their colleagues and to place common purposes ahead of individual service interests."[71] It was within this context that Sullivan chose to accept military counsel, mostly from his CIA Chief of Station and military attaché. He firmly believed that they were much more informed on the ground war in Laos, not to mention being more cognizant of the overall embassy's goals, than military officers stationed outside the country. As a consequence, military planners in Thailand and South Vietnam were required to submit their bombing targets to the U.S. Embassy in Vientiane for Sullivan's approval. The process, handled by the Air Attaché's office, produced a good deal of frustration and tension between the Air Force officers in Laos and their military colleagues working outside the kingdom.[72]

The Geneva agreements and the U.S. desire to conduct a "nonattributable war," set the stage for a major CIA role in Laos. The CIA, however, found itself bound by many of the same constraints that Sullivan had imposed on U.S. military operations there. In a conversation with CIA official Douglas Blaufarb, Sullivan confirmed that "The nature of the operation in Laos was by its very structure clearly so much more than a military operation, and so much of the military operation was itself under the control of the Agency [CIA] rather than the control of the Pentagon, that it became a simpler proposition for the Ambassador to keep a grasp on it."[73] And Sullivan maintained a very tight grip indeed.

2

"I Wonder If It Is Worth It"

A U.S. official commenting on the relationship between the U.S. Embassy in Laos and the United States Military Assistance Command noted that "The biggest job Bill Sullivan had was to keep Westmoreland's paws off Laos."[1]

While Ambassador Sullivan held serious reservations about the U.S. military and what he perceived as its designs on Laos, he was also determined to stem the ever-increasing flow of communist activity down the remote eastern spine of the country. On March 6, 1965, he proposed to Washington a new bombing strategy for southern Laos. As described by Air Force historian Jacob Van Staaveren, the plan "envisaged rebombing of vital traffic points and bombing saturation of selected routes . . . especially at night, to create a backup of enemy supplies. Thus exposed, the supplies could be attacked, slowing logistics movements."[2] Sullivan's idea was eclipsed, however, by the recommendations of General Harold K. Johnson, Army Chief of Staff, who had just returned from a fact-finding visit to South Vietnam. General Johnson's wide-ranging twenty-one point plan included an increase in Rolling Thunder bombing missions and a separation of the air war in Laos. The general proposed that the ongoing missions, called "Barrel Roll," be confined to northern Laos and a new program, called "Steel Tiger," be created to attack communist infiltration in the southern panhandle of Laos.[3] Although Sullivan was not completely satisfied with this new strategy, President Johnson ordered it implemented on March 20.[4]

Although the President had decreed an expansion of the air war in Laos, Sullivan was determined not to allow unchecked military operations. The Ambassador resolved that "air operations would be carried about meticulously with pilots aborting missions, for example, rather than inflicting damage on friendly villagers [who might be in the vicinity]." This policy explicitly included a ban on the use of napalm in Laos.[5] Following lengthy discussions between Sullivan and senior U.S. military officials, and a March 30 briefing to Prime Minister Souvanna Phouma, Steel Tiger was approved by the Royal Lao government. The first missions were flown on April 3, 1965, and within three weeks the U.S. Navy and Air Force had conducted nearly eight hundred sorties.[6]

The increased bombing brought into Laos large numbers of military aircraft, particularly faster and more complex jets. These airplanes required greater technical support and the pilots were understandably far less familiar with the terrain of Laos than the Air America pilots who had occasionally carried out bombing missions in propeller-driven T-28 airplanes.[7] In this regard the absence of navigational aids was a major limiting factor in flights over Laos and North Vietnam. In order to reach their destination pilots were forced to fly by dead reckoning and inertial navigation or were led to their targets by special "pathfinder" aircraft. This was a dangerous and inefficient practice the military sought to correct by the placement in Laos of portable tactical air navigation aids called TACAN. Using the TACAN system "the aircraft transmitted an interrogator pulse to a ground station, and received back range and bearing information."[8] While its accuracy was not precise, TACAN was the best ground navigation system then available in Southeast Asia.

In the fall of 1965 the U.S. formally asked the Royal Lao government for permission to install what they called "mobile" TACANs in several regions of Laos. Mobile was hardly the right word for the systems, however. Among their basic components were a beacon transponder, and an all-band antenna capable of furnishing information to 100 aircraft at a time. A sideband transmitter/receiver radio and three generators provided support. Taken together, these various components weighed several thousand pounds. The systems' line-of-sight range was 200 nautical miles.[9]

Air Force units stationed at Clark Air Base in the Philippines conducted site surveys in Laos in October, but final Lao approval for the installation was not received until January 1966. All equipment destined for Laos was ordered "sanitized," stripped of its military identification and serial numbers. For those installing and operating the system the following applied:

> Military personnel used to install, operate and maintain the equipment were required to wear civilian clothing and could carry no weapons for self-defense. In the event of capture, they were to inform their captors that they were installing U.S. Agency for International Development (USAID) equipment at the specific request of the Royal Laotian government.[10]

It was, with minor variations, the "cover story" used by most U.S. military personnel illegally serving in Laos.

The first mobile TACAN in Laos, designated "Channel 72,"[11] was installed in April 1966 at Phou Kate near L 44 and the southern city of Saravane. Code-named "Paula," like all the TACANs in Laos at the time it was manned by personnel on temporary duty sent from Thailand.[12] In May a second TACAN was installed in north central Laos on "Skyline Ridge," a mountain crest just above General Vang Pao's headquarters at Long Tieng.[13] Designated "Channel 79," it was also known as "Jane." On March 19, 1966, a survey team traveled to northeastern Laos and Site 85. Although the location was considered acceptable for a TACAN, it took several months for the U.S. Embassy in Vientiane to provide clearance to move the equipment to the site. Finally, on September 24, 1966, "Channel 97" went operational under the code-name "Clara." During September an Air Force team also installed radio equipment at Site 85. According to an Air Force study, "These radios were used only in the receive mode to provide intelligence information and to assist in the preparation of frag [deployment] orders for aircraft operating in the area and over North Vietnam."[14] A fourth TACAN was placed at Muang Phalane, also known as LS 61, in the central panhandle of Laos on March 26, 1967. Designated "Channel 77," and called "Nora," the location was deemed especially important because it allowed coverage over the Vietnamese demilitarized zone and the important American base at Khe Sanh, South Vietnam. This site experienced many problems, however, and eventually a second field visit was required. In June a team comprising an officer, a noncommissioned officer, and a civilian technical representative[15] were flown to the area via Air America. They quickly determined that the equipment had been placed in the wrong location; the site was relocated and became operational soon thereafter.[16]

On December 6, in preparation for the Tet offensive and encirclement of Khe Sanh, communist forces threatened Saravane town and caused the evacuation of L 44 and its TACAN. Continuing their efforts to silence these important navigational aids, on Christmas morning North Vietnamese and Pathet Lao units attacked LS 61.[17] By then the TACANs in Laos were being operated by Heavy Green personnel, and the consequences, as will be explained in chapter 5, were severe.

The placement of a TACAN at Phou Pha Thi, little more than a dozen miles south of the North Vietnamese border, attracted the attention of senior U.S. military leaders and underscored the possibilities for ground-directed radar bombing against North Vietnam. The success of Combat Skyspot missions in southern Laos and South Vietnam contrasted sharply with the ongoing struggle to fly effective, all-weather, Rolling Thunder sorties. Not surprisingly, records indicate that PACAF, CINCPAC and the Joint Chiefs of Staff were, as early as November 1966, actively pursuing plans to place MSQ-77 ground radar equipment in Laos.[18] Site 85 seemed the best candidate if the desired radar coverage were to be achieved. The military's primary obstacle, of course, was William Sullivan and his efforts to demonstrate U.S. compliance with the 1962 agreements. The deployment into Laos of a specialized bombing system manned by a dozen or so Americans did not fit the Ambassador's view of a deniable U.S. presence.[19]

On February 25, 1967, Admiral Sharp, CINCPAC, sent a private, "back-channel," top secret message to General Earle G. Wheeler, Chairman, JCS, titled "Installation of MSQ 77 in Northern Laos." Sharp outlined the advantages of deploying such a system to Site 85 and requested JCS support of the proposal. The Admiral noted Sullivan had been briefed on the idea at Udorn on December 10, 1966, by General Hunter Harris, Commander Pacific Air Forces. According to the message, "At the briefing Ambassador expressed keen interest in the tactical merits of an MSQ in northern Laos but again stated he had misgivings about its political acceptability." Sharp disclosed he had personally discussed the issue with Sullivan but concluded, "It appears that he did not intend to give his full support to this proposal at State level." Sharp then told General Wheeler:

Due to the significant increase in air operations capability which this MSQ will provide, I believe we must attempt to gain approval. This is no cure-all by any means, but we must do more now to increase the effectiveness of our air operations in the northern area. The Ambassador's original objection was based on doubts about the security of site which we have overcome to some degree. However, his later objections, which shifted to the political angle, may or may not be completely valid. This is something that will have to be flushed out at other levels.[20]

General Wheeler agreed and the JCS turned to the State Department and requested Ambassador Sullivan's views. The Ambassador responded on March 13, 1967, with a strong argument against the placement of the system in Laos. He based his opposition on the grounds that the MSQ-77 was an offensive system which, if it became known, would expose Prime Minister Souvanna Phouma to severe criticism. While Souvanna was privately a strong advocate of U.S. bombing efforts, the politics of "neutral" Laos required that he be able to plausibly deny knowledge of any U.S. military activity. If a radar was placed at Pha Thi, and the system's presence in Laos became publicly known, Sullivan believed Souvanna would have no choice but to strongly disavow the operation. Such a statement would be a major propaganda coup for the North Vietnamese and their supporters, leaving U.S.-Lao relations in a very vulnerable state.[21] There were also operational and security issues to consider.

For many years the CIA had successfully used Site 85 to recover Hmong reconnaissance teams from communist-controlled areas.[22] The Air Force also utilized the landing pad as an emergency refueling stop for helicopter rescue missions into and out of North Vietnam.[23] Although these activities were unaffected by the presence of the TACAN equipment, a constantly manned radar facility would quickly attract unfriendly attention. Theodore ("Ted") Shackley, CIA Chief of Station in Vientiane, recalls that he and Sullivan discussed this point and both concluded the radar would invite an enemy response and eventually force the CIA and Air Force to cease operations from Site 85. More importantly, however, both men held serious reservations about the ability of the CIA-directed Hmong units to provide such a facility with long-term protection. The Hmong, in keeping with guerrilla tactics and their own sense of security, often abandoned territory in the face of communist pressure. "Site 85's defense," says Shackley, "would never be a do or die situation." The Hmong were expected to provide warning and a brief shield, but "they could not be expected to hold it indefinitely."[24]

Many other CIA Lao specialists shared these concerns about security. Bill Lair, the architect of the paramilitary program in northeastern Laos, had visited the Hmong outpost at Pha Thi. Aware of the limited capabilities of the local defense forces, he was certain the presence of the MSQ-77 would quickly be made known to the North Vietnamese and that Hanoi would make its destruction a priority. Indeed, the CIA officer predicted that the Vietnamese would build roads to the site in order to bring in heavy weapons. "When you begin to see the roads, you'll know they are coming," he declared at the time. Nonetheless, he believed the site's remote location, steep cliffs, and extremely rocky terrain features would aid the Hmong in delaying any assault. Lair doubted the site would be in operation for very long, but felt confident that there would be sufficient warning to conduct an air evacuation.[25]

Despite Sullivan's opposition, the JCS went forward on April 25, 1967, with a formal memorandum from General Wheeler to Secretary of Defense Robert S. McNamara proposing the placement of an MSQ-77 at Site 85. The document began:

> Persistent inclement weather over the northern portions of NVN [North Vietnam] and the BARREL ROLL area of Laos continues to limit extensive air strikes against important targets in those areas. CINCPAC has recommended immediate measures be taken to increase his all-weather attack capability. The installation of MSQ-77, providing radar-controlled coverage over the northern portion of NVN and Laos is considered a desirable way of quickly providing CINCPAC with an increased all-weather bombing capability in this area.[26]

The memorandum, noting that a TACAN was presently located at Site 85, stipulated that this was "the only location in friendly hands from which the necessary coverage can be obtained," and advised that "an MSQ-77 can be emplaced by air and can be in operation on Site 85 within 60 days after approval." The proposed site would require "31 personnel, based at Nakhon Phanom [Royal Thai Air Base in northeastern Thailand], to support operations at Site 85 on an around-the-clock basis; however, no more than 14 personnel, comprising a shift, would be working on-site at one time." Acknowledging the political situation, the letter offered to place the MSQ-77 personnel under "shallow cover"(i.e., the men would wear civilian clothes and carry cards which identified them as civilians) in an effort to conceal their military status.[27]

General Wheeler stressed the accuracy and range of the MSQ-77 system when used with beacon-equipped aircraft (200 nautical miles) and explained that presently about 300 of these airplanes were deployed to Southeast Asia, with plans for an additional 600. The MSQ-77 was also touted as providing increased air protection for Lima Sites and other "key complexes in northern Laos," as well as being able to direct aircraft against fleeting targets, and to accurately position, within the radar's range, search and rescue units. The JCS also claimed that the system would reduce the possibility of "inadvertent attacks against friendly forces" and improve "avoidance of border violations." The principal mission of the site, located just 125 miles from Hanoi, was to provide heretofore unavailable radar coverage of high-priority targets in and around the North Vietnamese capital. According to the letter, the system provided the bombing aircraft "the added protection of operating above the heavy ground fire, thus enhancing aircraft and aircrew survivability."[28] This theme, that a radar at Pha Thi would prevent the deaths of many Americans flying the most dangerous Rolling Thunder missions, was often repeated during the Heavy Green program.[29]

Addressing Ambassador Sullivan's opposition to the plan, Wheeler stressed that a TACAN at Site 85 had been "operational for over six months without significant molestation." The general continued:

> The MSQ mission is not obvious from outward appearance of the installation or equipment and its identification as an aid to offensive operations is not readily discernible. If required, supplemental amendments could be made to existing plans for the emergency extraction of personnel and destruction of the MSQ to prevent the enemy's identifying the MSQ operators as US military personnel.[30]

The Joint Chiefs were insisting that the placement of a significant amount of electronic equipment, associated buildings and living quarters, and the presence of more than a dozen Americans, would evoke no interest from local villagers or communist forces operating in the vicinity. Moreover, the issue of "emergency extraction of personnel and the destruction of the MSQ" did not seem fully deliberated. These concerns will be fully developed in later chapters.

In closing, the letter stated that "The Joint Chiefs of Staff concur in CINCPAC's proposal to install MSQ-77 at Site 85 and consider this capability a valid military requirement in which the advantages outweigh the disadvantages." Secretary of Defense McNamara was asked to forward a memorandum to Secretary of State Dean Rusk so that action could be taken to obtain the consent of the Royal Lao government.[31] McNamara approved and the sensitive issue was moved to the State Department where it received further review.

In addition to the radar request, the Pentagon was trying to ease Sullivan's hold over other military operations in Laos. General Westmoreland wanted greater control and an expansion of air and ground activities against the "Ho Chi Minh Trail" in Laos. On May 1, while in Washington for periodic consultations, Sullivan answered his critics. Asked by William P. Bundy, Assistant Secretary of State for East Asian Pacific Affairs, to provide a paper on the limitations that influenced military actions in Laos, Sullivan quickly penned a cogent five-page critique of Westmoreland's latest proposals. He ended by expressing deep reservations about the political consequences "If we decide to ignore Souvanna's objections and go ahead with some of these proposals. . . . At the very least, these consequences would involve the withdrawal of Souvanna's collaboration on many matters of importance to us. . . . At the very worst, he could chuck in his job, retire to France and let the country degenerate into a Pathet Lao occupied, Communist controlled fief."[32]

In addition to his response to Westmoreland's call for increased ground action, Sullivan also expressed his views on placing an MSQ-77 at Site 85. He advised Bundy of his planned meeting with Secretary of the Air Force Harold Brown and Air Force Chief of Staff John P. McConnell to discuss the proposal, but reaffirmed his skepticism. He wrote:

In general, I think Souvanna would reject this if it were put to him honestly. He has agreed to the installation of the navigational devices in Laos and we have installed TACANs on Lao soil. However, the TACAN is a passive device. The MSQ 77 is a command radar which takes positive control of air strikes in North Vietnamese territory. Moreover, it involves several buildings and about 40 men. It would be very conspicuous. *I wonder if it is worth it.*[33] (Emphasis added)

Sullivan's deep reservations and solid support at the State Department, however, could not overcome strong military and White House pressure to improve the Rolling Thunder bombing program. Ultimately, President Johnson personally ordered Sullivan to present the request to the Lao government.[34] Heavy Green was about to begin.

3
Heavy Green

President Johnson's decision to proceed with the placement of a bombing radar at Site 85 sanctioned a major U.S. violation of the Geneva agreements. According to an official Air Force statement, "In early 1967, the Directorate of Operations, HQ USAF was involved with the establishment of a special project within Southeast Asia, in direct support of the Vietnam War. A plan was devised for the Air Force to contract the project requirements to a civilian Defense Contractor [and] officially discharge from the USAF all voluntary participants."[1]

Despite his personal opposition to the plan, in late June 1967 Ambassador William Sullivan was "instructed to seek authorization from the Prime Minister [Souvanna Phouma] for the installation of this site." Speaking in October 1969 to a classified session of the U.S. Senate Subcommittee on U.S. Security Agreements and Commitments Abroad, Sullivan recounted the meeting:

> [A]fter explaining it to him in some detail as to what it was and what it consisted of, he authorized the United States to establish it and to man it. At that time he told me that if the site were discovered, that is to say, if allegations were made by the North Vietnamese that it existed there, that he would take the public position that he was unaware of any such installation. If the site were compromised further and the Americans were captured there he would take the position that these people were there without his knowledge. The United States accepted these conditions.[2]

Sullivan, nevertheless, surrendered neither his authority nor resolve to prevent the public exposure of U.S. military activities in Laos. The implementation of the program, principally focused on how to construct a deniable military presence at Pha Thi, devolved to the Air Force and the U.S. Embassy in Laos. Actions moved quickly on two tracks: the procurement and installation of a suitable radar and the recruitment of technicians to operate it.

Anticipating the need for a radar system that was entirely air transportable, in April 1967 the Air Force issued a contract to the New York-based Reeves Instrument Corporation, the company that had developed the radar equipment and provided the Air Force with continuing technical support. One of the greatest challenges for Reeves was to engineer a system that could be built in components not to weigh more than 5,000 pounds. According to a government official who supervised the contract, the company embarked on an "intense 24 hour-a-day" work schedule to meet Air Force deadlines associated with the deployment of the radar to "a special location in Southeast Asia." The ensuing pressure was almost too much for one engineer, "who nearly had a nervous breakdown."[3]

A month later a Reeves team delivered a prototype system, serial number eight, to Bergstrom AFB, Texas, where helicopters and trucks brought the components to an isolated government airfield at Bryan, Texas. The Chinooks also allowed the men to practice the complicated task of receiving sling-loaded pallets of equipment from a hovering aircraft. Using a portion of the airfield as a mock-up site, technicians from the First Combat Evaluation Group and Reeves employees then assembled and tested the radar's performance. This rigorous process was followed by another month of modifications at the New York plant, including the removal of all markings and numbers traceable to the manufacturer. The result, prototype number thirteen, was sent to Bryan in July for final testing and evaluation.[4] Designated as TSQ-81, this was the equipment that would soon be perched on the western ledge of Phou Pha Thi.

While the equipment was undergoing development, an Air Force lieutenant colonel stationed in Saigon was being pulled into a hectic effort to verify that Site 85 was truly a suitable location for the bombing radar. Robert C. Seitzberg was the 7th AF coordinator for all Combat Skyspot missions. A veteran navigator who had served with the evaluation group and participated in the testing of the radar at

Matagorda Island, Seitzberg had the job of conducting a site survey at Pha Thi. Initially, Seitzberg flew to Udorn Air Base where he received a CIA briefing on the mountain's topography as well as an Air America identification card. He was also provided with a "cover story." If captured by enemy forces, he was told to say that he was surveying a new helicopter landing site. Carrying only the fake identification, the equivalent of ten dollars in Thai currency, his surveying equipment, and a Polaroid camera, the officer was flown to Long Tieng, Laos. Bad weather set in, however, and he spent the next four days trying to reach Site 85. Finally, a plane was able to land Seitzberg at LS 107, Ban Houayma, where an Air America helicopter completed the short ride to Pha Thi.[5]

Arriving at a small dirt landing strip[6] located near the mountain's eastern ridge, Seitzberg saw the navigation system, some tents, a small amount of military encampment, and a few indigenous soldiers. Although no one spoke, the officer was quickly approached by a young man who picked up his transit and other surveying equipment and led him up a steep, rocky path through thick undergrowth and bamboo. Walking for nearly 300 yards, the pair emerged into a clearing at an elevation of about 5,500 feet. Most of the mountain seemed to be a jumble of bedrock, stratified limestone of varying sizes and shapes, and dense scrub brush. The briefer at Udorn had correctly described a relatively open area near the southwestern rim which appeared to be about the size of two basketball courts. Cautiously approaching the edge of the mountain, which dropped off more than 3,000 feet, he looked down into a large valley. Scanning from south to north, Seitzberg examined Pha Thi's slowly rising ridge line which extended for more than a mile, ending with a jagged 5,800-foot peak. To the east he could see the mountains that led to North Vietnam and envisioned the bombing targets which, he quickly concluded, could easily be attacked with radar tracking provided from this vantage point.

Seitzberg was certain that positioning the radar along the southwestern cliff would provide the required unobstructed line of sight to the bombers and that sufficient space could be cleared and leveled for the operations and support buildings. To confirm his findings he surveyed angles for the entire 360 degrees and photographed the terrain at every 10 degrees. Seitzberg completed his inspection by taking photos of the surrounding area and grabbed a few handfuls of the local rock for further analysis. Recounting the experience, Seitzberg described Pha Thi as "technically perfect for the placement of the radar." Impressed by the panorama of the surrounding mountains and valleys he remembers saying to himself, "This will be the most beautiful RBS site in the world."[7]

Seitzberg, upon his return to Udorn, reported back to Saigon by telephone, only to learn that his five-day absence had caused some serious concerns over his safety and whereabouts. No one in Laos had reported the weather delays to 7th AF Headquarters. The Air Force leadership, anxious to learn the results of his survey, flew the exhausted officer back to Saigon in a special aircraft. Soon after his arrival he was questioned by the Commander of the 7th AF, General William W. "Spike" Momyer and then told to prepare to leave in four hours for Hawaii and then on to Washington. Over the next week Seitzberg briefed senior officers. When asked by a general in Washington how long he thought the site could remain in operation, he replied "Six months if they were lucky because the Skyspot operation would probably hurt them [the North Vietnamese] in bad weather." Seitzberg then traveled to Barksdale AFB, and the combat evaluations group for five days of in-depth discussions with operations personnel.[8]

When Seitzberg returned to Southeast Asia, he updated the senior staffs at 7th AF as well as the 13th AF in the Philippines. As the project moved forward 7th AF would play a major role in the operational activities of Site 85, while 13th AF would provide the program with critical communications and technical support. Seitzberg also traveled to Udorn to discuss the program with representatives from 7/13th AF, the CIA, Air America, and the U.S. Embassy in Vientiane. Over the next several months Seitzberg and the group would occasionally meet to discuss, plan, coordinate, and solve issues related to the construction and operation of the site. Despite the many organizational concerns, and the need to maintain top-secret security over the operation, project Heavy Green moved quickly through the bureaucracy.

Among Seitzberg's more unusual challenges was how to level a portion of the mountain's rocky and uneven landscape so that the radar could be properly positioned. Secrecy and the remoteness of the area precluded the use of laborers or mechanical equipment. After a good deal of thought and calls to explosive ordnance specialists, a U.S. Navy Seabee demolitions expert was located and dispatched to the mountain. Using dynamite the man quickly created a suitable area from a location that was relatively level and clear of large rocks and trees.[9] The resulting explosions, albeit controlled, surely did not go unnoticed by the local inhabitants and enemy forces operating in the area. While reports to the Pathet Lao and PAVN could only describe the creation of a flattened area along the western cliff, this activity must have raised questions about what the Americans and their Hmong forces were preparing at Phou Pha Thi.

Meanwhile, combat evaluation group officers had begun the process of screening records in search of a select group of qualified men who were willing to install the TSQ-81 radar equipment. A second complement of Air Force men would be asked to volunteer for an even more dangerous and highly classified assignment, the day-to-day operation of the radar. The commander of the latter group had already been selected, Lieutenant Colonel Jerry Clayton, the First Combat Evaluation Group's Director of Operations. A command pilot who had flown bombers in both World War II and Korea, Clayton had managed the installation of the MSQ-77 radars in South Vietnam and Thailand.[10] In the SAC electronic warfare community he was widely viewed as a rising star who "always got the job done."[11]

While the combat evaluation group sought its best and brightest for this unique mission, a significant complication surfaced at Air Force Headquarters. The problem—ironic in view of the Geneva agreements the U.S. was preparing to disregard—was that the USAF leadership wanted to assure protection for the men under the terms of the Geneva Convention. During a briefing on the project, General McConnell, Air Force Chief of Staff, raised a question regarding the rights of any Air Force personnel captured while working as "civilians" in Laos. "The AF Judge Advocate General's staff informed the general that under the currently envisioned circumstances of the project, the individuals concerned would have no official status under the Geneva Convention, and could be executed if captured."[12] The original plan, to have the radar operators wear civilian clothes and carry USAID identification cards, so-called "shallow cover," was now out of the question. Instead, General McConnell directed that the Special Plans Office of the AF Director of Operations be given the task of placing the TSQ-81 program into the "black world" of highly sensitive, so-called "special projects." Special Plans designated their new responsibility project "Heavy Green."[13]

In late July 1967 Colonel John T. Moore, head of the special plans office, contacted Duane O. Wood, president of the Lockheed Aircraft Service Company,[14] and proposed that:

> Lockheed employ certain active duty Air Force personnel as technicians for operation and maintenance of U.S. Air Force military communications and radar equipment at a classified location in Southeast Asia with the understanding that the personnel, although to be employed and paid by Lockheed, were to remain under Air Force control and supervision during the period of their employment. These personnel were to be involved in a classified assignment involving the national security interests of the United States and this contract was for the purpose of establishing a "civilian" status for the military personnel required to undertake the mission.[15]

Under the plan if any of the men were captured in Laos by enemy forces the U.S. could legally show their connection to a civilian employer and insist they be accorded protection under the Geneva Convention, thereby assuaging General McConnell's concerns. Mr. Wood and Colonel Moore came to "an agreement in principle" whereby Lockheed would "undertake the program in the interest of furthering the U.S. Government's objectives of bringing an orderly conclusion to hostilities in Southeast Asia."[16]

While today such an effort seems highly transparent, within the rules of the charade that ignored American and North Vietnamese daily activities in Laos, almost any pretense was acceptable. It is, however, instructive to note General McConnell's concern for the safety of the Heavy Green operators did not extend to other Air Force personnel wearing mufti in Laos. "Raven" forward air controllers were operating kingdom-wide with the barest of cover stories and the radar installation crew would spend several months at Site 85 with an equally weak explanation for their presence in neutral Laos.[17] General McConnell's insistence that the Heavy Green team be afforded far greater protection under the Geneva Convention seems a clear indication of his belief that there were special dangers associated with the operation.

Once Colonel Moore was assured in July 1967 that Lockheed would provide the necessary cover for the operations team members, the combat evaluation group and the Special Plans office moved forward to complete the selection, training, and deployment of the installation team. Lieutenant Colonel Alan C. Randle, the group's Director of Logistics, and Chief Master Sergeant A. J. Born, its Superintendent of Electronics, were chosen to head up this difficult phase. Both men had extensive Combat Skyspot experience in Thailand and South Vietnam, and Randle had worked for more than a month with the Reeves engineers in the development of the TSQ-81. Leading less than a dozen volunteers they practiced under simulated field conditions at the Bryan airfield mock-up for nearly a month, testing the radar and communications gear and mastering the assembly of the radar equipment and its associated buildings. Satisfied with their efforts, Randle had his men disassemble the buildings, repack the equipment, and crate everything for air transport. The men were provided special funds to purchase civilian work clothes and told they would enter Laos in the guise of civilian contractors.[18]

In August the installation crew and their cargo were deployed to Udorn, Thailand, while Randle was dispatched to provide a program update to senior officers at 13th AF Headquarters at Clark Air Base, Philippines, and 7th AF Headquarters, in Saigon. Upon arrival at Udorn he briefed Major General William C. Lindley, Deputy Commander, 7/13th AF, the senior U.S. military official responsible for Air Force support to the U.S. Embassy and CIA in Laos.[19] Strongly promoted by the Air Force leadership and blessed by the White House, Heavy Green was of enormous interest to many senior U.S. and civilian officials. Later, when tragedy struck, few would claim any responsibility.

Lieutenant Colonel Randle quickly instituted his work plan, sending Chief Master Sergeant Born and most of the team to establish living quarters and a construction base camp at Phou Pha Thi while he remained at Udorn, along with a few men, to prepare and manage the shipment of equipment and supplies to the mountain. Additionally, Randle was frequently called upon to provide his superiors with construction updates. The challenge was substantial as the men at Udorn were required to unpack each piece, determine when it was required on the mountain, and then repack it for helicopter transport on the designated day. Nevertheless, the Udorn workers had access to the considerable amenities available on and off base. Life at Phou Pha Thi was considerably more austere.[20]

Chief Born recalls that he and his men arrived at the mountain to find "three tents and a few Lao soldiers." The newcomers added large canvas and wood sleeping quarters, but preferred to sleep inside the helicopters whenever they were on site. Told that they would be "guarded by the Lao army," the Americans were prohibited from carrying any weapons. Oddly enough the sergeant never saw anyone else with a firearm either, despite "often hearing gunfire at night and wondering who was doing the shooting." With little else to do but work, and the added incentive that once they completed the living quarters they could move out of their tents, the men put in long days of exhausting physical labor. Heavy cloud cover and rain in northeastern Laos was a constant problem, however, often causing delays in the arrival of equipment and supplies. On several occasions during their three-month stay the team ran short of food and water, forcing the men to "put out tarps to catch rainwater." According to Born, on one memorable day a helicopter was finally able to land and promptly "blew over the tarps and our water barrels. It was a real bitch."[21]

Perhaps more importantly given the isolation and geographic harshness of Phou Pha Thi, the unpredictable weather also disrupted rest and relaxation visits by the crew to Udorn.[22] Since the men were ordered to avoid any contact with the local villagers and had only occasional encounters with other Americans, the twice-monthly trips to Thailand were important, and much anticipated, morale boosters. During these brief respites the men were able to send mail and even make telephone calls to loved ones, although phoning was very expensive.[23] But, for the vast majority of their assignment they were in near total isolation.[24] Additionally, there was the constant realization that they were working deep inside an area mostly controlled by enemy forces in a country where their government claimed there were no U.S. military men. In retrospect, Born's installation crew experienced many of the same irritants and stress which would later rankle the operations crews assigned to the isolated post. Nonetheless, it appears that no one at the combat evaluation group thought about or cared to learn from these initial experiences.

From an engineering perspective construction of the radar facility and living quarters progressed very smoothly. CH-3 "Jolly Green" helicopters from the Udorn-based 20th Helicopter Squadron ferried supplies to the landing strip and transported the men to and from the site.[25] The larger and heavier pieces were transported by a U.S. Army CH-47 Chinook helicopter.[26] The Chinook, used throughout South Vietnam for the emplacement of artillery pieces into small firebases, was especially well suited for this work. The aircraft's powerful engines and twin rotors allowed the pilots to safely maneuver in the thin air and often shifting winds of northeastern Laos, while the helicopter's cargo sling system was very effective in lowering awkward prefabricated building pieces and heavy materials to the confined construction area.[27] Although occasionally the cargo releases landed quite near the technicians, there were no serious injuries during the delivery of more than 150 tons of equipment and supplies.[28]

On August 20, however, the CH-47 was the target of hostile gunfire as it hauled cargo between LS 36 and Pha Thi. Three days later a CH-3 was shot down during a flight to Site 85, and another Jolly Green sent to investigate was fired on. No Americans were killed or wounded in the incidents. Commenting on the activity a message from 7/13th AF to 7th AF and Headquarters PACAF observed, "Area in vicinity of Site 85 is not always permissive environment and may become more hostile when OL [Operating Location] -28 is operational."[29] This would prove to be quite an understatement.

Following Lieutenant Colonel Seitzberg's recommendations, the radar facility was built some 20 feet from the edge of the southwestern cliffs.[30] Much as they had practiced at the Texas airfield, the technicians joined three 12 x 9 x 40-foot metal shelters, similar to intermodal ocean shipping cargo containers, to form an L-shaped building divided into a mission operations room and a communications and maintenance area. The radar cabinet, plotting board, computer, control console, and other associated equipment were placed in a single section located parallel to the cliffs. The radio, teletype, and cryptographic equipment, as well as storage rooms and maintenance work tables, were located in the double-wide segment facing perpendicular to the cliff. The structure had two doors located on opposite ends of the communications and maintenance area; one faced north along the ridge line, while the other opened south to the generator area and path to the living quarters. There were also several 2-foot by 2-foot "escape hatches" located on the sides of the building.[31]

Due to the weight of the radar gear, in some cases 1,500 pounds per piece, the units were hoisted onto the foundation and the remainder of the building constructed around the equipment. Similarly, one of the most difficult installation tasks involved the placement of the one-ton base and pedestal for the radar dish. Once the building was completed a U-shaped reinforced tower was erected around the outside of the radar operations area. Working within yards of the steep cliffs in often unpredictable winds, the technicians used a gantry crane gingerly to place the base, pedestal, and radar dish onto the tower. It was a proud moment for the men and a well-earned testament to their teamwork.[32]

The bathing and sleeping quarters, comprised of a single 12 x 9 x 40-foot metal shelter, were also constructed parallel to the cliff but located down an embankment approximately 30 feet to the east of the radar building. The four diesel generators used to power the entire operation were placed about 25 feet southeast of the radar building, while the TACAN equipment was relocated from the helipad area to the western cliffs some 20 yards directly south of the radar building. Two 400-cycle converters were positioned a few yards south of the generators. For added strength and protection, all of the buildings were reinforced with steel girders and sandbags.[33]

As the Phou Pha Thi crew completed the buildings and began the crucial equipment performance checks, at Barksdale AFB Lieutenant Colonel Jerry Clayton was about to make the final personnel selections for project Heavy Green. In recent weeks, however, the project had been expanded to include maintenance and operation responsibilities for all TACAN sites in Laos. According to Clayton, a senior Air Force official had determined that civilian contractors performing maintenance on the Phou Pha Thi-based TACAN might discern the mission of the radar facility and create security problems.[34] Consequently, despite having no connection with ground-directed bombing, TACAN operations and maintenance became the responsibility of Heavy Green. However, because no one in the evaluation group was qualified to screen and assess TACAN technicians, Clayton requested nominations from the Air Force Communications Service (AFSC), the command responsible for placing the navigational aids in Laos. AFSC then selected and sent a group of technicians to Barksdale for a final judgment by the group.[35]

In retrospect, adding the TACAN responsibilities to Heavy Green was a very poor decision. The First Combat Evaluation Group was a close-knit organization manned mostly by career personnel who had worked together in small detachments for many years. The men were a known quantity with demonstrated expertise, and Clayton could recruit from those who had served a Combat Skyspot Southeast Asia tour of duty. The inclusion of TACAN specialists, dedicated men to be sure, nonetheless introduced unknowns into the project's interpersonal chemistry.[36]

Despite the importance of the TSQ-81 initiative, Heavy Green was impaired from the very beginning by a single ill-conceived decision. A complete focus by the Heavy Green senior leadership on the radar bombing mission might not have averted the catastrophe that befell the program, but it certainly would have allowed these experienced managers to concentrate more closely on some serious personnel problems at Site 85.

On September 12, 1967, more than fifty Skyspot qualified personnel and about a dozen TACAN technicians assembled in a carefully guarded auditorium at Barksdale AFB. After the group received a tough security admonition about unauthorized disclosures of sensitive information, Major Robert A. Cornetti, from the Office of Special Plans, explained that participation in the overseas project he was about to discuss was "strictly voluntary." Several sergeants excused themselves, including one who explained that he was preparing for another assignment and had just shipped all his furniture to Europe.

Cornetti revealed that the men were being considered for a hazardous project which would require the participants officially to leave the military so they could be hired as civilian defense contractors.[37] The men were then provided with a three-page "Memorandum of Understanding" stamped "Top Secret Sensitive" which, among other things, defined how this program would be accomplished. This extraordinary document warrants quoting in its entirety.[38]

1. This Memorandum of Understanding between the United States Air Force and the Air Force member whose name appears above (hereinafter referred to as Member) will govern the terms and conditions of his assignment to Project HEAVY GREEN. The terms and conditions are set below:

a. The Member will submit a request for release from the US Air Force. The request will be approved by HQ USAF and the Member separated at HQ Command, Bolling AFB, Washington, D.C. During the period of separation from the US Air Force:

(1) All military pay, allowances, privileges, and benefits normally due a military member or his dependents while the Member is actively serving will be terminated.

(2) The Member will accept employment with Lockheed Aircraft Services Company (LAS), a subsidiary of Lockheed Aircraft Corporation.

(3) Pay and allowances during the term of employment with LAS will be equivalent to the Member's active duty gross pay in SEA [Southeast Asia] plus a gross monetary gain of $6,000.00 per year for a Member with dependents, $4,500.00 per year for a Member without dependents, or 50% of the Member's gross pay, whichever is greater. The amounts referred to in this paragraph are before taxes.

(4) Member and dependents will be entitled to all privileges and benefits due an employee of LAS, to include death and disability insurance for the member; hospital, surgical, supplemental accident, polio, and major medical expense benefits for dependents.

b. In the event a Member dies in any circumstance other than while serving under the documentation of a LAS employee, e.g., operating Site #85 and transiting between Site and Udorn, Thailand, employment to LAS will be terminated and the Member reinstated into the USAF. In this event, military benefits to the Member's dependents or other beneficiaries shall apply as in the case of the death of any officer or airman in ordinary circumstances.

c. In the event of death while under LAS documentation (as specified in b above) where the Member's body is recovered by friendly forces, b above applies.

d. In the event of death while under LAS documentation (as specified in b above) where the Member's body is not recovered, benefits shall apply to the Member's dependents or other beneficiaries as in the case of any LAS employee. In addition, the Member shall be reinstated to the rolls of the USAF and normal benefits to the Member's dependents or other beneficiaries shall also apply.

e. In the event of capture by enemy forces while under LAS documentation (as specified in b above) LAS will continue to pay the contractual salary to the Member's account and provide benefits to the Member's dependents under paragraph a (4) until the Member is restored to US control and reinstated to the rolls of the USAF or subsequent death of the member while under the control of the enemy is established. In the event of the latter, d above applies.

f. In the event a Member becomes "missing in action" while under LAS documentation (as specified in b above) he will be considered as captured, and e above will apply. This status will be reviewed under the applicable public law 12 months following the missing in action report. At that time, determination will be made to continue the Member's status under e above or declare the Member dead and invoke the provisions of d above.

g. Upon completion of the Member's assignment to Site #85, he will, upon authoritative direction, be discharged from LAS and reinstated to the rolls of the USAF. In this regard:

(1) The Member's military records will be corrected to void any indication that the Member had been released from military service. Military service in terms of longevity, accrual of time for promotion purposes and the like will be credited.

(2) A review of the Member's records will be conducted. The purpose of the review will be to ascertain if the Member would normally have been promoted while serving in the cover status. If the review is affirmative, a special board will effect the necessary promotion and establish an appropriate date of rank.

2. I have read and understand the foregoing, and I freely and voluntarily enter into this Memorandum of Understanding with the United States Air Force in accordance with the terms and conditions thereof.

Date Name/Rank/Serial Number

3. The Member whose name appears above has read the foregoing and has indicated his full understanding of its contents. I undertake on behalf of the United States to ensure that the actions which are the responsibility of the United States Air Force in this connection are promptly and adequately taken.

R.H. ELLIS, Major General, USAF Director of Plans
Deputy Chief of Staff/Plans & Operations

Forty-eight officers and enlisted men signed the above document and faithfully stepped out of the Air Force into the "black world." Many spent only a brief time reading the memorandum which, after being signed, was collected by Major Cornetti for safekeeping in the Special Plans office. Most of the volunteers were career military, a number with more than twenty years of service and eligible for retirement. Yet, they signed a paper that would lead to their discharge or resignation from the service without any benefits. As Jerry Clayton recalled thinking, "I just walked away from 24 years service with the stroke of a pen." He later joked to another volunteer, " I hope the Air Force comes through with their part of the deal."[39] But, despite the humor, Clayton and the others had no misgivings. The room at Barksdale was filled with many of the best technicians in the Air Force and these men were justifiably proud that they had been asked to participate in such an important project. Moreover, because many had served in Southeast Asia they clearly understood how a radar system based in northeastern Laos would substantially improve America's bombing campaign of North Vietnam. They accepted the danger, the separation from family and friends, and the knowledge that the work was so sensitive that it could never be disclosed publicly.

The married men were, of course, concerned that their decision to separate from the military would not adversely affect their dependents. They had all earned seniority and their military benefits, medical coverage, military family housing, and base exchange and commissary privileges were an important part of their total government compensation. It was, therefore, very important that the Air Force ensure that similar compensation and benefits were extended during their hiatus from the military. This seems to have been covered with the gross monetary gain and benefits described in paragraph 1, sub-paragraphs a (3) and a (4).[40] Similarly, in the event of death, capture, or "missing in action" status, the Lockheed arrangement assured the men would eventually be reinstated into the Air Force. This guaranteed the families would receive appropriate military benefits, as dictated by the situation. Lastly, upon return to the Air Force, the arrangement guaranteed the men promotions, if warranted, and military credit for their time as Lockheed employees. Under the circumstances, the Air Force and Lockheed created a fair pay and benefits package.

Once the Heavy Green personnel had been selected, Major Cornetti traveled to Lockheed headquarters at Ontario, California, for final contract negotiations with Duane Wood and Daniel Houghten, President of the Lockheed Aircraft Corporation. Houghten granted company approval and on September 29, 1967, the U.S. Air Force awarded Lockheed a single source contract to "Provide Non-Personal Services for the Operation and Maintenance of Designated Navigational Aids and to Perform Other Technical Services as required in Southeast Asia."[41]

Two days after the Barksdale briefing the men were given Permanent Change of Station (PCS) orders assigning them to Detachment

1, 1043 Radar Evaluation Group, Headquarters Command, Bolling AFB, Washington, D.C., with a reporting date of October 9, 1967. Under the orders the married men were authorized to move their dependents and ship household goods to a location of their choice within the continental United States.[42] While a few declined to relocate, the majority of the men moved their families to areas near relatives. For many of the families this three-week period was a very difficult time. Children were uprooted from familiar schools and neighborhoods and placed in new classrooms and surroundings. There were many quick goodbyes to friends and dozens of other details to contend with, all occurring at short notice and with little explanation. And, with their spouses about to depart for an overseas area, the wives knew that they would soon be very much alone to raise their children and contend with problems that would often require solutions long before an exchange of letters.[43] Moreover, throughout all of this disruption the husbands followed orders not to discuss the project with their wives. Then, in the week prior to the men's departure, the women were also brought into the black world. The Air Force had decided that the wives would be told what their husbands had signed up for and, if they did not consent, the men would be withdrawn from the program.

According to Air Force records, the implicit danger and the extraordinary requirement to separate the men from the military caused General McConnell to direct that "the wives of all the participants should be briefed completely on all details of the project to ensure that in the event of a loss of life, the individual's wives would be completely knowledgeable of all aspects of the program." The Air Force placed most of the women on military travel orders and flew them to Washington, D.C., for a top secret briefing at the Pentagon on October 10. The couples, according to Air Force records, were told "the administrative details of the program to include discharge from Service, employment by civilian contractor, to ensure protection of Geneva Convention, location of husband's employment and possible hazards of such employment to include the possibility of loss of life."[44] The wives were not, however, shown the memorandum signed by their husbands at Barksdale.[45]

Several of the participants recall that the briefing stressed the critical importance of the project to the country and praised the men for their selection. Captain Stanley J. Sliz, one of four officers picked for

Heavy Green, says they were told their efforts "would shorten the war." Ann Holland, wife of radioman Staff Sergeant Melvin A. Holland, remembers a very positive and upbeat presentation which included the statements that the "men were the cream of the crop" and that "the project would save lives."[46] As to the personal risks, the group was told "the location was secure" and that "friendly forces would be defending the area."[47] Indeed, Mary Hall, whose husband Staff Sergeant Willis R. Hall was a cryptographic specialist, describes a senior officer who downplayed the danger of the assignment. "We still had the right to quit at that point, but he said the discussion about risks was just a formality."[48] Nonetheless, Ann Holland recalls being very nervous about the entire plan and stubbornly insisted on a clear promise of protection for the families. "What if something happens, what happens to our military benefits?" she asked. An Air Force official responded "We can assure you nothing is going to happen, but if it does the men will be reinstated into the Air Force and you will get full military benefits."[49]

Following the briefing, all of the women were required to sign a secrecy agreement, witnessed and signed by Major Cornetti, which forbade them from discussing the Heavy Green project with any unauthorized persons.[50] Ann Holland at first refused to sign her agreement and tried to persuade her husband to decline the mission. He was adamant, however, and told her "If you keep me from going on this assignment I'll never forgive you." Against all of her instincts, she signed the paper.[51]

As the women left the briefing they were given a phone number at the Special Plans office and told to call if anyone in the family required assistance during their sponsor's overseas assignment.[52] Five months later it would be the Special Plans office calling the families to report eleven of the men missing.

Notwithstanding General McConnell's edict, at least two wives did not attend the briefing. Staff Sergeant Jack C. Starling, a TACAN specialist, was about to become a father for the seventh time. Starling assured the Special Plans officers that his wife agreed to the assignment and her presence in Washington was waived.[53] Later, Starling would have cause to reconsider his decision to join the Heavy Green program. Staff Sergeant Herbert A. Kirk , a teletype repairman, faced a much more serious concern. Once General McConnell ordered that the wives be informed of the project, the Air Force Office of Special

Investigations (OSI) immediately began a security review to verify their eligibility to receive a top secret briefing. The OSI and the Special Plans office determined that Mrs. Kirk, a German national, should not be granted a security clearance.[54] According to 1983 court testimony by Cornetti, the situation was explained to Sergeant Kirk and he agreed that his wife need not be informed of the classified project. Cornetti has said Kirk then assented "to a special waiver saying that, unlike the other members of the mission, in the event of his death, he would not be reinstated in the military."[55] Kirk was then processed out of the Air Force with the other members of Heavy Green.

Staff Sergeant Kirk, according to a newspaper interview with his stepson Klaus, explained to his family that he was leaving the military to become a civilian employed in Southeast Asia. However, Klaus insisted his father also said he expected to be reinstated in the military.[56] Clearly, Herb Kirk wanted to be a part of the Heavy Green project. Nonetheless, it strains credulity to believe a 38-year-old man who had served in the military for nearly twenty years would decline the same survivor benefits afforded his teammates. In writing, Kirk agreed to the project with the understanding he would be reinstated into the Air Force at its completion. Why would he make an oral agreement which, if he were killed, would deprive his family of significant military compensation? What seems more likely, is that a senior officer in the Special Plans office assured Kirk that in the event of his death his family would be properly cared for and Kirk accepted this pledge.[57]

While General McConnell, Air Force Chief of Staff, evidently felt a strong obligation to treat the other Heavy Green spouses with respect, insisting they be informed of the activity, Mrs. Kirk and her family were afforded no such consideration. There were scores of other qualified teletype repairmen in the Air Force; but, in its hurried efforts to get the Heavy Green program underway, the Special Plans office displayed supreme indifference to Mrs. Kirk and her children and accepted Herb Kirk. Again, it was expected security rules would forever prevent anyone from knowing the true circumstances. Herbert Kirk never returned from Site 85 and it would take more than a decade and a Federal lawsuit to have him posthumously reinstated in the U.S. Air Force. This subject is detailed in chapter 13.

Processing the men out of the Air Force was quickly accomplished at Bolling AFB, albeit with some quizzical looks. During the finance phase, Master Sergeant Francis A. "Frank" Roura, a senior administrative specialist who would serve as the Heavy Green "First Sergeant," encountered a former acquaintance. She questioned why Roura, close to retirement, would be asking for separation. Roura quickly took her aside and "formally suggested that she not pursue the subject with him or question any of the other men requesting release from the air force."[58] Although this anecdote underscores the flimsy nature of the project's "cover," the Air Force was really concerned only with being able to state factually if need be that the men were truly civilians. Ironically, as part of their cover while in Thailand the men would represent themselves as members of an Air Force radar evaluation team. This incongruity—one day military, the next day civilian—would eventually become a serious irritant to some of the Heavy Green men.

On Friday October 13 the men were flown on a military aircraft from Andrews AFB to Ontario, California for the Lockheed hiring formalities. The following day a Lockheed personnel specialist assisted the men in completing an "Agreement of Employment" and other paperwork assigning various health and insurance benefits.[59] According to a Lockheed statement:

> Lockheed . . . was instructed only to process the men for employment as they arrived and to issue them Lockheed identification, provide uniforms, and undertake normal employee indoctrination. It was clearly established in the pre-contractual briefings that Lockheed had no management authority, responsibility, or operational control over the men beyond the activity associated with the processing and that Lockheed's continuing responsibility extended only to payment of the employees' salary.[60]

Lockheed Aircraft Services designated the activity "Project 389" and named Jerry Clayton as the "manager of the field service group." Under this arrangement Clayton was required to notify Lockheed of any deaths or injuries to the men.[61]

Once the hiring process was completed, and the forty-eight men were officially civilian employees of Lockheed, most of the group donned their military uniforms and were flown by an Air Force C-130 transport to Udorn, Thailand. Clayton, accompanied by four of his top technicians, headed to Hawaii and the Philippines to update senior military officials on the status of Heavy Green. The briefings created a sense of optimism that this new initiative would boost the Rolling

Thunder campaign and thereby, perhaps, convince the U.S. political leadership to support an expanded bombing program.[62]

Indeed, as the Heavy Green program was being finalized there was increasing international and domestic debate on America's bombing of North Vietnam. As Mark Clodfelter has written, "[M]any nations saw it as an exercise of American aggression. In the United States, student protesters castigated Rolling Thunder, and in October 1967 thirty Congressmen sent [President] Johnson an open letter urging him to stop the bombing. Yet to most Americans the air offensive was a source of confused anger. Baffled by the bombing restrictions, they called for heavier raids on the North."[63] The U.S. military was determined to be prepared to carry out the latter.

The Heavy Green team arrived at Udorn air base much like any other group of airmen on temporary duty and assumed their military cover as members of Detachment 1, 1043 Radar Evaluation Squadron (RES).[64] The unit was organized into four functional areas, administration; supply; radar operations and support teams for the TSQ and TACAN duties at Phou Pha Thi; and maintenance and repair teams for the Lao-based TACAN sites. Senior positions were as follows: Lieutenant Colonel Clayton and Lieutenant Colonel Clarence F. "Bill" Blanton were, respectively, commander and deputy commander of the squadron. Major Donald R. Layman and Captain Stanley J. Sliz each supervised a nine-man radar operations and support team. Master Sergeant Roura served as First Sergeant and chief of administration, while Master Sergeant Granville C. Norton headed the supply section, and Master Sergeant Robert E. Myers was the senior TACAN specialist.[65]

In an effort to shield their comings and goings, the detachment established offices in a Quonset hut located inside the Air America compound. The location would provide uncomplicated and mostly unobserved access to the aircraft used to transport them to and from Phou Pha Thi, a period when they would be in civilian clothes. Since they were no longer in the military and eligible for government housing and meals, the men lived in rented bungalows in the city of Udorn and purchased their own food. This arrangement also reduced their contact with other Americans, lessening the possibility of a security breach. Otherwise, while at Udorn the men conducted themselves like any other airmen.[66]

In all outward respects, a casual observer would have concluded that the detachment was just one of many small units supporting the

Southeast Asia air war. After less than two weeks in Thailand, the Heavy Green team was ready to go to work "dropping bombs."[67] Arrangements for the turnover at Site 85 were nearly complete.

Ground-directed radar bombing required a precise knowledge of the radar's location and in early October a U.S. Defense Mapping Agency (DMA) team had been dispatched to Laos to determine this data. Advised that there was a French-installed benchmark[68] located somewhere in the royal capital of Luang Prabang, the DMA specialists and Lieutenant Colonel Randle were flown to the area by the 20th Helicopter Squadron. Fortuitously, one of the helicopter pilots was able to communicate in French with the local Lao army commander and the team was quickly led to the mark.[69] The surveyors were not so lucky at Pha Thi, however, where they sat for several weeks until clear skies finally permitted the celestial sightings necessary to determine their exact location.[70] Nonetheless, by mid-October the TSQ-81 was ready to undergo a final equipment evaluation with test aircraft.

Seventh AF in Saigon directed Colonel John C. Giraudo, Commander, 355th Tactical Fighter Wing (TFW),[71] Takhli Royal Thai Air Force Base, to provide F-105 "Thud" fighter-bombers for two weeks of Combat Skyspot trials. For Giraudo, a fighter-pilot who had been shot down and taken prisoner-of-war during World War II and Korea, the task became decidedly onerous. Upon assuming command two months earlier, Giraudo says General Momyer, Commander 7th AF, told him "That crew at the 355th have been a bunch of glory seekers, more interested in chasing MiGs [enemy fighters] than in taking out the targets I've assigned them. I expect you to get out there and change things."[72] Colonel Giraudo responded with a program he called "Bombs On The Target" or BOTT, which emphasized different bombing tactics and the use of wing-mounted electronic jamming pods.[73] He also gained Momyer's approval for his wing to discontinue the 7th AF practice of flying combat missions with the Identification Friend or Foe (IFF) system engaged. The IFF emitted a signal which, when "interrogated" by a friendly aircraft, allowed a positive identification. Although Giraudo had no specific evidence, he believed the North Vietnamese and their allies might be using the IFF signals to track and shoot down American aircraft. Others, who supported flying with the IFF turned on, claimed that it allowed U.S. fighters to quickly identify the F-105s and prevented accidental friendly fire shoot downs.[74] When notified of the Combat Skyspot testing, Giraudo immediately recognized that his new strategy was in conflict with the tenets of radar bombing. He decided, therefore, to personally participate in the calibration flights.[75]

The flight testing began with a few unarmed missions and then progressed to controlling actual bomb drops over northern Laos. Accuracy was determined by photo missions and reports from Hmong ground teams sent in to inspect the bombed areas. Almost immediately, however, Colonel Giraudo objected to instructions from the radar team. In order to assist in tracking the aircraft, the team asked that the IFF be switched on. He agreed, but only for flights operating over Laos. After the first bomb drops were evaluated, the F-105's were directed to operate in closer formation. Flying in a spread-out defensive configuration caused each of the pilots, when the controller directed bomb release, to drop their ordnance in a slightly different area. Because 7th AF was attempting to obtain the greatest possible accuracy, the 355th was told to tighten up their formations. Giraudo voiced his objections, but complied. The final stage was an actual bombing mission against North Vietnam.

The 355th was directed to attack the Yen Bai railroad marshaling area located northwest of Hanoi. Known to be heavily defended by anti-aircraft artillery (AAA), the wing was told to conduct the operation in two four-aircraft formations. Colonel Giraudo immediately voiced his objections by telephone to Major General Gordon F. Blood, 7th AF Director of Operations. After listening to the Colonel's concerns, including his belief that flying the strikes as directed might well cost lives, General Blood pointedly asked Giraudo if he was "refusing the Yen Bai frag [order]." Giraudo replied that he would fly it, but would "see him and General Momyer personally the day after."[76] The mission against Yen Bai was tense for both the TSQ-81 controller and the pilots of the 355th. According to Giraudo:

> We briefed as Sky Spot directed: Lead IFF on, close formation on the bomb run, straight and level until bomb release. Just like a big B-52 formation. There was very bad weather in the target area, complete overcast with tops at around 9,000 feet. Communications between the controller and I were terse. I took each of his constant course corrections resentfully. Our RHAW gear [radar warning equipment] indicated a few radars were tracking us, soon scattered AAA appeared, none real close. We were well settled down when the controllers gave us the drop command.[77]

The Thuds returned uneventfully to Takhli, but Colonel Giraudo carried out his promise to discuss with his superiors the fallacy of radar-directed bombing by F-105 fighter-bombers. Unbeknownst to Giraudo, Momyer was one of Heavy Green's greatest supporters.

In Saigon Colonel Giraudo argued that if the radar bombing was continued every one of his recently implemented defensive measures would have to be "abandoned, despite the now proven fact that the 355th loss rate was half of the 388th's against the same targets." He repeated his concerns about the IFF, flying in close formations "we were looking like the Thunderbirds over Las Vegas," and the vulnerability of such maneuvers to attack by enemy fighters and surface-to-air (SAM) missiles. "With all due respect, and to protect the pilots of my wing," Giraudo has recalled, "I officially requested that the 355th no longer be fragged on a Sky Spot mission because I knew losses would dramatically increase." Giraudo says General Momyer then directed that the 355th be exempt from any radar bombing missions. When the Colonel expressed the opinion that no wing should fly such bombing strikes, he received a curt "thank you" from Momyer.[78]

When asked in 1994 to reflect on his truncated involvement with the 7th AF ground-directed radar bombing campaign, General Giraudo expressed "near disgust about the political air war we were fighting." In his view,

> B-52's with extensive fighter cover and ECM [electronic countermeasures] screen should have been fighting the NVN [North Vietnam] air war, not the mosquito pricks which the F-105 and F-4 fighter bombers were inflicting. In recognition of this I felt no responsibility to heroically sacrifice precious American lives by playing phony B-52.[79]

Commanding an F-105 fighter bomber wing in his third war, Giraudo was committed to the fewest possible pilot losses. Moreover, he was intent on evaluating and, if found useful, instituting new technologies. Giraudo quickly determined that ground directed bombing, as ordered by 7th AF, was fundamentally unsafe for his pilots and he took steps to remove his wing from the program. By default the 388th TFW would carry on and, as discussed later, would soon suffer the losses Giraudo had forecast. Why did 7th AF continue with a program one of their most experienced wing commanders found to be highly dangerous? Unfortunately, in the fall of 1967, the Air Force had no other means by which to conduct all-weather bombing operations. Brigadier General Rockly Triantafellu, PACAF's senior intelligence officer from 1966 to 1969, recalls, "It was embarrassing for the Air Force that only the A-6s could do the job. We were very concerned about the lack of an all-weather bombing capability, but nobody wanted to bring in the B-52's at that time."[80] General Blood has acknowledged the dilemma and said, "We saluted and did what we were told."[81]

For the forty-eight men who had signed up for a program they were told would "save pilot's lives," the reality, at least according to John Giraudo, seems to have been very different. Was Heavy Green part of an effort to make do with fighter bombers, "phony B-52's," because the White House lacked the political will to use the real thing over North Vietnam? And what of the senior Air Force leadership, which accepted unsound civilian-directed military decisions and responded by cobbling together a temporary and highly problematic bombing program? Sadly, the worst was yet to come.

The radar was now fully operational and the installation crew was preparing for the arrival of the Udorn crew. One final engineering task provided this TSQ-81 with a very special feature—14 x 14-inch sheets of thermite[82] rigged for the emergency destruction of the equipment. According to Chief Master Sergeant Born, he personally affixed the one-inch thick squares to the pedestal and each of the radar components. The thermite, when ignited by an electrical charge, was expected to burn and melt the metal and any surrounding electronics. In more than twenty years of military service it was the only time the sergeant would ever be called upon to place a destructive device in a radar system.[83] The site was now ready for turnover to the permanent operating crew.

In a bid to prevent the installation team from discerning the identities of the operating crew, a carefully controlled changeover occurred the last week of October. Major Layman and his crew, dressed in civilian clothes and carrying Lockheed identification cards, were flown to the mountain by helicopter.[84] Prior to the aircraft's arrival, Chief Master Sergeant Born directed his men into tents and ordered that they remain inside, out of sight, and make no attempt to observe the arriving men. Born met the helicopter and led the Heavy Green team, most of whom he had known from earlier assignments, up the path to their new working and living quarters. The senior sergeant then conducted a tour of the facility and provided briefings on the status of the equipment while the installation crew left the tents and loaded their personal gear onto the helicopter. Some three hours later Born wished the Heavy Green team well and joined his men for their long awaited trip to Thailand and onward to the United States.[85]

In less than eight months the Air Force had conceived a bold plan, convinced senior military officials of its merit, gained White House support to overcome the misgivings of a wary ambassador, developed and installed the specialized equipment, and formed and deployed a dedicated group to carry out the mission. Heavy Green was ready to make its mark on the Vietnam war.

4

"Commando Club"

TSQ-81 operations at Site 85, under the code name "Commando Club,"[1] officially commenced on November 1, 1967. With the onset of the northeast monsoon and an early October presidential decision to permit increased bombing in the Hanoi area, the timing was very good news for 7th AF.[2] Although unusually clear weather conditions in October allowed the Air Force to conduct nearly a thousand sorties, poor flying conditions over North Vietnam would soon severely impede U.S. bombing efforts.[3] Despite Colonel Giraudo's misgivings, the senior leadership at 7th AF believed they now possessed a technology that would allow Air Force pilots to conduct an all-weather bombing campaign against North Vietnam.[4] Commando Club, recalled Major General Gordon F. Blood, 7th AF Director of Operations, was "one of many technologies we were trying. We wanted all the new equipment we could get."[5] 7th AF would waste little time putting the radar to work.

In just a few months Pha Thi's summit had been transformed from a small Hmong guerrilla encampment occasionally used to recover Hmong reconnaissance teams and refuel Air Force rescue helicopters to a significant permanent American presence. Prior to the installation of the TSQ-81 CIA paramilitary officers rarely remained overnight on the mountain, instead commuting from their northeastern Laos operations base at Na Khang (LS 36).[6] When the Heavy Green technicians arrived, however, the CIA stationed two officers at Site 85. The agency also brought to the mountain a seven-man Thai Police Aerial Reinforcement Unit (PARU) team to serve as radio operators and inter-preters.[7] To accommodate the paramilitary officers and security forces the CIA constructed tin-roofed, wooden sleeping and working quar-ters just south of the helipad near the trail leading up to the radar facil-ity. A generator supplied electrical power to what the Heavy Green technicians called the "CAS" area.[8]

Certain the increased activity at Pha Thi would become known to enemy forces, the CIA officers, Terry Quill and John Spence, known by their nicknames "TQ" and "Woody," quickly established an early warning security program. Hmong teams were sent to collect intelli-gence on communist intentions and to patrol the surrounding valleys in search of any approaching enemy soldiers. This would be the "trip-wire" or first line of defense for Pha Thi. If detected, North Viet-namese and Pathet Lao forces would then be attacked with U.S. air strikes. Meanwhile, some 800 Hmong soldiers, many of whom lived with their families in the village of Pha Thi, were expected to hold the eastern approach to the summit against any ground attack. Sheer and rugged cliffs to the north, south, and west were considered impassable and deemed safe from enemy assault.[9]

The plan seemed to provide reasonable security; none of the CIA personnel envisioned the need for more than a brief Hmong delaying action to permit the destruction of the radar equipment and air evac-uation of the technicians, the Thais, and themselves. This CIA assess-ment was briefed to the Heavy Green commander, Lieutenant Colonel Clayton, who was assured that his men would have at least 24-hours notice "to blow up the site and get out before any significant attack."[10] Once the Americans and Thais were safely away the Hmong would fade into the surrounding mountains and the communist forces would be left with just another abandoned Lima Site.[11] In the event LS 85 was lost, senior American officials expected to locate new equipment on another mountain site and begin Heavy Green anew.[12] At least that was the plan.

Major Layman and his team settled easily into their new assign-ment. Although most of the men were somewhat startled at the loca-tion, one man recalling that it was "desolate, isolated, and I wondered what I had gotten involved with," the equipment and mission was sec-ond nature. Moreover, the men expected that they would soon be controlling the first ground-directed bombing strikes ever launched against the North Vietnamese capital.[13] These volunteers were at Pha

Thi to make a major contribution to the air war, or so they were led to believe, and it was time to go to work.

Commando Club missions began with the receipt of a daily mission outline, commonly called a "frag." Transmitted to Pha Thi in code from the Air Force communications center at Udorn air base, the frag provided the Heavy Green unit with detailed target information as well as the type of aircraft and munitions to be used in the attack. The target coordinates were loaded by the data operator into the radar computer, allowing the controller and crew chief to depict the target and the bomb run track on the plotting board. Concurrently the radioman set the mission frequencies, as designated in the frag, while the cryptographic technician ensured proper encryption of all transmissions. Lastly, the generator technician conducted an equipment check to determine the availability of all required power.

As the strike aircraft approached a predetermined location, known as the initial point (IP), the two radar technicians began a search and "locked on" to the lead aircraft. Tracking of the strike force commenced and the board operator, supervised by the crew chief, plotted the movement of the aircraft. Upon arrival at the IP, the controller provided the pilots with required course corrections.[14] From this moment until the order to drop bombs, the aircraft were under the direction of the controller. At ten seconds to bomb release any final course corrections were transmitted and the controller called out the final five seconds. The aircraft leader then verified "bombs away" and the strike force departed the target area.[15]

Using these procedures a team of just nine men,[16] working in a small metal building in northeastern Laos, added a new and significant dimension to the Rolling Thunder campaign: Air Force all-weather bombing of North Vietnam was now a reality.

Within a few weeks, however, serious questions were raised about the risk versus gain of ground-directed bombing. On November 18, 1967, Colonel Edward B. Burdett led an F-105 strike force of sixteen aircraft against Phuc Yen airfield, North Vietnam's primary MIG-21 fighter base and the occasional home of Hanoi's small squadron of IL-28 light bombers.[17] Burdett's aircraft, along with another, were downed by a barrage of "10–12" surface-to-air missiles that were fired into the formation. The remaining aircraft then jettisoned their bomb loads before reaching the targets.[18] The shootdown provided grist for pilots like Colonel Giraudo, who believed that flying at a constant speed and course, as required during the final minutes of radar bombing, markedly increased pilot vulnerability to enemy defenses.[19]

Despite the loss of Colonel Burdett, the following day Site 85 again controlled aircraft striking targets near Hanoi. Although no pilots were lost, Air Force officials termed the missions "costly" and "directed that strikes operating under the COMMANDO CLUB system be limited to a more permissive environment—until such time as problems associated with the system were resolved." General John D. Ryan, the commander in chief Pacific Air Forces, a strong proponent of ground-directed bombing and acutely aware that the Air Force desperately needed an all-weather strike capability, ordered a complete review of the tactics, techniques, and technical capabilities associated with the TSQ-81 program.[20] Ryan's order brought about the following changes to Commando Club missions:

> Strikes against targets in the Hanoi/Phuc Yen area were limited to one mission per day. Optimum strike times would be selected daily varying times on target. The size of the strike force would be controlled to keep them as small as possible and still accomplish the mission objective. Electronic countermeasures support . . . anti-SAM forces and MIGCAP [combat air patrol against MIGs] would be maximized. Maximum radio silence would be employed. Poststrike reconnaissance would be conducted only when supporting forces were available.[21]

Satisfied that these modifications would provide reasonable safety for the attacking pilots, 7th AF resumed the Commando Club missions. Official Air Force records confirm the early difficulties, but point to overall satisfaction with the program. In his end-of-tour report Major General William C. Lindley, Deputy Commander, 7/13th AF, observed, "After initial operational problems were overcome, the site began to pay dividends."[22] An Air Force study of the war reported, "These [initial] problems were resolved shortly and COMMANDO CLUB missions were successfully employed in the high threat areas."[23]

Indeed, during the eighteen weeks Heavy Green was operational, ground-directed bombing was often the only method by which the Air Force could successfully strike high-priority targets in North Vietnam.[24] While unexpected clear weather allowed considerable flying activity in October, poor conditions in November and December forced the cancellation of numerous Rolling Thunder missions.

Weather conditions in the new year were even worse. According to Air Force records, "1 January through 31 March 1968 was probably the most frustrating of all ROLLING THUNDER periods."[25] In the first three months of 1968 the overcast sky in North Vietnam precluded many non-Commando Club bombing missions, particularly in the northern part of the country where visual bombing came to almost a complete standstill. "February brought the poorest flying conditions in three years, and March was little better with the Northeast Monsoon prevailing nearly the entire month."[26] During this three-month period there were only four days when weather conditions over Hanoi and the surrounding areas allowed visual bombing, making it "necessary for nearly all missions to be conducted using radar bombing techniques, and results could not be observed through the undercast."[27] But, how many strike missions were actually controlled by Heavy Green and what were the specific targets?

During November, Site 85 directed seventeen missions over North Vietnam, involving 130 sorties. Targets included airfields at Yen Bai, Hoa Loc, Kep, and Phuc Yen, two storage facilities in western North Vietnam, and an army barracks located some fifty nautical miles northwest of Hanoi. Citing communications problems with the aircraft, Headquarters Pacific Air Forces rated six of the missions (more than seventy sorties) as unsuccessful.[28] In December, the number of sorties flown against North Vietnamese targets dropped to ninety-three as the focus of Commando Club shifted to strikes on communist positions in Laos. Specifically, eighty-four missions, 346 sorties, were flown in December against targets in northeastern Laos. Overall, sixty-nine of the North Vietnam sorties and 316 of the Laos sorties were rated as successful. While information is incomplete on the Lao targets, at least sixteen sorties struck enemy positions near Phou Pha Thi. In North Vietnam, Heavy Green continued to direct strikes at airfields, railroad yards, and three army barracks.[29] In the new year, TSQ-81-directed missions against North Vietnam were nearly equal to the December levels. Nineteen missions, ninety-nine sorties, flew against Yen Bai airfield and a storage area located in western North Vietnam. In Laos, thirty-eight missions, 152 sorties, struck unspecified communist targets. Success rates are unavailable.[30] February saw a substantial increase in the number of ground-directed radar missions against Lao targets; 417 sorties. About half of these attacks hit enemy strong points in the vicinity of Site 85. Against North Vietnam, there were twenty missions involving seventy-six sorties. Again, success rates are not reported.[31]

During its final ten days of operation, Site 85 directed three missions against North Vietnam and 153 missions at Lao targets. On March 4, Commando Club controlled strikes on the Ha Dong boat yard located some five nautical miles south of Hanoi. The following day, Heavy Green sent U.S. aircraft to hit the Tien Cuong railroad yard located about 35 nautical miles northwest of Hanoi. On March 10, Commando Club controlled its final strike against a North Vietnamese target, the Thai Nguyen railroad yard located some 40 nautical miles north of Hanoi. Both railroad yards had been attacked in December, while the boat yard was a new Heavy Green target. In Laos, nearly all of the missions were flown in defense of Site 85. There is no complete information available on the success of these missions.[32]

A central question remains. Did the system achieve bombing results commensurate with the danger to the lives of the Heavy Green team and the Air Force pilots being controlled by the TSQ-81? The answer is complex: some details are still available only in classified government documents, so the complete truth may never be known. Nevertheless, declassified materials and interviews with many of the central participants confirm that the radar at Site 85 filled an important lacuna in the Rolling Thunder air campaign. Unquestionably, the Heavy Green team made a unique contribution to the air war in North Vietnam, guiding American bombers in poor weather to most of North Vietnam's major airfields and important railroad and storage facilities. Still unresolved, until additional Vietnamese documents are released and examined, is whether the bombing results justified the risk of placing so many men in harm's way.[33] Based on my recent work with records in Laos, Cambodia, and Vietnam I have little doubt that the materials exist. Obtaining the required government approvals and access required for a meaningful scholarly examination, however, remains elusive. Absent information from Vietnamese sources, measuring the true efficacy of America's Rolling Thunder bombing strategy (let alone the Heavy Green program), is an overwhelming, if not impossible, task.

A complete assessment of U.S. materials related to the Heavy Green program is similarly onerous. The very nature of the bombing, missions flown at night and in poor weather, made it difficult and sometimes impossible to determine the damage and accuracy of these attacks. Nonetheless, the U.S. government possesses significant materials related to the Heavy Green project.

For more than thirty years, however, many facts known to the Air Force have been concealed or distorted from the general public and the families of those who served in the Heavy Green project. An official U.S. Air Force history published in 1978, *Air Power in Three Wars*, appears to have intentionally downplayed the Heavy Green operations. The author, retired General William W. Momyer,[34] based much of the monograph on Air Force materials collected under Project "Corona Harvest" which, due to their classified nature, could only be read by those with the proper security clearances and the "need to know."[35] As such, Momyer and his staff had access to many of the most sensitive secrets of the Vietnam war. In effect, Momyer and his assistants became the filter through which the Air Force examined the lessons of air power and warfare. This self-appraisal is an important process and all of the military services have, in most cases, performed an excellent job in sifting through their records to produce otherwise unavailable written perspectives. On the issue of project Heavy Green, Momyer chose to exclude from his comprehensive study some very important facts.

In Momyer's account of Site 85 he briefly discusses the political problems associated with having the "MSQ"[36] in Laos and the dangers faced by strike aircraft as they approached a target at a steady speed and bearing. He then reports:

> However, to keep pressure on the enemy during bad weather, the Air Force tried this technique [radar bombing] on 18 and 19 November 1967 in the Hanoi area. These missions were unsatisfactory because the MSQ was unreliable at its range limits. Because of these limitations of the MSQ, further attempts to bomb by MSQ in the high threat area were canceled.[37]

A careful reading of this passage would, logically, leave one with the impression that following the November 18 and 19 missions the program was deemed a failure and ground-directed radar bombing was not used again "in the high threat areas." Of course, as detailed above, Site 85 did continue after November 19 to direct USAF bombers into high threat areas near Hanoi.

There are a number of possible, and overlapping reasons why, in 1978, Momyer would obfuscate the true role of Heavy Green.[38]

Although the monograph was published a decade after the loss of Site 85, some Air Force leaders were still doubtless unwilling for security and political reasons to publicize the loss of the men and equipment. Momyer acknowledges the initial presence of the site in Laos and its purpose, but he does not disclose the site's continuing importance and eventual capture by communist forces. Was there a legitimate security rationale for these omissions? The system's basic technology had been available since the Korean war, suggesting the TSQ-81 equipment was sensitive only because it was located in Laos. In 1978 the Vietnamese and Laotian communists were celebrating their third year in power and they were very much aware of Site 85's existence and how it was destroyed.[39] Why, then, would Momyer obscure the details surrounding the Heavy Green mission? Since the communists were already aware of the details, what was the purpose in withholding this information?

In a 1974 memorandum Momyer argued that a Corona Harvest study of U.S. air activity in Laos laid bare a multitude of issues he believed were "somewhat of a problem." The sensitivity, according to the general, was not with the public release of technical secrets but with the political differences inherent in the Lao war. In Momyer's words:

> Since it [the study] covers the interdiction in Laos, it must and does treat with the problems of the divided responsibilities between the 7th Air Force and Embassy Vientiane. Probably the most controversial element is that pertaining to the rules of engagement which had a major impact on the effectiveness of the effort. These rules were detailed and varied from time to time which made it extremely difficult for air crews. As a consequence . . . I recommend that the second book [dealing with Laos] remain top secret with limited access. This should not preclude, however, some [military] student access for special monographs.[40]

Momyer vigorously opposed any public access to documents on the war in Laos, keenly aware that any detailed review would raise embarrassing questions about U.S. military activity in the "neutral" kingdom. In turn, this exposure would likely have spread to the subject of Heavy Green, an initiative the Air Force forced into Laos against the better judgment of the U.S. ambassador and the CIA. At Momyer's strong recommendation, therefore, the Air Force invoked the "top secret" security classification to prevent the dissemination of records on the war in Laos and the bloody loss at Site 85. Later, this was the very body of classified information the general appears to have selectively mined for inclusion in *Air Power in Three Wars*. These actions created a false history of the Heavy Green project which, because of the general's recommendation to have the source documents classified, could never be publicly examined or challenged. Or so it seemed at the time.

Paradoxically, a year before the publication of Momyer's monograph, the Office of Air Force History released *The United States Air Force in Southeast Asia: An Illustrated Account*. In the acknowledgments Momyer is described as having reviewed the study, providing the authors with "an especially helpful commentary." The loss of LS 85 is mentioned, but there is no discussion of the site's involvement in bombing. Instead, a passage states "Late in 1967 the Air Force replaced the original facility [TACAN] with an all-weather navigation system, operated and maintained by 19 USAF personnel."[41] The TSQ-81 was not a navigation system, it did not replace the TACAN, and it was not manned by nineteen personnel. Moreover, with regard to the post-attack recovery of American personnel from Site 85, this official account contains serious factual errors.[42] Nonetheless, these mistakes continue to be present in a 1984 "revised" edition.[43]

There is at least one other possible explanation for Momyer's abbreviated and misleading account on Site 85. In July 1975, after seven years of unsuccessful efforts to learn the fate of her husband, on behalf of herself and five children, Ann Holland filed a $1.6 million dollar wrongful death lawsuit against the Lockheed Aircraft Corporation and the United States government. Thus, at the time Momyer was preparing his study the Air Force was defending against this lawsuit, denying any liability, and fighting to maintain the secrecy of the Heavy Green program. The Holland lawsuit, including contradictions between these two official accounts, Air Force legal statements rebutting the suit, and the reaction of the U.S. government, will be examined in chapter 13.

Despite initial difficulties the TSQ-81 radar at Site 85 provided the Air Force a heretofore unavailable capability to carry out all-weather, round-the-clock, air strikes against important targets in North Vietnam and northeastern Laos. For the communist forces, dependent upon periods of poor weather and darkness to cover their movements and bomb damage repair efforts, this new American weapon posed an immediate and serious threat. A PAVN counterstrike, as forecast by CIA official Bill Lair at the program's inception, seemed a certainty.[44] Moreover, in the fall of 1967 Hanoi was in the midst of deploying forces and materiel for a major campaign in South Vietnam—the resulting Tet offensive and the battle for the U.S. Marine Corps base at Khe Sanh would soon irrevocably shatter America's perceptions of the Vietnam conflict. TACAN equipment in southern Laos, now operated by Heavy Green personnel, was providing critical navigation information for U.S. aircraft attacking communist positions around Khe Sanh and in other areas just south of the demilitarized zone.[45]

In late 1967 communist forces set out to destroy all of these radar and navigation facilities, seeking to "blind the eyes" of the American bombers. Hanoi's initial efforts would include a brutal assault in late December on a two-man TACAN facility in southern Laos and, in one of the most unusual air attacks of the Vietnam war, biplane bombing runs against Phou Pha Thi in January 1968. We now turn to a review of these well documented events, a significant foreshadowing of the successful March sapper assault on Phou Pha Thi.

5

Sowing the Wind, Reaping the Whirlwind

Shortly after the deployment of the Heavy Green unit to Udorn, Lieutenant Colonel Clayton, traveling as a Lockheed civilian employee, flew to the Lao capital of Vientiane for a critical meeting in the American Embassy. Clayton knew from his conversations with CIA and Air Force officials in Washington and Udorn that Ambassador William Sullivan exercised tight control over all U.S. military operations in Laos and those who ignored or misunderstood his instructions did so at great peril to their careers. He was uncomfortably aware that the presence of his men and their equipment in technically neutral Laos, if publicly revealed, would likely cause an international furor and great damage to U.S. interests. Lieutenant Colonel Clayton also understood that Ambassador Sullivan, as the de facto U.S. military commander in Laos, would be the ultimate decisionmaker on the continued operation of Heavy Green. Clayton had, in addition, been advised the CIA would supervise the indigenous forces that would provide site security, which only added another layer of unorthodoxy to this already peculiar situation. In the event of serious enemy pressure, CIA officials at Udorn assured the Air Force officer, there would be "an orderly evacuation and sufficient time to destroy the radar equipment." Clayton was also aware that senior Air Force officers in Saigon and Hawaii were closely watching the program and he wondered what role they would have in Site 85's continued operation. Further, he knew that Heavy Green's Lao targets would be approved through the air attaché's office.[1] Given these extraordinary political and military circumstances, Jerry Clayton sought a face-to-face meeting with the Ambassador and the CIA station chief.[2]

Despite the presidential-level interest in the Heavy Green program, however, the visit caught the Vientiane embassy unprepared. According to CIA station chief Ted Shackley, Clayton arrived at the embassy and asked to speak with him regarding a sensitive issue. Once in Shackley's office, Clayton began to provide an update on the radar bombing program. The station chief briefly listened and then directed Clayton to Colonel Paul Pettigrew, the Air Attaché.[3] After discussing the matter with Pettigrew, the two Air Force officers and Shackley met the same day with the ambassador. In Sullivan's office Clayton explained the program's equipment status, manning, and how he intended to comply with the ambassador's desire for a "deniable" presence. Sullivan, although still unconvinced the program's gain was worth the risk, was satisfied with Clayton's planning and had few comments.[4]

Lieutenant Colonel Clayton then asked two questions central to his responsibilities as the unit commander: "What happens when the site is threatened?" and "When would he know when to shut down operations?"[5] Nearly three decades later Shackley and Sullivan are clear and unambiguous in their recollections. "Clayton," says Ted Shackley "was told explicitly that we [CIA-directed forces] could not provide a static defense for Site 85."[6] Ambassador Sullivan recalls, "Shackley and I were in agreement. Site 85 could not be held by the Hmong. And Ted had his own people up there to worry about."[7] Clayton affirms total consensus at the meeting; there was no intention to stand and fight for the privilege of using Phou Pha Thi. "Ambassador Sullivan assured me that in the event of any serious enemy threat he would order the site closed. He said we would have plenty of time to carry out an evacuation. It was a great burden off my shoulders to hear those words. I knew the ambassador would make the decision and I was reassured it would not be done at the last minute."[8] The Heavy Green team chief returned to Udorn convinced his men were in safe hands.

But what of the curious initial reception afforded Lieutenant Colonel Clayton? It seems incongruous that none of the involved organizations at Udorn (Air America, CIA, or 7/13th AF) advised Vientiane that Clayton's team was poised to begin operations and that he wished to discuss the project with Ambassador Sullivan. The station chief insists no one notified him of Clayton's visit.[9] In any case, Shackley stressed, "The radar bombing initiative was an Air Force program.

The Air Attaché was the proper embassy entry point and that is where I sent him."[10]

Whatever the exact circumstances of the visit, the awkward nature of this initial contact suggests the lines of communication and authority between the U.S. Embassy in Laos and the Heavy Green team were poorly drawn and understood. There is no doubt Sullivan and Shackley had considered the security of Site 85 and decided there would be no heroic efforts to maintain a U.S. presence on the mountain. Yet, Shackley considered the overall program an Air Force responsibility. In practice, beyond validating bombing targets through 7/13th AF at Udorn, the attaché's office would have very little to do with Lima Site 85. Site security was a direct CIA responsibility and logistical support, transport of the men and their supplies in and out of Laos, would mostly be accomplished by the CIA proprietary airline, Air America.[11] Moreover, CIA personnel were stationed at Phou Pha Thi in order to facilitate these duties.

Perhaps the episode says something about the embassy's culture of operations. The CIA and air attaché offices were certainly busy prosecuting the war; in hindsight, were they too preoccupied to properly monitor such a high-risk venture? And who at the U.S. embassy was really responsible for Heavy Green oversight? These tough questions, and many others, would be asked in the aftermath of the fall of Site 85.

Remarkably, once Commando Club operations were underway, Clayton's attention was quickly diverted to air navigation problems having nothing to do with the initial Heavy Green concept. The last-minute Air Force decision to place all of the Laos-based TACAN sites under Clayton's command had turned into a management disaster. Instead of focusing his complete energies on the supervision of his radar bombing team, Lieutenant Colonel Clayton was being barraged by irate senior officers in Thailand and South Vietnam complaining about malfunctioning TACAN equipment. Selected for Heavy Green because of his radar bombing expertise, within weeks Clayton was on the verge of losing his command because of faulty TACAN operations—a system he knew virtually nothing about.[12]

Leaving his deputy, Lieutenant Colonel Blanton, to deal with Site 85 issues, Clayton soon determined that nearly all of his young TACAN technicians were unqualified for these unique field operations. Indeed, prior to the arrival of Heavy Green this specialized TACAN maintenance work had been performed by seasoned military technicians and factory-trained civilian contractors.[13] The switch in the fall of 1967 from these highly skilled and experienced personnel to the less qualified Heavy Green men resulted in an almost immediate breakdown in TACAN maintenance and repair. In a vigorous effort which probably saved his career, Clayton established a two-week training program for his people with the 1st Mobile Communications Group (1 MCG), at Clark Air Base, Philippines, the unit that had initially installed and operated the TACAN equipment. Although Clayton's technicians soon returned TACAN operations in Laos to respectable levels of reliability, problems persisted and the program required almost constant command attention. The Heavy Green men simply did not have the same level of maintenance expertise and access to parts as that enjoyed by the communications group and its contractor civilians.[14] The Air Force, in an effort to reduce costs and maintain the secrecy of the program, had been a little too clever for its own good.

Clearly the radar systems had an impact on communist operations: while Clayton was struggling to resurrect the malfunctioning navigational aids, Hanoi was busy devising plans to eliminate the systems in place at Muang Phalane, Phou Kate, and Phou Pha Thi. Discerning American dependence on the TACANs, on the eve of the Tet offensive the North Vietnamese military sought to frustrate U.S. air power by destroying these vulnerable ground stations. In October communist military forces began to deploy the necessary men and weapons into the target areas.[15]

As CIA official Bill Lair had forecast, in preparation for the assault on Site 85 the communists began building roads from eastern Sam Neua province toward Phou Pha Thi.[16] Although the construction and associated military activity was an obvious indication of their objective, a successful conventional attack on the mile-high base required heavy weapons (e.g., artillery, rockets, mortars) and considerable ground troops. Sustained transport along a dependable route was essential. So, despite the loss of surprise and the risk of U.S. air attacks, the movements continued. There was little doubt the North Vietnamese and their Pathet Lao allies were intent on destroying the enemy equipment atop Site 85.

Two hundred miles away at Udorn, Air Force and CIA officials tracked the movements and frequently requested air strikes against the closing forces—strikes that would prove largely unsuccessful. As was often the case on the Ho Chi Minh trail, mountainous terrain, dense jungle, and hazy and smoky conditions obscured the enemy and his materiel from American attacks. Moreover, these factors regularly precluded or reduced effective post-strike reconnaissance, resulting in delayed or unusable damage reports. Nonetheless, for the most part, the available intelligence showed that the road work continued.[17]

Once Hanoi made the decision to strike the sites, Pathet Lao and Vietnamese reconnaissance and intelligence collection operations were quickly set into motion. All three radar installations were located near civilian populations, where agents and sympathizers could easily gain first- and second-hand information on daily operations and security arrangements.[18] While the full extent of their initial collection against Site 85 remains unclear, one incident bears recounting and examination. On October 20, Hmong security forces seized two Buddhist monks near the mountain's helipad. According to CIA officer Woody Spence, the monks were attending a festival at the village of Pha Thi when it was suggested by a local Lao official they might reach their next destination by "hitching a ride" on a departing Air America helicopter. Unfortunately for the two men, Hmong security forces discovered that one of the monks was carrying a camera. The revelation raised obvious questions about their exact purpose on the mountain and the monks received an immediate ride—to Vang Pao's headquarters at Long Tieng. Interrogation, and a full review at Udorn of their developed film, revealed no ill intent and the two were eventually released.[19]

Although ultimately deemed benign, the "monks incident" did raise at least two security issues. First, the local population had frequent and extensive access to most areas on Pha Thi. While the TACAN and TSQ-81 areas were off-limits to the villagers, Thai and Hmong defenders daily walked around and near the equipment. The normal interaction of these forces with the local population presented numerous opportunities for communist intelligence agents to elicit information. Indeed most of the Hmong soldiers lived in the adjacent villages.[20] And, while the people of Pha Thi were deemed friendly to the government, the loyalty of the people in the numerous villages in the surrounding area was uncertain.[21] The presence and general activities of the Americans, along with the locations and configuration of the main buildings, could not have been much of a secret to anyone who cared to ask.

Indeed, both long-range and local-area Hmong reconnaissance

patrols, sent out by Spence and fellow CIA officer Terry Quill, were reporting increasing numbers of enemy forces to the east and southeast of LS 85. A December CIA briefing for General John D. Ryan warned:

> All available intelligence which we believe to be reliable and relatively complete indicate that the enemy plans to capture the following objectives during the coming dry season: Site 220, Site 205, Site 36, Site 85, and Site 201 . . . . . during November the enemy trucks and troops entering Laos have increased at an alarming rate.[22]

While these communist movements raised security concerns for the Americans at Pha Thi, the enemy concentrations were also viewed by Air Force officials at Udorn air base as "lucrative" targets. In a November 24 message to General Momyer, 7th AF, Major General Lindley, Deputy Commander 7/13th AF, reported a five-fold increase since early November in the number of trucks moving down route 68 toward Xiengkhouang. Lindley stressed "the obvious estimate of objectives is LS 36 [Na Khang] and LS 85" and requested additional night bombing sorties by A-26 aircraft.[23] There was little doubt the North Vietnamese and Pathet Lao were moving methodically to silence Site 85.

7th AF headquarters responded in late December by devising a Site 85 "self-defense" plan which was coordinated with CIA and Air Force officials at Udorn and Vientiane. Under the concept the Local Area Defense Commander (LADC),[24] was responsible for collecting targeting information on the movements and locations of the closing communist forces. The LADC would then provide this information to the air attaché in Vientiane who, after coordination with the ambassador, had the authority to authorize TSQ-directed self-defense air strikes. The bombing, however, could take place only if 7th AF had available aircraft.[25]

In southern Laos, communist forces were also moving against two other TACANs. On December 6 enemy troops threatened the town of Saravane and the nearby TACAN located at Phou Kate (LS 44). While operations were disrupted for a time, the two Heavy Green technicians escaped injury and the equipment was undamaged. LS 61, the Muang Phalane TACAN providing coverage over the Vietnamese demilitarized zone and the American base at Khe Sanh, was not so fortunate.

At 1:30 A.M., Christmas day, enemy forces launched a combined mortar and ground attack against a Royal Lao army infantry battalion command post located near the Muang Phalane airstrip. Scattering the Royal Lao forces, the attackers fired B-40 rockets into the TACAN equipment and living quarters of Heavy Green technicians Staff Sergeant John D. Morris and Sergeant Peter W. Scott. Expecting to spend that afternoon enjoying a specially prepared meal sent in from Udorn, the unarmed Americans were caught by complete surprise and killed. The assault then shifted to the town where an Air America radio station and USAID office were destroyed. Four Thais were reported killed at the station and a Filipino radioman taken prisoner, but an American USAID employee and his wife managed to escape. The Royal Lao forces "offered token resistance before fleeing west, leaving behind a 75mm recoilless rifle, three M79 grenade launchers, an M60 machine gun, and a Toyota truck."[26]

Reaction from the CIA and Air America was swift—and nearly catastrophic. Unsure if there were any survivors, an Air America H-34 piloted by Thai national Sariphan Bhibalkul flew CIA officer Mike McGrath to LS 61 where the adviser conducted a dangerous and inconclusive search of the Heavy Green living quarters. Meanwhile, the waiting helicopter came under mortar and small arms fire, wounding Sariphan in the head. Returning at a run, McGrath clambered aboard as the barrage continued and the bleeding pilot successfully fought to raise his damaged aircraft to a safe altitude. Suffering more than a hundred hits, the H-34 rapidly lost oil pressure and was forced to land some ten kilometers west of Muang Phalane. After an uncomfortable evening in the midst of enemy forces, the men were retrieved by an Air America helicopter.[27]

The following evening, Washington time, presidential adviser Walt Rostow judged the events significant enough to alert President Johnson at his Texas ranch. "Preliminary reports," Rostow advised, "suggest that the attack was specifically aimed against the U.S. presence at Muong Phalane. Two American technicians who manned a navigational station which assists U.S. air operations in southern Laos are missing."[28]

The U.S. Embassy in Vientiane, absent the bodies, was proceeding with the possibility the two men might have been captured. More practically, the embassy was also developing plans to recover any bodies and survey the damages. Lieutenant Colonel Clayton was provided with the basic circumstances of the attack and recalls the embassy dispatching the U.S. Army Attaché to southern Laos to oversee the follow-up operation. Clayton remembers, "The Lao forces claimed the North Vietnamese had moved tanks into the area and were very reluctant to move back toward Muang Phalane. It was days before the Lao and Americans got back in there."[29] During the delay, the U.S. Embassy in Vientiane was dealing with a possible breakdown in the Heavy Green "cover story."

On December 28, Deputy Chief of Mission (DCM) Robert Hurwitch[30] requested immediate "press guidance" from the State Department regarding public disclosure of the Muang Phalane attack. At issue was Washington's apparent reluctance to release any details which identified the Heavy Green casualties as civilian employees of Lockheed. In his cable Hurwitch reminded Washington that the men carried Lockheed identification cards. If the men had indeed been captured, Hurwitch pointed out, the Lockheed cover story would be critical in order to maintain plausible deniability of U.S. military operations in neutral Laos.[31] Foggy Bottom reconsidered and agreed to the original plan; the Americans lost at Muang Phalane were described as Lockheed employees.

Royal Lao military forces finally took control of Muang Phalane on December 31, and found the corpses of Morris and Scott in the burned out living quarters. Rushed to the now secure area, a communications group survey team reported nearly all the equipment destroyed by B-40 rockets and declared the site a total loss. Anticipating the worst, 7th AF had already decided to replace the TACAN and ordered site surveys for a new location. Within the week technicians decided to place the navigation aid at Phou Mano, located about four miles south of the Mekong River city of Mukdahan, Thailand. The locale, which looked down across the river onto the Lao town of Savannakhet, proved capable of providing coverage over Khe Sanh, some 125 miles distant. Designated Channel 99, and assigned the code name "Nancy," the site became operational on January 8, 1968.[32]

An Air America helicopter returned the bodies of Staff Sergeant Morris and Sergeant Scott to Udorn air base where Lieutenant Colonel Clayton had the gruesome task of identifying the highly decomposed remains. He also took on the onerous duty of accompanying his fallen men back to the United States for burial. In accordance with the top secret agreement they signed at Barksdale AFB,

John Morris and Peter Scott were quietly reinstated into the United States Air Force and their families were provided all government and Lockheed survivor benefits.[33] No one ever publicly claimed that the men were in the Air Force. In fact, a comprehensive classified Air Force history, prepared in 1976 by the U.S. Air Force Communications Service, says of the deaths, "Apparently, these were not military personnel."[34]

In operation less than ninety days Heavy Green had been bloodied. Communist soldiers had destroyed a military target and killed two Americans. The location of the deaths was somewhat problematic for the U.S., but only if the North Vietnamese or Pathet Lao chose to publicize the American presence in Laos. Of course, highlighting America's illegal activities in Laos might well have drawn unwanted attention to the thousands of North Vietnamese troops who were daily violating Lao sovereignty. Ultimately, Hanoi determined it would serve no useful purpose to expose the American activities at Muang Phalane. And so, the charade of Lao neutrality continued.

While the destruction of the LS 61 TACAN was a rather straightforward mortar and ground assault, it did come as a surprise to U.S. and Lao officials. In contrast, enemy movements toward Site 85 were well known and considered predictable. In the wake of the Muang Phalane attack, however, security at LS 85 was reevaluated. Reporting to CINCPAC on January 3, the U.S. Embassy advised:

> CAS [CIA] has done an analysis . . . there are 200 troops in immediate vicinity of site; an additional 800 troops in the lower portion of the mountain . . . believe reasonable security exists and feel that adequate warning will be provided in case evacuation is determined necessary. An emergency plan for evacuation . . . exists.[35]

The cable continued, nonetheless, to warn "There is always the possibility that a small skilled commando/sabotage team could penetrate and damage any of the three [TACANs]. It is the consensus here that . . . all reasonable precautions are being taken to safeguard the sites."[36]

Ten weeks later this prescient statement would be viewed as both a warning, perhaps unheeded, and an attempt to fix responsibility for the loss of Site 85. The exact meaning of "adequate warning" and "reasonable precautions" would be hotly debated in Air Force, State Department, and CIA offices. Moreover, in the coming years the

Heavy Green families and POW/MIA interest groups would clamor for a full explanation.

In the days following the message communist activity near Pha Thi was relatively light. To the east, however, the enemy had driven Vang Pao's forces out of the key infiltration corridor located along the North Vietnamese border with Sam Neua province. A CIA report of January 8 noted this important loss of intelligence collection capabilities and suggested Vang Pao might soon attempt to move his forces back into the area. Two days later a five-man Pathet Lao patrol was spotted less than two miles north of Pha Thi, but the incident was deemed insignificant and reported five days later.[37] Despite the lack of movement, the North Vietnamese had indeed decided to rid themselves of another troublesome U.S. presence in Laos. The lull was about to be shattered—in a most extraordinary effort.

On January 11, 1968, Air America pilot Theodore H. Moore was flying supplies to various Hmong villages and defensive positions located near Site 85. Moving food and ammunition in his Huey (UH-1D) helicopter, before the day ended Moore would conduct nineteen landings. Even though he was flying within a dozen miles of the North Vietnamese border, this was considered rather mundane work. Captain Moore and a select group of other Huey pilots were often called upon to fly extremely dangerous missions into North Vietnam to infiltrate and exfiltrate CIA-controlled road watch teams.

The sudden appearance of a Soviet-built jet aircraft streaking over Site 85 reminded everyone at Pha Thi that the enemy also possessed aircraft and, according to Moore, appeared to be using the MIG to take photographs of the radar facility.[38] The following day the purpose of the probable reconnaissance mission became more clear.

Four dark green North Vietnamese Air Force biplanes departed Duc Thang airfield,[39] on January 12, headed west toward Laos.[40] According to an official Vietnamese account, the aircraft were under the direction of Company Commander Phan Nhu Can on a mission to destroy the Pha Thi radar being used to "conduct [U.S.] planes from Thailand against North Vietnam."[41] Following a flight plan that took them south of Sam Neua city, the slow-moving "Colts" were observed splitting into two formations above Ban Houei Soui, some 11 miles southeast of Pha Thi. While two of the aircraft orbited in the area, the other planes turned toward the mountain.[42] During this critical period, according to Vietnamese sources, Ngo Quang Ngoc served "nearby the enemy base" as the ground controller for the air assault.[43] Understandably, once the aircraft arrived in the area of Site 85, the Vietnamese wanted to ensure they could direct the "bombers" to the correct target.[44] Changing weather conditions were just as challenging for the Vietnamese as for the American flyers.

Beginning at about 1:20 P.M., the biplanes conducted separate single bombing and strafing passes. John Daniel, a Heavy Green radar board operator, was at the helipad when the airplanes attacked. "I could see the aircraft very clearly, only a couple of hundred feet above the site. I saw one dropping bombs and a Thai soldier emptied a full ammo clip at the plane."[45] TACAN specialist Jack Starling was working inside the TACAN building when the attack began. He remembered, "One of the bombs hit close enough to "twist the TACAN building and knock the antenna off-course. [The antenna was required to be set at true north]. I ran outside and saw the planes in slow motion."[46] Although the damage was limited, for several days the TACAN was out of commission.

The extensive bombing and strafing was confined mostly to the CIA area near the helipad, indicating the pilots may have been attracted to the shiny tin-roofed buildings.[47] The TSQ area was untouched. However, Roland T. Hodge, a power specialist assigned to Heavy Green, was working on a CIA generator near the helipad and was slightly wounded by flying debris. Elsewhere, the attack killed four Hmong (including two women) and wounded two soldiers.[48]

Ted Moore, moving 105mm artillery shells at Site 85, saw the biplanes attack and recalls, "It looked like World War I." Moore, flying with flight mechanic Glenn Woods, began to chase the first Colt as it attempted to head north to the Vietnamese border. Moore climbed above the target as Woods pulled out an AK-47 rifle and began firing at the lumbering airplane. The pursuit continued for more than twenty minutes when the second AN-2 flew underneath the helicopter and both airplanes began an attempt to gain altitude. Moore and Woods watched as the first AN-2, apparently hit by gunfire, dropped and then crashed into a mountain ridge less than two miles west of the North Vietnamese border. Minutes later, the second Colt hit the side of a mountain located some three miles further north of the first crash and only a few miles west of the border.[49] Ted Moore and Glenn Woods gained the distinction of having shot down a fixed-wing aircraft from a helicopter—a unique aerial kill in the entire history of the Vietnam war.[50] The two biplanes orbiting to the southeast did not take part in the attack and, presumably, elected a tactical retreat back to North Vietnam.[51]

At the time of the attack Ambassador Sullivan remained out of the country and, coincidentally, Deputy Chief of Mission Robert Hurwitch was in the Air America operations center when the bombing was first reported. In his initial message to Washington Hurwitch advised, "Continuing to check in order be [sic] absolutely certain this new departure in war in Laos has in fact occurred although indications are so far that such is the case."[52] In an updated message sent several hours later, Hurwitch advised, "No indications as of now regarding enemy ground follow-up although we have noted an increase in enemy pressure in this area in past weeks." As to the worrisome possibility that the North Vietnamese might have initiated a new tactic and, thereby were escalating the war in Laos:

> At present we can only speculate on location of launch point of attacking aircraft which appeared to come from northeast. Loaded Colt AN-2 has a range of about 250 miles which opens a myriad of possibilities in North Vietnam. However, cannot rule out possibility aircraft flew from strip in Laos. There have been recurring unsubstantiated reports in past months that AN-2 type aircraft have been operating during evening hours in northern PDJ [Plain of Jars].[53]

Within hours a CIA-controlled ground team reached the crashed aircraft and found bullet holes in both. The first airplane had burned on impact and was nearly completely destroyed. The second aircraft, which bore tail number 665, was in far better shape. Three dead bodies which "appeared to be Vietnamese" were found in the wreckage. Two of the bodies were removed, while the third was "wedged in the aircraft." Aeronautical charts, which marked the inbound route from Duc Thang to Pha Thi and a return home, were found along with notebooks and a Soviet-manufactured HF radio.[54]

An examination of the aircraft by a 7th AF intelligence team revealed "that 120mm mortar rounds had been converted to 'bombs.' Dropped through tubes in the floor of the AN-2, the 'bombs' became armed in the slip stream and detonated on impact. The rockets were 57mm, and were carried in rocket pods under the wing of the AN-2."[55] Captain Moore estimated that nearly fifty of the mortar "bombs" were dropped on Pha Thi.[56] Clearly, had the pilots been even slightly more proficient in their bombing and strafing, the attack at Site 85 would likely have been costly in both lives and equipment.

Following an analysis of the available intelligence, on January 13, Hurwitch suggested to Washington that Site 85's location made it a unique target requiring unconventional efforts.

> We can conclude that aerial attack represented enemy effort to get at navigational facility which could be reached on the ground only at heavy cost. Theoretically, enemy could resort to this technique again, either at Site 85 or elsewhere. We regard aerial raid as highly unusual variation in normal pattern of enemy tactics and do not believe this one incident necessarily introduces a new dimension to war in Laos.[57]

Nonetheless, the message advised, "We are presently reviewing questions of air defense at Site 85."[58]

The PAVN air attack against Site 85 was unprecedented in the history of the Vietnam war. At the time, the U.S. Embassy was most concerned with the possibility the North Vietnamese were embarking on "a new dimension to war in Laos." The unique location of the TSQ-81, its close proximity to the Vietnamese border, and the difficulty of launching a conventional ground attack on a mile-high base, gave credence to the theory that this was a one of a kind venture. And, since the effort was a disaster, there is no reason to believe the North Vietnamese would have undertaken another such foray into Laos.

Unfortunately, the cable does not address an obvious and key question.[59] The decision to reconfigure and launch the AN-2 Colts into neutral Laos required approval from the most senior echelons of Hanoi's political and military leadership. Who, specifically, gave the order for this bizarre bombing raid? Again, the very nature of such an unorthodox attack ensures that this was an operation closely monitored at senior levels of the North Vietnamese leadership. The progress of such a unique undertaking was undoubtedly the subject of regular reports. It is the ultimate in prevarication for U.S. and Vietnamese officials to now claim the North Vietnamese knew, or know, little about the events at Site 85 (see chapters 14 and 15).

In the aftermath of the attack the American Embassy was also concerned with controlling public information on this new development; the U.S. and Lao governments wanted no press spotlight on Phou Pha Thi. Given the extraordinary circumstances, however, it was obvious the story would soon be spread by any number of pilots, soldiers, humanitarian aid workers, and villagers. Turning the incident into a propaganda campaign, on January 15, the Royal Lao government announced that four AN-2 "fighter-bombers" had attacked the northeastern town of Muong Yut.[60] The press release noted it was "the first known use of Hanoi's planes against ground positions" and that two of the planes had been shot down.[61] On January 19, the second Colt was lifted from the jungle by a U.S. Air Force helicopter and eventually transported to Vientiane where it was put on display near the That Luang temple.[62] In mid-January, however, the surprising air attack at Pha Thi was overshadowed by events involving the Lao army some 75 miles to the west.

6
Folly at Nam Bac

The January 1968 military fiasco at Nam Bac demonstrates that the flawed decisionmaking employed there may well have had an effect on later U.S. judgments regarding the continued operation of Site 85. Since 1966 the *Force Armées du Royaume* (FAR) had worked to coordinate operations in Military Regions I and II to block and harass communist troop movements northwest of the royal capital at Luang Prabang. The plan envisioned a solid defense across this traditional invasion route that would "change permanently the tactical balance of power in northern Laos."[1] The key to this strategy was Nam Bac, a small outpost in a valley located 60 miles north of Luang Prabang and only 40 miles southwest of the Vietnamese border. In mid-1967 the normally timid FAR General Staff, faced with ominous North Vietnamese road building to the north of Nam Bac, began deploying 7,500 troops to the area. Hanoi responded in December by sending "the entire 316 Infantry Division and elements of the 335 Independent Regiment" to Nam Bac. Nonetheless, the FAR retained a numerical advantage.[2] More importantly, the Lao army enjoyed the logistical support of Air America fixed-wing and helicopter transports, air strikes by Royal Lao Air Force T-28s, and tactical advice from CIA officers and U.S. military attachés.

All of this assistance, nevertheless, did little to counter the typical extraordinarily poor FAR leadership and the inevitable dismal performance of the line troops. Despite indications that the communist forces were closing around the base, the Laotian defenders refused to patrol outside their perimeter. In early January a North Vietnamese squad easily moved into firing distance and pounded the airfield and adjoining area with mortar fire. Morale, what little there was of it, quickly crumbled, and by January 13 the North Vietnamese and Pathet Lao launched a full-scale assault. Within a day the Laotian forces were in full rout.[3] In their haste they abandoned heavy weapons and ammunition valued at more than a million dollars and another $125,000 in communications equipment.[4] This bonanza of materiel was quickly recovered by the communist forces and transported to their units in north and northeast Laos. Personnel losses were equally devastating; half-hearted rescue efforts resulted in the recovery and regroupment of less than half the Laotian forces. More than five hundred survivors would eventually be moved to northeastern Laos, where they were put to work supporting Pathet Lao units.[5] Fortunately for the residents of Luang Prabang, the communists were not yet ready to attack the royal capital and the city was spared.

The loss of Nam Bac was a source of deep embarrassment for the Royal Lao government and the U.S. Embassy. Not surprisingly the Americans blamed the Lao military, while some Lao officials decried a lack of U.S. support.[6] A number of observers have identified Ambassador William Sullivan and CIA Station Chief Theodore Shackley as being especially culpable in the debacle. Lao specialist Roger Warner, who has interviewed many of the American principals, has written, "In Vientiane, the U.S. Embassy tried to absolve itself of blame. Nam Bac, Sullivan declared, had been a Lao plan all along, not a Country Team plan." The plan, Sullivan told Warner, was nonetheless pursued "in full recognition that it was going to be a fiasco, which it was."[7] Why would William Sullivan, known to be proud, extraordinarily professional, and very engaged in all facets of the embassy's operation, be complicit in such a high stakes campaign? Failure was anathema to William Sullivan. What, then, might explain the Ambassador's approval for a "doomed" operation?

According to several of his subordinates, shortly after arriving in mid-1966 Shackley declared the Lao war had been run like "a country store" and he "was going to turn it into a supermarket."[8] Shackley has disavowed the remark,[9] but his predecessor, Douglas Blaufarb, has described an embassy position paper developed during Shackley's tenure which appears to have enunciated a moderate expansion of the Lao war. Titled "U.S. Policy with Respect to North Laos," the 1967 paper determined "that a carefully measured and limited expansion [of Lao military and paramilitary operations] served U.S. and Lao purposes, but generally not north of a line connecting Muong Sing,[10] Muong Sai,[11] Nam Bac, and Phou Pha Thi." The report went on to urge caution, "Refrain from actions which could provoke serious enemy retaliation." Blaufarb also notes the plan "called for strong defense of bases where USAF operations were supported and from which certain intelligence operations were mounted."[12] Shackley's involvement is further confirmed by the comprehensive work of journalist David Corn, who cites the recollection of a senior embassy official that the station chief and the embassy's senior military attachés developed a strategy intended "to really bloody the nose of the North Vietnamese." Nam Bac would be, they believed, part of "an iron arc of bases in northern central Laos."[13] These remarks seem to indicate that a fairly cautious formal plan had been informally modified to include a new aggressive posture on the part of the Lao military and the Hmong irregulars under the command of Major General Vang Pao.

Years later, when questioned about his role in the Nam Bac affair, Shackley placed responsibility on the U.S. Army Attaché. Recounting the decisionmaking process, Shackley explained "The instigator/primary proponent and planner of that operation was the military attaché. . . . Now within the mission council we were all asked to contribute to that operation. And I did agree that we would make a contribution with the forces that we had. . . . But that was not our operation."[14] Ambassador Sullivan, however, during November 1969 testimony in front of a U.S. Senate subcommittee, denied there was any formal U.S. planning involvement in the Nam Bac affair and suggested it was a CIA responsibility.[15] Further, Sullivan has recalled Shackley being "pretty much single-minded" about the decision to reinforce and hold Nam Bac and wanting "to get the North Vietnamese off Lao territory as quickly as possible, and those who didn't get off, get them killed."[16]

It seems clear, Shackley's protests notwithstanding, that the station chief and the military attachés in the Vientiane embassy were advocating a more conventional military strategy in Laos—a move that would have tragic consequences at Nam Bac. While many of his former colleagues have attributed Shackley's motives to naked ambition, why would William Sullivan risk Laos's precarious political and military

position by antagonizing the North Vietnamese army? For those familiar with the Laotians' capabilities, or lack thereof, the suggestion they
could eject the North Vietnamese from Laos was ludicrous. For the
Hmong mountain fighters, it seemed suicidal. A veteran CIA officer
has offered a blunt assessment of this change of course.

> There was a very conscious decision to turn this very effective and com
> petent guerilla organization into something for more conventional that
> served the purposes more of Vietnam than Laos, the purpose of tying
> down more and more NVA soldiers in Laos. That was the price that Ted
> Shackley and William Sullivan paid. In order to keep the program from
> going over to the [U.S.] military, they juiced up the Hmong to fight in
> the more conventional manner, and it would be a total . . . disaster for the
> Hmong.[17]

When Ambassador Sullivan arrived in Vientiane in November 1964
he was determined to keep the American military out of Laos.[18] As the
North Vietnamese presence in Laos escalated, however, so too did
efforts by senior U.S. military officers to increase U.S. bombing and
ground activities in eastern and southern Laos. By 1967 Sullivan was
being pressured by General Westmoreland to allow increased "ground-
oriented, anti-infiltration" operations in Laos. Sullivan largely opposed
these operations, originally called "Shining Brass" and later "Prairie
Fire."[19] In a notable message to the State Department on July 4, Sullivan declared his annoyance with one such request by saying it came
"purely out of the opium pipe" and suggested he might grant approval
so the military could "try and demonstrate . . . failure."[20]

Sullivan's response to a proposed increase in military operations in
southern Laos sounds very similar to his reaction to the CIA/attaché
efforts to strike at North Vietnamese forces in northern Laos—go
ahead, show it won't work. After three grueling years, Sullivan may
have grown tired of fending off General Westmoreland's efforts to take
control of the war in Laos. Moreover, now he was faced with an ambitious CIA station chief. Ever the pragmatist, the Ambassador knew the
war was changing and, as suggested above, perhaps he decided to
allow increased CIA efforts in lieu of an expanded U.S. military presence. As I have written elsewhere, at least as early as 1969 Sullivan
approved complex CIA-directed ground operations involving large
numbers of Air America and U.S. Air Force aircraft.[21]

Another explanation for the Nam Bac disaster may be as simple as the timing; Sullivan was out of the country during the final weeks of the affair and returned after the rout. Had he been in Laos, given his cognizance of the royal Lao army and penchant for frequent briefings on the status of every operation, it seems probable he would have ordered a withdrawal prior to the final communist assault. While Sullivan may have decided to demonstrate to the CIA and U.S. military the consequences of mixing operational zeal with the Lao army, it is unlikely he would have knowingly permitted such a costly lesson. In any event, Sullivan and Shackley understood that personal blame was to be avoided at all costs—and in this regard Nam Bac became a subject to be avoided.

The Nam Bac affair sheds light on the changing, more confrontational, philosophy of the CIA station chief and the embassy's military attachés. Moreover, after-the-fact quibbling over accountability suggests the two offices were entangled in ambiguous roles and responsibilities. Nonetheless, Ambassador Sullivan seems to have reached a point where he was willing to allow the attachés and CIA station greater sway in the initiation of offensive operations involving the Laotian forces and General Vang Pao's Hmong forces. The record shows, however, that Sullivan remained mostly skeptical of these activities and positioned himself to avoid direct responsibility if they went awry.

Given the growing seriousness of the North Vietnamese threat to Site 85, where security was supervised by the CIA, Heavy Green's self-defense missions were approved through the air attaché's office, and the Ambassador held the ultimate power to close down the site, who was really in charge?

7

The Heights of Abraham

There are striking parallels between the assault on Phou Pha Thi and an incident that took place during the French and Indian War, in September 1759. At that time British forces successfully climbed the "unscalable" Heights of Abraham and captured the city of Quebec. The French commander-in-chief, the Marquis de Montcalm believed "the steepness of the cliffs made an assault unlikely." "We need not suppose that the enemy has wings," Montcalm said, "A hundred men posted here could stop their whole army." Unconventional thinking on the part of the British army commander, Major General James Wolfe, and the presence of a "cleft in the cliffside" below the city, proved the marquis quite wrong.[1] Montcalm, might well have done better had he heeded the words of the contemporary French military theorist Pierre Joseph Bourcet, who warned that "Every plan of campaign ought to have several branches and to have been so well thought out that one or other of the said branches cannot fail of success."[2] Two centuries later, the U.S. military also might have done well to have heeded Bourcet.

When the Joint Chiefs of Staff lobbied for the placement of a radar bombing facility and U.S. military technicians a dozen miles from North Vietnam, the chairman wrote "[T]he MSQ mission is not obvious from outward appearance. . . . If required, supplemental amendments could be made to existing plans for the emergency extraction of personnel and destruction of the MSQ to prevent the enemy's identifying the MSQ operators as US military personnel."[3] While arguably the presence of the radar equipment (or at least the creation of a new and important U.S.-manned facility) had been known for months to the communists, the attack had erased any possible doubt Hanoi knew about the radar site. What became of the JCS assurances regarding evacuation of the men and the destruction of their equipment?

The JCS had successfully presented the Heavy Green program as a "valid military requirement in which the advantages outweigh the disadvantages."[4] In late December, 7th AF had issued a self-defense plan for Site 85, but there was no discussion of removing the men and closing the operation.[5] In mid-January, with the site being encircled by enemy forces and under threat of additional aerial attacks, there was no doubt the men and equipment were in jeopardy.[6] Nevertheless, there was no move to reevaluate the risk versus gain of continued operations. A trend had developed; the radar equipment was now being used to attack far more targets in Laos than in North Vietnam. Instead of directing missions against high-priority facilities in North Vietnam, Heavy Green had increasingly become a means by which to lure in, and then attack, communist forces. The advancing North Vietnamese forces, whose very presence should have triggered closure of the radar facility, had become a reason to maintain it. The opportunity to kill large numbers of North Vietnamese and Pathet Lao soldiers was irresistible.

For the two paramilitary officers assigned to Site 85, Terry "TQ" Quill and John "Woody" Spence, the decision to continue or end the radar facility rested "far above their pay grade."[7] They were told to continue collecting intelligence and to supervise the mountain's defensive operations. Beyond the U.S. air strikes, over which they had little authority, the officers relied on the mountain's natural defenses and the Hmong and Thai soldiers assigned to Phou Pha Thi.

There were about 1,000 CIA-controlled Hmong guerrillas in the immediate vicinity of Pha Thi, of whom nearly eight hundred were spread around the eastern and southern upper approaches to Site 85. The highlanders, many of whom would be defending their own families in the village of Pha Thi, were expected to delay the enemy attack long enough for the Americans to be evacuated by air. Most of the Hmong troops and their families would then withdraw from the mountain to designated recovery points and await airlift. The CIA case officers, who believed that the communists would be satisfied with the destruction of the radar site and the capture of the helipad, deemed it unlikely that any significant casualties would result. Little would be gained, they believed, by pursuing the Hmong. At least this had been the experience in other engagements between the guerrillas and the North Vietnamese.[8]

In an early February, however, a command shake-up may have caused discontent and dissension among the LS 85 Hmong forces. General Vang Pao, seeking more aggressive leadership, supplanted Captain Gia Tou, the native born Local Area Defense Commander (LADC),[9] with an outsider, Major Soua Yang.[10] Soua Yang, a highly regarded field commander, was ordered to develop a 12 kilometer defensive perimeter around Pha Thi and to retake from the communists several nearby key terrain features. While the guerrillas did step up their patrolling, they failed to gain control of these strategic locations.[11]

In addition to the Hmong, two twelve-man special forces teams were deployed in defensive positions around the Heavy Green facilities, the CIA operations area, and the helipad. A seven-man Thai PARU team assisted the case officers as radio operators and interpreters.[12] The unit was essential as a liaison between the CIA officers and the Hmong, but the security role assigned the Thai special forces was at best problematic. While many of the Thai soldiers were ethnic Lao, sharing a common culture and language with the lowland Lao, they felt no such kinship with the Hmong. Indeed, like most of their Laotian cousins, they held the tribesmen in contempt and viewed them as no better than savages. As a result, the Thai and Hmong developed little rapport or teamwork in their collective duties to protect the mountaintop. Also, while the Hmong were often cited for their unwillingness to defend fixed positions against the North Vietnamese, the Thai combat record was mostly undistinguished. In fact, the presence of the Thai troops was the less than satisfactory result of an effort to place U.S. combat forces at Pha Thi. Ambassador Sullivan's steadfast refusal to allow U.S. special forces to guard Site 85 meant the Thais were the next best option.[13] Later, few would be surprised at the Thai performance under fire.

In reaction to the aircraft bombing and the need to counter the heavy weapons of the surrounding communist troops, the CIA increased the firepower at Phou Pha Thi. A captured anti-aircraft gun was positioned in a Thai-manned bunker on the southwestern edge of the mountain just south of the TACAN and, farther to the south, a communist-manufactured mortar was placed in another Thai outpost. The technicians, unbeknownst to Lieutenant Colonel Clayton, were even given instruction and allowed to practice fire the anti-aircraft gun off into the valley.[14]

On the southeastern edge of the mountaintop, a 105mm howitzer was helicoptered into place about 300 yards south of the CIA operations area. From this position the gun overlooked the village of Pha Thi and a trail to the base of the mountain. A communist-manufactured 85mm field gun, captured by Vang Pao's forces on the Plain of Jars, was set up a few yards north of the helipad.[15] Another, much more unorthodox weapon, also made its way to Pha Thi. In February two officers from the CIA's Technical Services Division (TSD)[16] devised and installed a portable launching apparatus that fired white phosphorus rockets. The device was set up on the southeastern corner of the helipad and loaded with a pod of seven rockets. Cases of refills were stacked alongside.[17] This Rube Goldberg device would play a brief, but lively role in the defense of Site 85. This weaponry augmented the mountain's own natural defenses which, while considerable, had flaws.

During the latter part of January, concerned by the steady encroachment of the Vietnamese and Pathet Lao forces, Quill and Spence conducted a walking inspection of the Site 85 perimeter. As discussed in chapter 3, the TSQ-81 and TACAN buildings were placed on the western edge of the mountain on solid rock a few yards from a nearly vertical 3,000-foot cliff. This working and living area, encompassing about one-quarter of an acre, was located on a relatively flat bluff some 200 feet in elevation above the CIA operations area and helipad. The mountain was heavily wooded and there was a single steep and rocky path that connected the helipad and operations area to the TSQ-81/TACAN site. From the helipad, there was a path down to the village of Pha Thi. To the north and south of the site, however, the ridge line was less abrupt. Although a difficult climb, the CIA officers considered that a determined force might attempt to use these route to gain access to the mountaintop. As a result, concertina wire and land mines were placed throughout the area.[18]

On the western ridge line the review revealed a more disconcerting feature—a path leading down a steep, but traversable gully along the western face of the mountain. The track, which showed no signs of current use, appeared to lead off toward the west and Houei Houk, a Lao Theung village considered loyal to the Royal Lao government. Although the two paramilitary officers thought it unlikely an enemy could find and use the path, they ordered the placement of a Thai fighting position on the ridge line near the path's approach, just north of the TSQ-81 buildings. Mines and concertina wire were added to support the defense of this locale. This increased to three the number of Thai and Hmong defensive positions located around the site's perimeter.[19]

Following the loss of Site 85 the CIA and their defense forces would be roundly criticized in many quarters, from the Air Force to the Heavy Green families, for a lack of preparation and vigilance. Whatever the faults of the CIA, and there were errors to be sure, they did not rest with the paramilitary officers at Site 85. Like most of the other CIA veterans of the Lao war, the men assigned to Pha Thi never believed the mountain could be defended against a concerted PAVN assault.

While the AN-2 attack caused great momentary excitement amongst the technicians, it seems to have created little concern. Radar operator Harold Summers recalls his team placing a man on "enemy aircraft look-out duty," sitting on a raised chair facing to the west. The effort was short-lived, however, and manned only when Summers' team was on the mountain.[20] Enemy ground movements toward Pha Thi, increasingly targets for TSQ-directed strikes, were similarly dismissed. According to radar technician John Daniel and TACAN specialist Jack Starling, despite the Colt attack and the surrounding communist forces, the men believed the top of the mountain was secure.[21] Much like the French soldiers who defended Quebec in 1759, the surrounding cliffs lulled the men at Site 85 into a fatally false sense of security.

And, after nearly three months of operations most of the technicians were more focused on their jobs and what was going on in the U.S. than personal security. They truly believed their safety was guaranteed. Not once in any of my lengthy discussions with former Heavy Green personnel, including both crews, was I told that the men feared for their lives.[22] Indeed, everyone involved with Site 85—from the lowest to the highest level—seemed so certain of a safe helipad evacuation that no other contingencies were ever considered.

Confined for ten-day periods[23] to an area the size of a few football fields, the men had little to occupy their time but work, letter writing, card games, and thinking about their families. Except for the official communications with Udorn, they were very much cut off from the outside world. While relations with the CIA officers were cordial, there was little need for regular interaction between the two groups. Most of the technicians, in fact, believed their neighbors were U.S. Army special forces. Communication with the security forces was limited to a few of the English-speaking Thais.[24]

Living conditions were quite spartan and a number of the men recall water being a constant concern. In addition to bringing water with them from Udorn, occasionally helicopters were used to ferry water from a nearby stream to the mountaintop. During one especially memorable tour of duty water became so scarce that the men bathed in the drippings collected from their air conditioning units. Food, on the other hand, was never much of a problem. The men, who were required to purchase their own supplies, shopped at the base commissary and on the local economy. Several became very proficient cooks, and even managed to bake a cake in a jury-rigged oven outside the radar building.[25]

As time went on, the men became less conscious of the security rules laid down by Ambassador Sullivan. Established procedures dictated that prior to departure from Udorn the men be "sanitized." To comply with their cover story they changed from Air Force uniforms to Sears work clothes and were supposed to remove any items that would identify them as military personnel. This restriction also included personal letters or written matter which, if captured by the enemy, would provide evidence of their illegal presence. Increasingly, this effort at deniability was ignored as the men carried all manner of materials to northeastern Laos. This included tape recorders, to listen to and record "audio letters," books, magazines, musical instruments, and even a family cookbook and a wife's prized skillet. While the men were trying to make their surroundings more livable, they were also building a considerable cache of potentially compromising materials.[26] After the war the Vietnamese, who routinely captured and often placed on public display any American-associated items, would claim their forces recovered nothing from the site.

The sloppy security practices were a symptom of larger problems— a breakdown of leadership at the site and the difficulties of this dual life. The men were expected to act as obedient military personnel while, in reality, they were no longer bound by military regulations. There was a gradual slide toward inappropriate familiarity amongst the team, which sometimes made it difficult for the officers and supervisors to enforce their directions. These men, after all, were now legally civilians.[27] Assembled in haste, many of the Heavy Green personnel were unprepared for the psychological challenges of this unique assignment. Most adapted to the situation, but several would develop serious reservations about their participation in the Heavy Green project.[28]

In order to evaluate the site's self-defense capability, on January 25 Udorn directed the technicians to initiate an unannounced "test exercise." Lacking prior notification and authority, however, personnel at 7/13th AF headquarters refused to provide any aircraft for the TSQ-directed strikes. In the midst of genuine requirements for air strikes elsewhere in theater, the Udorn command post was unwilling to divert scarce aircraft for a surprise test. This failure brought about a number of procedural changes and Air Force records claim, "When circumstances called for actual implementation, there was no repeat of the difficulties experienced in the test."[29]

Indeed, when properly coordinated, the site received significant strike support. Over the first three weeks of January some sixty sorties attacked communist positions within 30 kilometers of the site. And a surge during the last week of January added an additional hundred strikes against targets to the east of Pha Thi.[30] Advance notice was the key, a luxury not available in an emergency situation.

Ambassador Sullivan and his advisers always viewed the site as a short-term location for operations. From its inception, Sullivan and CIA station chief Shackley acknowledged that once placed on the mountain the radar was certain to elicit a communist response.[31] Indeed, if this ground-directed bombing system were as effective as the Air Force anticipated, Hanoi would have been compelled to take immediate action to destroy the facility. Phou Pha Thi, therefore, was never envisioned as an outpost that would be defended against concerted North Vietnamese pressure.

The State Department's understanding of the risks at Site 85, and belief that the facility would soon be evacuated in response to the North Vietnamese threat, was made clear in a February 1, 1968 memorandum.

> The most recent reports of enemy action around Site 85 (Phou Pha Thi) indicate that an attempt to seize the site is imminent. . . . When the decision was made to install these facilities it was understood that no last ditch

stand would be made to defend them. Although this equipment is costly, it is expendable—the men who service it are not and they will be removed prior to the fall of the site, if the situation becomes hopeless.[32]

While the mountain offered a special vantage point looking into North Vietnam, there were other viable operating locations in northeastern Laos. Heavy Green was to be a kind of electronic guerrilla warfare unit whereby a small group of men would direct air strikes against North Vietnam until, faced with enemy pressure, they would simply relocate before any counterattack. Senior decisionmakers, in much safer surroundings, had decided to push the envelope with the continued operation of Site 85.

8
Imminent Threat

On February 25, 1968, a CIA report warned that "It is clear that the enemy will continue to attempt to consolidate his gains in the Phou Pha Thi area during the next two weeks while making arrangements for his final assault."[1]

The communist noose was tightening. Since early February 1968 four North Vietnamese battalions had entered northern Laos and taken up positions around Site 85. These forces increased the total number of North Vietnamese battalions in the Pha Thi area to five, or about two thousand men. Another two battalions were operating within an easy march of the site.[2] Adding to the apprehension, on February 18 a Hmong patrol ambushed a small North Vietnamese unit and killed a number of enemy soldiers. A notebook recovered from one of the bodies contained specific details regarding a proposed attack on the site and the word "TACAN" in English with an exact location of the equipment. Although the enemy plans referred to a ground assault "preceded by an air strike plus howitzer and mortar barrage," there was no indication of any sapper threat.[3]

During this same time, the defense of LS 85 was bolstered by the arrival from Thailand of Technical Sergeant James Gary, an experienced combat controller. Gary had been dispatched to the mountain to direct "responsive airstrikes" against the encircling communist forces. Using the call-sign "Rainbow," the Sergeant developed an excellent working relationship with the CIA and Heavy Green personnel.[4] In February, 473 strike sorties were flown within 30 kilometers of

Pha Thi; while about a third were radar-directed, many were close enough to the mountain for Gary to control them visually.[5] By comparison, during the same month Heavy Green directed just twenty strike missions against targets in North Vietnam.[6]

Inasmuch as Site 85 was now involved in a relatively small number of missions against North Vietnam, was the growing risk to the men and U.S. interests worth the continued presence of the Heavy Green program? According to senior Air Force leaders the facility was crucial to their bombing operations, especially, as they noted, during the northeast monsoon season, when the weather was poor. Indeed, on February 13, Headquarters PACAF provided CINCPAC with a grim weather forecast and stressed the unique capabilities of Site 85. The message, for all its technical language can be considered the "smoking gun" message, as it laid out the basis for keeping the site open.

> Climatology analysis for 90 day period Feb, March, April indicates only 16 days operational weather suitable for visual strikes in RPV [Route Package V] and only 9 days in RP VI [Route Package VI]. Using this as basis, our forces could only strike visually in RPV on 18 PCT [percent] of days in this period and on only 10 PCT in RP VI. Loss of Site 85, with its TACAN and TSQ-81, would result in substantial impairment of capability of our strike and support forces to carry out their missions against enemy in NVN and Laos during all seasons, and particularly during Northeast Monsoon.[7]

While the message underscored the purported military advantages of continued operations, an increasingly uneasy William Sullivan directed that Ted Shackley, his CIA station chief, prepare a risk assessment of Site 85. Shackley recalls that the Ambassador "wanted a cable that would focus attention on Site 85. But, this would not be just an estimate of when an attack might occur. He wanted a date certain."[8] Shackley put his men to work calculating many variables (e.g., road-building time, weather, personnel required, etc.), and on February 25, released this forecast of Hanoi's intentions. "As a result of the enemy's penetrating the 12 kilometer radius around Phou Pha Thi in force and occupying key positions . . . he represents an imminent threat to the security of the TACAN site and other installations at Phou Pha Thi."[9]

The assessment also observed that the TACAN and TSQ-81 radar could remain in operation during this two-week period if Hmong guerrilla units continued "to harass successfully the enemy on the ground and if aircraft continue to strike enemy concentrations." Concluding with an extraordinarily prophetic comment, the report warned: "It is not possible to predict, however, the state of security at Phou Pha Thi beyond 10 March because of the enemy's willingness to continue to escalate his commitment in this area."[10]

Moved by the stark judgment,[11] the following day Ambassador Sullivan personally conveyed the CIA findings to General John P. McConnell, the Air Force Chief of Staff, emphatically reminding him that, "You will recall that, when we arranged this installation, I made clear our principal defense effort would rest upon guerrilla units who operated with mobile tactics and that we could not . . . guarantee a static defense. Therefore, the moment of truth may be approaching for this site." Ruling out the introduction of reinforcements, and expressing doubts that TSQ-directed air strikes against local targets could turn back a determined communist assault, Sullivan concurred with the CIA judgment that Site 85 would soon be in enemy hands. He went on to advise McConnell, "[W]e are in touch with USAF authorities on evacuation and destruction plans. We are fairly confident both should be able to be carried out in an orderly fashion." And, as if to underscore the inevitability of Pha Thi's capture, the ambassador revealed that the embassy was already "examining possibilities of finding another useful site in the same general area which will provide roughly the same coverage."[12]

Preparations for an evacuation of Site 85 were under way, but available records and the ultimate results suggest that an emergency extraction of personnel from Pha Thi was a far more difficult and dangerous undertaking than any of the planners were willing to admit. CIA and air attaché representatives, in coordination with Air Force officials at 7/13th AF, decided that once Ambassador Sullivan gave the evacuation order[13] a mix of Air America and U.S. Air Force helicopters would be used to remove the Americans, Thais, and Hmong from atop Pha Thi. A February 24, 1968, CIA memo to the 7/13th AF Director of Operations outlined the use of five helicopters, three USAF and two Air America. The Americans were to be given priority during the evacuation, but the use of five aircraft would permit the airlift of more than 150 people—an indication that the CIA was anticipating the removal of more than just the summit defenders. Air America helicopters would be pre-deployed to Lima Site 98[14] while USAF aircraft would respond from airfields in Thailand. Although it was expected that the operation would be conducted during daylight hours, the plan stated that the Air America helicopters had a "limited night evacuation capability." And, "Weather permitting," A-1E/H "Sandy" aircraft would be scrambled for air cover and ground suppression fire and, if necessary, would act as forward air controllers for any additional air strikes. CIA officers and the recently assigned combat controller at Pha Thi were to assist in the direction of air strikes.[15]

If this strategy were to be followed, however, it would be at least several hours before all the rescue forces could reach Pha Thi. Reacting to this concern, a week later 7/13th AF suggested to Ambassador Sullivan that the two Air America helicopters be placed directly at Site 85, rather than LS 98. This proposal was disapproved in Vientiane on March 4, as the CIA correctly reasoned that any Pha Thi-based helicopters would themselves become "lucrative targets" and encourage communist attacks.[16] Left unsaid was the fact that the Air America helicopters were unarmed and lacked any protective armor plating. No matter what time of day, with communist heavy weapons aimed at Pha Thi's summit, the Air America crews would be flying into a potential death trap. The faith placed upon these men and aircraft was a testament to Air America's well-deserved record of pilot initiative and tenacity in rescuing endangered personnel.

Despite the grave warnings contained in the February 25 CIA assessment, three days later Ambassador Sullivan yielded to military pressure and approved a 7th AF request to increase the number of on-site personnel to "facilitate around the clock capability of the TSQ facility."[17] Additional manning at Site 85 was not easily accomplished, however. The living quarters were built to house a crew of about fourteen people, and the water and food supplies were also based on this number. Moreover, considering the ongoing enemy activity, it appeared that resupply flights would become increasingly dangerous and sporadic. Clayton deemed it impractical, therefore, simultaneously to house and feed two complete crews on the mountain. Instead, he decided to send just two complete radar teams, a total of ten men. The six non-radar positions, computer, teletype, cryptographic, generator, radio, and TACAN, would have to be singly manned. "It was not an ideal situation," recalled Clayton, "but until additional sleeping quarters could be built and the food and water problems solved, it was the best we could do."[18]

On Monday, March 4, after two frustrating days of weather delays, this new hybrid crew was delivered to the Pha Thi helipad.[19] As it turned out, from this day forward they would conduct just three missions against North Vietnam before PAVN commandos silenced the radar.[20]

The men quickly climbed the trail to the top of the mountain, knowing that the on-duty crew was eager to return to the comfort and safety of Udorn, Thailand. None of the arriving men displayed any fear, but a number of them approached the awaiting equipment vans with mixed feelings.[21] David Price, one of the unit's youngest members, jumped out of the helicopter onto the hard rock of Pha Thi and began an assignment he had only heard about. When the two Heavy Green teams were originally constituted it was decided that Price, a radar technician, would serve in a logistics position at Udorn. After four months of working in the supply section, he was finally on the mountain. Bill Blanton, the deputy commander of the Heavy Green program, had never served a Pha Thi crew rotation. While he had previously visited the site, Blanton's primary responsibility had been to assist Jerry Clayton with the myriad administrative and logistical duties at Udorn. For several months, however, Clayton had heard rumors that the two teams were having personal disagreements during crew changeover. There had been no serious difficulties but, given the increasing workload, Clayton thought it prudent to have Blanton serve as the site commander for this rotation. He instructed Blanton to take a hard look at the operation and return with suggestions on how the current procedures might be improved. Although it was conceded that enemy pressure would soon cause the relocation of the Heavy Green operation, there was no indication that the mission itself was near termination. Anticipating new and stressful challenges, Jerry Clayton wanted the strongest possible team. Still, he also knew there were far greater personnel problems than simple grousing.[22]

A month earlier, in violation of explicit orders, a number of off-duty Heavy Green personnel had ventured down the mountain to the village of Pha Thi. In keeping with their cover story, which required "plausible deniability," Ambassador Sullivan had insisted the Heavy Green personnel were to have little contact with other Americans in Laos, and especially limited exposure to indigenous people. The technicians, including an officer, had walked down to the village and participated in a traditional Lao *baci* ceremony. During this Buddhist rite the villagers and technicians joined together in a blessing ceremony for the continued good health of all. The Lao tied amulets of white string on the wrists of their guests, warning them that to receive the full protection of the ceremony the strings should not be removed for at least several days. And so, when many of the errant technicians returned to Udorn wearing the tattered souvenirs of their unauthorized foray, the village visit and the lack of discipline and leadership it demonstrated was soon known throughout the Heavy Green program.[23]

At the time Jerry Clayton hoped it was an isolated instance of poor judgment.[24] This was not the case, however. While the Heavy Green personnel had been ordered by their commander to minimize contact with the Pha Thi villagers, a senior CIA officer has reported that the *baci* event was not the first visit by the technicians to the village. In fact, the local CIA case officers may have encouraged the visits. They certainly posed no objections. Despite Sullivan's misgivings, the CIA officer believed the presence of the technicians reassured the local military and their families of continued CIA support. The Hmong could expect to be well provisioned and allowed to occasionally travel on resupply helicopters: a major benefit for the isolated villagers. This, in turn, would likely encourage the Pha Thi forces to mount a more spirited defense of their positions.[25] Nevertheless, the willingness of the technicians to disregard orders is a robust symptom that some of the men assigned to Heavy Green were ill-suited for such a sensitive program.[26]

There were other, more serious, personnel problems. Weeks earlier Melvin Holland had approached the unit's administrative supervisor, Frank Roura, and asked to be relieved from the program.[27] From the inception of Heavy Green the men had been told that at any time they could ask for release and immediate return to the Air Force, no questions asked. Holland had been considering resignation since at least early January when he wrote his wife, "Let me know when the bills are cleared up. I may be coming home early."[28] Roura was sympathetic with Holland and told him that as soon as replacements arrived from the United States he would be released.[29] Holland agreed and went one last time to Site 85.

Upon his return to Pha Thi, Mel Holland spoke briefly with Donnell W. Hill, a radar operator and friend assigned to the other team. Hill and Holland had known each other from a previous assignment and both were dedicated, family-oriented men who had hoped to share the same shift. When the team assignments were announced, and the men found themselves on separate duty cycles, both were deeply disappointed. And, according to Hill, as the months passed Holland became increasingly unhappy with his Heavy Green assignment. In particular, recalls Hill, Holland often expressed to him his disillusionment with the less than professional attitude displayed by some people on Holland's crew. Hill, who had served an enlistment with the U.S. Marine Corps, agreed that his team was much more mature and security conscious than several of Holland's teammates.[30]

While the two friends unloaded food and water from the helicopter and carried it to the living quarters, they discussed the latest bombing activity, with Holland stating that he had heard "things were pretty busy." Hill recounts that Holland then announced, "This will be my last rotation," explaining that "the visit to the village by some of the men on my crew was the last straw." It was clear that Holland had made up his mind and Don Hill wished him well. Soon afterward, the shift change was completed and the departing team climbed aboard a helicopter. As they lifted off the helipad none of them realized that they were seeing Site 85 for the last time. Hill, who would be departing Thailand within days for leave in the United States, hoped that his friend Mel would also soon be reunited with his family.[31]

Holland, however, was not the only man to return reluctantly to the mountain. At the time he was approached by Holland, Frank Roura had also recently engaged in a long and serious discussion with another team member. The man, remembers Roura, had concluded that "he was a really a civilian and didn't have to put up with the military crap." Earlier the man had refused to purchase life insurance for his family and, until explicitly ordered to stop by Lieutenant Colonel Clayton, had carried a personal handgun while at Pha Thi. Claiming "pangs of remorse" and voicing "the sentiments of a conscientious objector," Roura says the man asked to be released from the program. As with Holland's request, Roura explained that the unit would soon receive new people and asked the obviously troubled airman to remain with Heavy Green a little longer.[32]

Shortly after the increase in technician manning, there were two other American personnel changes at Phou Pha Thi. Site 85's combat controller, Technical Sergeant Jim Gary, was replaced by Sergeant Roger D. Huffman. For the 22-year-old Huffman, the transition had come about very quickly. A relatively junior controller who had been training Thai Border Patrol Police units in northeastern Thailand, he was suddenly ordered to the American Embassy in Vientiane. Huffman received a short briefing from an assistant air attaché and was presented with a U.S. government civilian identification card. Within a few days "Mr. Huffman" found himself standing on the rocky Pha Thi helipad, meeting Jim Gary for the first time, and learning that he was to be responsible for directing air strikes in defense of this top secret base. After a few days of familiarization, Technical Sergeant Gary departed for Udorn, Thailand, and his eventual reassignment to the United States.[33] Huffman found himself looking down the mountain into jungle occupied by thousands of communist troops.

Given the potential for loss of life and international exposure of a U.S. activity that clearly contravened the Geneva agreements, the impending North Vietnamese assault on Site 85 seems to have been handled with great composure and confidence by Ambassador Sullivan and his staff. Sullivan's mood was reflected in a March 1 cable to the American Embassy in Saigon announcing his intention to attend an upcoming SEACOORD (Southeast Asia Coordinating Committee) meeting at Cam Ranh Bay, South Vietnam. "In view of the current respite from active enemy military drive in Laos," Sullivan wrote, "I consider prospects Vientiane attendance SEACOORD March 7 appear more bullish." He did, however, condition his attendance by saying that a final decision would depend upon an examination of the "local situation early next week." Included in the message were Sullivan's proposed agenda topics, among which were an update on the situation at LS 85 and plans for an alternate TSQ-81 site.[34] As discussed earlier, Sullivan believed that Phou Pha Thi would soon be under enemy control, but he accepted assurances from his staff that there were adequate plans to remove the men and destroy the equipment prior to any serious attack. As to continued TSQ operations from another site, Sullivan understood there would be "some delay and disruption while new equipment was brought in." Eventually, however, he expected the radar-guided bombing to continue from another northeastern Laos location.[35]

Ambassador Sullivan's confidence in the safety of the men at Site 85 may be explained by recent changes he approved to the rules of engagement for air strikes in defense of Pha Thi. U.S. aircraft had been authorized to increase the use of anti-personnel weapons against the communist forces surrounding the site, and the Pha Thi-based forward air controller and the Heavy Green radar operators could now direct attacks against any validated target within the 12-kilometer radius of the defensive perimeter. Moreover, with advance permission from Vientiane and "under threat of imminent attack," the radar technicians were now permitted to direct strike aircraft in clear voice (nonscrambled) transmissions.[36] In other words, the site was no longer required to camouflage its true location and role through the use of a relay aircraft flying over the Gulf of Tonkin. Lifting this restriction, which would permit the enemy to intercept and record the Heavy Green transmissions and therefore prove America's gross violations of the Geneva agreements, was a major concession to the gravity of the situation.[37]

Sullivan also agreed to arm the Heavy Green personnel with M-16 rifles. According to a senior CIA officer, "The Ambassador had been reluctant to approve issuance of firearms to the technicians. T.Q. [CIA officer Terry Quill] and others consistently argued for a change to this policy and about a week before the attack the technicians received M-16's. There was only time to familiarize and informally fire the weapons on the site." This brief exposure was hardly sufficient for the technicians to develop any level of confidence and proficiency with these new rifles. Indeed, recalls the officer, "The technicians were uncomfortable with civilian clothes, civilian ID cards, and weapons."[38] The M-16's, along with Air Force issue survival vests containing flares and ground-to-air radios, were stored in the Heavy Green living quarters located behind the radar building.[39] At least one of the men, against the explicit orders of Lieutenant Colonel Clayton, may also have been armed with a handgun.[40]

As the days passed, the "respite" to which Sullivan alluded in his cable to Saigon was short-lived. On March 4, the same day the additional technicians arrived at Site 85, the CIA station in Vientiane reported an unprecedented buildup of North Vietnamese forces in northern and southern Laos. Intelligence sources indicated that a recent influx of more than 3,000 troops had raised to 37,000 the total number of North Vietnamese assigned permanently to Laos. The growing communist presence suggested that the Hanoi leadership had decided to expand the war in Laos and, in the name of their Pathet Lao allies, intended to capture a number of key geographic areas. The current NVA objective in north Laos, according to the agency, "was clearly the capture and elimination of Phou Pha Thi as a TACAN and navigational site and as a major Lao guerrilla support base in northeast Laos." The report went on to speculate that the enemy might add another three or four battalions "before he makes his final move on Phou Pha Thi. Given the short distance over which the enemy has to move his troops from North Vietnam to Laos this buildup could be completed by 10 March 1968."

Equally disconcerting was the judgment that several previously unidentified PAVN battalions had moved into southern Laos and now posed direct threats to the towns of Saravane and Attopeu. While it was unclear that the North Vietnamese would carry out such brazen attacks under the nose of the International Control Commission, at a minimum the deployments consolidated their hold on several key segments of the southern Ho Chi Minh trail.[41]

With regard to LS 85, the latest CIA assessment was particularly blunt. "In the case of Phou Pha Thi the enemy will undoubtedly eliminate it as a TACAN and navigational site primarily by harassing mortar/artillery fire." However, the appraisal concluded with the observation that "The effort to take Phou Pha Thi should tie up North Vietnamese forces in north Laos to the extent that they will not be able to address themselves fully to other objectives."[42] This judgment, that it might be tactically advantageous to prolong the defense of Pha Thi, suggests that some U.S. officials considered Site 85 a useful lure to attract and occupy the attention of large numbers of communist troops. Indeed, on March 9 the CIA released a detailed estimate of the security at Site 85 and declared a beneficial aspect to the PAVN activity.

> The irregulars on top of Phou Pha Thi are ready to hold Site 85 as a terrain feature. They can hold it, if given tactical air support in depth, long after the TACAN and other navigational aids have been put out of commission by mortar or artillery fire. The length of time which seven enemy battalions can be tied down in an assault on Site 85 will significantly affect the enemy's ability to exercise other aggressive attack options in northeast Laos. It is thus in the best interest of the Lao government to keep the enemy tied down in the Site 85 area . . . and in so doing to bleed enemy forces in northeast Laos.[43]

When asked in a 1995 interview about this effort to "bleed enemy forces" Ambassador Sullivan responded that it "sounded like someone trying to place the best face on the situation."[44] But the report ends with the comment, "The ambassador has read and approved this cable."[45] Further, in an official interview conducted in 1970, Sullivan recounted one of the reasons why he was reluctant to order an earlier evacuation of Site 85.

> 7th Air Force felt that the defense capability of the unit itself, that is to say, its ability to vector aircraft in on the targets, was something we should maintain as long as possible. I think that had some merit to it, because they did have a mosaic of the area around it that they were using the TSQ-77[46] controls on [nearby targets].[47]

Sullivan's statement suggests that 7th AF had come to the same conclusion as the CIA and was using the encirclement of Pha Thi as an opportunity to place air strikes on large concentrations of PAVN forces. Ironically, the declared *raison d'être* for the TSQ-81, the bombing of high-priority North Vietnamese targets, had all but disappeared. As discussed in chapter 4, during the first ten days of March Heavy Green directed only three missions over North Vietnam. By contrast, during the same period the radar controlled more than 230 strike sorties against communist targets within 30 kilometers of Pha Thi.[48]

In the face of an imminent communist assault on a facility that had outlived its stated purpose, why would U.S. military leaders urge Ambassador Sullivan to delay the evacuation of Site 85 and accept an enormous risk to Americans lives and U.S. foreign policy interests? The military was under significant pressure from the White House to improve the effectiveness of Rolling Thunder and Site 85 had provided a distinctive contribution to this air campaign. As discussed in chapter 1, the USAF was struggling to maintain a credible bombing campaign against North Vietnam. While communist forces encircled Pha Thi, American aircraft were contending with North Vietnam's northeast monsoon, the worst flying conditions of the year. Because of extensive cloud cover over important North Vietnamese targets, Heavy Green's radar had often meant the difference between USAF aircraft dropping bombs or remaining grounded. The Air Force leadership, intent on protecting its image as a dominant air power, refused to concede that bad weather could render impotent a major part of its vaunted air power[49] Thus, while the danger to the Americans at Pha Thi and the international consequences of a public exposure of this clear U.S. violation of the Geneva agreements were considered, the military leadership claimed that Heavy Green's unique capability—albeit little employed—outweighed these concerns.

While it is unclear if Ambassador Sullivan knew the North Vietnam missions had all but evaporated, in the weeks leading up to the loss of Site 85 the ambassador frequently discussed the facility with senior officers at 7/13th AF in Udorn and 7th AF in Saigon. The generals, Sullivan says, repeatedly and consistently vouched for the importance of the TSQ-81 radar. Recalls Sullivan, "I was being told that the site was critical to the bombing campaign over North Vietnam and that it should be kept open until the last possible moment."[50] The 7th AF view was made explicit in a March 5 message to PACAF headquarters. "[D]ue to the desirability of maintaining air presence over NVA [North Vietnam][51] during present inclement weather period, Site 85 probably would not be evacuated until capture appeared imminent. The fact that complete security could not be assured in the original plan is noted."[52]

Saigon's apparent lack of concern was not, however, shared in Hawaii. Later the same day General John D. Ryan Commander in Chief of Pacific Air Forces, directed that Major General Lindley, Deputy Commander of the 7/13th AF, contact local CIA sources and provide "your estimate of threat, including anticipated time of attack, and friendly capabilities to defend." Clearly alarmed by the rapid communist buildup around Pha Thi, Ryan authorized 7/13th AF to "direct evacuation of site and destruction of equipment when in your judgment such action is necessary. Your plan, OPLAN [Operational Plan] 439–68, is approved for this purpose. Insure that all preparations are made for emergency evacuation as required."[53] While General Ryan's concern was well-founded and he was within his authority to express this concern to Lindley, he did not have the final vote on abandoning Site 85. Indeed, adhering to the views of General Momyer, his immediate superior, on March 6 Major General Lindley advised General Ryan, "Believe consideration of moving the MSQ is out of the question for 6 to 9 month period due to non availability of an appropriate new site and the forthcoming South West Monsoon." He then recommended to Ryan "that pressure be maintained on Amb [Ambassador] Vientiane to protect site at all cost. Evacuation plans for Site 85 will be implemented only as a last resort."[54] Faced with such an aggressive stance from his in-theater commanders, General Ryan appears to have taken no further actions to close down Site 85. Notwithstanding the views of Generals Momyer and Lindley, as documented earlier, Heavy Green does not appear to have ever been critical to the U.S. bombing of North Vietnam, let alone in the early days of March 1968.

By his own admission, this was a very troubling period for William Sullivan.[55] Armed with presidentially approved authority, the Ambassador exercised firm control over all U.S. military activity in Laos.[56] He rarely delegated this power and, in the case of Pha Thi, evacuation planning discussions between 7/13th AF representatives and the CIA clearly indicated Sullivan would personally give the order. According to the escape scenario, "the decision to evacuate was reserved for the Ambassador, Vientiane. . . . Following a decision to evacuate, the Ambassador was to notify 7/13 AF TACC [Tactical Air Control Center] at Udorn AB, Thailand who could in turn notify 7AF."[57] Lieutenant Colonel Clayton has also said he was told in Washington that Sullivan was the only one who "could close the site," a statement the Ambassador confirmed in an interview with me.[58] Still, the Ambassador has not always been consistent on this point. In 1970, when asked who was empowered to make the decision to close Site 85, Sullivan stated:

> That was 7th Air Force, but I probably could have over-ridden it. I mean I not only probably could have, I could have, and probably should have. I probably would have had some squawks from 7th Air Force, but they would have behaved, I mean they would have done it, I'm sure. As it was I left it up to 7th to determine when they thought they wanted it shut down, and they pushed it a little too far. So I blame myself for not having acted in advance.[59]

Based on the available evidence, including Air Force records and Sullivan's own actions after the attack began,[60] I am persuaded that these comments were simply Sullivan's awkward attempt to avoid direct responsibility for the loss. As his words show, he was torn between admitting he did not have complete authority over the military and wanting to show they shared culpability for the incident. And, although he admits blame here, it is unclear what this really means. As will be discussed later, Sullivan believed the Heavy Green losses were caused by the personnel themselves.[61]

Despite the CIA warnings, well known to senior civilian and military officials throughout Southeast Asia and in Washington, the facility continued operations. Ambassador Sullivan says, in the end, he was given no other option. "A week or so prior to the attack on Site 85," Sullivan recalls, "I received a cable with instructions which could not be overruled. The site was to be kept open." When pressed for the author of the cable, Sullivan would only repeat that it was someone whose authority was absolute. In short, Sullivan was assured, and then directed, that the imminent risk to American lives and U.S. interests in Laos was more than offset by Site 85's singular capability to direct all-weather bombing strikes over North Vietnam. The Ambassador had now been twice overruled on the issue of Heavy Green. Despite what he says were serious personal reservations, Sullivan says he had no choice but to maintain the U.S. presence at Phou Pha Thi.[62]

On Friday, March 8, Terry Quill departed Site 85. He was scheduled for time off and wanted to visit his girlfriend Diana, an American nurse working at the Sam Thong refugee center. Because CIA station policy required the presence at Pha Thi of two case officers, however, it was agreed that Quill would be replaced by his supervisor, Howard "Howie" Freeman. A very experienced officer who was normally stationed at LS 36, Na Khang, Freeman was no stranger to Pha Thi. He was well aware of the surrounding enemy forces and the pressure being placed by the Air Force on his station chief to keep the site open. Freeman and Spence knew also that an attack on the site was impending and the Hmong and Thai forces were incapable of providing little more than a brief fixed defense. When the time came to "bug out" they hoped that an air evacuation of the nineteen Americans, themselves included, would go smoothly; the case officers had no desire to take to the jungle with a group of technicians untrained in escape and evasion procedures.[63]

By March 9 the CIA was advising that, "it was becoming increasingly difficult to estimate enemy strengths and fix their locations because they had deployed into numerous small concentrations."[64] The same day, in a different report, the agency estimated, "The enemy is now in position with sufficient strength to launch his attack at any time. Site 85 is now vulnerable to a major artillery mortar barrage followed up by a ground assault and a possible air attack at any time. In view of this . . . Site 85 . . . is in grave jeopardy."[65]

On Saturday afternoon, March 10, Howie Freeman and Woody Spence were trying to make some sense of the ever increasing communist moves on Pha Thi. Villagers were reporting enemy movements from the south and west of "about 1,000 enemy troops" and "an enemy force about eight kilometers south and southwest of Phou Pha Thi was laying telephone wire for use with field phones."[66] Despite the authority to direct self-defense bombing missions against nearby enemy forces, the CIA case officers and their Thai and Hmong forces at Pha Thi were decidedly uneasy, knowing full well that their loose defensive perimeter was constantly being probed and often breached. Villagers and Hmong guerrilla units were reporting large numbers of North Vietnamese and Pathet Lao troops, many armed with artillery and mortar pieces. Increasingly, the irregulars were engaged by the communists in brief firefights. The case officers knew that if confronted by a determined enemy assault, the eight hundred or so Hmong guarding the approaches to the mountain would abandon their fixed positions and scatter into the surrounding hills. Expert at hit and run tactics and intelligence collection, the Hmong had never embraced the tenets of conventional warfare, i.e., to hold key terrain as part of a larger strategy. Indeed, in the past a number of the long-time Lao case officers had found it advisable to join their Hmong troops in a hasty retreat from attacking communist forces.[67] Months of Vietnamese activity had created an overwhelming and indisputable certainty—within hours Site 85 would become the objective of an unprecedented communist assault. Ultimately, then, an orderly evacuation from the mountain would rest upon the uncertain arrival of Air America and USAF aircraft and the skills and determination of the Heavy Green radar operators, two case officers, a young forward air guide, and a relatively small contingent of Thai and Hmong troops.

The nervous case officers called the radar site on the land line telephone and asked the on-site commander, Bill Blanton, to join them at the CIA operations building for a threat assessment briefing. Blanton, accompanied by Dick Etchberger, was soon listening to a grim recitation of enemy movements. Howie Freeman and Woody Spence then went on to express their growing concern over the continued presence of the Heavy Green personnel and their strong view that the technicians should be evacuated prior to the attack. Nothing, however, could be settled in the cramped CIA outpost, and a radio call was placed to Bill Lair, CIA Chief of Base at Udorn.[68]

Lair, the "godfather" of the covert army in Laos, was intimately familiar with the capabilities of the Hmong and Thai forces guarding Pha Thi. And, as discussed earlier, from the first mention of placing the TSQ-81 in Laos, he had predicted that Hanoi would move rapidly to locate and destroy any such equipment.[69] Lair listened to the case officers' assessment and quickly sent for Lieutenant Colonel Clayton. Woody Spence recalls the remainder of the conversation as follows, "Bill got hold of Jerry Clayton and had him talk to the commander [Blanton] in our shack. Clayton told him to stay on the mountain and defend it. We thought it was a poor decision."[70] Jerry Clayton's recollection differs slightly on the content of this crucial and final verbal conversation between the long-time friends.

> I told Bill that he was there and I was here, and to do what he thought best. Of course, we both knew that the operation could only be closed down by Ambassador Sullivan. Once the explosive charges were set and the equipment blown-up, there was no turning back. We were military people and you couldn't just mutiny. The final say had to come from Vientiane and I still believed we would have a minimum of twelve hours notice to blow-up the equipment and get out.

Clayton did, however, tell Blanton to prepare for a limited crew extraction, tentatively scheduled for the following morning.[71] Meanwhile, until directed by the Ambassador, Clayton and Blanton were powerless to end the Site 85 program.

What no American realized at the time, despite all the varied intelligence collection efforts, was the impending onset of a well-planned commando-style attack on the radar and TACAN itself. For more than a month, according to a postwar interview, a North Vietnamese sapper team had trekked from the headquarters of North Vietnam's Northwest Military Region, located in Son La province, to the base of Phou Pha Thi. Led by Truong Muc,[72] a 37-year-old first lieutenant from a minority tribe in Yen Bai province, North Vietnam, the team had been given the task of destroying the American "radar equipment." Late in the afternoon of March 10, Truong Muc and his men lay hidden in the jungle between Houei Hok village, LS 198, and the southwestern base of Phou Pha Thi. Loaded down with ropes, explosives, and automatic weapons, the *Dac Cong* awaited the order to begin a climb timed to coincide with a mortar and artillery attack. Under cover of the barrage, their immediate objective, according to Truong Muc, was to reach the northwestern summit at "a point between the U.S. TACAN/TSQ Site and the Thai unit" located just to the north of the radar buildings. Once on the mountaintop the sappers would encircle the enemy positions and kill or destroy everything in their path.[73]

Set to ascend the very path discovered by Woody Spence and Terry Quill during their late January security review,[74] the *Dac Cong* were about to employ Sun Tzu's ancient dictum of war, "All warfare is based on deception. Attack where he is unprepared: sally out when he does not expect you."[75]

9

"Everything to Defeat the U.S. Aggressors"

At the CIA operations area Freeman and Spence decided to send an "after-dinner message" to the surrounding Vietnamese troops. A little harassment, the Americans believed, might well upset any ongoing enemy artillery and troop movements and temporarily place the communists off-balance.[1] The rocket launcher constructed and placed at the site by the CIA Technical Services Division seemed ideal for their purpose. At 6:00 P.M., the case officers fired several of the 2.75-inch white phosphorous rockets toward the east—and immediately found themselves under a heavy mortar, artillery, and rocket attack![2] According to Spence, "Even before we saw the flash of our impacting rockets, the Vietnamese had fired at us and scored a near direct hit on the site's 105mm howitzer—only about 300 yards from our rocket launcher."[3] The enemy round, believed to be from a captured 105mm howitzer,[4] shredded a large tree adjacent to the gun as the startled CIA men and their Thai and Hmong troops ran for the safety of nearby bunkers. Roger Huffman, who had been cleaning his M-16 rifle in the CIA building, ran across the helipad to his bunkered radio position. En route Huffman ran into a large rock and bruised his knee, but was otherwise unhurt.[5]

The shelling continued for some time, with rounds landing near the CIA and Thai living quarters and operations area. The accuracy of the attack, coming from positions many miles to the east, left no doubt that local spies had drawn a detailed map of the site for the North Vietnamese. Woody Spence wondered if the two rockets had acted as a signal for the enemy gunners, or if it was merely a bizarre coincidence that both sides had begun firing at the same time.[6] No matter; the Site 85 defenders realized that, vastly outgunned, they could only radio for help, huddle in their cold bunkers, and hope for quick assistance.

Six miles to the northeast at Site 111, in anticipation of a North Vietnamese attack USAID refugee worker Ernie Kuhn and Hmong leaders were preparing for a civilian evacuation of the area. Their meeting cut short by the Site 85 explosions, the senior Hmong official and Kuhn grabbed their radios and tried, respectively, to contact village authorities at Pha Thi and the defenders at the mountain's summit. No one at the village responded, and the ominous silence began to panic the Hmong at Site 111. Kuhn was only slightly more successful. Using an HT-2 survival radio, he finally reached Roger Huffman and learned that the young combat controller was dug in near the eastern edge of the helipad. Huffman reported that shells were hitting near the helipad but, because he had no current communications with the CIA command bunker, he was unable to confirm possible casualties. Fearing that the CIA officers had lost their radio link to the outside world, Kuhn called U.S. Embassy officials in Vientiane via his USAID single-sideband radio and reported his conversation with the forward air guide. Thirty minutes later a single U.S. aircraft reached Site 85 and, directed by Kuhn and Huffman, attempted to bomb the enemy's artillery and rocket positions. In the absolute jungle darkness, however, the pilot was unable to determine exact targets and could only drop his ordnance on suspected enemy areas. Bombs spent and low on fuel, the lone airborne defender soon departed.[7]

Unbeknownst to Ernie Kuhn, the CIA and Heavy Green representatives at Udorn had promptly received word of the emergency from their respective personnel at the mountain and were working nonstop to save their men and equipment. USAF Major Richard "Dick" Secord,[8] the CIA air operations officer at Udorn, along with CIA officers Pat Landry and Tom Clines, had for months been monitoring the enemy's encirclement of Site 85. Secord has written that upon learning the facility was under attack he repeatedly telephoned 7th AF officials in Saigon to request that they immediately divert aircraft from other missions to defend Pha Thi. He asked specifically for one of the deadly AC-130 "Spectre" gun ships which, according to Secord, "had been in the theater only a few months and were rapidly becoming the terror of the skies." Mightily upset when told that a Spectre could not be diverted from a "priority mission" on the Ho Chi Minh Trail, the flamboyant Secord claims he screamed over the telephone at an uncooperative one-star general, "Are you aware of Site 85? Are you aware of what it is? What the hell is your name?" He alleges that the general responded with his name and asked whom he was speaking with. Secord replied that he was a "major" trying to defend Site 85 and "a sizable contingent of American and Allied troops, and a ton of classified gear, was about to go down at Pha Thi." After repeating his request for aircraft "urgently and emphatically," Secord says he hung up the phone.[9]

While Secord's account contains the kind of flair and bravado some might hope for in a critical situation—the earnest young major railing against an uncaring and uninformed general—it is, charitably, a flawed "war story." The author has interviewed two U.S. Air Force generals who served at 7th AF during the period of Secord's supposed berating of the general he identifies as "General Arnold C. Craig." Both officers stated that they knew of no general by that name and, quite forcefully, expressed the view that it was very doubtful that the event could have transpired in the way Secord has described.[10] Although it is possible Secord chose to use a pseudonym for the "general," as he does with other characters in his book, it is more likely that he never spoke to a general at all.

More important, a comprehensive official USAF history states that on March 10, 1968, there was a single AC-130 in all of Southeast Asia, and it was a prototype. At the time of the Pha Thi assault the gun ship, stationed at Ubon Royal Thai Air Force Base, was only two weeks into a combat evaluation test program. Routine AC-130 gun ship activity in Southeast Asia did not occur until the December 1968 deployment of four AC-130s to Ubon.[11] Secord may have confused the AC-130 with AC-47 "Spooky" gun ships, which were active in South Vietnam during this time and had been used in Laos up until July 1966. It is worth noting, however, that the AC-47s were withdrawn from Laos missions after four were shot down by communist anti-aircraft fire.[12] It is doubtful the vulnerable AC-47s would have been returned to Laos. While it is possible the lone AC-130 was airborne on the night of March 10, no competent officer would have risked the dispatch of this experimental aircraft and its crew to northeastern Laos.[13]

It is thus clear that Secord, for reasons unknown, has provided a faulty account of the loss of Site 85. Unfortunately, his version has been accepted by some writers and incorporated into their accounts of the attack. Nonetheless, from a number of reliable sources it is clear that as a young officer Secord often behaved with great bluster. A senior CIA officer has said, "I have heard Secord be quite forceful in phone conversations and briefings to USAF officers quite senior to himself. His sharp comments were always a surprise to CIA officers who understood what was considered acceptable conduct between a subordinate and a senior. In total, Secord was most effective and productive in getting USAF support for CIA programs in Laos."[14] To be sure, Secord was deeply involved in U.S. military operations in Laos at the time and, given his reputation for action, it is not hard to imagine him trying to organize some sort of defense for Site 85. Nonetheless, his written account is greatly flawed.

At about 6:00 P.M., when Woody Spence and Howie Freeman were preparing to fire their 2.75-inch rockets, Bill Blanton had just concluded a team meeting up on the radar site. Looking into the faces of the fifteen men gathered in the operations/maintenance building, the lieutenant colonel repeated what he had heard at the CIA briefing. Summing up, he announced they were "pretty well surrounded," and asked if any of the men wanted immediate evacuation or, if they were "willing to stay and kill some of the SOBs."[15] No one asked to leave. Blanton then said that some of the "non-essential" men would probably be airlifted out the next morning and there was some discussion as to who would go. John Daniel recalls that there was no hint of panic and he personally viewed site security as "very adequate. There was only one way up to the radar and the path was guarded."[16] Jack Starling, the only TACAN technician at the site, silently observed that he would not be among those soon departing.[17]

The meeting broke up and the men began to prepare for a special dinner. Beef steaks had been included with the food supplies the men brought with them from Udorn, and Daniel, the nominal site cook, had earlier started a charcoal fire near the northwestern corner of the living quarters. This Sunday evening the Heavy Green team planned to dine on grilled steak. Just as some of the men were leaving the meeting an enemy shell landed squarely on the barbeque pit and "steaks were flying everywhere."[18] The 7/13th AF Tactical Air Control Center (TACC) at Udorn was immediately advised by radio of the attack and told that "Wager"[19] would be off the air. Using a portable radio, emergency communications were established between the technicians and the CIA bunker.[20] Meanwhile, Stan Sliz and several others ran toward their lone bunker located between the radar and the living quarters. They quickly realized the bunker had suffered a direct hit—the communist gunners were either very lucky or very good—and turned and ran for the living quarters. Sliz went to his bunk in search of cigarettes, only to find that shrapnel had raked the building.[21] At this point, the technicians gathered up their weapons and survival radios and decided to take cover in a small trench located near the edge of the western cliff. Bill Blanton soon made radio contact with the CIA command bunker and was told that the area was under a rocket and mortar attack. According to Stan Sliz, the men then decided to climb down along the side of the mountain "because of the lack of any real good protection in any other area."[22]

The scramble over the side of the mountain was not a pre-planned decision, but the instinctive act of men who had served in South Vietnam and knew the dangers of rocket, mortar, and artillery attacks. The firing was coming from the east and, they reasoned, they were at risk if they remained unprotected in the flat area near the radar and the TACAN. Lying among the large rocks just below the ridge line, still only a few yards from the equipment, they were shielded from shrapnel. Moreover, from this position, any shells that passed over the site would continue beyond the men and fall thousands of feet to the base of the mountain.[23] It was a logical response to the barrage. During the next phase of the attack, however, it provided the men a terribly false sense of safety.

Throughout the attack Freeman and Spence maintained radio contact with John Rodman,[24] CIA Chief of Base at Lima Site 20A (Long Tieng). In turn, Rodman was relaying the information to his superiors in Vientiane. Woody Spence believes these radio transmissions were also being monitored by CIA personnel at LS 36, at Udorn air base, and at the CIA station in Vientiane.[25] The key figures in Vientiane, Ambassador Sullivan, Air Attaché Colonel Pettigrew, and CIA Station Chief Shackley, were all quickly informed. At 7:10 P.M., the Rescue Coordination Center (RCC) at Udorn air base, call-sign "Compress," was alerted for a possible evacuation of LS 85.[26] Half-way around the world the White House communications room received notification of the attack and President Johnson was shortly thereafter informed "Site 85 was under enemy pressure."[27]

Log entries made at the Udorn TACC indicate that upon learning of the attack 7/13th AF personnel quickly diverted to the site several U.S. Air Force C-130 Lamplighter flare ships, A-26A Nimrods, and F-4 Phantoms.[28] Spence recalls that at about 7:30 P.M., some ninety minutes into the bombardment, a Lamplighter arrived above the mountain. The surrounding area was quickly bathed in the eerie light of huge flares suspended from slowly descending parachutes. Almost simultaneously, the firing ceased, and it appeared the Vietnamese had recognized that the roles were about to be reversed. Soon they would become targets for the U.S. Air Force.[29]

Crouched down along the western face of the mountain, the Heavy Green personnel greeted the end of the shelling with intensity and determination. Quickly returning to their duty positions they discovered that, despite the initial damage to the bunker and living quarters, both the TSQ-81 radar and TACAN remained operational. More important, there were no injuries to any American personnel. At 7:45, "Wager" reported to the 7/13th AF TACC that they were ready and able to direct bombing strikes against the surrounding communist forces. Indeed, after receiving bombing coordinates from Freeman, Spence, and Huffman, two A-26s and five F-4s were placed under TSQ-control and began striking nearby targets.[30]

The enemy locations came, ironically enough, from a map found on the body of a dead Vietnamese officer. Recovered nearly a month earlier by a Hmong guerrilla team, the drawing listed the geographic positions for those units scheduled to participate in the Pha Thi attack.[31] John Daniel recalls that the air strikes were uncomfortably close to the site. "I told some of the guys near me that I hoped none of the bombs has a bent fin. Everyone laughed. We actually went outside the building and watched the explosions." Morale was high and the Heavy Green team was "back to dropping bombs."[32] The attack did, however, remind the men of the thermite charge located on the radar pedestal above their heads. Fearing that more shelling might ignite the thermite, destroy the radar, and perhaps injure nearby personnel, the incendiary material was removed and thrown over the side of the mountain.[33] It was a spontaneous decision which would have long-term, unforeseen consequences.

At 7:55 P.M., Air Attaché Colonel Pettigrew declared in a cable to the Defense Intelligence Agency (DIA):

> Site 85 situation critical. Enemy troop concentrations closing. 1828L [6:28 P.M.] Site 85 received incoming rounds. Evacuation not yet considered but if situation deteriorates will be mandatory. Small arms fire reported being received. TSQ commo [communications] out. Personnel presently in bunkers. Further sitreps [situation reports] as available.[34]

This was followed by a CIA Vientiane cable of 9:04 P.M., which stated in part:

> By about 1835 [6:35 P.M.] hours . . . Site 85 . . . was under heavy enemy mortar fire. TACAN personnel reported that their commo shack had received a direct hit and they were going to their bunker. About 40 rounds of heavy mortar fire landed on or near the 105 howitzer position. All personnel at Phou Pha Thi were in bunkers, and the defense effort at Phou Pha Thi was well organized.[35]

By the time the CIA released the above cable, however, Ambassador Sullivan "had judged circumstances serious enough to authorize the site to conduct the direction of sorties via clear voice transmissions."[36] This was a clear acknowledgment that, although defense efforts were "well organized," the situation had turned critical and immediate external support was needed to defend the site. Air strikes, unfortunately, failed to deter the second phase of the communist attack. Woody Spence remembers that renewed shelling, this time from the south, commenced at 8:00 P.M.., and continued for about one and a half hours. During this phase of the attack an enemy round landed some eighteen inches from the CIA bunker, causing Spence permanent hearing loss.[37] Hmong defenders were involved in heavy fighting at the village of Pha Thi, located on the eastern slopes of the mountain. Freeman recalls that the Hmong forces, protecting their families and home village, mounted a very strong defense. "If the Hmong had failed to hold I feel certain the North Vietnamese would have made it to at least the helipad area and we would have been in very serious trouble."[38]

Freeman's observations raise a number of questions regarding the attack. Was the communist artillery and mortar barrage from the east simply a diversion so that the *Dac Cong* could assault the radar vans? Or did the Vietnamese, unsure that their commandos could successfully climb the western face of Pha Thi, always intend to use conventional ground forces to attack and hold the mountain? Based on the number of communist forces deployed around Site 85, it seems reasonable to conclude that they had every intention of seizing and controlling the mountain and surrounding area. If so, the Hmong defenders at the village of Pha Thi may well have disrupted Hanoi's timetable and saved a number of American lives. It also seems probable the North Vietnamese were following the doctrine of alternative objectives, and planned for different modes of success.[39]

Increasingly nervous staff officers in Vientiane and Udorn followed the events at Pha Thi, reviewed their evacuation plans, and made a tentative decision to recommend an evacuation of the site at first light. This message was conveyed to the Udorn Rescue Control Center at 9:50 P.M., which logged the brief comment "possible [evacuation] first light."[40] Senior Air Force officials, however, were reluctant to carry out such a mission. The subject was discussed in a telephone conversation between Major General William C. Lindley, Jr., Deputy Commander, 7/13th AF, and an officer assigned to the air attaché office in Vientiane. According to an entry in the TACC log General Lindley directed:

> . . . evacuation should only be effected as a last resort if the situation became untenable; furthermore, the situation should be followed on an hour to hour basis. These views were to be expressed to the Ambassador. Any decision to evacuate was to be relayed to the Deputy Commander at once.[41]

Lindley seems to have been following the March 5 orders from 7th AF directing that evacuation of Site 85 not take place "until capture appeared imminent."[42] But, again, the Air Force showed little understanding of Sullivan's longstanding view, and control, of the U.S. military presence in Laos. Indeed, by the time Lindley called Vientiane, the Ambassador had already made a decision to evacuate some of the Heavy Green men. A Site 85 update message sent by the U.S. Defense Attaché office in Vientiane states that shortly after 9:21 P.M., Sullivan ordered that nine of the technicians be removed by helicopter at 8:15 A.M. the next day.[43] A 10:30 P.M. log entry at the rescue center in

Udorn noted, "First light effort will be made to evac 8 personnel. 2 SJG's [Super Jolly Greens][44] will be used."[45]

As discussed earlier, active evacuation planning had been underway for several weeks. Once the RCC had been notified, the rescue operation sprang into motion. 7th AF headquarters in Saigon directed that the rescue be carried out by Detachment 2, 37th Aerospace Rescue and Recovery Squadron (ARRS). Flying HH-3E "Jolly Green Giant" helicopters from Nakhon Phanom Royal Thai Air Force Base and HH-53B "Super Jolly Green Giant" helicopters from Udorn air base, Detachment 2 had primary responsibility for the recovery of military aircrews in Laos and North Vietnam.[46] On the Detachment 2 duty roster for March 11 "alert"[47] were Captain Russell L. Cayler, pilot, and Captain Joseph A. Panza, co-pilot. They were assigned the radio call sign "JG 67." A second Super Jolly crew was commanded by Captain Alfred C. Montrem, with call sign "JG 69."[48] Late on the evening of March 10, the Jolly pilots and several A-1H "Sandy"[49] pilots reported to the Udorn TACC for a detailed pre-mission briefing. Cayler recalls that a number of men in civilian clothes, whom he presumed were CIA, showed the pilots aerial photographs of the site, explained the physical layout, and told the rescuers the recovery would take place from the helipad. Sobered by the difficulty of the mission that lay ahead, the men headed for their bunks and tried to gain a few hours of sleep.[50]

Meanwhile, at Pha Thi the Heavy Green technicians and Roger Huffman, from his position near the helipad, were busy directing all available bombing aircraft at the surrounding communist forces. The site's original intent, to strike at the heart of North Vietnam, had now shifted entirely to self-preservation. In the midst of this activity, sometime after 8:00 P.M., Bill Blanton decided that his radar team would remain on duty while Stan Sliz and his men would try to get some sleep. While it was understood that some of the technicians would be evacuated in the morning, it appears that Blanton anticipated the site would continue in operation and, therefore, wanted to ensure the availability of a fresh crew for the following day's bombing operations.

Judging that the shrapnel-damaged living quarters were unsafe, the men of radar team two grabbed their sleeping bags and some food and "decided to spend the night on the side of the hill [mountain]."[51] They also carried with them M-16s and survival radios.[52] John Daniel and Monk Springsteadah descended some twenty feet down the western side of the mountain to a rock overhang located just south of the radar buildings. It was the spot where Daniel, during his off-duty hours, had often spent time writing letters and recording audio tape messages home. The path to the overhang was not steep, but it ended abruptly and then dropped off several thousand feet. Daniel recalls that there was no thought of a ground attack "because there was no way for the enemy to get to the top of the mountain." Therefore, there was no fear that the men were trapped at the end of the path. Sheltered under the outcropping, bundled up in their sleeping bags, the two men "all keyed up, watched the flares, and fell asleep off and on."[53] Stan Sliz, Dick Etchberger, and Hank Gish decided to remain closer to the vans at a point just below the ridge line and some twenty yards to the south of the operations building. Sliz has reported that he set up a portable high frequency radio, notified the Blanton crew and the Heavy Green office at Udorn that they were monitoring the radio, and eventually fell asleep at about 1:00 A.M.[54]

On the southwest corner of the site, Jack Starling was inside the TACAN enclosure completing a series of maintenance checks. Gratified that "Channel 97"[55] was still on the air, Starling closed up the equipment and wondered how much longer he and the others would remain on the mountain. Alone, he walked north to a point some 30 yards beyond the operations building and then climbed down to a flat area just below the crest of the cliff. Finding shelter next to a large boulder, he, too, was soon asleep.[56] In the darkness, Starling was unaware that radar team two was just a dozen yards away, on a separate outcropping.

Inside the radar building, sitting in front of the teletype machine, Mel Holland sent an operational status report to Jerry Clayton in Udorn. The message ended with Holland's name and the comment, "See you later, I hope." Reading the words off the printer in the security of his Udorn communications room, Clayton sighed and silently prayed for the safety of his men. It would be the final written message from project Heavy Green.[57] From Udorn to Vientiane, everyone was now settled in for a tense night, hoping that the combination of air strikes and Hmong ground forces at the base of Pha Thi would prevent the North Vietnamese from reaching the Americans. All eyes were focused on the presumed locations of the Vietnamese main force units and their artillery and rocket forces. At ten minutes past midnight the Rescue Control Center at Udorn was advised "Back up Helio will be Durax[58] 11, 12 located at L-36 [Na Khang]." Five minutes later, the rescue center was told that only six personnel would be evacuated. Two hours later the rescue controllers were told that "Any wounded will be [evacuated] regardless of nationality."[59] The CIA wanted it made clear that, if at all possible, their Thai and Hmong forces would not be left behind.

Shielded by the artillery, mortar, and rocket barrage, North Vietnamese Lieutenant Truong Muc and twenty-six of his men made their way to the western crest of Phou Pha Thi. Emerging at about 2:00 A.M. in an area about one hundred yards north of the radar buildings and just to the south of a Thai-manned defensive position, Truong Muc says he personally "disarmed three or four trip-wire anti-personnel mines" which were "deployed above ground and were not a significant obstacle." The commandos then divided into two "cells," with "five or six men" directed at the Thai position and Truong Muc and the remainder of the group concentrated on the Americans and the radar/TACAN buildings. The smaller team "found it did not have sufficient time to attack the Thai unit, so it withdrew to positions where it could block any attempt by the Thais to reach the U.S. TACAN/TSQ site." Meanwhile, Truong Muc and his cell moved toward the east and began a clockwise movement around the American facilities. Reaching a point "approximately mid-way between the north and south ends of the site and opposite the cliff—with the Americans between the sappers and the cliff," Truong Muc's cell split into three attacking forces. Two groups continued their clockwise movement, placing men near a "generator shed" and positioning men "facing the entrances to other structures so they could shoot any Americans that might try to rush out." Several other raiders were sent to the southwest perimeter of the Heavy Green area. The encirclement completed, the *Dac Cong* were now prepared to "intercept any Americans attempting to flee towards the helicopter landing pad, as well as intercept any forces that might try to move toward the TACAN/TSQ site from the direction of the helicopter pad." The time, according to Truong Muc, was between 3:30 and 4:00 A.M. Ordered to "kill any Americans inside the operations vans, living quarters, and bunkers," Truong Muc and the larger group moved toward the center of the Heavy Green area and began the slaughter.[60]

Mentally and physically drained from the enemy bombardment and more than eight hours of preparing and directing air strikes, radar team one and their support personnel were caught completely unaware. Bill Blanton, Jim Calfee, Pat Shannon, Don Worley, and David Price were likely at or near their consoles inside the radar building. The support personnel, Mel Holland, Herb Kirk, Jim Davis, Willis Hall, and Bill Husband, were probably working or sleeping in the operations van.[61] According to the official U.S. Air Force report, "Shortly after 0300L [3:00 A.M.] . . . either automatic weapons fire, shelling, or both . . . caused the crew to abandon the facility in haste. At this point all radio contact with the TSQ location and personnel was severed."[62]

Truong Muc says that he and his team entered the operations building. With their assault rifles they "immediately opened fire on any American they encountered" and "killed some Americans on the spot, while other Americans were able to react and return fire." His men then "killed some Americans in or near the command [operations] building and bunker." Elsewhere on the site, the commandos "killed one American near the generator shed, and a group of five or six Americans in [a] defensive position near the edge of the cliff."[63]

Jarred awake by the initial commando attack, Jack Starling recalls that he was soon joined by Willis Hall and both attempted to conceal themselves behind the large boulder on the western cliff. According to Starling, within minutes Bill Blanton, Mel Holland, Pat Shannon, and David Price were also seeking safety in the small flat depression some "20 to 30 feet" from Starling and Hall's location. Many of the technicians had weapons and were firing at the pursuing Vietnamese. Starling was also shooting, but his M-16 soon jammed. Trapping the men in a small area with no escape route, the *Dac Cong* pressed the assault with automatic weapons fire and grenades. The results, according to Starling, were devastating. "Holland's arm was blown off and he was on the ground, moaning with pain. Price was lying next to Holland, dead. Blanton and Shannon were lying together on the ground, neither was moving." During the barrage Starling was struck by bullets in the right thigh and his right big toe, while Hall also received undetermined wounds. Starling recalls hearing shouts from the Vietnamese and then the commandos rushed toward the men, firing their weapons. Defenseless, Starling played dead as he heard the *Dac Cong* sweep over the area. At one point, a Vietnamese even stepped on his ankle, but Starling remained silent. Attracted by the groans of the wounded Americans, the *Dac Cong* began firing into each of the prone and defenseless men. "I heard them open up with a machine gun, and then it got quiet. They killed the man next to me and how they kept from hitting me, I'll never know."[64] Starling was certain the enemy executed every other American in the depression.[65]

Awakened by shooting that seemed to be coming from several locations around the site, and "hearing strange voices directly overhead," Sliz, Etchberger, and Gish quickly made their way down the path and joined Daniel and Springsteadah near the protective rock overhang. The five men tried to squeeze into this "grotto-like affair," desperately trying to conceal themselves from an enemy they could sense was walking just a few yards above their heads. Struggling to find safety, Stan Sliz made his way around John Daniel and pressed into the cold limestone next to Monk Springsteadah. Sliz recalls being so cold that he accepted Springsteadah's sleeping bag and pulled it over himself. The five men were now arranged on the path as follows: Etchberger was closest to the top of the path, followed by Gish, Daniel, Sliz, and Springsteadah. Within "five or ten minutes" of the initial attack there was a lull in the firing and then "five or six" of the enemy began walking down the trail toward the trapped men. At the direction of Sliz, Dick Etchberger opened fire with his M-16 and provoked a furious Vietnamese response. "This was probably when they first realized we were down there," recalled Sliz.[66]

The Vietnamese retreated up the trail and positioned themselves on the edge of the cliff above the overhang, directing their rifle fire and grenades at the technicians' shallow hiding spot. Hank Gish was killed during the first burst of enemy fire, while Stan Sliz and John Daniel were struck in the legs by shrapnel and bullets. Grenades were landing on the path and the men desperately tried to kick them away, all the while calling out warnings to each other. One grenade, however, landed near Gish's body and, according to Sliz, "blew him in half, two pieces of his body laid on my legs." Another grenade "blew him [Gish] off down the side of the hill."[67] Shortly thereafter, John Daniel heard Sliz call out, "Monk's gone," whereupon Sliz passed out from his wounds. Daniel yelled over to Dick Etchberger, "Looks like it's just the two of us."[68] In less than an hour Hanoi had annihilated project Heavy Green.

10

"One Day Too Long"

On March 11 Ambassador Sullivan messaged the State Department news he suspected it already knew: "As Dept has probably learned from military sources, enemy has effectively eliminated air navigation facilities at Site 85."[1]

Early that morning, with dawn still an hour away on the beleaguered mountain, rescue aircraft at Udorn air base began launching for Site 85. Unaware of the deadly PAVN commando assault, at 4:26 A.M. the Rescue Center dispatched the two primary Jolly Green rescue helicopters. Although air refueled by a C-130 tanker, the Jollies would still require more than two hours to reach the mountain. Two A1E/H escorts departed Udorn some ninety minutes later. Following established procedures, upon reaching the general vicinity of Pha Thi all rescue aircraft would establish an orbit and await further instructions. In order to provide additional firepower, the rescue planes would be supported by a number of A1E/H "Firefly" strike aircraft already en route.[2]

Atop the mountain, the fight was far from over. Although Lieutenant Colonel Truong Muc claims that by 5:00 A.M. he and his team had killed all the Americans and gained "complete control" of the site,[3] there were at least five Heavy Green personnel still alive and hiding. Dick Etchberger, John Daniel, and Stan Sliz were huddled on the mountain ledge below the TSQ buildings. For unexplained reasons the *Dac Cong* had failed to press their attack down the path. To the north, surrounded by slain or wounded teammates, Jack Starling was playing dead. Unknown to Starling at the time, Bill Husband was concealed in an area above and to the north of Starling's position.[4] What happened over the next several hours on the top of Pha Thi mountain remains most uncertain.

Muc alleges that after securing the TSQ/TACAN area he evacuated his casualties, five killed and an unspecified number of wounded, to the western base of the mountain. Carrying these casualties in the darkness down the steep path would have been a difficult and time-consuming process.[5] Muc says he then took verbal reports from his men and learned that "more than 10" Americans were killed during the attack. According to his statements, Muc and his men then walked around the site and viewed a number of American bodies. At about 7:00 A.M., before the lieutenant and his men, he says, "could begin collecting weapons, documents, and equipment, or begin burying the American bodies," U.S. aircraft began bombing the area. The *Dac Cong* then "took refuge in crevices and [among] rocks on the face of the cliff, a few meters below the crest of the hill and away from the TACAN/TSQ site." At about 9:00 A.M., recalls Muc, the bombing ended and a helicopter arrived to rescue one American from "a ledge on the cliff below the TACAN/TSQ site." Muc says that one of his men attempted to prevent the rescue and was shot and killed by either the American on the ground or the rescue force. The rest of the Vietnamese team then fired upon the helicopter, but failed to prevent the recovery. As the helicopter departed, according to Muc, the air strikes resumed and the commandos were forced to remain in their hiding places. The bombing continued until late afternoon, at which point Muc says he and his men continued with their efforts to search the site.[6]

Down at the CIA operations area, Howie Freeman had decided to lead a reconnaissance team to the Heavy Green site. According to Freeman, the case officers maintained landline communications with the TSQ operators until about 2:00 A.M. At this point, after numerous calls to the radar team went unanswered, Freeman presumed the shelling had severed the connection. Later, he and Spence heard gunfire from around the cliffs and realized that somehow the enemy had reached the technicians. At 5:45 A.M., as dawn broke, Freeman grabbed his shotgun and, accompanied by Major Souya Yang and eight Hmong, carefully advanced up the path to the site. Freeman first went to the living quarters, approaching from the east, and found the door locked. By now it was daylight and he noted no apparent damage to any of the buildings and saw no bodies. One of the generators, however, was on fire and it was spewing a great deal of black smoke. The team then began to move toward the radar area. At this point a lone Hmong patrol member ventured to the north of the living quarters and was immediately wounded by gunfire. He withdrew and was assisted by team members back down the path. Meanwhile, Freeman and several Hmong were moving to the west and the location of the generators. Suddenly, an enemy soldier wearing a green uniform and carrying an AK-47 came around the southeast corner of the operations building. Freeman fired his shotgun and the man disappeared. The case officer, now alone, quickly scampered to the southwest and around the TACAN. From this vantage point he had a clear view north between the cliff side and the buildings and, although there were a few low rocks, Freeman felt he could have seen any survivors or bodies. None were visible. Freeman then saw two enemy soldiers in the 12.7mm gun position located between the southern end of the TSQ building and the cliffs. Both of the men had AK-47s and were standing as he fired into their backs. They dropped down and then, from an unknown direction, Freeman was himself shot. Wounded in the left leg by either a direct gunshot or piece of splintered rock from gunfire, Freeman recalls hearing additional firing but saw no other enemy forces. He then threw a phosphorous grenade at the machine gun position and began to withdraw. Cursing a jammed shotgun, a limping Howard Freeman and the remaining patrol members made their way back down the path to the CIA operations area.

Reflecting at length on his survey of the Heavy Green area, Freeman believes he had an unobstructed view of the eastern side of the living quarters, the area between the radar buildings and the living quarters, and the area between the cliff side and the TSQ buildings. He saw no Americans and at no time did he see any bodies—either enemy or friendly.[7] This recollection is at variance with Truong Muc's, who claimed to have killed at least one American in an area searched by Howard Freeman. Lieutenant Colonel Truong Muc's version and other post-attack information made available to U.S. government investigators will be further examined in chapter 15.

While Freeman was surveying the Heavy Green area, Woody Spence remained in the CIA bunker to maintain communications with the outlying Hmong defensive units, the CIA bases at Long Tieng,

Vientiane, and Udorn, and with the Air America operations center. Sometime after 7:00 A.M. Spence was able to speak by radio with Sergeant Huffman, the forward air controller. It had been a difficult night for the young airman who had bravely remained at his post and directed air strikes throughout the attack. Indeed, according to Huffman, between 4:00 and 5:00 A.M. he heard a great deal of friendly gunfire directed at two to three figures he could see running across the helipad. At the time, Huffman believed that his Hmong comrades were shooting at enemy soldiers who had overrun the helipad and CIA operations area. Consequently, at daybreak Huffman decided to heed the instructions of several Hmong defenders who motioned him to follow them north along the eastern ridge line. After traveling for several hundred yards, Huffman stopped and attempted to gain radio contact with the CIA bunker. Finally, Spence's voice came through and directed Huffman to return to the helipad and prepare for evacuation. Relieved that the CIA men were still alive and that the helipad was safe, Huffman and his Hmong group returned and searched the helipad area to the north of his bunker. They found no bodies, and Huffman concluded that the figures he had seen during the attack were most likely retreating Hmong or Thai defenders. At no time did Huffman ever see any Americans crossing in front of his bunker.[8]

Upon his return to the CIA operations area, Freeman reported back to Vientiane and was told to prepare for evacuation on the hour. In no uncertain terms he was directed to insure that all known American and Thai personnel were removed from the site forthwith. He was further instructed that "if they came under fire to walkout if necessary." Freeman, concerned that his leg wound would hamper any ground escape, told Spence that he would leave by the first available helicopter with the other wounded. Spence was to remain as long as feasible and then get out by helicopter. If air rescue was impossible, then he was to escape with the Thai and Hmong into the jungle and evade until they could be recovered by friendly forces.[9]

At about 7:15 A.M., a flight of A1E/H "Sandys" and "Fireflys"[10] arrived, along with a PC-6 Pilatus Porter carrying case officer Frank Odum. Almost immediately the aircraft came under fire from the 12.7mm gun located near the radar vans. Fearing that the Porter would be shot down, Freeman called Odum on the radio and told him to pull away. Believing that none of the technicians had survived, Freeman then ordered Huffman to direct the A1E/H's to begin bombing the guns and the TSQ site. The efforts proved very inaccurate, however, and the bombs began to fall to the southeast of the CIA operations area. Fearing friendly fire, Freeman demanded a halt to the air strikes.[11] During this time at least one A1E/H also strafed the area below the radar vans, wounding a number of Hmong and Thai defenders.[12]

Incredibly, there were still at least five Heavy Green technicians who were very much alive and desperately seeking help. Throughout the strafing and bombing Dick Etchberger, John Daniel, and Stan Sliz remained huddled together on the small path under the rock overhang and, farther to the north, Bill Husband and Jack Starling were hugging the ground and praying for rescue. Freeman, prevented by enemy fire from searching the area north of the vans and unable to see the western cliffs, had unknowingly been within yards of the trapped men. Fortunately, one of the technicians had activated the emergency beeper on his survival radio and an Air America helicopter was about to attempt an extraordinarily dangerous rescue.[13]

On the early morning of March 11, Captain Ken Wood and flight engineer L.M. "Rusty" Irons lifted off from Long Tieng airfield and pointed their "Huey" toward LS 36 and what they supposed would be a normal day of ferrying people and equipment to and from various Lima sites. Wood was a former U.S. Army pilot who had been flying for Air America less than a year, while Irons had left the U.S. Army in 1965 to join the better paying civilian airline. As was the custom with most Air America crews, the men monitored the military "guard"[14] frequency on their radio and almost immediately after takeoff heard the distinctive beeper of an activated survival radio. Using the aircraft's airborne radio direction finder (ARDF), Wood located the source of the signal and turned the aircraft to the northeast. Remarkably, despite CIA and USAF planning for the evacuation of Site 85, Wood and Irons had no idea at the time that Pha Thi was under attack. Captain Wood's decision to head toward the source of the emergency beeper was purely instinctive.[15]

At 7:35 A.M., Ken Wood, flying from the right seat with "Rusty" Irons spotting from the right door, closed on the southwestern cliffs of Phou Pha Thi. The A1E/Hs maneuvered in and out trying to silence the 12.7mm gun, while JGs 67 and 69 remained five miles away in a holding pattern.[16] Wood was the first to spot the men on the ledge; slowly he maneuvered the unarmed helicopter, nose facing south, along the mile high cliffs. With no place to land and unsure of where the enemy might be located, Wood courageously maintained a hover as Irons began to play out a cable attached to a "Breeze" rescue device.[17]

Rusty Irons recalls, "As I ran the hoist back up the survivors would come into the door and I pushed each one to the left side of the aircraft. The hoist was very hot and there was a lot of cable laying around on the floor."[18] To Wood, "It seemed like it was taking forever to get them aboard."[19] If it was an eternity for the pilot, it was certainly a lifetime for the technicians. John Daniel, struggling to remain conscious, recalls hearing the helicopter. "All of the sudden I hear this chopper, what a sound. It was in a hover right over us." As the hoist came down Dick Etchberger, who amazingly was not wounded, assisted Daniel onto the seat and Irons immediately retracted the cable. Etchberger then helped Sliz aboard and, when the cable dropped back down, he prepared to be pulled up.[20]

During the rescue Captain Ken Wood was fighting to hold the aircraft in a hover which, Irons recalls, had the helicopter "tucked into" the side of the cliff, providing a limited degree of protection from any enemy gunners. Looking back on the event Wood believes, however, that they were probably more shielded from attack by a lingering ground fog.[21] And it was the lifting of the fog that resulted in tragedy. Bill Husband, who had been hiding in an area to the north of the radar vans, heard the helicopter and began running toward the rescue point. He then saw Jack Starling, who was shot and unable to move. According to Starling, Husband said that he was "going to try and get on the chopper." Since Starling was unable to walk, let alone run, he told Husband "Tell them I'm here." Husband reassured his teammate and then ran to the cliff side and down the path to where Etchberger was about to be pulled away.[22] Husband grabbed onto the cable and he and Etchberger were pulled up together. Just as this third hoist was in progress, the helicopter began to take gunfire from below. The Air America pilot immediately began to pull away from the mountain while Irons dragged the two technicians inside and shoved them to the other side of the aircraft. Bill Husband, wounded by shrapnel, lay on the floor. Dick Etchberger came to rest on a canvas seat, sitting astride Irons' personal weapon, an AK-47 assault rifle. Within seconds, six armor piercing bullets smashed through the Huey's belly, nearly striking the fuel control system. Several of the rounds came up directly under Etchberger, splintering the AK-47's stock. One round entered the sergeant's lower body.[23] The flight to LS 36 took less than thirty minutes, but Etchberger was already in critical condition.

At any moment during the rescue the enemy might have fired into the defenseless helicopter or, quite literally, thrown any object into the whirring rotor blades and sent the aircraft crashing down the mountainside. Moreover, aside from the enemy, Wood had to contend with winds and foggy conditions. It was truly an act of remarkable heroism and flying ability for which Wood, Irons, and Air America, have remained mostly unrecognized.[24]

Minutes after Ken Wood began his hover over the Heavy Green technicians, another Air America pilot, flying a STOL aircraft (Helio Super Courier U10A, call-sign "Durax 11") attempted to land at the helipad located on the eastern side of the mountain. Although the enemy did not fire on Wood's aircraft hovering on the western edge of the mountain, a 7:45 A.M. entry in the Udorn Rescue Center log reported, "Durax acft pulled out due to gunfire." Nonetheless, the rescue forces persevered and at 8:20 A.M. an Air America Huey was finally able to touch down at the helipad.[25] Howie Freeman directed that a number of Thai and Hmong wounded be placed on the aircraft and then he climbed aboard for the brief flight to LS 36. Upon landing at Na Khang, Freeman was met by a very angry General Vang Pao who demanded to know why the site was being evacuated. Freeman explained that Ted Shackley had ordered the removal of all Americans and Thais from LS 85 and that was exactly what he was doing. Vang Pao was not pleased. Freeman then saw, for the first time since the attack began, the five Heavy Green survivors. The technicians, along with Freeman, were transferred to a waiting C-123 transport and flown directly to Udorn air base.[26]

In 1968, communications technology was far from instantaneous, even cables destined for the White House. At about the same time Howard Freeman was being evacuated from Site 85, President Johnson was receiving his first detailed information on the Pha Thi attack. Walt W. Rostow, national security advisor to the president, prepared the following memorandum at 8:00 P.M., Washington time:

> We have been informed tonight by Ambassador Sullivan that he has ordered the evacuation of the 18 Americans because the operations at the Site is impossible. The Site is under heavy mortar and small arms fire. . . . Steps are being taken to destroy all the remaining equipment prior to

evacuation. Site 85 has been a thorn in the side of the Communists because it provides an advanced staging base for guerrilla operations and contains communications and navigation equipment that supports U.S. air operations over North Vietnam. I will report tomorrow the alternative arrangements for filling the functions which were carried out at Site 85.[27]

Thus, some fourteen hours after the attack began, the President and his advisers were just receiving the news that the facility was being evacuated. Indeed, while decisionmakers in Washington were being assured that an orderly evacuation was underway, sensitive equipment would be destroyed, and the Heavy Green program would soon emerge in a different location, in Vientiane and Udorn the full scope of the tragedy at Pha Thi was becoming painfully obvious.

While Rostow's memorandum would appear to indicate senior level interest in the facility, a rigorous search by the author has failed to locate any additional White House correspondence on the radar bombing program.[28] And, when Rostow was shown in 1994 a copy of his memorandum to the President, he insisted that he could not even recall the TSQ-81 facility or the loss of the site.[29] Rostow's recollection notwithstanding, there is little doubt that the fall of Site 85 and the loss of so many Americans in Laos posed potentially serious political, if not military, problems for the United States. One reason for this curious lack of White House concern was the siege at Khe Sanh, South Vietnam. During the period leading up to and including the loss of Site 85, some three North Vietnamese divisions were arrayed around the U.S. Marine Corps base located just south of the demilitarized zone. President Johnson's fixation with the battle, brought about by widely publicized but inaccurate comparisons to the 1954 Viet Minh victory over the French at Dien Bien Phu, may well have overshadowed the loss of a small radar site in Laos.[30] Another explanation, that the site had become mostly irrelevant because the Johnson administration had decided to undertake a bombing halt, is discussed in the following chapter.

The rescue work at Pha Thi continued as JG 69, piloted by Captain Al Montrem, dropped onto the helipad at 8:46 A.M. Spence recalls that although the wounded had been placed near the helipad for evacuation, once the helicopter landed the aircraft was quickly inundated with troops seeking to get off the mountain. Quick and decisive action by the helicopter crew members and a not so gentle Major Souya Yang got the situation under control and the wounded were placed on board. Montrem then departed for LS 36 with thirty-two indigenous soldiers, including three wounded.[31] Nine minutes behind JG 69, an Air America Huey arrived at the helipad to extract Woody Spence and Roger Huffman. Spence had been told by radio to prepare for evacuation and to bring out with him all the CIA records. Much to Spence's chagrin, when the Huey touched down his Thai and Hmong counterparts clambered on board, leaving the case officer with the unenviable task of making six trips to and from the CIA operations area and the waiting helicopter. No one, it seemed, wanted to risk losing his seat by assisting Spence.[32]

When the exhausted case officer reached LS 36 he was also interrogated by Vang Pao, who still wanted to know why the site had been abandoned. And, moments later, a Thai officer approached Spence and angrily asked why all the Thai forces had not been evacuated. The now exasperated Spence retorted that except for those "who had run away, all the Thais had been brought out." An hour later he accepted a ride with USAID official Edgar "Pop" Buell, and departed for Long Tieng.[33] Back at Phou Pha Thi, however, the most unusual rescue of the day was about to occur.

For more than two hours, JG 67, with Captains Cayler and Panza at the controls, had been on orbit near Site 85 listening to the radio chatter and waiting for orders to move in. As the "High Bird," JG 67 was assigned to stand by while the "Low Bird," JG 69, landed at the helipad. In the event of an emergency, JG 67 could then offer assistance to the other helicopter. Following the evacuation of Etchberger, Daniel, Husband, and Sliz, word was sent back to the rescue forces that "one person might still be alive." Bill Husband had told his rescuers about Jack Starling. Acting on this information, an Air America Huey led JG 67 toward Pha Thi's western cliffs and Starling's probable position. Scanning the rocks, Captain Cayler's attention was quickly drawn to a flashing light. At 9:37 A.M. Russ Cayler placed the aircraft into a hover just off the cliffs and pointed the helicopter to the southeast. From the right seat he looked across copilot Joe Panza and saw the radar buildings off to his left. Turning his attention to an area further north, he spotted what appeared to be a "dead or wounded enemy soldier slumped over in almost a sitting position." Looking down along the cliff, Cayler saw "many bodies, many Americans" in a flat area with large boulders. Twenty-seven years later, Cayler could still "see" three of these American bodies grouped together near one of the boulders. Nearby another American was lying on his side, signaling with a flashlight. As the crew prepared to lower the pararescueman,[34] Sergeant James J. "JJ" Rogers, Cayler decided not to employ any suppressive fire. "We were there to perform a rescue, not get into a firefight." And, according to Cayler, during the course of the rescue no shots were fired at the Jolly.[35]

"JJ" Rogers had been in Southeast Asia since September 1967, but this would be his first combat save. As the Jolly Green approached the cliffs he was manning a machine gun mounted in the left window. Rogers's initial view of Pha Thi, therefore, was to the north and away from the Heavy Green area. As he stepped to the doorway on the right side of the aircraft, however, Rogers could see the radar vans off to the left. People, "crouched and hunkered down," seemed to be moving around the buildings. By their demeanor the pararescue specialist "sensed they were enemy," but they took no threatening action and he immediately focused on the task at hand. Rogers had been told of a single, seriously wounded survivor and, based on what he observed from the window during the approach, expected that he would be dropped into a heavily wooded area. Instead, looking out the door, he observed a drop of several thousand feet down a rocky slope. Weighted down with a survival vest, medical kit, flak jacket, and an M-16 slung over his shoulder, Rogers climbed onto the hoist and was lowered some 75 feet to a small ledge, no more than 30 inches in width. Encumbered by his equipment and thrashed about by the Jolly Green's powerful rotor wash, the young sergeant fought to gain a sure footing. Dragging the cable with him, he began to make his way south, laterally across the cliff face, toward the vicinity of the bodies some thirty feet away. As he approached the casualties, however, the ground gave way and he slipped several yards down the cliff. In the process, his rifle dropped off his shoulder and fell some twenty feet before becoming entangled in some small bushes. Rogers quickly decided not to retrieve the weapon and began to climb back up toward the bodies. Pulling himself up on to the flat depression he could see a number of figures in two groups, lying very close to one another. Recalling the scene, Jim Rogers estimated there were at least "5–7 bodies" and, perhaps, "twice that number" dressed in "similar, dark clothing." He had the feeling they were "Oriental" and "everyone was dead," although there was not a great deal of blood or trauma associated with the bodies. Moving forward for a better look, Rogers was stunned when a hand reached out and grabbed his right shoulder.[36] Recalling the shock of the incident, Rogers said, "It was a good thing I had lost my M-16. I probably would have shot him."[37] It was Jack Starling.

Rogers quickly gained his composure and, having been told that there was but a single survivor, directed his complete attention to the wounded sergeant. Trained to recover only the living and aware that any moment they could become an easy target, Rogers could not afford to devote time to an examination of the adjacent bodies. He lifted Jack Starling onto the hoist, locked his arms and legs around the wounded man, and radioed for them to be pulled up. Instead of immediately raising the two men up into the hovering aircraft, however, the Jolly Green pulled away from the cliff with Rogers and Starling suspended below. At a safe distance from Site 85 the aircraft slowed and the two men were winched to the door. While Rogers remained on the cable, a second pararescueman carefully pulled Starling to safety and laid him in a metal litter. Rogers was then brought aboard as the helicopter sped toward LS 36. At 9:46 A.M., JG 67 reported, "picked up one wounded. Could not recover three dead roundeyes." The rescue had lasted an eternity of less than ten minutes.

Arriving at LS 36 some twenty minutes later, the crew of JG 67 was ordered to remain inside their aircraft as "Americans in civilian clothes" off-loaded the wounded technician and carried him to a waiting fixed-wing aircraft. Within thirty minutes the TACAN specialist was on his way to Udorn air base.[38] Meanwhile, JG 69 and JG 67 were being directed to return to Site 85. An interpreter was placed aboard JG 67 and at 10:20 A.M. the two Jolly Greens lifted off toward Pha Thi. Reaching the mountain, however, had become extremely risky. A1E/H "Sandys" and "Fireflys" reported heavy enemy fire and advised the helicopters to "get the hell out of the area." JG 69 and JG 67 complied and, being told there was "no parking at LS 36," continued on to Long Tieng. Landing just before noon, the crews received only a few hours rest before being ordered back into a rescue orbit near Pha Thi. Finally, at 4:15 P.M., the Jollies were released from their duties and turned toward Udorn air base. After more than fifteen tension-filled hours, the crew of JG 67 reached home and some well deserved rest.[39]

As the Jolly Green Giants were touching down at Udorn, the CIA was still trying to make some sense of the tragedy at Site 85. The agency's photo reconnaissance aircraft, a specially modified Beechcraft turboprop, was dispatched to photograph the area. Piloted by Berl King, the aircraft conducted numerous passes along the western cliffs and successfully took pictures of the relatively undamaged radar buildings as well as the western cliffs. Later, this photography would play an important role in trying to determine where some of the technicians may have died.[40]

At the same time, flying aboard a PC-6 Pilatus Porter, case officers Jerry Daniels and Terry Quill were conducting surveillance over Pha Thi.[41] While making a final pass along the western face of the mountain, Quill recalls that Daniels called out, "looks like three bodies." Although Quill did not observe the bodies, he believes that Daniels was quite certain of what he saw. Meanwhile, USAF F-4s were flying bombing missions on and near the mountain. According to Quill, these high speed aircraft "were not having much luck in trying to destroy the radar and TACAN equipment." Daniels and Quill returned to LS 36 where they remained for several days assisting in the regroupment of the dispersed Hmong units. For the next five months, until reassigned to Langley, Terry Quill continued to work with the Hmong. He has no recollection of any reporting that indicated Americans were captured at Pha Thi. However, he does not rule out the possibility that some of the technicians could have been captured and moved down the western side of Pha Thi.[42]

Earlier in the day, just before noon, in a state of near shock and disbelief, Jerry Clayton stood on the runway at Udorn air base as the C-123 transport touched down with Stan Sliz, John Daniel, Bill Husband, Howard Freeman, and Dick Etchberger. Tragically, the latter, who had valiantly fought off the North Vietnamese and risked his life to protect his fellow airmen, had died en route. The single bullet had caused massive internal bleeding. As the aircraft jerked to a stop, Clayton, along with other personnel from Heavy Green, the CIA, and 7/13th AF, rushed forward. Howard Freeman recalls that he and the other survivors were immediately transported by ambulance to the base hospital.[43] Etchberger's body was then carried off the aircraft and, at first, Clayton could not see the man's face. The internal injuries were deceptive, leaving Etchberger with a relatively unscathed outward appearance. As Clayton moved closer, however, he saw that it was his friend of many years. Clutched in the man's right hand, the

colonel found a pair of wire cutters. Clayton surmised that Etchberger, aware that the thermite charges had not been activated, had
intended to return to the radar vans to complete the connections and
destroy the equipment. It was an act of personal courage and responsibility which typified the sergeant's career. For his actions at Site 85,
Chief Master Sergeant Richard L. Etchberger posthumously and
secretly received his nation's second highest decoration, the Air Force
Cross.[44]

Arriving at the hospital the technicians were inundated by Air
Force men with tape recorders and scores of questions.[45] Meanwhile
the bearded Howie Freeman, who had personally surveyed the radar
buildings and exchanged gunfire with the attackers, was virtually
ignored. Once his wound was treated, however, Freeman was moved
to a secure area where he was thoroughly debriefed by CIA personnel,
including Vientiane Station Chief Ted Shackley.[46] According to official
government sources, the records related to the debriefing of Howard
Freeman "have been misplaced or lost."[47]

Several hours later, Jack Starling, who had played dead and lived
through the horror of listening to the North Vietnamese kill several of
his wounded teammates, became the fifth and final technician returned
to Udorn. He, too, was transported to the base hospital. Eleven others, Bill Blanton, Jim Calfee, Don Worley, Mel Holland, Don Springsteadah, Hank Gish, Willis Hall, Jim Davis, Herb Kirk, Dave Price, and
Pat Shannon, were unaccounted for. Dick Etchberger was dead. For
the Air Force leadership this final rescue from Lima Site 85 would mark
the end of the Heavy Green program. Or so they thought. For many
others, principally the families of the eleven men who did not return
from the mountain, a long nightmare of uncertainty and government
misinformation was just beginning.

In Vientiane, Ambassador William H. Sullivan was immersed completely in a still unfolding catastrophe which, beyond the tragic loss of
life, posed an enormous political maelstrom for those directing America's Laos and Vietnam war policies. The calm and careful diplomat,
who for nearly four years had worked fervently to limit and contain the
U.S. military presence in neutral Laos—and had consistently questioned the risk versus the gain of placing the TSQ-81 at Pha Thi—was
now faced with explaining the disaster at Site 85. Sullivan began with a
FLASH[48] cable to Secretary of State Dean Rusk. In part, the cable
read:

Evacuation plans have been seriously disrupted by enemy activity and several "Lockheed" [Heavy Green] employees have apparently been dispersed from pre-planned evacuation sites. Because of confused situation at site and withdrawal our CAS [CIA] personnel . . . it will doubtless be some time before we have clear picture. At first glance, however, it appears we may have pushed our luck one day too long in attempting to keep this facility in operation.[49]

The questions, recriminations, and coverup began immediately.

11

Deniability

[c]overt activities were a way of life under the guidelines with which we
were fighting the war in Vietnam. I can recall several of those projects, and
I guess I should say no more than I can see how they can get out of control
real fast if people aren't on top of them.[1]
—GENERAL RICHARD H. ELLIS, USAF, RETIRED, AUGUST 1987.

On the late afternoon of March 11,
the "Sandys" and "Fireflys," which
only a day earlier had operated under the site's control, were attacking
Phou Pha Thi and providing direction to jet aircraft bombing the
TSQ-81, TACAN, and CIA facilities atop the mountain. Dropping
unguided bombs on this small area, with thousands of North Vietnamese soldiers defending the surrounding terrain and the *Dac Cong*
firing a captured machine gun, was no small feat. Fearing further loss
of American lives the aircraft were forced to withdraw without inflicting major damage to the facilities.[2] Meanwhile, as CIA case officers
and USAID workers evacuated Hmong civilians to safer areas, on the
slopes of Pha Thi Vang Pao's forces fought delaying actions against
North Vietamese elements.[3]

William Sullivan, the consummate diplomat, quickly assessed the
Pha Thi crisis and its potential damage to U.S. interests in Southeast
Asia. Based on CIA photography, visual reconnaissance by case officers
Jerry Daniels and Terry Quill, Howard Freeman's debriefing, and the

recollections of several Heavy Green survivors, on March 12, Sullivan reported to Washington that "eight [technicians] . . . are known dead. Three are unaccounted for, although one of these . . . may be presumed dead." Concluding "none of missing personnel are likely to be alive," the Ambassador's immediate goal was to deny the North Vietnamese access to the damning physical evidence left behind at Site 85.[4] With every passing hour the chances increased that the communist forces would find and remove the incriminating equipment and associated materials.

The same day Sullivan convened a meeting in Udorn with Major General Lindley, Deputy Commander, 7/13th AF, to discuss the loss and develop a response plan. According to a summary cable, Sullivan directed the following actions: The Air Force was to conduct search and rescue operations for "personnel still unaccounted for," using napalm to destroy "all remaining structures and equipment." The U.S. Embassy in Vientiane would attempt to create a news blackout on the incident and the Ambassador would personally brief the Lao prime minister on the site's capture. Next of kin notifications were to proceed according to the cover story. Ever pragmatic, Sullivan also agreed that a USAF survey team should quickly begin work to establish another TACAN site in northeastern Laos. As to another ground-directed radar site, the ambassador declared "installation was result [of] one-shot agreement with Prime Minister, we will have to wait out developments before we can judge whether it can be reconstituted."[5]

Although the cable reported an intent to conduct search and rescue operations for missing personnel, this action was clearly inconsistent with Sullivan's concurrent decision to immediately proceed with bombing attacks against the Site 85 facilities. Moreover, the choice of napalm further underscored an effort designed for maximum destruction, not the recovery of bodies or rescue of possible survivors. In fact, within 24 hours of the Udorn meeting the Ambassador would declare, "Latest interrogation and discussion with survivors has led to firm conclusion that three previously carried as missing were indeed seen dead by one or more survivors. Therefore, we are no longer carrying any personnel as missing, but consider all those who were not rpt [repeat] not extracted to be dead."[6]

Sullivan has said he was comfortable with the decision,[7] but the facts show this crucial finding was based on incomplete and faulty information. Once the declaration was made, however, there would be no reconsideration. This was a situation best forgotten and then denied—so the Lao facade of neutrality could continue.

Over nearly four years William Sullivan and Souvanna Phouma had successfully crafted and maintained an image of American purity in Laos. In truth the Prime Minister approved, and the Ambassador directed, a prohibited U.S. military assistance program of massive proportions. The communist capture of Site 85 greatly jeopardized their efforts to maintain plausible deniability for all American military involvement in Laos.

Ambassador Sullivan took great pride in the close relationship he had developed with the Prime Minister; accordingly, a March 13 discussion about Site 85 was frank and to the point. "I told him that destruction of equipment had not rpt [repeat] not been as thorough as we had expected because thermite plungers appear not to have been activated before facility abandoned." The Ambassador went on to explain that rescue forces had failed to recover all of the American personnel, but all of the missing were believed to have been killed. Souvanna was visibly shaken by the news, commenting that the "enemy would be able, if he chose, to make some pretty damaging disclosures." Sullivan agreed, but advised that neither the North Vietnamese nor the Pathet Lao radio stations had mentioned the attack. Nonetheless, Souvanna urged the ambassador to "destroy as much evidence as we can rapidly."[8] Both men recalled Souvanna's conditions for installation of the site; "If the site were compromised further and the Americans were captured there he [Souvanna] would take the position that these people were there without his knowledge."[9] Faced with the possibility that the Prime Minister would publicly disavow the project, fracturing U.S. probity in Laos, the Ambassador was under enormous pressure to eliminate the remnants of Site 85 and the remains of the American dead.[10]

Bad weather hampered air attacks on March 12; however, the next day "Fireflys" conducted napalm strikes and "Sandys" directed sorties by jet aircraft on Site 85. The pilots reported several fires and destruction of "a bunker and several buildings." North Vietnamese defense of the area remained intense, however. At about 9:35 A.M, two "Sandy" aircraft were circling Pha Thi approximately 60 feet below the crest when the lead aircraft, "Sandy 1," disappeared. "Sandy 2" did not observe the crash but the pilot heard a rescue beeper tone for some five seconds. There was no voice contact with the downed pilot and no parachute was observed. Although American helicopters were flying in the area at the time of loss, the location was deemed too hostile for a rescue attempt.[11] Twelve American airmen were now missing on or in the vicinity of Phou Pha Thi.

Unofficial reports on the North Vietnamese capture of Site 85 had already made their way to the news media in Vientiane, but there were currently no references to American losses or the true nature of the facility. Nonetheless, Washington was anxious to prepare a "contingency" press statement. The State Department proposed the following response to any media questions: "It is my understanding that some Americans are missing at a small village in North Laos that was overrun by North Vietnamese troops. These personnel were Lockheed Aircraft Company employees who were in Laos to repair communication facilities belong to USAID."[12] Sullivan, in a testy response, counseled patience and requested Washington to refrain from any public statements on the loss. The Ambassador, a master at controlling the message, was greatly concerned that premature comments could expose the U.S. and Royal Lao government to a whole series of undesirable questions about U.S. activities in Laos. "It seems to me rather impossible to plan . . . until and unless we know what they're going to say and what evidence they produce to back up their story." Sullivan then reminded his seniors of "damaging" documents left behind which, in the hands of the North Vietnamese, would shred the credibility of the Lockheed cover story.[13] The State Department backed off, commenting "Although many details of final attack on Site 85 available to press here via UPI ticker item from Vientiane, it contains no mention US presence at Phou Pha Thi and no inquiries received to date."[14] Reflecting on his mood at the time, Sullivan has said "There wasn't much more we could do. We had to deal with it as it emerged."[15] In many respects this would also become the manner in which the U.S. government dealt with the Heavy Green families.

Following procedures outlined in the U.S. Air Force agreement with the Lockheed Aircraft Service Company, on March 12 Lieutenant Colonel Clayton communicated the known facts and the names of the eleven missing to a company representative.[16] Within hours an officer from the Special Plans office, which was closely monitoring the situation, informed the affected families by telephone that Site 85 had been captured and a number of men were missing. The wives were cautioned to say nothing to anyone about their husband's status and await formal notification from the Lockheed company.[17] That afternoon a Lockheed employee contacted the families by telephone and followed up the next day with a telegram.[18] The following message sent to Ann Holland is representative.

> It is with sincere regret that we must notify you that your husband Melvin has been reported missing while performing an important assignment for our company in Laos. Please be assured that we are doing everything possible to obtain further details concerning your husband's welfare and we will inform you immediately of any additional information we receive.[19]

For the next several weeks the Special Plans office was in daily contact with the wives, but the women were consistently told there was no new information. The calls became less frequent and the families settled into a period of great uncertainty and isolation. Because the wives had signed secrecy agreements they were forbidden from discussing their situation with anyone outside of the Special Plans office. This prohibition encompassed members of the clergy, relatives, and even the other Heavy Green family members.[20] During 1968 more than 14,000 American servicemen would forfeit their lives in the Southeast Asia war. While the families of these men had the armed forces casualty system to provide support and assistance in their time of grief, the Heavy Green wives had a figurehead representative at Lockheed and a telephone voice at the Special Plans office in Washington. Nonetheless, the cover story seemed to be holding together.

In Southeast Asia, Ambassador Sullivan and General Momyer were engaged in some post-attack posturing. Momyer began the exchange on March 14:

> I am concerned about the need for a postmortem. . . . In terms of assessing whether future sites should be established believe it important to determine how a relatively small force was able to take such an allegedly well defended installation. No indications have been received here as to what efforts if any were made by local defense forces on site to defend installation, especially in view of clear indications of impending attack.[21]

Considering the months of nearly daily message traffic detailing the growing threat to Site 85, all of which was available to Momyer and his staff, these comments were at best highly disingenuous.[22] Two days later Sullivan responded:

> Believe you should understand . . . that enemy force was not . . . 'relatively small.' Our intelligence indicates their numbers between five and seven battalions, with artillery and rocket support, considerably outnumbering local defense forces, which never numbered more than 1,000.[23]

The Ambassador also emphasized in this cable that he had "made clear from the beginning" the inability of the Hmong forces to defend against a serious North Vietnamese threat. He reminded Momyer (and everyone else reading the message) of numerous and regular embassy and CIA estimates of the site's growing vulnerability and the prophetic CIA estimate that site security could not be guaranteed beyond March 10. "Therefore," Sullivan asserted, "its fall should have come as no surprise to anyone."[24]

The ambassador also restated to Momyer several concerns voiced in his initial flash message to Washington:

> There may be some lessons . . . with respect to length of time technical personnel should be required to stay at their posts after installation falls within artillery range. In hindsight, it seems to me we should have pulled all technicians out morning March 10 even if this meant losing the last several hours of the installation's capabilities. What concerns me most is not the defensive action, but the disruption of preplanned evacuation procedure. It is still not clear why technical personnel went over cliff to a narrow ledge rather than down trail to chopper pad.[25]

Sullivan was suggesting none too subtly that, despite a well-documented artillery threat, 7th AF continued to request the site be kept in operation.

Because the evidence is clear that by March the site was almost exclusively working against so-called "self-defense" targets, air strikes on enemy forces encircling Phou Pha Thi and not targets in North Vietnam, what purpose was really served by keeping the men at Site 85? Momyer and his staff were daily briefed on the North Vietnamese and Laotian targets. Momyer knew, or should have known, Heavy Green was no longer being actively used for its primary purpose. Nonetheless, even as the rocket and artillery attack was underway on the evening of March 10, Momyer's subordinate commander, Major General Lindley, was telling the air attaché office in Vientiane that "evacuation should only be effected as a last resort if the situation became untenable; furthermore, the situation should be followed on an hour to hour basis."[26] In fact, as discussed in chapter 9, by the time Lindley called Vientiane the Ambassador had already directed a partial evacuation. It is unpleasant to speculate on how many other men might have been lost if the rescue forces had waited for Lindley to give the rescue order, presumably some time the next morning. Moreover, it was 7th AF that insisted the site remain open, despite the knowledge it was no longer involved in anything except self-defense. Perhaps the perceived opportunity to kill by air large numbers of communist troops in Laos, or at least "tie them up," was irresistible. Was it worth the lives of the men at Site 85, who were told they would shorten the war by directing aircraft to high-priority targets around Hanoi? Given the background information known to 7th AF, Momyer's March 14 cable to Sullivan was extraordinarily fallacious.

Another issue Sullivan raised, the failure of the technicians to follow "preplanned evacuation procedures," deserves special review. The Ambassador's understanding of the Site 85 attack was shaped by the information he received from CIA and Air Force sources. In a 1970 oral history interview he provided his thoughts on the loss of the Heavy Green technicians:

> As far as the loss of our personnel up there is concerned, quite frankly, I think that those losses were due to a failure on the part of the people at the installation to follow exfiltration procedures that had been laid out for them. The ones that were killed used this strange arrangement they'd worked out by themselves, with leather straps to lower themselves over the side of the cliff down onto a ledge where they were just sitting ducks for hand grenade attacks by the North Vietnamese. We'd had drills with them about the method in which to get out. And had they followed that method I think they would have been extracted safely.[27]

Sullivan's sincere, but quite faulty, version raises serious concerns about the rigor and depth of the post attack inquiry. In fact, there is no evidence to support his description of the Heavy Green team's alleged actions.

While recent interviews with a number of Heavy Green personnel confirm that they expected to be evacuated from the helipad, none recalls any drills or tests on how this was to be accomplished. Practice sessions, they say, would have been unnecessary because there was just a single path from the Heavy Green area to the landing zone.[28] As to the "straps," this was actually part of the netting used to conceal the equipment. According to Heavy Green survivor Stan Sliz, "That's what those . . . slings were, it was just camouflage netting. So it was no escape route, the only escape route we had was the helicopters. But that would have just gotten us to the bottom of the hill [to the CIA area] and in more trouble. So that really wasn't an option as far as we were concerned."[29]

The rocket and artillery attack caused the Heavy Green personnel to seek safety along the side of the western cliffs just below the TSQ equipment.[30] Unaware the shelling was anything more than a standoff attack, the men had no reason to believe access to the helipad would be blocked. And they certainly never expected a ground assault from the west. When ordered, the technicians fully expected that they would make their way to the helipad for a controlled departure. The losses at Site 85 were not self-inflicted. Indeed, instead of abandoning the facility and fleeing toward the CIA area, the men remained on duty or went on crew rest. Ambassador Sullivan, apparently, never had the benefit of an accurate and reasoned report on what the rescued Heavy Green technicians did, and did not, witness during the attack.

Like the CIA debriefing of Howard Freeman, there is no longer any record available of statements made by the technicians upon their return to Udorn. Interviews with Heavy Green personnel at Udorn and an examination of statements made by three[31] of the technicians, however, permits an accurate reconstruction of these critical events.

Jerry Clayton and Frank Roura, the Heavy Green "First Sergeant," spoke with Stan Sliz and John Daniel after they were rushed to the Udorn base hospital. Roura recalls that he and Clayton were told "a number of men were killed and fell off the mountain," leading to the conclusion that most of the casualties occurred on or near the ledge occupied by Sliz and his radar team. They also heard of the extraordinary heroism displayed by Dick Etchberger in defending his fellow team members against the *Dac Cong* fire and placing the wounded men onto the helicopter hoist.[32] The two survivors were then briefly questioned by intelligence officers from 7/13th AF.[33] These statements, taken from wounded and dazed men, became the cornerstone for the presumption that none of the technicians had survived the attack. An official report, citing "interview with survivors" provided the following scenario:

> As the technicians came running out of the operations structure, they were met with a hail of small arms automatic weapons fire from close range. These men scrambled for safety down the slings which were only a few feet away. But apparently three Americans were killed at once — among them the TSQ senior officer and commander [Blanton].
>
> Subsequently, enemy troops at the site discovered the escape slings leading down the slope and . . . [began] lobbing some fifteen to twenty grenades onto the slope and then intermittently spraying the area with automatic weapons' fire. It was deduced that most of the American casualties were suffered at this time.[34]

As detailed in chapter 9, hours before the ground assault Stan Sliz and his radar team had moved to the ledge below the TSQ buildings and remained in this area throughout the *Dac Cong* attack. Sliz and Daniel could not have observed this activity and no other technicians joined them on the ledge during the attack. Following the initial assault against the buildings, the North Vietnamese discovered this refuge and, in the resulting firefight, Monk Springsteadah and Hank Gish were killed and John Daniel and Stan Sliz were wounded. From their position on the mountainside, no one could have observed the buildings or any movements around the radar equipment. As to the fleeing technicians, a detailed interview with John Daniel confirms that no member of the Blanton team was ever observed on the ledge below the TSQ.[35] Who, then, was the source of this information?

Stan Sliz has said Starling and Husband told him about the purported deaths of Bill Blanton and his crew.[36] But, when could these discussions have occurred? Bill Husband, Stan Sliz, and John Daniel were all evacuated together from Phou Pha Thi and could have discussed the attack en route to Udorn, although all were wounded and in shock. But Starling had not yet returned to Udorn, which left Husband as the only available witness to the supposed movements of Blanton and his team. Frank Roura, however, says neither Husband nor Starling were interviewed at Udorn and he never saw Starling with the other survivors.[37] Starling supports this version, saying no one in Thailand ever interviewed him about the attack.[38]

As to the conversation between Sliz and Starling, it did not take place for at least several days. Within hours of their return to Udorn, Sliz and Daniel were transferred to the U.S. Army's 31st Field Hospital, Korat, Thailand, for treatment of their gunshot and shrapnel wounds.[39] Bill Husband, with hip to head shrapnel wounds on the left side of his body, was evacuated to the U.S. Air Force hospital at Clark Air Base, Philippines.[40] Jack Starling arrived at Udorn about two hours after the other survivors and was treated at the base hospital. Later, he traveled to Korat where he and Sliz discussed the attack.[41] According to Sliz:

> The stories that I got from Jack Starling and Willy [Bill] Husband . . . they both told me the story of how Bill Blanton and [Jim] Calfee, and Pat Shannon came running out of the equipment to face these guys with guns, and that Bill said hey, wait a minute and he reached for his wallet so he could show these guys his Lockheed service I.D., and that's when they shot him. They shot all three of them. Both of these stories I got from Husband and Starling at separate occasions, so I know that's true.[42]

While Sliz accepted the accounts, he was in no position to have judged their credibility.

In their interviews at Udorn Sliz and Daniel provided both first- and second-hand information about the missing personnel. This critical distinction was somehow overlooked—which should have been obvious to the 7/13th AF investigators. Bill Husband and Jack Starling were the only two survivors who might have seen the movements of the missing technicians. Inexplicably, it appears neither was interviewed at Udorn. Later, when the facts were more closely examined by the Special Plans office, it became clear that there were no multiple U.S. witnesses to the movements of the Blanton crew. And, given the ferocity of the assault, darkness, and physical barriers, it is highly unlikely anyone could have reliably observed movements beyond more than a few yards.[43] By then it was too late. Sullivan had long since concluded all the unaccounted for Americans at Site 85 were dead.

On March 11, in the fog and friction of war, the story of Bill Blanton's death and his team climbing down the side of the mountain became accepted fact. Under the political circumstances, one might conclude it was simply expedient to believe all the men had perished.

But there were also post-attack eyewitness accounts and photographic evidence to support a presumption of numerous U.S. casualties.

The Jolly Green crew that rescued Jack Starling reported seeing numerous bodies in the area,[44] while CIA officer Jerry Daniels observed "three bodies."[45] Jerry Clayton and Frank Roura have a clear recollection of a March 12 review of CIA photography which showed bodies at several locations on the side of the mountain.[46] "After the attack the CIA continued to photograph the mountainside, to assess bomb damage and to see if any of the bodies moved. None did."[47] Unfortunately, the quality of the photos was insufficient to determine with any degree of certainty if the bodies were American or North Vietnamese.[48] Nonetheless, given the available information, Clayton and Roura concluded there was little likelihood of survivors.[49] This was also the consensus of the 13th AF, CIA, and air attaché personnel who briefed the situation to Ambassador Sullivan.[50]

Even so, someone in authority should have examined the circumstances of the attack and weighed the evidence—or lack thereof—much more carefully. Howard Freeman's brave foray, during which he was unable to see any of the five technicians located just yards away, should have illuminated the possibility that some of the missing men might also have survived the initial North Vietnamese assault. Similarly, a detailed questioning of Sliz, Daniel, Starling, and Husband would have exposed the flaws in Sliz's statements. Instead, there was a rushed judgment which explained the loss of all eleven missing technicians and placed no blame on any of the senior civilian and military leaders responsible for Site 85's continued operation. Apart from the Sullivan-Momyer exchanges, highly classified messages with limited distribution, the Pha Thi debacle seemed headed for obscurity.

On March 17, however, a Pathet Lao radio broadcast recounted the successful capture of Site 85, setting off alarms in Washington. In a cable to Sullivan the State Department reported communist claims of "78 killed, including some American advisers, 73 wounded, and 16 captured. PL claims also to have captured large quantities of weapons, supplies, and 'important documents.' " The department advised that this was the "fourth or fifth time in past year PL radio has alleged US advisers killed in various parts of Laos," and observed "Although we could in most cases deny charge, standard reply to press queries referring to such allegations is that we do not comment on communist propaganda."[51]

In response, Sullivan assured Washington he was also following the radio broadcasts and advised "Press at this end has evinced singular lack of interest in these broadcasts, probably because PL have cried wolf so often about killing U.S. advisors." Given the media indifference, Sullivan agreed with the strategy of refusing to respond to "propaganda." Nonetheless, he warned that the claims of captured documents might well be genuine proof of an American military presence. "This evidence could, for example, consist of Air Force code books which were left behind in the MSQ [TSQ] site or voice code book which was left behind in bunker by Air Force Forward Air Controller." In closing, the Ambassador once again recommended "all the nervous Nellies sit tight and wait till we see what develops."[52]

While the Johnson administration was understandably nervous about possible disclosures of illicit U.S. military activities in Laos, there is no record that anyone at the White House expressed any dismay over the loss of radar bombing capability.[53] In addition to being rocked by the Tet offensive and anxiety over the continuing siege at Khe Sanh, the White House was struggling with increasingly strong domestic political opposition to the war. President Johnson, even as the communist forces were completing their encirclement of Site 85, had "accepted the idea of a reduction of the bombing and a new peace initiative." Secretary of State Dean Rusk, in the days following the site's loss, spent eleven hours in front of the Senate Foreign Relations Committee answering questions on the administration's Vietnam policy. Adding to Johnson's discomfort was a strong showing by Senator Eugene McCarthy in the New Hampshire primary and the decision a few days later by Robert Kennedy to enter the presidential race. The President declared to his advisers, "I will have overwhelming disapproval in the polls and the election. I will go down the drain."[54] Meanwhile Johnson was also hearing an unexpectedly bleak assessment on the war from a bipartisan group of elder statesmen, the so-called "Wise Men." As Richard Immerman has described, the president was "devastated" and "infuriated" by their recommendation that he abandon the military option, begin to disengage from the war, and seek a political settlement. "Everybody is recommending surrender," he complained.[55]

Shortly thereafter Lyndon Johnson decided on a bombing halt—and the end of his political life.

On March 31, in a nationally televised broadcast, President Johnson declared "Tonight I have ordered our aircraft and our naval vessels to make no attacks on North Vietnam, except in the area north of the demilitarized zone. . . ." He then revealed his decision not to seek another term in office.[56] Hours prior to the broadcast the State Department notified key U.S. ambassadors of the bombing halt. As was so often the case, bad weather was cited as a principal obstacle to effective bombing.

> In view of weather limitations, bombing north of the 20th parallel will in any event be limited at least for the next four weeks or so—which we tentatively envisage as a maximum testing period in any event. Hence we are not giving up anything really serious in this time frame.[57]

The State Department's judgment on the length of the bombing halt would prove quite incorrect, as the pause would continue until November when a North Vietnam-wide suspension of U.S. bombing went into effect. Although there has been speculation in the past about a connection between the loss of Site 85 and this bombing pause, I have found no evidence to support this conclusion.[58]

Despite longstanding plans to relocate the TSQ-81 program to another site in Laos, Heavy Green never recovered from the March 11 assault. The President's decision to order a bombing halt had rendered a Lao-based radar program unnecessary.[59] Moreover, under the codename "Commando Nail," the Air Force was successfully flying modified F-105F, F-4D, and F-111A airplanes in a limited number of all-weather bombing strikes. During March, Commando Nail aircraft flew eighty-six sorties against area targets.[60]

Within days of the site's loss Jerry Clayton escorted the body of his long-time friend and colleague, Dick Etchberger, back to the United States. Don Layman and Frank Roura took charge of the Heavy Green support unit at Udorn, and began preparations to close down the program. Because the continued operation of the Laos-based TACAN systems was a constant concern and high Air Force priority, many of the navigation aids specialists were asked to temporarily continue their maintenance duties. Most of the TSQ-related technicians, however, left Udorn within the next sixty days. By July, Frank Roura had seen enough. The program still maintained its own housing and vehicles, in addition to the extra pay and benefits the men received as Lockheed employees. Roura believed Heavy Green, or what remained of it, had become "a lot of money for nothing." Disenchanted with the program he returned to the U.S., regained his military status, and continued with his Air Force career.[61]

Leaving the covert world was a matter of several days processing in Ontario, California. In accordance with the agreement they had signed in Washington, the men simply resigned from Lockheed and made a seamless return to the U.S. Air Force.[62] On paper, it was as if they had never left the U.S. military.

And, in keeping with military tradition, Heavy Green paid tribute to Dick Etchberger's extraordinary heroism. Frank Roura was overwhelmed, but not surprised, to hear of the senior sergeant's courageous efforts in those final hours on the mountain. Based on the recollections of Stan Sliz and John Daniel, who said they witnessed their colleague fight off the North Vietnamese forces and repeatedly risk personal exposure to enemy fire as he placed each of the wounded men on the rescue hoist, Roura wrote a recommendation that Etchberger receive the Medal of Honor. Following a review at Headquarters U.S. Air Force the recommendation was changed to the Air Force Cross Medal.[63] In December 1968, in a closed Pentagon ceremony General McConnell, Air Force Chief of Staff, presented Dick's widow, Katherine J. Etchberger, with the U.S. military's second highest decoration. Also in attendance were the Sergeant's mother and father, brother, three sons, Lieutenant Colonel Jerry Clayton, and "a room full of generals."[64] They all listened as an officer recounted the uncommon heroism, but never mentioned where and how the events transpired. In part, the citation to accompany the medal stated:

> His entire crew dead or wounded, Sergeant Etchberger continued to return the enemy's fire thus denying them access to his position. During this entire period, Sergeant Etchberger continued to direct air strikes and call for air rescue . . . thereby enabling the air evacuation forces to locate the surrounded friendly element. When air rescue arrived Sergeant Etchberger deliberately exposed himself to enemy fire in order to place his three surviving wounded comrades in the rescue slings.[65]

Because the Heavy Green program remained top secret, Etchberger's posthumous award received no formal publicity.[66] In a similarly subdued fashion, John Daniel, Bill Husband, Jack Starling, and Stan Sliz were presented with Purple Heart medals.[67]

While completing the writing of this book, however, I learned that Chief Master Sergeant Etchberger's official personnel records did not include any documentation on the award of the Air Force Cross. Consequently, his name had never been included on the list of Vietnam-era airmen who received the medal and his extraordinary bravery has never publicly acknowledged.[68] I began a search for Etchberger's family and, with the assistance of many private citizens,[69] finally established contact with his brother, Robert, and the sergeant's three sons, Steven, Cory, and Richard. The family was able to provide me with a copy of the original order awarding the medal, and this documentation was sent to Air Force personnel officials.[70] Dick Etchberger's official file now reflects the award of this decoration and the Air Force Enlisted Heritage Research Institute in Montgomery, Alabama, plans to create a display to honor Etchberger.[71] Moreover, in April 1998, Dick Etchberger was publicly recognized in *Air Force Magazine* as one of only twenty-one enlisted members to have received the Air Force Cross.[72]

For reasons that remain unclear, the Air Force waited more than two months to complete their investigation of the Site 85 loss. On May 31, 1968, the State Department advised the U.S. embassy in Vientiane to process "presumption of death" certificates for the eleven unaccounted for Heavy Green technicians.[73] After an exchange of cables, it was agreed the forms would contain the following declaration:

[name] is considered to have been killed by communist forces during an attack on March 11, 1968 while he was repairing navigational equipment in Laos. Circumstances involved led to the conclusion that [name] is dead. The remains have not and are not expected to be recovered because the area has continued to be under communist control.

Although the statement carefully avoided mention of the Lockheed company or the presence of any other personnel, Washington emphasized the "suggested declaration is based on discussion with lawyers and insurance representatives and is intended to strengthen case for NOK [next of kin]."[74] The forms were dated June 6, and mailed to Washington for distribution to the families.[75]

On June 10, Major Thomas M. Hoskinson, Air Force Special Plans Office, began a six-day cross-country trip to brief personally the ten families on the situation at Site 85 and provide them with background on the issuance of the death certificates.[76] In a carefully scripted presentation Hoskinson told the family members the area of the loss was still under communist control, the U.S. was exploring "resources via intelligence nets and contacts," and awaiting press and propaganda statements which might "state capture of personnel." The major explained that there had been no positive developments in any of these areas.[77]

Hoskinson did, nonetheless, offer hope that one day some of the men might return home. He also confirmed that the U.S. government never possessed conclusive evidence that the missing men were killed at Site 85 on March 11. Reading from prepared remarks, Major Hoskinson revealed that air reconnaissance photos were unable to make any positive identifications so that the bodies could as easily have been those of the enemy as of the missing Americans. He then explained it was "'possible" some of the men might eventually "walk out" of the area, adding there "was nothing as of today" on this potentiality.[78] This last comment was especially important to the families, because it indicated the government was daily monitoring the possibility that a survivor could emerge from the area. In view of information certainly known to the Air Force, that after nearly three months the men would either be dead or in a captive situation with virtually no chance of escape, this was a cruel misrepresentation.[79]

The remainder of the briefing pertained to legal and security matters. Hoskinson explained the entries on the death certificate and procedures to apply for Social Security, life insurance, and California Workmen's Compensation benefits. As to the last two payments, the major reminded the women that their husbands would be officially reinstated into the Air Force, eventually providing the families with both civilian and military compensation. The wives, who were still receiving their husband's Lockheed salary, were advised to expect a final check within a week and then payment of $60,000 in civilian life insurance.[80] Until the men were reinstated, the families were told they would have to rely on California Workmen's Compensation and Social Security benefits. Once the men were returned to Air Force status they would be declared dead and the families would then receive all military entitlements, including $10,000 in life insurance and survivor benefits. The payments from California Workmen's Compensation and Social Security would continue, unless someone neglected "to live the same [Lockheed] cover."[81]

Hoskinson reminded the wives of their signed secrecy agreements which, he underscored, "were still valid and applicable," and prohibited them from discussing the project with anyone—including other Heavy Green participants. In this time of great stress these families were told to maintain their silence, or face financial hardships and possibly criminal prosecution. The Special Plans office doubtless believed they could pull off yet another covert program. They had not, however, counted on a young woman with five children and a fervent desire to learn the truth about her husband's reported death. Ann Holland's campaign against an overwhelming U.S. bureaucracy is reviewed in the following chapter.

Contact with the family of Herb Kirk, whose German-born wife was deemed a security risk and ineligible for the Heavy Green briefing, was handled by a Lockheed representative. Like the other wives, she was led to believe her husband might have survived the attack. The impact of the news, however, caused her to suffer a mental breakdown. After receiving a life insurance settlement from Lockheed she returned to Germany with her eldest son. Although the Air Force planned to reinstate the other ten men, and had informed their families of the additional military insurance and survivor benefits, the Kirk family was excluded. It would take nearly fifteen years, and a lawsuit originated by Ann Holland, to obtain justice for Herb Kirk and his family. The U.S. Air Force made no effort to inform Mrs. Kirk or her two sons of the true circumstances of her husband's presumed death. Moreover, the Air Force that Staff Sergeant Herb Kirk had served so loyally quickly undertook a calculated effort to cheat his survivors—all in the name of national security.[82]

While Ambassador Sullivan and the Air Force had decided not to establish another TSQ-81 site in Laos, the loss of the Pha Thi TACAN created navigation problems for U.S. aircraft flying in northeastern Laos and western North Vietnam. Moreover, General Vang Pao and the CIA were anxious to reassert a Royal Lao government presence near LS 85 "for the psychological effect and for a staging area for future guerrilla operations." Beginning in June, Vang Pao's forces began a push to recapture Phou Pha Thi and the surrounding territory. Aided by thousands of USAF sorties, the Hmong soldiers fought a series of battles through the summer and fall of 1968. While a number of nearby airstrips were retaken, after more than four months the North Vietnamese remained in control of Phou Pha Thi.[83]

In a bold move to counter an anticipated communist dry-season offensive, in late November Vang Pao assembled more than 1,500 men and launched operation PIG FAT directly at Phou Pha Thi. According to U.S. intelligence officials "such an audacious strike against LS-85 required sizable air support, both for troops in contact and to disrupt enemy reinforcements and resupply around Sam Neua." Communist forces, many of whom had participated in the attack on Site 85, were now part of "the largest concentration of men, equipment, and material on the Indochina Peninsula" outside of North Vietnam.[84] Nevertheless, 7th AF in Saigon was unwilling to authorize the more than 400 sorties over four days deemed necessary to carry out a successful bombing attack. Specific requests for AC-130 "Spectre" gun ships and A-26 "Nimrod" bombers were also disapproved. 7th AF was concentrating on enemy forces further south along the Ho Chi Minh trail which, in the headquarters view, posed a more immediate danger to U.S. and allied forces in South Vietnam.[85]

Although Vang Pao had to settle for less air power than he wished, on November 28 he began a four-pronged attack on Phou Pha Thi.

For several miles around the mountain, the Lima Sites fell one after another to the guerrillas. The units pushing north toward the mountain enjoyed the greatest success by capturing all the sites in its area except LS-85 itself. Air Force FACs directed ground fire and airstrikes into the enemy position.[86]

For a week the communist forces fought back and, armed with heavy weapons and the 12.7-mm machine gun located near the TSQ buildings, successfully repelled the attack. Vang Pao then called in additional air strikes and artillery fire on the mountain. During this period prisoners reported "two NVA battalions fought at LS-85, and that Chinese advisers were hiding in a cave below the karst."[87]

On December 18, with significant air support, the Hmong captured the original airstrip located southeast of Pha Thi and the approaches to the southern summit. Prisoners reported that air strikes had "killed half" of North Vietnam's 927th battalion at Pha Thi, while a defector said the 148th Regiment was hit by air and "suffered 128 killed and more than 250 wounded."[88] Over the next several days the soldiers were able to seize control of the former CIA area and adjacent helipad. "Dug-in" enemy forces, however, maintained the high ground near radar equipment. Poor weather, aircraft maintenance problems, and conflicting U.S. priorities in southern Laos reduced close air support and it soon became obvious Vang Pao's initiative had

"bogged down." On Christmas day the NVA began a series of coun-
terattacks and by January 7 PIG FAT was at an end.[89]

Although Vang Pao's operation failed to regain control of Phou
Pha Thi, Air America aircraft moved more than 5,000 Hmong from
the mountains of Sam Neua area to the safety of the Long Tieng valley thereby reducing "the enemy's potential labor source and political
control over the population." Air Force intelligence officials also
believed the Hmong operation delayed the onset of the communist
dry-season offensive.[90]

Regrettably, these CIA-directed forces were never able to examine
the former Heavy Green area and there is no record that they received
any information regarding American prisoners in the area of Pha Thi.
Additionally, the air and artillery strikes added to the destruction previously visited upon the western cliffs below the former radar site. In
March 1994 I surveyed and photographed these cliffs while circling the
ruins of the site in a Soviet-built MI-8 helicopter. A comparison with
pre-March 1968 photography shows a considerably altered western
face. If there were any American remains still located on the cliffside,
where Monk Springsteadah and Hank Gish are known to have perished, it is entirely possible they were destroyed or dispersed during
the Vang Pao offensive.

There were no more U.S. or Hmong efforts to retake Phou Pha
Thi. Communist forces, including a strong Vietnamese contingent,
remained at the summit and deployed around the mountain's
approaches. Designated a special security zone, access to Pha Thi was
strictly controlled. Nonetheless, the Hanoi and Vientiane governments continue to this day to claim they recovered no remains and no
material from the site. What, then, happened to 150 tons of equipment
and the remains of as many as eleven Americans? These issues are further examined in chapters 15 and 16.

12
Oath of Secrecy

Although President Nixon would state in 1970 that "no American stationed in Laos has ever been killed in ground combat operations,"[1] one woman, Ann Holland knew otherwise and would not let the matter rest

Staff Sergeant Melvin A. Holland, a 31-year-old radio specialist, had served fourteen years in the U.S. Air Force when he volunteered for project Heavy Green. Myrtle Ann, then 27, was his partner in a strong and loving eleven-year marriage. Mel and Ann Holland had spent their entire adult lives together and, although raising three girls and two boys on his enlisted salary was difficult, they had a happy family. Sergeant Holland was honored when senior officers recommended him for the top secret project and an opportunity to make a difference in an increasingly frustrating and divisive war. He was going to join other Strategic Air Command technicians in the operation of a radar facility that would allow the Air Force to effectively bomb North Vietnam. The placement of a ground-based radar system in Laos, they were told by superiors, "would save airplanes and airmen." Ultimately, this "would cause the Hanoi government to end the Vietnam war." For Mel Holland and the other volunteers who had already spent time in Southeast Asia, this was particularly heady stuff.[2] Nonetheless, many of the wives were filled with grave doubts—especially Ann Holland.

She was standing in the kitchen of a house filled with Cub Scouts when she learned by telephone that her husband was missing. She was sternly admonished not to discuss with anyone Mel's true employment status. A voice at the Pentagon, in the Air Force Special Plans office, which had only months before assured her and the other wives that the project was safe, was the only authorized link to any information about her husband. Unable to share her pain with family and friends, avail herself of the military casualty affairs system, or even talk to a minister, Ann Holland forced herself to focus on the upbringing of their children. However, convinced the Special Plans office was withholding information on the loss of Site 85, she vowed to learn more about the fate of her husband.[3]

A month later, Mrs. Holland read an Associated Press news article in *The Columbian*, a Vancouver, Washington newspaper. Titled "Reds cool off Laos drive apparently under orders," the story mentioned "radar stations in Laos" manned by "American civilians." At the conclusion of the article, almost as an afterthought, it was reported "Eight of the 12 Americans technicians at one station were killed March 11 when the North Vietnamese overran the post, which was in Sam Neua province 15 miles from the North Vietnamese border." She immediately telephoned Major Hoskinson at the Special Plans office, only to be told a day later "there was no connection between the news story and her husband's loss." In later years Mrs. Holland would point to this conversation as "the first of many lies" she was told by her government.[4]

What Mrs. Holland did not know at the time, and what Major Hoskinson did not reveal to the Heavy Green wives during his June briefings, was that similar articles had appeared in other U.S. newspapers. On May 2, the Baltimore *Sun* provided many details on the communist attack, including the misspelled name of the mountain. "The United States maintains radar sites inside Laos to guide American bombers and reconnaissance planes to North Vietnam. One such outpost, located on a mesa-like mountain top at Pou Phaty . . . was overrun by North Vietnamese troops March 11. Eight of the twelve American technicians at the post were reported killed. The other four escaped."[5]

Because the Air Force was in a damage control mode, and intent on maintaining the project's secrecy, the Special Plans office misled the Heavy Green families and deliberately withheld information already widely known to the press. Counseled by the Air Force to strictly abide by their secrecy agreements, the wives were forced into a world where they had no rights and no guardians. Dealing with women under great stress and mostly unaccustomed to questioning authority, the Air Force found especially vulnerable targets. In a military system where the families should have found protection and trust, they were instead abused and written off as part of an idea gone bad. Senior Air Force officers decided the dual compensation benefits were sufficient relief; there was no need to be honest in explaining the circumstances surrounding the loss of the eleven men.[6]

A careful examination of the facts would have revealed the negligent decisionmaking that, despite explicit enemy threats, allowed the continuation of the Site 85 operations. Exposing the truth would have brought into question the flawed process that rushed to conclude there were no survivors and allowed the Air Force to attempt the destruction of Site 85 and any evidence, human or otherwise. Officers in the Special Plans office, who should have been advocates for the wives of their lost subordinates, protected Air Force interests and their own careers. If the wives violated their oath of secrecy, it was clear there would be much to answer for.

On August 5, 1968, Ann Holland signed a "Release and Agreement" for the Lockheed Aircraft Service Company and received a $35,000 life insurance payment. Six months later she received a second and final settlement from Lockheed in the amount of $25,000. Under the terms of the agreement she was required to reimburse the insurance carrier "if Melvin A. Holland is subsequently found to be alive." This was a phrase of great import because, based on the information received from Major Hoskinson, Holland believed her husband "could still walk out of the jungle." Forced to use some of the insurance money to purchase a home, she banked most of the settlement under the presumption "we would have to repay the money when he came home."[7] Overwhelmed with the pain of the loss and frightened by the uncertainty of their future, nonetheless, the Holland family tried to establish some sense of normalcy.

In the fall of 1968 Ann Holland took her children to visit several Air Force families they had known prior to the Heavy Green assignment. Upon hearing Holland express the belief her husband might have survived, one of her husband's former coworkers, disregarding the security implications, took her aside. Saying that he had learned about the attack through unofficial channels, he told her "the Air Force is lying," the attack was "no surprise," and the site was "bombed the next day." The obvious implication was that there was no possibility Melvin Holland or the others had survived; the Air Force had taken steps to destroy the evidence. Holland quickly contacted Major Hoskinson and pointedly asked if U.S. aircraft had bombed the site. She was told efforts were taken "to destroy just the equipment, but only after none of the bodies had moved for three days."[8] Her faith in the Air Force was being sorely tested.

In December another news article on Laos caught Holland's attention. Soth Phetrasy, the Pathet Lao spokesman in Vientiane, was quoted in a United Press International story as saying "None of the 96 Americans and British prisoners in Pathet Lao hands will even be allowed to receive packages or letters sent to them at Christmas."[9] Holland took direct action, writing to the man who had signed her husband's death certificate, Michael V. Connors, Vice-Consul, U.S. Embassy, Vientiane. In her January 10 letter, Holland enclosed a copy of the article and asked if her husband was one of the prisoners on the Pathet Lao list. It would be two months, however, before she received a reply, as Connors had recently been posted to the U.S. Consulate in Algeria, where the forwarded letter reached him in mid-February. He returned the letter to Vientiane and in mid-March Mrs. Holland received a brief response from the U.S. Embassy's Second Secretary, James P. Murphy, stating "we have no information about your husband Melvin A. Holland. He is not on the list of U.S. personnel missing in Laos that has been handed to the NLHS [Pathet Lao] representative." The letter ended by saying Holland's request would be forwarded to an official in Washington for further review.[10] On March 25, Holland was informed by Thomas J. Barnes, U.S. State Department Country Officer for Laos that "The Department of Defense list does not include your husband, Melville [sic] A. Holland, as being missing anywhere in Southeast Asia, let alone Laos. Additionally, his name does not appear in the Embassy list of both American military and civilians missing in Laos." It was suggested that Holland gather additional facts, "date, location, and circumstances of his disappearance," and forward them to Frank A. Sieverts,[11] Special Assistant to the Under Secretary, U.S. Department of State.

Three weeks later, however, Barnes wrote Mrs. Holland to say her earlier letter to Vientiane had not included sufficient detail to permit a proper response. Having recently received "a report of your husband's presumptive death," the officer could now confirm the Pathet Lao official was merely referring to a list provided by the United States.

"Your husband's name, therefore, would not have been on this list since the United States Government does not carry him as missing in Laos." Barnes then provided this update:

> Although Lao government forces made an effort a few months ago to retake the area where your husband had been working, they were unsuccessful. The area has thus been continuously in enemy hands since the attack on March 11, 1968. It is extremely unlikely that government forces will be able to reoccupy that sector within the foreseeable future.

The letter ended with an apology for the "scant information about the circumstances of your husband's presumed death."[12]

Mrs. Holland was still being told there was no conclusive proof of her husband's death, sustaining the possibility he may have survived the attack. Yet, her government was undertaking no formal efforts to learn more about his fate. Because Melvin Holland was not officially in the U.S. military, his name, and those of the other Heavy Green personnel, was not included in POW-MIA queries to the Pathet Lao, Hanoi, and third-country diplomats. No one was asking about the eleven missing Americans, so there was no pressure or incentive for the communists to provide any available information. For Ann Holland the message seemed clear: the U.S. State Department and Air Force could not be trusted to pursue the case of her missing husband.

In February 1969 the Air Force began the process of bringing ten of the eleven missing Heavy Green personnel back into the U.S. military.[13] A blank form, signed by each man in Washington and left with the Special Plans office, was now completed to reflect continuous military service. In effect, the October 1967 discharges were voided. Those who were eligible for promotion during their Heavy Green assignment were also advanced in rank on the appropriate date. For example, Mel Holland was actually discharged on October 16, 1967, but his records were revised to show another enlistment beginning the following day. Additionally, his promotion to Technical Sergeant was made official as of November 1, 1967. These "corrections" were approved at a very senior level by Assistant Secretary of the Air Force for Manpower and Reserve Affairs J. William Doolittle.

Once the men were returned to military status they were reported as having been killed on March 11, 1968, and their records were changed to reflect standard notification to the families at the time of loss. A casualty report form, dated March 25, 1968, was placed in their personnel records indicating the men were "killed in action in Southeast Asia" and each was posthumously awarded a Purple Heart Medal for "wounds incurred as the direct result of an act by a hostile foreign force." Once these formalities were complete, military life insurance and survivor benefits were paid to the families and they were processed for military dependent identification cards allowing them access to military medical, commissary, and base exchange (BX) facilities.[14] A year after the loss at Site 85 the ten families were again part of the military system.

Although the Special Plans office hoped this would complete their dealings with the Heavy Green project, reinstating the men in military service did nothing to answer continuing questions from many of the wives. There were still no reports of capture or of remains and, therefore, the families continued to question when, or if, they would ever gain closure.

Holland continued to press for answers and in the spring of 1969 with the guidance of James E. Carty, a local attorney, requested assistance from her congresswoman, Julia Butler Hansen. She was told the site had been bombed by U.S. aircraft, and was particularly interested in learning exactly when the air strikes were initiated. Despite a series of correspondence between Representative Hansen and the Pentagon, however, Holland received little satisfaction. Indeed, the Air Force was now backing away from any possibility of survivors. The Air Force Office of Legislative Liaison responded, on May 16, 1969, that Melvin Holland's name was not placed on the list provided to the Pathet Lao because he was considered killed. As proof they cited a March 21, 1968 Pathet Lao propaganda broadcast which claimed "nearly 20 Americans killed" and no reports of captured U.S. personnel. In response to the question of bombing the facility, the Air Force replied "Security precautions preclude discussions about the air operations in question. [You] may be assured, however, that the United States Government would not conduct air operations against American personnel." This carefully worded letter, which never acknowledged Holland had been in the Air Force at the time of his loss, closed by saying, "We hope the foregoing will be helpful and deeply regret our inability to provide even the slightest ray of hope that there were survivors."[15]

Desperate to contain Holland's inquiries, the Air Force knowingly misled Representative Hansen, who passed along these patently false statements to her constituent. As discussed in the previous chapter, U.S. air strikes on Site 85 began on the morning of March 11, even before the first helicopter rescue, and specific attempts to destroy the equipment (close by the last-known locations of the Heavy Green personnel) began on the afternoon of March 11 and continued for at least a month. As to "security precautions," the Air Force was understandably nervous about this entire line of questioning. In 1969 the U.S. Air Force was flying more than 500 sorties in Laos per day, but for five years the U.S. government had acknowledged nothing more than "armed reconnaissance flights in northern Laos."[16] The Air Force could hardly be honest in admitting the bombing of Site 85. With regard to the facile no "ray of hope" closing remarks, senior officers in the Special Plans office knew there were serious problems with Stan Sliz's claims, and a year earlier Major Hoskinson had admitted they could not be sure everyone had been killed. The response was obviously designed to convince Holland's congresswoman and attorney that her suspicions were unfounded, she should consider her husband dead, and it was time to get on with her life.

One can imagine Air Force officials were more than a little piqued that a sergeant's wife had shown the temerity not only to doubt the veracity of the Special Plans office, but to also involve the State Department and a Member of Congress in their highly classified project. Rather than treating her questions with honesty and respect, the Air Force saw Holland as a threat to be silenced. While those in the Special Plans office hoped the response to her congressional representative would end Holland's inquiries, they would soon learn the mother of five would not go quietly.

Holland's inability to learn more about America's little known war in Laos was a frustration shared by many Southeast Asia watchers in the government, news media, academia, and general public. Although for years the Central Intelligence Agency had briefed the Lao paramilitary program to key congressional leaders and their staffs, in Washington and during visits to Laos, few Americans had any conception of the deep and longstanding U.S. involvement in this neutral country.[17] Official Americans in Laos, to include Air America employees, were forbidden to discuss any U.S. military-related activities. Journalists, stymied by a lack of roads and private air transportation, were rarely allowed access to areas outside of Vientiane. In short, while there was a good deal of tantalizing bar chatter in the capital's many nightspots, there was little verifiable proof of the vast American presence. This shroud of obfuscation and denial, however, was about to unravel.

Shortly after Richard Nixon took office, Pentagon officials warned the State Department that diplomatic efforts to bring about a bombing cessation in South Vietnam,[18] without a similar ban in Laos, would expose the United States to intense international criticism. The problem, of course, was that the U.S. had never publicly admitted to more than "armed reconnaissance" flights in Laos. As one senior official explained, giant B-52 bombers could never "by any stretch of the imagination be considered . . . reconnaissance aircraft." To gain support for military actions clearly prohibited by the Geneva Agreements, in February a senior Pentagon official suggested the State Department ask Prime Minister Souvanna Phouma publicly to reveal his knowledge and support of the air strikes. The request was quickly rejected, citing the likelihood that an acknowledgment of the prohibited bombing would invite condemnation by the Soviet Union and other Eastern Bloc countries. Additionally, it was believed "any official admission of our bombing . . . would considerably increase the pressure on our own government as well as Souvanna to implement a bombing halt in Laos and, therefore, increase rather than diminish the problem of interdicting what appears to be undiminished traffic along the Ho Chi Minh Trail."[19]

But, to Washington's great consternation, it was Souvanna himself who soon broached the subject and created a major credibility problem. In June the *New York Times* and *Washington Post* quoted Souvanna Phouma as confirming U.S. air strikes in Laos. Perhaps the Lao prince had become tired of the fiction or, more likely, he was sending a strong message to the communist countries supporting the trespass of his country. In any case, the State Department soon devised a rather absurd public response. The U.S. government had "no quarrel" with the Prime Minister's statements, but there would be no further clarification or comment on these activities.[20] Given the growing uncertainty and debate about America's Indochina involvement, the White House should have realized this major violation of the Geneva agreements would not be ignored by either the press or anti-war activists.[21] Indeed, when a State Department spokesman invoked the new policy during a June 17, briefing, "the assembled reporters laughed in derision."

Nevertheless, a month later Under Secretary of State Elliot

Richardson remained convinced that if the truth came out "we would then stand before the world as the sole foreign force there . . . A change in our public position would [also] be unpropitious following . . . DRV [Democratic Republic of Vietnam] allegations at the Paris talks that we are the aggressors in Laos."[22] Continuing policies established in the Kennedy and Johnson administrations, the executive branch was consigned to maintaining the secrecy of U.S. military operations in Laos. But, after seven years of relative obscurity, rigorous congressional and press scrutiny was about to illuminate America's war in the shadow of Vietnam.

As I have elaborated elsewhere,[23] on October 20, 1969, a subcommittee of the Senate Committee on Foreign Relations began four days of hearings on U.S. involvement in the kingdom of Laos. William Sullivan, then serving as a deputy assistant secretary of state, was the premier witness, but there was also an impressive array of military and civilian authorities brought in from Laos. Senior Defense and State Department officials were also present. On the fourth day CIA Director Richard Helms presented especially sensitive testimony about the agency's Lao operations. Concurrently, *Time* and *U.S. News & World Report* carried stories on the American presence in Laos and the *New York Times* published a remarkably detailed three-part series on the "twilight war" in Laos.[24] Americans were suddenly reading about U.S.-sponsored armies, airlines, and a massive economic assistance program in a country without even a railroad. Spurred by the publicity surrounding the Senate hearings, Holland's attorney sought the assistance of Washington Senator Warren G. Magnuson (D., Washington), who forwarded the letter to Senator Stuart Symington (D., Missouri), the subcommittee chairman. The request was simple: Mrs. Holland wanted a determination of "the status of Mr. Holland, and if dead, the place of burial."[25]

Symington, William Sullivan's guest during a 1966 visit to Vientiane and several up-country Lima Sites, was well informed on the U.S. military's deep involvement in Laos and had supported the clandestine activity.[26] Still, as the Southeast Asian war continued, the Senator began to doubt the wisdom of the Lao operations. Symington began the hearings by asserting, "If there is any . . . area where it would appear that the American people need and deserve more information, it is with regard to U.S. commitments and involvement in this small distant kingdom."[27] These would have been very welcome words to

Holland, if she and the rest of the American public had been allowed to hear them. At the insistence of the Nixon administration, the hearings were closed to all but those with security clearances and a need to know the information.

On the second day of testimony Senator Mike Mansfield (D., Montana) asked Colonel Robert Tyrrell, the current U.S. Air Attaché to Laos, for the number of U.S. casualties at Site 85. Tyrrell, who was on his second attaché tour in Laos but not in the country in March 1968, deferred the question to Brigadier General Donald Blackburn, representing the Joint Chiefs of Staff. Blackburn, undoubtedly briefed by lower ranking officers on key subjects likely to be raised at the hearings, said he did not have the figure.[28] The general offered to provide the information for the record and the line of questioning on Pha Thi was dropped. Subsequently the military provided the committee this statement: "The radar facility at Phou Pha Thi (Site 85) was lost as a result of enemy action on 11 March 1968 and resulted in 12 USAF personnel killed."[29]

Later in the day Tyrrell was questioned on the Christmas Day 1967 loss of the Muang Phalane TACAN site. Again, the Colonel claimed ignorance. When Blackburn was queried, however, on how the Pentagon maintained the secrecy of U.S. military deaths in Laos, he correctly stated "They were reported as lost in Southeast Asia."[30] In a follow-on exchange regarding Site 85, Ambassador Sullivan was asked by committee counsel, "Do you believe that the North Vietnamese discovered the nature of this facility before it was taken or not?" Sullivan replied, "This would have to be a speculative guess. My guess would be, yes." At this point the conversation on Pha Thi continued, but was deleted from the official transcript and remains classified.[31]

The final questioning on Site 85 was raised in conjunction with the post-attack communist offensive and General Vang Pao's response. When asked by counsel if there had been an effort to regain control of Site 85 Sullivan stated, "No, there was no effort to retake it."[32] This was a complete falsehood. As the Ambassador was fully aware, in the fall of 1968 a major U.S.-Hmong operation nearly seized the mountain.[33] Clearly, Sullivan was in no mood to drag out old business and risk more unwelcome questions. Similarly, the uniformed officers in attendance thought more about their own careers than the families of those who had agreed to shed their uniforms and serve in obscurity at Phou Pha Thi. In retrospect, their silence was deafening.

The hearings succeeded in exposing substantial U.S. wrongdoing in Laos, albeit in response to what amounted to a North Vietnamese takeover of eastern Laos, and set the stage for further congressional and press investigations. Nonetheless, at the time no one in an official capacity seems to have been suitably outraged by the losses at Muang Phalane and Site 85 to seek further information. Most glaring in the publicly released testimony is the absence of any questions regarding how death was determined and what may have become of the bodies. In fact, the transcripts give no indication that the subcommittee members and their staff even realized the "12 USAF personnel killed" included eleven men whose bodies had not been recovered.[34] Doubtless, it never occurred to any of the questioners that the U.S. Air Force and Department of State would be concealing pertinent details on the largest single ground combat loss of Air Force personnel in the entire Southeast Asian war. And the witnesses who did know about the coverup were certainly not inclined to elaborate on their responses. There wasn't much honor in revealing an operation that ended with eleven Americans, missing or dead, left behind by their government on a mountain in Laos.

Despite what was revealed in the hearings, on October 30 Senator Symington replied to Holland's request for assistance, "I do not know what our subcommittee could do in this matter and would suggest that you write to the Secretary of Defense. It just is not the type and character of matter that comes before our subcommittee."[35] Under the circumstances the tone of the letter appears especially callous and high-handed. Because Senator Symington was well informed on the true status of the Americans at Site 85, I can only speculate that an uninformed staffer was responsible for the reply. There is also the possibility that, because the testimony was considered classified, Symington was unwilling to release any sensitive information.[36] In any case, he took no further steps to assist with the case of Melvin Holland or any of the other men missing from Site 85. Ann Holland's efforts to learn more about the fate of her husband had, it seemed, come to an impasse. And then the President spoke out on American activity in Laos.

On March 6, 1970, the White House, attempting to contain rising press and public criticism, released a detailed presidential statement on U.S. involvement in Laos.[37] In the introductory remarks Nixon explained, "North Vietnam's military escalation in Laos has intensified public discussion in this country. The purpose of this statement is to set forth the record of what we found in January 1969 and the policy of this administration since that time."[38] Further in the declaration, after a discussion of recent press accounts on U.S. ground combat in Laos, the President said, "Because these reports are grossly inaccurate, I have concluded that our national interest will be served by . . . a precise description of our current activities in Laos."[39] Nixon followed with nine detailed "facts" which, as pointed out in a 1972 essay, "The Pentagon Papers and U.S. Involvement in Laos," "failed to mention the extensive CIA operations in Laos, the recent use of B-52s in northern Laos, or the full extent of American military advisory operations in the Lao army and air force."[40]

For the purposes of the discussion here, the most misleading assertion was "No American stationed in Laos has ever been killed in ground combat operations."[41]

After a flood of incredulous press inquiries, the White House released a revised statement[42] saying U.S. dead in Laos numbered about 200, with another 193 missing or captured.[43] The media were led to believe these figures were all related to aircraft losses and, therefore, the President's statement was technically accurate. Even after a story in the *Los Angeles Times* revealed the February 10, 1969, death of Captain Joseph Bush, a U.S. Army adviser killed while serving in northern Laos, the White House continued to dissemble. Captain Bush was not a "combat" loss: he died as the result of a "hostile action."[44]

Mrs. Holland was stunned by Nixon's declaration. Having failed to gain any support for her inquiry from the State Department, Air Force, or members of Congress, she now learned the President of the United States was disavowing her husband's loss. Years later, testifying in front of a congressional committee, she recalled, "I knew then that he either did not know about my husband in which case he could not do anything to bring him home, or he did know about him and was not going to do anything to bring him home. He was being abandoned. My greatest fear had come true."[45] In anger and despair Ann Holland called a local newspaper editor to voice her frustration. The national media picked up the story and soon reporters were asking the government to explain the Site 85 losses.[46] While White House spokesmen confirmed American civilians were killed at Pha Thi in 1968, they claimed the President could not be responsible for events occurring in an earlier administration. "Reporters grumbled, but, lacking further details, said little more."[47]

The publicity about Site 85 did, however, cause the Air Force to quickly marshal an information containment campaign. Alarmed the still top secret Heavy Green program would be further exposed by conflicted family members, a carefully selected Air Force team was directed to meet with each of the eleven[48] families. The following statement was used during the initial telephone contact:

> This is Major Zielezienski . . . I have replaced Major Hoskinson in matters concerning the death of your husband. During Major Hoskinson's last visit, he made the promise that the Air Force, when it was able, would provide you and your family facts regarding the death of your husband. With recent publicity which, I might add, is based primarily on unofficial sources, you may have become further puzzled. Therefore we would like to provide you and your children with the official facts as they exist.[49]

The group comprised Colonel Jerry Clayton,[50] Major Joseph A. Zielezienski, Special Plans, and Major Dannie M. Jackson, a personnel specialist. Clayton was to provide his personal knowledge of the circumstances surrounding the loss and subsequent Air Force actions, the personnel representative was to explain and assist with any survivor benefits issues, and Zielezienski was to represent the interests of the Special Plans office.[51]

Colonel Clayton began each of the visits, which occurred March 20–28, 1970, by stating the team was acting at the request of the Secretary of the Air Force and the Air Force Chief of Staff to provide a summary of the "official facts and circumstances" surrounding the loss of their loved one. A statement was then read by Major Zielezienski, which included the following information. "We can tell you that he volunteered and was selected for a highly important mission in Laos. This mission was to operate an electronic site consisting primarily of radar and communications which supported our tactical operations in SEAsia and assisted in the recovery of U.S. aircrew personnel who were shot down. All personnel had in their possession guns, ammunition and survival kits including individual survival radios." This careful declaration, avoiding any mention of the bombing of North Vietnam or Laos, also included a brief, and generally accurate, overview of the site's physical characteristics, defense forces, and helicopter support.[52]

While it may have made the families feel better to hear the site was performing humanitarian assistance in recovering downed aircrews,[53] there was no connection between Heavy Green and any rescue activity. With regard to the issuance of individual weapons and survival gear, as discussed earlier, Ambassador Sullivan had consistently denied the men weapons. When the M-16's and survival vests were finally provided, days before the attack, there was little time for training. At the time of the attack only a few of the technicians were able to reach their weapons and survival equipment.[54] But the most important factual errors were contained in a summary of the attack. "True" facts were not necessarily "official" facts. The families were told:

> [At] approximately 4 o'clock . . . enemy ground forces attacked and over-
> ran the site killing all of the men on duty. For the next 3 to 3 1/2 hours,
> intensive attacks were made on . . . airmen support personnel [the Sliz
> team] by the North Vietnamese. At approximately 7 o'clock that morning
> (at daybreak), rescue helicopters arrived on the scene and extracted all sur-
> vivors. Intensive enemy fire (literally a wall of bullets) precluded recovery
> of the remains of personnel who had been killed. Extensive aerial recon-
> naissance . . . ; public statements by the enemy; and other intelligence
> establishes the fact that there were no survivors of this attack. Prior to this
> time, because of security implications, the Air Force has been unable to
> make statements surrounding these events.[55]

In fact, the initial *Dac Cong* attack on the vans occurred around 3:00 A.M. and, as detailed earlier, the Air Force had no evidence even to determine positively who was even in the vans, let alone to declare everyone had been killed. The families were not told CIA officer Howard Freeman had surveyed the site at about 5:45 A.M. (the actual time of daylight, not "7 o'clock"), before withdrawing with a bullet wound. After this, the Air America helicopter arrived to remove only four of the survivors. Jack Starling, picked up by an Air Force helicopter, was not rescued for another two hours. As to the "recovery of the remains," it was Air Force policy not to risk rescue teams in recovering bodies. Although pararescueman Jim Rogers saw bodies in the vicinity of Jack Starling, he was trained to concentrate on the living and correctly took no action to recover any of the dead.[56] As to the issue of "public statements by the enemy,"[57] as discussed earlier in this chapter, the U.S. Embassy and State Department routinely dismissed Pathet Lao broadcasts as propaganda. Why would suspect stories about dead Americans at Site 85 be treated as believable? They were convenient.

The Air Force was intent on creating the impression among the families that this was an unfortunate accident; the men were conducting a humanitarian mission, were properly defended, equipped, and a rescue was conducted immediately. Most of all, the Air Force wanted to leave no doubt the missing men were dead—all killed during the early hours of the attack.[58] In truth, the Air Force had no witnesses to the attack on the vans and, except for the deaths of Springsteadah and Gish, no multiple witnesses to any other losses. They did, however, know Freeman had searched the area without seeing any Americans, living or dead. Yet, just yards away, Bill Husband was hiding just north of the vans and five technicians (in two locations) were located on the cliffside. During the attack the North Vietnamese were unable to capture or kill these men. Could there have been other technicians who also escaped the initial attack? Rather than considering the possibility that some of the men may have hidden in areas away from the vans and cliffside, the Air Force had readily conceded the missing were killed in and around the radar equipment. There was good reason for this—the U.S. bombing of Phou Pha Thi.

The most egregious omission in the presentation was the decision not to fully inform the families of the U.S. air strikes. As detailed earlier, the attacks began even before the arrival of the first rescue helicopter. Howard Freeman and Stan Sliz, while under North Vietnamese assault, had boldly requested the first air strikes to save lives. The later bombing, beginning on the afternoon of March 11, but most intense on March 13, had been undertaken to destroy the U.S. equipment and any other evidence of an American presence.[59]

A concluding phrase read to the families by Major Zielezienski appears to have been both a plea to their patriotism and a veiled threat.

> We are proud to have been able to serve . . . with airman such as your (son/husband) who have valiantly given their lives in defense of their country and fellow airmen. The Secretary of the Air Force and the Chief of Staff personally wish to express their gratitude for your silence which, which among things, has permitted the Air Force to protect and maintain security and has also served to protect those benefits that have been received from other sources.[60]

Colonel Clayton then told the families of the aerial photography of the site and survivor reports that had convinced him "none of those on-duty personnel in the radar building survived even though no one had actually seen the casualties." If some of the men had escaped the enemy, Clayton explained "the unlikelihood of a Caucasian American surviving among the natives in Laos for this length of time." Clayton then "repeated the President's statement regarding not releasing the names of personnel killed in Laos during a previous administration, taking the opportunity to point out the possible loss of civilian benefits which might occur if the dual role status were to surface."[61]

The families were being asked to remain silent in order to protect national security which, in turn, would guarantee them continued dual survivor benefits. For the ten families, most with young children, there seemed little alternative. The Special Plans team made it clear the secrecy agreements remained in force; going public might well result in loss of benefits and even criminal prosecution. The officers also stressed there could be no communication between the families or with the former Heavy Green participants. Colonel Clayton would be their sole source of information about the attack and immediate aftermath. In this way the Air Force sought to further limit information exchanges about the program and its demise.[62] Unable even to discuss their possible options with anyone, most of the families quietly accepted what they were told. After all, the Air Force system was there to protect them.

As documented in Major Zielezienski's trip report, each stop was carefully recorded, including questions asked, mood of the family, and length of the visit. The Etchberger family visit was perfunctory, since Chief Master Sergeant Etchberger's next of kin had been presented with the Air Force Cross Medal and an accompanying citation detailing his last moments. Discussions with the former[63] Mrs. Gish and Mrs. Springsteadah were brief and straightforward, their husbands had been killed in the presence of two survivors.[64] At Mrs. Hall's home the team explained "one of the survivors had observed a North Vietnamese shoot her husband at close [sic] with a machine gun and . . . [the Air Force] found this to be conclusive proof of her husband's death." Mrs. Shannon was told "no survivors had seen her husband after the attack or had actually seen her husband shot." Nonetheless, the report stated "the facts as outlined were of sufficient substance to allay any doubt that she may have had. She is now apparently firmly convinced that her husband is in fact dead."[65]

Mrs. Calfee was told the Air Force had "conclusive proof of her husband's death . . . one of the survivors had seen Sgt Calfee badly wounded with his right arm blown off and multiple body wounds." Although Mrs. Calfee "accepted these facts" she told the officers her in-laws were having trouble understanding "the exact circumstances surrounding her husband's death" and one sister-in-law had written the President on the matter. As a result, the team also presented a briefing to Master Sergeant Calfee's mother, his four sisters, and their husbands. According to the report, "The family apparently had received information concerning the fall of Phou Pha Thi from sources other than Mrs. Calfee and asked several pointed questions." The family wanted to know if the site was bombed, if it was secure, why the men were not evacuated earlier, and if the friendly forces had defected. Calfee's mother then asked about the possibility of a remains recovery and if she might be able to speak to the survivor who last saw him.

The team responded by saying "approximately 3 days after the fall of Phou Pha Thi when we were assured there were no survivors, or Americans at the site, we destroyed the site with bombs and rocket fire to insure highly classified sensitive equipment was destroyed." Colonel Clayton explained the security and evacuation arrangements, known intelligence, and his belief the Lao forces were loyal. He also stressed he would "make every effort" to have any found remains identified and returned to the families. The family members "appeared to be satisfied with this." As to the request to speak with a survivor, the group was told he was "no longer in the continental limits of the United States" but that "the facts presented them were complete."[66]

In addition to providing a grossly inaccurate answer to the bombing question, the team also misled the Calfee family about the availability of the surviving witness. Jack Starling, the source of the information on Master Sergeant Calfee, was indeed outside the United States. But, in a manner of speaking, he had been in touch with the Special Plans office. Following a brief hospitalization and an abbreviated tour of duty at Randolph Air Force Base, Texas, Starling was reassigned to the Philippines. According to Starling, after his arrival in Manila his commander stressed the Site 85 assignment remained top secret and he was "not allowed to discuss it."[67] Moreover, after the briefing team returned to Washington, the Special Plans office recommended "all surviving personnel assigned to Project Heavy Green be contacted . . . and briefed on the official U.S. Government position." According to the report, "This briefing should serve to put a stop to apparent loose talk emanating from unidentified members."[68] In order to ensure the primacy of their "official facts" the Air Force sought to block contact between the family members and the survivors.

A discussion with the former Mrs. Davis,[69] according to the report, makes no reference to any specific details on the location or cause of Staff Sergeant Davis's death and she asked no questions related to his loss.[70] During a visit with Mrs. Worley and Staff Sergeant Worley's mother and father, there is no indication the family was provided any specific information regarding his death. The trip report did note, however, "the parents were aware of the cover. Therefore, the entire arrangement was explained to them . . . and a suggestion was made that revealing this arrangement . . . might possibly jeopardize some of the benefits being received by the widow. They . . . assured us of their confidence."[71]

The visit with Mrs. Price and her in-laws followed much the same pattern as the Worley discussions. There were no specific details provided on Staff Sergeant Price's death. But, it became obvious to the team that Price's mother, father, and sister were "completely aware of the cover arrangement." Again the rationale for secrecy was stressed, along with the concern any security leaks "might possibly jeopardize benefits." The team noted "the family apparently had received information from unknown sources since they asked pointed questions." Their questions focused on Price's location at the time of the attack and the fact he was lost on his first assignment to Site 85. Colonel Clayton assured the family that Staff Sergeant Price "had died fighting for his country."[72]

Discussions with Mrs. Blanton were cordial. Lieutenant Colonel Blanton, the site commander, and Colonel Clayton had been longtime friends. She was presented with no specific evidence of her husband's loss but, according to the report, accepted his death.[73] Mrs. Blanton did say, however, that her husband's father and daughter should receive the briefing. The team contacted the two and learned they too were aware of the cover story. They were briefed on the loss and explained the reasoning for the Lockheed arrangement. For Mr. Blanton it was a particularly painful session; years earlier his other son had been killed in a military plane crash.[74]

Both sides expected the Holland family visit to be tense—and it was. From the perspective of the Special Plans office Ann Holland was a troublemaker who had repeatedly violated her secrecy agreement by

contacting the press, non-Air Force government officials, and other
Heavy Green families. Holland was "guilty" as charged, but had
become convinced the Air Force was lying to her about the loss of her
husband. Quite simply she believed her obligation was to Mel Holland, not the U.S. Air Force. Not surprisingly the Special Plans trip
report entry on the Holland visit began, "Mrs. Holland's opening
remark was "What made you people finally come out here to tell me
what happened after all this time?" After explaining the delay was
caused by "security considerations," the team proceeded with their
briefing. Colonel Clayton then told Mrs. Holland he had spoken with
a survivor who reported "Sgt Holland had been wounded and cried
out for help during the entire night in a gurgling voice . . . and that in
the later stages of the battle, Sgt Holland fell silent and no other cries
or indications of life were heard." Clayton then said he was certain
"there was no possibility that Sgt Holland could be alive."[75] Mrs. Holland then asked to speak with the survivor. She was told he remained
"too ill" to discuss the battle.[76]

According to Major Zielezienski's report, "These comments and
the official statement apparently convinced Mrs. Holland that her husband was in fact dead. Mrs. Holland stated she anticipated no further
action regarding this matter with the press or her attorney."[77] Having
failed for two years to gain any new information on her husband's case,
Ann Holland was prepared to acquiesce and accept this official determination of her husband's fate. It was a terribly difficult decision to
make, but like the other wives, what choice did she really have?
Requests to the State Department, Congressional inquiries guided by
an attorney, and calls to the press had failed to provide a detailed and
believable account of her husband's death. Now, in part because of her
press contacts in the wake of Nixon's statement, Mel's former commander had come to say he had died at Site 85. "Why," she wondered,
"could they not have done this two years before?" Conflicted, she
nonetheless decided it was time to end her private war with the U.S.
Air Force.[78]

The Special Plans team completed its mission and returned to
Washington confident they had contained the potential security problem. Major Zielezienski wrote in the trip report:

All persons we talked to knew their . . . [loved one] had volunteered for
an important classified mission, that he genuinely felt this project, if suc-

cessful, would help shorten the war, and that considerable risk was involved in the assignment. They all appeared to be very patriotic Americans who believed in our efforts in SEAsia. The majority did not desire the public notoriety of this incident and spoke openly against the news media role. I concluded all were proud of their deceased members' role in the USAF mission and genuinely appreciated being officially told the facts and circumstances surrounding the death of their . . . [loved one].[79]

This all sounded quite nice; loyal citizens so accepting of the Air Force position and even some who were anti-press. They were also good people who had a misplaced faith in those who had presented the "official facts."

A careful review of their presentation reveals a vague story with serious shortfalls. Of the ten missing men, the Special Plans team presented only five families with specific details on the deaths of their loved one. Of these, only the Gish and Springsteadah losses were witnessed by more than one survivor. The purported deaths of Calfee, Holland, and Hall were exclusively based on the statements of one man, Staff Sergeant Jack Starling. Unbeknownst to the families, the Air Force had accepted Sullivan's determination that all eleven had perished during the battle. And, as detailed in the previous chapter, Sullivan's conclusion was based on hurried and incomplete information developed in the midst of an overwhelming desire to destroy as quickly as possible Site 85 and all its incriminating evidence.

It should have also been clear to the Air Force that Jack Starling's recollections were not credible. According to Sliz, Starling had observed the North Vietnamese kill Blanton, Calfee, and Shannon as the Americans exited the radar vans.[80] But Starling has also said Blanton, Calfee, Hall, Shannon, Holland, and Price died within feet of his location.[81] The Calfee family was told the survivor (Starling) reported Master Sergeant Calfee as having "his right arm blown off." At other times, Starling has said it was Holland who lost an arm in the battle and makes no mention of Calfee.[82] While there is little doubt some Americans were killed near Starling's locale, there is considerable question over the actual identities of these men.

In March 1970 no one realized the Holland visit was simply a truce and that five years later an all-out war would break out. Thwarted by the Air Force, ignored by the State Department and Congress, but convinced she was being deceived, Ann Holland would expose the Heavy Green program in federal court.

Six weeks after the family visits, for reasons that remain somewhat unclear, Senator Symington conducted an interview on the Site 85 losses. On May 8, 1970, his subcommittee summoned survivor Stan Sliz, recently promoted to major. In a classified session, with no other senators present, Symington and the subcommittee counsel questioned Sliz for less than thirty minutes. After Sliz provided an overview of the attack, including the deaths of Gish and Springsteadah, the Senator mostly asked about the actions of the defending and attacking forces. Finding that Sliz knew little about this, he turned to questions about the bombing of northern Laos and the use of napalm. Even Sliz's recounting of the January AN-2 Colt attack evoked little interest. In closing comments to Sliz, Symington suggests he had received an earlier, if faulty, briefing on Site 85. "Well, it is a sad and fine story of the way you handled it. We heard about it, we were getting some testimony and so when we heard you were a survivor, we were told there were no survivors, and we wanted to talk to you about it."[83]

Although Sliz's testimony should have at least provoked some questions about the recovery of the bodies, Senator Symington and his subcommittee declined to pursue the Site 85 losses. This is all the more odd when considered against the backdrop of the controversy surrounding President Nixon's March 6, 1970 declaration. While there was a great deal of public discussion regarding dead American military personnel in a neutral southeast Asian kingdom, Symington curiously remained silent on the most egregious case of all.

Ann Holland remarried in 1971, becoming Ann Dettloff, but continued to follow developments on the war in Laos. Occasionally she would call the Special Plans office to ask questions, but there was never any additional information. As the years went by the calls became fewer. Even so, the tone in Washington had become testy. Eventually an officer said she was "obsessed with the loss" and should put the episode in the past lest people think she was "unbalanced."[84] She could not let go, however, and in 1975 she received news which sent her straight to an attorney's office.

13

An End and a Beginning

In the spring of 1975 the second Indochina war moved inexorably to its conclusion. Nearly 600 American former prisoners of war celebrated the second anniversary of their release from communist captivity,[1] U.S. combat forces in Southeast Asia were a bitter memory and, as the North Vietnamese prepared to capture Saigon, President Gerald Ford proclaimed the war "finished as far as the United States is concerned."[2]

The war was far from over, however, for Ann Holland Dettloff. Technical Sergeant Melvin Holland had not returned and, although she had remarried, he was never far from her thoughts. In early 1975 a mutual acquaintance placed Dettloff in contact with a man who seemed to have remarkably accurate information on the loss of Site 85. He correctly described the general physical layout of the site, the presence of a 105-mm howitzer, and the emergency destruction devices placed on the TSQ-81 equipment. He told Dettloff the North Vietnamese had given the Americans "ample notice" to leave, the local defense forces had "sold out" to the North Vietnamese, the site was bombed a day after the North Vietnamese attack, and there were rumors of "six prisoners taken off the hill." The man did not know the nationality of the captured men.[3]

Shaken by the information, Dettloff confronted an officer in the Special Plans office with what she had learned. Upon mentioning "L-85" and "Channel 79," designators provided by the source, she says the officer exclaimed "You have been talking to one of the men who came back from over there, haven't you?" Reminding the officer of his repeated assurances the Air Force had waited several days before attacking the site, Dettloff then asked if, as the source claimed, "the site had been bombed the next day?" She was told Colonel Clayton's recollection was "several days" but, unfortunately, he was now retired and could not be contacted for further clarification.[4] Convinced she was being intentionally misled and having exhausted every other possible means of equity, Dettloff retained an attorney and began a seven-year legal battle.

On July 22, 1975, Dettloff initiated a $1.6 million lawsuit in the King County Superior Court, Washington State, against the Lockheed Aircraft Corporation. Represented by Howard Pruzan, a partner in a well-respected Seattle law firm, the suit alleged, "Defendant Lockheed, acting in concert with the United States Government, wrongfully and actionably caused the death of decedent and actionably subjected plaintiff and the minor children of decedent and plaintiff to prolonged and unnecessary mental anguish and suffering."[5] Concurrently, Dettloff filed a $1 million "Claim for Damage or Injury" against the U.S. Air Force for negligence in the death of Melvin Holland and "inflicting of mental anguish and suffering upon decedent's widow and minor children."[6]

Lockheed's attorneys acknowledged the suit on August 22, 1975, saying they had insufficient information to answer the complaint but, following an investigation, would answer the allegations.[7] In response, on December 10, 1975, Pruzan served Lockheed with a detailed set of interrogatories.[8] Meanwhile, the U.S. Air Force Judge Advocate General denied Dettloff's $1 million claim. She fired back on February 24, 1976, with a $1.6 million lawsuit against the U.S. government. Soon thereafter, Lockheed attorneys successfully consolidated their defense with this new suit and had the action moved to Federal court. Pruzan responded on April 1, with a set of interrogatories for the U.S. government.[9]

According to a May 3, 1976, memo prepared by the Special Plans office, the lawsuits caused U.S. Air Force attorneys to query the U.S. Justice Department "to determine if a precedent existed for defense of the matter entirely within a classified context." The Air Force was told, "The Deputy Assistant Attorney General after consultation with his superiors opined this would be impossible."[10] Based on this opinion, the Special Plans office developed and recommended a plan to declassify parts of the Heavy Green project. On April 22, 1976, representatives from the Special Plans office briefed Roger Shields, Deputy Assistant Secretary for POW/MIA Affairs, about the project and the ongoing litigation. Shields agreed with the declassification strategy and requested the Assistant Secretary of Defense for Public Affairs be informed in order to prepare for any media inquiries. Shields's position was reported to the Air Force Office of General Counsel, which in turn informed the Air Force Vice Chief of Staff and the Under Secretary of the Air Force. On April 30, the Special Plans office was informed that the Under Secretary had approved their recommendation to "declassify portions of the project in plateaus."[11]

On August 27, 1976, the Air Force responded to the April interrogatories, providing the first public acknowledgment of the Heavy Green program. Nonetheless, much of the information was imprecise, misleading, or simply fraudulent. For example, the Air Force stated, "The most knowledgeable persons would be the five survivors."[12] The Air Force then correctly named Sliz, Daniel, Husband, and Starling but, for reasons that remain unexplained, included Roland T. Hodge, the technician injured in the January 12, 1968, AN-2 bombing.[13] Hodge, who was not even at Pha Thi the night of the *Dac Cong* assault, was hardly a "knowledgeable" person. Some of the responses were more than just sloppy; they advanced notions which were obviously untrue.

Answering the question "When and under what circumstances did either Lockheed or the Government first learn of an impending attack . . . ," the Air Force responded:

> The United States rejects the concept of an attack having been "impending." All information known suggests that *the attack was a matter of complete surprise with no advance warning*. While it is true there was enemy ground activity in the surrounding territory, none of this activity was thought to be directed at the decedent's location. (italics added).[14]

The Air Force did not disclose the numerous CIA and U.S. Embassy Vientiane cables warning of a North Vietnamese attack or the Air Force cables directing an increase in Site 85 manning to permit additional air strikes on communist forces surrounding the mountain. Most damning was the omission of the March 5 message from 7th AF to Pacific Air Forces Headquarters that stated, "[D]ue to the desirability of maintaining air presence . . . Site 85 probably would not be evacuated until capture appeared imminent. The fact that complete security could not be assured in the original plan is noted."[15] Further, in a post-attack message General Momyer pointedly asked Ambassador Sullivan to explain friendly defensive actions "in view of clear indications of impending attack."[16] Reminding the general of the prescient CIA judgment that site safety could not be assured beyond March 10, Sullivan shot back, "its fall should have come as no surprise to anyone."[17] Clearly the government was lying, but believed these top secret materials would never be made public. And, with the truth safely locked away, who would be able to contest these official statements? Although submitted to the court as fact, these responses were part of a continuing deception and coverup.

Replies to questions regarding the U.S. bombing of Phou Pha Thi were similarly inaccurate. "At any time either before, during or after the attack upon said installation, did airplanes . . . controlled by the Government . . . take part in any air strike—bombing, strafing, or dropping weaponry of any kind—on said installation?" The government answered, "The known information is that on March 11, 2 USAF A-1 planes attacked with anti-personnel equipment and on March 14 (about) an unknown number of USAF planes were sent over the site to completely destroy the equipment. The sole purpose of the air strikes [on March 11] was the destruction of the enemy attack force after our personnel were off the hill."[18] The reply was silent on Sullivan's hurried March 12, decision to destroy the American equipment. Secrecy rules, the Air Force believed, would prevent Dettloff and the public from ever learning about the Ambassador's conversation with Souvanna Phouma, the heavy bombing on the afternoon of March 11, the attempted air strikes on March 12, and the loss of a pilot during the March 13 napalm bombing to destroy the "evidence" at Site 85.[19]

Seeking additional information and clarification of the government's answers, on September 23, 1976, Dettloff's attorney filed a second set of interrogatories.[20] Although all of the questions dealt with facts readily available to the Special Plans office, the U.S. Attorney's office delayed its response until June 30, 1977. When questioned on the Air Force's claim that there was no notice of an "impending attack," the government responded, "Enemy activity had built up to the extent that it was possible for a surprise attack to be launched at almost any time. There was no warning of the particular attack which overran the site."[21] The answers also continued to include careless mistakes, including the misspelling of the names of several technicians and the inclusion of Roland Hodge as a survivor.[22] More sloppiness, or outright misrepresentation, is found in the Air Force statement, "The State Department has no record of any contact by Mrs. Holland with the Embassy in Laos."[23] This silly falsehood was easily exposed when she provided copies of the correspondence she had received from the State Department and the U.S. Embassy in Laos.[24]

Answering additional queries on the U.S. air strikes, government lawyers said "General Momeyer [sic] was the authority" for the bombing.[25] Further, "All survivors were removed by helicopter shortly before the air strike by United States Air Force aircraft." On the question of photography, the Air Force said "We have been unable to locate any permanent record of the results of the photographic missions."[26]

Misspelling Momyer's name was simply stupid, but the Air Force knew four of the five technicians had been rescued by an Air America helicopter and crew. As to the lost photography, it is more than curious that the Air Force claimed it could not locate these photos. A November 1969 official Air Force study includes pictures of the site and the adjacent cliffs, with the caption "Close study of the bottom photo shows U.S. personnel hiding in rocks on side of cliff below radar site."[27]

One of the more troubling responses in this second set of interrogatories was the startling, and incorrect, government assertion that Stan Sliz was the survivor who "recalled observing Sgt. Holland being wounded and that Sgt. Holland's vocalizing thereafter during the night always had a sound consistent with internal hemorrhaging and then the sounds died and there were no more . . . indications of life from Sgt. Holland."[28] In fact, it was Jack Starling who claimed to have been near Melvin Holland and witnessed his presumed death. Such a gross error goes beyond mere incompetence; so what else might explain the statement? While it is difficult to believe the Air Force was actually seeking to substitute Sliz for Starling, perhaps the Special Plans office believed Major Sliz would make a better witness than the inconsistent Staff Sergeant Starling.[29]

Whatever the case, the facts demonstrate the government's response to these interrogatories was both slipshod and disreputable. If anyone discounted the challenges faced by Melvin Holland's wife in her struggle to pry truthful information out of the Air Force, these actions left no doubt about the baseness of her adversaries. Shielded by national security, these egregious actions would go mostly unchallenged. Justice, unfortunately, would not prevail.

On September 28, 1979, U.S. District Judge Morell E. Sharp dismissed Dettloff's case against the U.S. Government. He ruled:

> Plaintiff's claim of tortious misconduct against defendant United States of America stems from the allegation that defendant failed to candidly inform plaintiff of the facts surrounding her former husband's condition after the North Vietnamese Army attacked his Laotian outpost. In 1970, however, plaintiff was provided with a detailed account of the death. There can be no doubt that this visit . . . apprised plaintiff of her former husband's demise.

On the second cause of action for mental suffering, the judge said:

> Plaintiff's cause of action accrued when plaintiff discovered . . . the Government's concealment of the facts confirming Sergeant Holland's unfortunate death. This occurred on March 25, 1970. Plaintiff waited until July 25, 1975, to file her administrative claim. Because plaintiff was required [by law] to process her tort claim within two years after the claim accrued, plaintiff is time-barred from bringing suit for mental suffering.[30]

An appeal was filed the following month, but on June 1, 1981, the Ninth Circuit Court of Appeals affirmed the ruling.[31]

Ann Holland, the name she was using again,[32] saw her case against the government for misconduct dismissed because, as detailed above, the Air Force lied and she had no way to prove otherwise. As to her cause of action for mental suffering, this was dismissed because in 1970 she wanted to accept the information provided by the Air Force briefing team. While she had never truly believed their version of the attack, short of a lawsuit, she had exhausted all reasonable avenues to learn the truth. In effect, she was penalized for hoping the Air Force had been truthful. Unfortunately, it took another five years to discover she had been misled and turn to the legal system. Ann Holland's instincts were good; the Air Force was not telling the truth. Still, she was overwhelmed by a military system and government bureaucracy determined not to accept responsibility for eleven missing men.

The lawsuit against the Lockheed corporation labored on for

nearly another year. On March 30, 1982, U.S. District Court Judge Barbara J. Rothstein, acting on Lockheed's request for a summary judgment, ruled:

> [T]he court could find nothing to support a finding that Holland was an employee of defendant Lockheed. It is clear that the role was limited to providing "cover" . . . and that all true control and direction remained with the United States Air Force. The court finds as a matter of law that there was no employer-employee relationship between defendant Lockheed and . . . Holland. Lockheed's motion for summary judgment is granted.[33]

Holland's determination, however, resulted in an unexpected result. A second lawsuit, filed by another Heavy Green family member, was now before the federal court. Mostly based on the information developed during her legal actions, the outcome would be quite different.

Klaus R. Kirk, the stepson of teletype repairman Herbert Kirk,[34] was living in the Seattle, Washington, area when he read in a local newspaper about Holland's lawsuit. After contacting and retaining Howard Pruzan as his attorney, in April 1976, Kirk filed an administrative claim against the United States. When this proved ineffective, he initiated a lawsuit against the U.S. Government and Lockheed on behalf of himself, his mother, and his brother, for mental suffering, wrongful death, and deprivation of veteran's benefits.[35]

On April 2, 1982, Lockheed succeeded in gaining a motion for summary judgment. Three weeks later, however, the same judge delivered a split ruling in Kirk's case against the U.S. government. Kirk, who had earlier agreed to a dismissal of the wrongful death claim and the severing of his mother and brother from the suit, prevailed on the claim of mental suffering and loss of veteran's benefits. Ironically, because of Holland's perseverance, Kirk learned of the government's misconduct and was able to file his suit within the two-year requirement. Klaus v. United States of America was going forward.

On May 12, 1982, during a pretrial conference, Judge Rothstein urged the U.S. Air Force to reinstate Herbert Kirk. Six days later, representatives of the Special Plans office, the Air Force Staff Judge Advocate, and the Air Force Public Affairs office discussed how to proceed with the declassification of project Heavy Green. Apparently, the Air Force had decided to publicly disclose some details about the project in the hope this would prevent further legal action. On May 20, 1982, Heavy Green was officially declassified and a half-page summary of the loss was developed for any press inquiries. The statement made no mention of Lockheed and claimed "twelve USAF personnel were killed while operating a TACAN site."[36]

Seven years after the communists seized Indochina, the Special Plans office was still unwilling to admit there had been a bombing radar at Site 85. The absurdity of this continuing charade is reflected by the 1978 publication of General Momyer's official history, *Air Power in Three Wars*. Although, as discussed in chapter 4, there are serious misrepresentations in this monograph, Momyer had written, "In 1967, a radar bomb facility was established at Site 85 in Laos. A detachment of skilled Air Force personnel manned the radar which provided guidance to targets within 30 miles of Hanoi."[37] In another publicly available study, in 1977 Air Force historians said the Site 85 TACAN was replaced by "an all-weather navigation system, operated and maintained by 19 USAF personnel." According to a following passage, "in hand-to-hand combat" the North Vietnamese were able to reach the radar site. "12 [technicians] managed to escape and were rescued by helicopters, 4 bodies were seen in the ruins of the facility, and 3 remain unaccounted for."[38] Although these two sources were neither consistent nor accurate, the Air Force had disclosed much about Heavy Green prior to the official "declassification."[39]

More than fourteen years after his presumed death the Air Force reluctantly fulfilled its promise to Herbert Kirk.[40] He was reinstated in the military, without promotion or any decorations, and a Report of Casualty was completed on June 23, 1982. The action was filed with the Veteran's Administration and Klaus Kirk was allowed to submit a request for survivor benefits. In mid-January 1983, he received a check in the amount of $1,565.23 and a certificate for educational assistance which contained the statement, "As a child of a veteran, you have a maximum of 45 months if used prior to 12–2–77."[41] Because it was five years past this date, the stipulation made the paper worthless. The Air Force also paid Kirk's widow his government life insurance which, with accumulated interest, had increased from $10,000 to nearly $24,000.[42] If the Air Force anticipated the allocation of these benefits would end the lawsuit, however, they were quite mistaken.

On March 28 and 29, 1983, Kirk's case was presented to District Court Judge Daniel H. Thomas. Called to testify was Lieutenant

Colonel Robert Cornetti, one of the Special Plans officers instrumental in the development of the Heavy Green program.[43] Cornetti, under questioning by Judge Thomas, affirmed that because Mrs. Kirk was a German national she could not be told about the top secret project. Nonetheless, according to Cornetti, Kirk wanted to proceed and verbally agreed that "unlike the other members of the mission," in the event of his death he would not be reinstated into the Air Force. Cornetti acknowledged, however, that unlike the basic agreement signed by all the team members, this "special waiver" of Kirk's death benefits was not in writing.[44]

Judge Thomas ruled against the United States on August 12, 1983.[45] The U.S. Air Force was found negligent in failing to inform Mrs. Kirk of her husband's death which, in turn, prevented the Kirk family from receiving proper survivor benefits. In part, the judge declared, "The Court sees no justification for the Air Force's negligent failure to inform Sgt. Kirk's family . . . and its negligent failure to reinstate him so that his family could reap the proper benefits for his dedicated service."[46]

Assessing and granting appropriate damages to Klaus Kirk was a difficult task and Judge Thomas made clear his wish to underscore the Air Force's misconduct.

> The Court feels that the government had handled the Kirk situation in an inexcusable fashion, and were there sufficient evidence to indicate the value of the additional lost benefits, such as health care and commissary privileges, the Court would not hesitate to award the equivalent of their value to the plaintiff.[47]

Based on the evidence provided at trial, the loss of an estimated $452 per month in educational benefits over a period of 45 months, the judge ordered the government to pay Klaus Kirk the sum of $15,390.[48]

Although Holland's lawsuit was dismissed because it was "time-barred," ultimately her efforts resulted in the official declassification of the Heavy Green program and the reinstatement of Staff Sergeant Kirk. Moreover, it documented how the Air Force had long deceived and mistreated the families of those lost at Site 85.

Two years after Heavy Green was declassified, the U.S. Air Force awarded posthumous Bronze Star medals to the families of the eleven missing technicians. An Air Force public relations officer explained the delay by saying, "Until the incident was declassified there was no basis for awarding the Bronze Star." Notwithstanding this bizarre logic, the family of Melvin Holland agreed to receive the medal in a March 29, 1984 ceremony at McChord Air Force Base, Washington. Attending along with their mother and three sisters were John and Richard Holland, both sergeants in the United States Air Force.[49]

Over the coming years the pain of not knowing the truth would continue to haunt many of the Site 85 families. Hope and anguish would clash as additional information, both accurate and false, would emerge on the fate of the eleven men left on Phou Pha Thi. Astonishingly enough, the Heavy Green men were not even added to the U.S. government's official list of Personnel Missing in Southeast Asia roster until September 1980.[50] Until then no one in the U.S. government was looking for information related to the eleven. Thus, even if any of their names or information associated with the incident had been given to U.S. officials, a check of the list would have revealed no such loss. In many cases, no further action would be taken. The government has a list of names, and if a person is not on it, they are not considered unaccounted for.[51] Seven years after the last U.S. combat forces departed South Vietnam, and eleven years after the eleven men had been reinstated in the United States Air Force, how was such gross negligence possible?

In January 1973, the Joint Casualty Resolution Center[52] (JCRC) was formed under the command of CINCPAC "to assist the Secretaries of the Armed Services to resolve the fate of those servicemen still missing and unaccounted for as a result of the hostilities throughout Indochina." Initially established in Saigon and manned by about 140 personnel under the command of Brigadier General Robert C. Kingston, the unit was primarily designed to undertake field searches. While the majority of the personnel were U.S. Army Special Forces, all four military services were represented.[53] Shortly thereafter, as part of the reduction of U.S. forces in South Vietnam, the resolution center moved its headquarters to Nakhon Phanom Royal Thai Air Force Base in Thailand. Nakhon Phanom's proximity to Laos and North Vietnam made it an excellent launching point for projected search operations in these countries.[54] A small detachment remained in Saigon and performed difficult search and recovery work in South Vietnam. Meanwhile, other resolution center personnel consolidated and compiled records for more than 2,600 American losses.[55]

In 1976, after the fall of Saigon and the emergence of political difficulties between the United States and Thailand, the JCRC moved its headquarters to the Barbers Point U.S. Naval Air Station, on the island of Oahu, Hawaii. Concurrently, a resolution center liaison office was established at the U.S. Embassy in Bangkok. During this period the center also began a close working relationship with the U.S. Army Central Identification Laboratory (CIL), which had also been relocated from Thailand to Hawaii. The laboratory was responsible for recovering and identifying U.S. remains and, in the years to come, its personnel would accompany U.S. investigative teams on extraordinarily difficult work throughout Southeast Asia.[56]

In June 1980, Holland was interviewed by a reporter for the *Daily Astorian*, a local Oregon newspaper. Although the resulting article was similar to many previously published on the circumstances of her husband's loss, it set off alarms at the resolution center. A news-clipping service had routinely forwarded the report to its analysts who, believing they had folders on every American loss, were puzzled to find no record of Melvin Holland or anyone else lost at Site 85. Seeking assistance, the center's commander, U.S. Army Lieutenant Colonel Joe B. Harvey, queried the Defense Intelligence Agency (DIA), the organization responsible for all intelligence collection on POW-MIA matters.[57] Although Harvey recalls that the agency "did seem aware of the losses," the resolution center would wait more than a year to receive formal notification of the eleven missing men.[58]

The resolution center's query landed in the agency's POW-MIA office which, according to declassified records, quickly validated the basic information found in the Oregon newspaper article. The Phou Pha Thi losses were assigned a case reference number (REFNO) 2052, and added to a data base September 17, 1980. Nonetheless, the Defense Intelligence Agency still lacked official details on the loss. While there were at least several officials who had knowledge of the Site 85 attack,[59] apparently no one in the government ever questioned why these losses had been excluded from the roster. Now that the problem had surfaced, the Defense Intelligence Agency was obligated to formally ask Air Force Headquarters to provide information on the Site 85 incident.

Nothing about Heavy Green, however, was ever straightforward. For more than a year the Air Force and DIA wrangled over access to the material. Despite the obvious consequences involved in such a lengthy delay—the resolution center and the agency might well be losing opportunities to resolve these losses—the Air Force refused to turn over copies of their files. Finally, on November 17, 1981, the center received formal notification of the eleven missing personnel. However, the information did not come via DIA, but rather from an office a dozen miles away at Hickam Air Force Base. According to a resolution center memorandum, an Air Force officer delivered to the center a listing of "Air Force personnel engaged in a sensitive mission and declared KIA [killed in action] in 1968. The representative indicated that records concerning these individuals are presently retained by PACAF DOXZ [plans office] and are not available to JCRC due to security considerations."[60] Even though DIA had privately added the eleven names to the database fourteen months earlier, DIA and the resolution center were still without the information necessary to properly investigate these losses.

Ann Holland's newspaper interview had quite belatedly alerted the JCRC to the single greatest ground combat loss of U.S. Air Force personnel during the entire history of the Vietnam war. And yet, the Air Force refused to assist in any efforts to investigate the loss of these men. Although the JCRC leadership now realized the eleven men should be added to the list, the memorandum ended soberly:

> No effort will be made to establish a definite connection between the name list and the Phou Pha Thi incident. If, however, unidentified remains or reports of remains are received from that area, a query to PACAF for further information could be in order.[61]

The resolution center's responsibility to "resolve the fate of those servicemen still missing and unaccounted for as a result of the hostilities throughout Indochina," was not extended to project Heavy Green. Considering the timing, it appears the ongoing litigation by Ann Holland and Klaus Kirk had caused the Air Force to delay providing critical information.

Finally, in May 1982, when the Air Force was compelled by the Kirk lawsuit to declassify Heavy Green, the agency and the center were provided a few more details on the loss and allowed to publicly add the eleven names to their databases. Significantly, the Air Force did not forward any post-attack details. In particular, the critical post-attack debriefings of Stan Sliz and John Daniel were withheld and, to date, have never been read by POW-MIA investigators.[62] Similarly, the CIA has been unable to locate their March 11, 1968, interview of case officer Howard Freeman. Until my 1995 discussions with Freeman, no one involved with casualty resolution had ever had the benefit of this case officer's special perspective.[63]

Thus, fourteen years after the *Dac Cong* attack, the U.S. government was finally affording the eleven men lost at Pha Thi the same investigatory consideration given more than 2,000 other servicemen unaccounted for from the Vietnam war. Inclusion in the process, however, only ensured the case was available for analysis, considered for intelligence collection and, if the opportunity presented arose, could be raised in discussions with the governments of Laos and Vietnam.

Not surprisingly, resolving the Heavy Green losses presented peculiar challenges. Because identified PAVN units were known to have attacked the facility and then remained at the site for many years, it was clear Hanoi could provide answers about the fate of the eleven men. Unfortunately, the decade-long Laotian charade had left behind a complicating legacy of deceit. Just as the United States had denied combat operations in Laos, so, too, did the North Vietnamese. If the Vietnamese responded truthfully to questions about the attack, they would be admitting their illegal presence in neutral Laos. Such a concession would also bruise the pride of the Pathet Lao veterans who are constantly praised in government propaganda releases for their heroic armed struggle against the powerful U.S. and Royal Lao forces.[64] Indeed, for many years the Lao communists have publicized "their" successful attack on Phou Pha Thi with no mention of the Vietnamese whatever.[65] This issue is further discussed in chapter 15.

Still, 1982 was an important watershed for the Heavy Green families. Although Ann Holland's lawsuit was dismissed, the depositions and interrogatories conclusively demonstrated that the government had no compelling evidence to show all eleven men had been killed at Phou Pha Thi on March 11, 1968.[66] Far from being discouraged by the legal setback, Ann Holland redoubled her efforts to learn the truth about the attack on Site 85. Declassification of the Heavy Green program allowed the families to avail themselves of the Air Force casualty affairs system. The case was assigned an Air Force casualty representative at the Air Force Military Personnel Center, Randolph Air Force Base, Texas, whom the families were free to contact for any information. In turn, the casualty office was responsible for updating the families on any developments related their case. Holland and the other wives were no longer restricted to a contact in the Special Plans office. Just as important, the wives felt free to discuss the case with each other and to participate in national POW/MIA support groups.[67] As a result of these contacts, Ann Holland became acquainted with Mary Hall, whose husband Willis was also missing from Site 85. The wives were no longer alone, but able to share their experiences, concerns, and sources of possible information.

Holland, spurred by the inconsistencies presented by the government during her legal action, filed a Freedom of Information Act request with the Defense Intelligence Agency to view her husband's case file.[68] In December 1985 she received a set of materials, including a copy of a stunning November 17, 1972 DIA Intelligence Information Report prepared by a U.S. Army attaché in Vientiane, Laos. The report stated that in March or April 1968, "Following the NVA seizure of Phou Pha Thi, Source [a Pathet Lao defector] encountered a small armed Pathet Lao element taking a male Caucasian to the Headquarters area at Ban Na Kay [located 34 miles east of Site 85]. The individual was bound, did not seem to be injured, was in his early 20's and was wearing light colored frame glasses." According to the report, the guards, assigned to the Pathet Lao 613th infantry battalion, had captured the "American" near the base of Phou Pha Thi. In the document's comments section, the U.S. reporting officer added additional information received from a North Vietnamese defector. The man, claiming to have been a company commander with the forces who took control of Phou Pha Thi following the *Dac Cong* attack, reported he "saw no Americans . . . although he did hear that all Americans had been thrown over the cliff by the NVA sappers." To these allegations the American reporter observed, "This is the first report this office has seen that one of the US personnel (all presumed killed) at Phou Pha Thi may have been captured. JPRC records do not indicate any prior report concerning US personnel captured, missing, or killed at Phou Pha Thi."[69]

Attached to the intelligence report was a February 2, 1978 DIA evaluation which began, "This report was previously evaluated on 10 January 1973. It is currently being reevaluated in light of further analysis." The evaluation then discussed the case of Major Donald E. Westbrook, the pilot lost near Site 85 on March 13, 1968.[70]

The evaluator concluded it was "unlikely" the report was related to Westbrook because there was no mention of the captive being a pilot, the circumstances of loss indicated Westbrook had not survived the crash, and Westbrook "was in his early 40's at the time of this incident." The final sentence in the evaluation read, "Moreover, it is believed there were no survivors of the Phou Pha Thi attack."[71]

Ann Holland now had written confirmation of one of her worst fears. The U.S. government had received information from an intelligence source that seemed to correlate directly to Site 85 and the possibility of at least one survivor. There was also information, of unsure reliability, that detailed post-attack PAVN activities related to the Americans at Site 85. However, as the reporting officer observed in 1972, because the Americans associated with Site 85 were "presumed dead," no one was pursuing the information. And, six years later, the evaluation repeats the belief there were no LS 85 survivors.[72] Curiously, the presence of the report in Melvin Holland's file was an indication someone in DIA thought there might be a connection.

As extensively documented in earlier chapters, this presumption of death was based upon highly questionable sources and an incomplete investigation. And, without cooperation from the Air Force, DIA probably had no way to know there was no clear proof of how, where, and if all the missing Heavy Green personnel had died at Site 85.[73]

In any case, in 1978 the Defense Intelligence Agency and the Joint Casualty Resolution Center could only continue to collect and analyze information from a distance. Both organizations developed useful programs to "screen" thousands of refugees for POW/MIA-associated information.[74] Nonetheless, while the screening projects have proved important in resolving some cases, few of these people would have possessed definitive information on the Heavy Green losses. The answers were in Hanoi and Vientiane and it would be sixteen more years before the U.S. government was permitted to conduct a meaningful investigation of these losses.

Although these revelations infuriated Ann Holland, there was little she could do beyond publicly telling her story and hoping that additional details would surface. Four years later, a comprehensive, formerly top secret, document on Heavy Green suddenly appeared.

During a discussion with her Air Force casualty officer Mrs. Holland was told about the existence of an August 1968 Air Force report, "The Fall of Site 85." She formally requested access to the material and in September 1986 was provided a declassified, but not redacted,[75] copy of the report.[76] A minor firestorm ensued. Written as part of the

U.S. Air Force Contemporary Historical Examination of Current Operations (CHECO) project, the study was authored by an Air Force captain who received access to many key documents and interviewed a number of Air Force personnel with first-hand knowledge of the Heavy Green program and the loss of Site 85. He did not, however, talk with any of the survivors.[77] Considering the sensitivities involved, the CIA, State Department, a top secret Air Force bombing project, all taking place in supposedly neutral Laos, it is remarkable the document was even allowed to be written. Perhaps the Air Force leadership decided, in documenting an otherwise successful bombing program, it would be useful to have a record that indicated the Heavy Green technicians were judged to have been culpable in their own deaths. Neither of these findings was true, of course.

The release of the CHECO report caused a brief media reaction. On October 5, 1986, *The Sunday Oklahoman* published a major story on the report complete with photos of Ambassador Sullivan and Prime Minister Souvanna Phouma. The paper excerpted passages, including Sullivan's message to Momyer disputing the general's characterization that the Site 85 attack had been a "surprise." An accompanying story featured the recollections of Major Stan Sliz, with quotes from his May 1970 classified discussions with Senator Symington.[78]

On November 23, 1986, the newspaper followed-up with a story based on formerly classified DIA documents obtained through a Freedom of Information Act (FOIA) request. In addition to documenting the 1972 report of a Caucasian prisoner captured near Site 85, the paper disclosed a gruesome 1980 refugee account. According to the report, a Pathet Lao propaganda film showed American bodies at the site while the accompanying narrative claimed the remains were thrown over the cliff. The 1980 report was further delineated by a May 1974 DIA intelligence summary which stated "The NVA supposedly threw the captured U.S. personnel off of the cliffs to be dashed to death on the rocks below. Reportedly, the NVA sapper company involved was withdrawn to NVN to avoid having the atrocity publicized; the NVA sapper company commander was subsequently court martialed."[79]

Nevertheless, this extraordinary story quickly faded away. There was momentary outrage over the loss of the men; the larger story of a coverup, and the possible abandonment of live American serviceman in Laos, was yet to fully emerge.

14

"The Highest National Priority" [1]

Like the Vietnam War itself, U.S. efforts to gain the fullest possible accounting for the families of those who remain missing continues to be a deeply emotional subject for the American public.[2] Reconciliation between the United States and the communist governments of Laos and Vietnam was delayed, in part, because of this highly charged topic.[3] Deep suspicion exists on both sides. Professor Allen E. Goodman of Georgetown University has written, "Vietnamese leaders have tended to think that the MIA issue was a veil behind which successive U.S. administrations were seeking to impoverish the country and overthrow the government. U.S. leaders saw the limited steps the Vietnamese took between 1975 and 1989 to cooperate with American investigators as evidence of 'callousness and deceit' on the issue."[4] As succinctly described by a Pentagon analyst involved in the negotiations process:

The initial post-1975 position taken by the Vietnamese on the POW/MIA issue was fundamentally uncooperative and inflexible. In part it may have been a visceral response to the thought of assisting American invaders to account for their missing in the face of so much devastation inflicted on Vietnam by the United States. Another decade would pass before significant internal political changes, shifting regional alignments, changing Western interests, Sino-Soviet rapprochement, and progress towards a nonmilitary settlement of the Cambodian conflict would bring Hanoi to the point of rethinking its . . . need to take steps to resolve the POW/MIA issue.[5]

Further, as the analyst continued, although publicly framed by both sides as a humanitarian matter, "For Vietnam, economic calculations were often at the core of decisions to improve cooperation with the U.S. in efforts to account for missing Americans."[6]

In other words, the stimulus for Hanoi had little or nothing to do with any beneficent impulse to locate and return American remains. Vietnam, understandably, was simply undertaking a pragmatic policy designed to advance its own national interests. Some Americans, however, have interpreted Vietnamese assistance as complete cooperation. As discussed later, Hanoi and Vientiane have carefully controlled the pace and level of access to significant wartime witnesses and archival materials. Moreover, while the Vietnamese and Lao governments carefully staff their "missing persons" offices with trained security and intelligence personnel, the U.S. has regularly assigned these important investigative matters to well-meaning but often poorly qualified active duty and retired military personnel.

The communist government of Laos has an especially difficult political problem vis-à-vis the POW-MIA issue. The Pathet Lao military forces played a limited combat role in the "liberation" of their country. In northern Laos the North Vietnamese shouldered the great majority of significant ground actions against Royal Lao forces; mostly Hmong soldiers under the command of General Vang Pao and the CIA.[7] In southern Laos, the North Vietnamese exercised even greater dominance: they essentially annexed the panhandle of the country for their transportation and supply efforts into South Vietnam and Cambodia. As a result, more than 80 percent of U.S. losses in Laos are judged to have occurred in areas under Vietnamese control.[8] Because their party history is built on the pretense of a long and glorious armed struggle, Pathet Lao veterans are loath to admit their relatively minor wartime military role. Queries to the Lao, therefore, must be couched in language that does not highlight their wartime subordination to the Vietnamese.

Nonetheless, Pathet Lao forces did work closely with the North Vietnamese forces and the present Lao government has or could easily acquire information of significant POW-MIA accounting value. Although the U.S. has repeatedly requested permission to examine relevant wartime archival materials and to interview informed Lao veterans who served in areas of known American losses, the Lao have consistently refused. Likewise, U.S. attempts to follow-up Lao press reports or to view films containing details of U.S. losses are routinely turned away. Ironically, with regard to permitting access to wartime witnesses and archival materials, the Lao have been far less cooperative than the Vietnamese.[9]

Credible research on the second Indochina war must involve access to communist wartime veterans and their records. In August 1990, I traveled to Laos to interview senior Pathet Lao officials.[10] My goal was to obtain recollections of their military and political response to the vast U.S. wartime assistance effort in Laos.[11] I interviewed former defense minister General Khamouan Boupha and General Singkapo Sikhotchounamaly, formerly commander of the Pathet Lao military forces. I also spoke at length with Sisana Sisane, Chairman of the Social Sciences Research Committee and an important wartime official. While interviewing General Singkapo in the company of U.S. Deputy Chargé Karl E. Wycoff, also a Lao speaker, Singkapo quickly and casually responded to a general question on the battle at Phou Pha Thi.[12]

The General's answer remains a subject of great controversy. He declared that he had been the commander of the Pathet Lao forces assigned to the Pha Thi area and "about one hundred Pathet Lao and more than two hundred North Vietnamese were involved in the attack. Some injured Americans were captured at the site and sent to North Vietnam."[13] Singkapo further asserted that the Lao communists, as a matter of policy, always turned over captured Americans to the North Vietnamese. Wycoff and I were both taken aback at these statements and, to ensure there would be no misunderstanding, Wycoff then restated the general's comments. Singkapo affirmed that these were his recollections. Wycoff asked if the general would be willing to be interviewed by U.S. specialists on this subject, and he unhesitatingly agreed.

This was the first instance of any informed senior Lao communist official discussing the Pha Thi battle and alleging that some Americans had survived. There were many obvious follow-up questions, but Wycoff and I felt assured of Singkapo's future cooperation. I had no idea that our brief discussion would be the only useful talk any American would have with him on the topic of LS 85. I then changed the subject and continued with the interview.

Two weeks later I again interviewed Singkapo but did not raise the issue of Pha Thi. Because the purpose of my research was to learn more about the Pathet Lao response to U.S. support for the Royal Lao government, and I was not officially involved in POW-MIA work, further questioning on the subject seemed inappropriate. During both sessions I found him to be consistently clear and precise in his recollections of specific wartime events. Indeed, Singkapo took great pleasure in recounting his contributions to the revolution. I believe he perceived our talk as an opportunity to place his personal history in an American study of the war. He was quite open and, doubtless, did not consider the full ramifications of his remarks.[14]

Upon completion of my research in Laos, I flew to Bangkok for a brief layover en route to my home in Honolulu. I reported to the U.S. Embassy and discussed Singkapo's remarks with the resolution center liaison office commander, an Air Force lieutenant colonel. Seemingly oblivious to the importance of these statements, he told me to "debrief myself" on the meeting. Relatively new to the job, and apparently intimidated by his subordinates, the officer was unwilling to assign anyone to interview me.

Because I was scheduled to depart the next morning, I contacted a friend in the Bangkok DIA POW-MIA intelligence collection office, called "Stony Beach."[15] I then discussed the matter by secure telephone with a senior DIA POW-MIA official in Washington. Based on the phone call and a just-received State Department cable on the subject, he told me DIA had sufficient information to follow-up the Singkapo meeting. The next morning I departed for Hawaii where, some weeks later, I was interviewed by a resolution center sergeant.

Upon my return to Honolulu I learned that Singkapo's Phou Pha Thi remarks had created quite a stir in various U.S. government agencies. DIA's POW-MIA office quickly asked the State Department to request an official interview with the general. When news of my discussion with the general reached the Lao government, the immediate reaction was to disavow the remarks and characterize Singkapo as an ignorant old fool.[16] An especially well educated Lao, who had served the Pathet Lao for more than thirty years and risen to become a member of the Lao Communist Central Committee and commander of the Lao military, the general was now being dismissed as insignificant and uninformed.[17]

DIA had reason to be very interested in General Singkapo. The agency had at least three intelligence reports that placed him in direct contact with American prisoners of war and another where he related specific knowledge of U.S. prisoners. One case involved U.S. Navy

Lieutenant Charles Klusmann, shot down near the Plain of Jars on June 6, 1964. Klusmann was captured by Pathet Lao soldiers and held for three months before successfully escaping with the assistance of a Lao prisoner to a friendly area. According to Klusmann, Singkapo paid two visits to his jail camp and asked if he was being properly treated.[18] In February 1965 an intelligence source reported that Singkapo had assured the Pathet Lao spokesman, Soth Phetrasy, of the "well-being" of five American prisoners.[19] In an April 1967 intelligence document it was reported that in May 1965 "Two American pilots in flight suits with the insignia of rank removed were being held under armed guard in the general's [Singkapo] house."[20] Moreover, on March 23, 1973 the U.S. Embassy related discussions with a Swedish television crew just returned from the Pathet Lao headquarters in Sam Neua. According to the Swedes, they had spoken at length with Pathet Lao leader Prince Souphanouvong and Singkapo. On the subject of American POWs, the communist leaders said the issue was "too delicate" to discuss. Nonetheless, the media crew was told by another official that the Pathet Lao did hold some U.S. prisoners.[21] Clearly, Singkapo had been in a position to be aware of policies and information related to American POWs.

On October 25, 1990, in anticipation of an interview between a Resolution Center linguist and Singkapo, the DIA POW-MIA office sent Resolution Center headquarters a message with five pages of questions. The introduction to the queries began, "It is our feeling that he [Singkapo] is one of the most knowledgeable Lao officials with regard to the PW [prisoner of war] issue. This may be the only opportunity for years to address the PW issue openly with a senior LPDR official."[22] In spite of pledges of POW-MIA cooperation, however, the Lao government steadfastly refused to allow any reinterview.

Frustrated by the Lao intransigence, on April 29, 1991, a DIA message summarized the Lao attitude and proposed another approach.

In August 1990 . . . General Singkapo made one of the most significant LPDR government revelations in the PW issue since the end of the Vietnam war. Despite the sincere efforts of AMEMBASSY, Vientiane; State Department; JCRC Liaison; and DIA/PW-MIA among others to investigate . . . the Lao government has successfully stonewalled all USG attempts. Their claims that General Singkapo is senile, or that he knows nothing of the PW-MIA issue, and their inferences that he will be "busy" the next time we ask to see him are shallow. DIA PW/MIA recommends that since efforts to reinterview Singkapo have gone nowhere, that we abandon the effort to interview him in Laos. We would suggest that an effort be undertaken to interview him outside Laos.[23]

Meanwhile, pressure was growing at senior levels in the administration of President George Bush to force the Lao hand. In what was surely a calculated government leak, on June 3, 1991, *The Washington Times* published a lengthy article "Laos Blocking Queries on MIAs." Quoting from the still-classified message, the reaction of "Bush administration officials," and an official Pentagon spokesman, the paper reported Singkapo's August 1990 comments and the Lao government's refusal to make him available for an interview. The article also noted a possible correlation between the general's statements and the 1972 report of a Caucasian with glasses captured by the Pathet Lao shortly after the loss of Site 85.[24]

Two weeks after the newspaper's criticism, the U.S. Embassy in Vientiane gained an appointment with Vice Foreign Minister Soubanh Srithirath, the U.S. government's principal interlocutor on POW-MIA issues. Deputy Chargé Wycoff stressed the importance to U.S.-Lao relations of resolving the impasse and permitting U.S. specialists to question General Singkapo. Ignoring the fact that the Chargé had heard the exchange, Soubanh insisted Singkapo was senile and had been misunderstood. Although Wycoff assured the vice minister he personally monitored the talk and there was no mistaking Singkapo's words, Soubanh would not budge.[25] It was the typical Lao reaction to U.S. evidence of Lao "knowledgeability" of POW-MIA information—deny, obfuscate, and refuse to answer.

Two months after the Soubanh-Wycoff meeting, and nearly a year after his Pha Thi comments, Singkapo was finally made available for a brief statement. D. Warren Gray, DIA's senior Lao analyst and Master Sergeant William Gadoury, a Resolution Center Lao linguist, flew to Vientiane to conduct an interview. After several days of delay with no interview in the offing, Gray decided to return to Washington. Shortly thereafter, Gadoury was allowed to meet briefly with Singkapo whereupon the general said the information gained from the August 1990 interview was "incorrect" and he had been "misunderstood."[26] The Lao government considered the matter closed and, indeed, the U.S. government has never asked for another meeting with the general.

Several points must be made with regard to my interview with General Singkapo. First, as indicated earlier, I did not probe him on the loss of Site 85. I believed he would soon be questioned by a POW-MIA investigator who, with the proper preparation and access to U.S. government materials, could conduct a much more informed interview. Had I suspected the Lao would block access to him, I might well have attempted to gain further information in our second meeting. Gregarious and anxious to frame his place in history, Singkapo loved to talk about his contributions to the revolution.

A thorough and truthful discussion would likely have answered many troubling questions about the captured Americans. Clearly, he was following the Lao communist practice of excising out Vietnamese military involvement in favor of Pathet Lao exploits; there is no doubt the North Vietnamese surrounded, attacked, and overran Site 85. It is, therefore, unlikely the Pathet Lao would have been in a position to capture any of the Heavy Green personnel. However, given Singkapo's military and political position, it is quite likely he would have been informed of any American prisoners. In an effort to inflate his own role he may have appropriated the actions of the North Vietnamese. His second statement, that there was a Pathet Lao policy to release U.S. prisoners to the Vietnamese communists, was a significant admission. This acknowledgment, which confirmed what many intelligence specialists had long suspected, allowed the general to claim the Pathet Lao had captured Americans but could not account for them because the men were no longer in their custody.[27]

I am convinced General Singkapo, a senior Pathet Lao wartime leader with impeccable Lao Communist Party credentials, has detailed knowledge of the attack on Site 85. Moreover, I believe he knows what became of the bodies, any survivors, and the equipment and personal effects of the Heavy Green team. Although I do not think Singkapo was present at Phou Pha Thi during the attack, I am confident the North Vietnamese provided him and other senior Pathet Lao leaders with a detailed account of the events. It is important to recall that the Lao communist headquarters was located in a cave complex at Vieng Sai, only thirty miles from Site 85.[28]

Notwithstanding their stonewalling on General Singkapo's Site 85 remarks, the Lao government was sophisticated enough to understand the United States was not going to walk away from efforts to achieve an accounting for the more than five hundred men still listed as unaccounted for in Laos.[29] While archival research and interviews with wartime veterans were off-limits, the resolution center had been allowed to undertake limited field work. In December 1983 a joint Lao-U.S. team surveyed a crash site near Pakse in southern Laos. However, the Lao dragged out permission for an actual excavation until February 1985. The twelve-day recovery operation "yielded a sizable quantity of highly fragmented skeletal and dental remains." Secretary of State George Schultz, seeking to commend the Lao political elite for their cooperation, sent a personal thank-you letter to the Lao Foreign Ministry.[30] Apparently, the recognition missed its target audience. Like the Vietnamese, the Lao publicly spoke of the humanitarian nature of the work but privately demanded an economic *quid pro* as the price of searching for America's missing. In mid-December 1985 the U.S. Congress enacted legislation permitting bilateral U.S. development assistance. Several weeks later the Lao government allowed a survey of another crash location near the southern town of Muong Phine. A successful excavation of remains followed the next month, but by year's end there had been no further field operations in Laos. A resolution center report observed there was "scant hope for meaningful progress when Laos allows only one excavation per year."[31]

The collapse of communism in eastern Europe,[32] however, was having a significant impact on fraternal economic and military assistance to Laos and its principal ally, Vietnam. During the second half of the 1980s the Soviets were annually providing between $40 and $50 million in economic aid and up to $100 million in cash and military hardware to the Lao armed forces.[33] Moscow's military and economic aid to Vietnam has been estimated in the billions of dollars.[34] In turn, from 1975 to 1985 Hanoi provided Vientiane with some $133 million in economic assistance. Although exact figures on Vietnamese military aid to Vientiane are unavailable, up to 50,000 North Vietnamese soldiers are known to have remained in Laos until the late 1980s.[35] The collapse of the Soviet Union triggered a significant economic and political domino effect on Hanoi and Vientiane; in order to survive they were forced to seek other sources of assistance, including from the United States.

In 1989, after U.S. humanitarian aid funds were used to construct a medical clinic in a southern Lao village, the Lao expanded bilateral discussions on POW-MIA matters and other issues. A former resolution center official has opined, "Lao cooperation may also have benefitted from and been stimulated by the improved atmosphere . . . with Vietnam."[36] Indeed, in 1987 President Ronald Reagan had appointed retired General John W. Vessey, Jr., former Chairman of the Joint Chiefs, to be a special POW-MIA emissary.[37] Vessey had led a vigorous campaign to gain Vietnamese assistance and, while the general and his staff focused their attention on Hanoi, these activities were closely watched in Vientiane.[38] By 1991 the Lao government was slowly developing a cordial working relationship with the United States on a number of other important bilateral concerns, including increased U.S. economic assistance and the institution of counter-narcotics programs in the opium-rich mountains of Laos. Nonetheless, the decision not to make Singkapo available for a serious interview was an important signal that Lao cooperation on the MIA-POW issue would have very defined limits.

American public interest in resolving the Southeast Asia POW-MIA conundrum, however, had been growing for several years, and there was now considerable political pressure to learn more about the fate of America's missing. On August 2, 1991, a *Wall Street Journal*/NBC News poll revealed that 69 percent of Americans believed that U.S. prisoners of war were still being held in Indochina. This was a shocking indication of the public's lack of faith in nearly two decades of U.S. POW investigations, doubtless encouraged by a spate of absurd Hollywood action movies depicting American POWs in Southeast Asian prison camps.[39] The POW-MIA issue has always been plagued by such foolishness which, inevitably, reduces the impact of credible sources of information. In the years to come genuine photographs, from Vietamese archives, would provide irrefutable evidence that Vietnamese officials had knowledge of unaccounted-for Americans.[40] On the same day the *Wall Street Journal*/NBC poll appeared, the U.S. Senate established a Select Committee on POW/MIA Affairs. The staff work and publicity associated with the committee, led by a number of influential and ambitious senators, mightily influenced significant changes in the accounting of those missing in America's wars and conflicts.[41] After fifteen months of world-wide travel, comprehensive hearings, and detailed investigations, the committee issued a 1,200-page report. A review of the document by the Library of Congress Congressional Research Service concluded, "Although it was possible some POWs were not returned at the end of the war, there was no compelling evidence that any remain alive in captivity; and that although there was no 'conspiracy' to cover up live POWs, there was serious U.S. government neglect and mismanagement of the issue."[42] The latter statement came as no surprise to Ann Holland and others who had been victimized by the Air Force and the POW-MIA accounting system.

One immediate result of the committee's work and the administration's desire to demonstrate progress on the issue was the formation of Joint Task Force-Full Accounting (JTF-FA). Established in January 1992 under the command of CINCPAC and based at Camp Smith, Hawaii, the JTF-FA quickly grew to a strength of some 150 military members[43] and civilian personnel commanded by an army brigadier general. The resolution center, at the time comprising about forty people, was assimilated into the new organization.[44] The joint task force, which was envisioned as a temporary operation,[45] soon grew to include small detachments in Vientiane, Hanoi, Phnom Penh, and a significant logistics hub in Bangkok. There would be plenty of desirable military and civilian assignments, most with promotion potential. As one serious researcher has noted:

> Launching a new "joint" command was an unprecedented step in the fall of 1991, the period that has come to be known as the official end of the Cold War. Elsewhere in the U.S. military establishment individual armed service commands and joint units were being rolled up and abolished. So the creation of the JTF/FA was a real windfall for the Pacific Command. As the rest of the military was shrinking, CINCPAC's empire was waxing fat.[46]

During this same period, DIA increased manning authorizations for the Bangkok-based Stony Beach operations that had been underway since May 1987. Stony Beach officers and enlisted men now sought information in Vietnamese refugee camps in Hong Kong, Singapore, Indonesia, Malaysia, and the Philippines. In Thailand, Stony Beach linguists interviewed thousands of Lao, Cambodians, and Vietnamese for POW-MIA information at refugee camps throughout the country.[47] They also carried out special investigations, mostly related to purported sightings of live American prisoners. One of the most widely publicized cases involved a photo, dubbed "The Three Amigos." In August 1990 Stony Beach investigator George Scearce wrote the first report on a photo of three purported American prisoners. Supposedly the men were being held by the Vietnamese, but could be ransomed for $2.4 million. Although DIA believed it was a scam, several family members came forward to say the photo showed their loved ones. Indeed, the middle-aged men in the photo did bear a striking resemblance to artist's depictions of how the men might look after two decades. POW-MIA activists demanded answers and in July 1991, the photo appeared on the cover of *Newsweek* magazine. A year later Stony Beach investigators searching the National Library in Phnom Penh found the original photograph in a 1989 edition of *Soviet Life*. The picture, actually taken in 1923, showed three farmers celebrating a harvest in Uzbekistan.[48]

In the midst of this heightened public interest, CINCPAC and the joint task force were scrambling to put together an effective accounting plan that would respond to the concerns of the Senate Select Committee and be acceptable to the governments of Laos, Cambodia, and Vietnam. In April 1991 General Vessey had succeeded in gaining Vietnamese permission for the establishment of a U.S. POW-MIA office in Hanoi. The joint task force took over this operation, created similar offices in Vientiane and Phnom Penh, and began to undertake a robust schedule of field investigations, remains recovery operations, and archival research.

Unlike the earlier low-key operations, the the joint task force was being driven by a hard-charging general who demanded "results."[49] Brigadier General Thomas Needham was a lifelong bachelor, "married to the army," as he once told his Cambodian counterpart. He was under considerable pressure from CINCPAC and Washington to demonstrate success and, for those who worked for or around him, it was often a very unpleasant experience. Disdainful of language-qualified area experts and intelligence officers, the infantryman quickly alienated scores of long-term Indochina watchers who marveled that someone with so little intellectual curiosity could have risen to such a senior position. The answer was that Needham was considered an operations expert with an extraordinary capacity to develop and oversee complex military endeavors. Devoted to knowing the smallest details, he was the quintessential micro-manager. The General knew how to make the trains run on time.[50]

While this expertise had presumably worked well in the infantry, Needham's one-dimensional perspective quickly brought him into conflict with some of his subordinates. However, as General Needham soon made clear his willingness to end the career of any military member or civilian employee who did not comply with his instructions, most people within Needham's grasp did not dare question his methods or vision.[51] With remarkable single-minded intensity he moved the new organization forward.

The joint task force had to be capable of deploying people and equipment to some of the most inhospitable and dangerous areas in the world. Working in the mountains and jungles of Vietnam, Laos, and Cambodia, constantly on guard against unexploded ordnance, reptiles, other wild animals, and disease required well trained personnel. These talents were available in the military services and, in fact, the joint task force detachment commanders were selected for their ability to command troops in remote and challenging conditions. Nonetheless, the joint task force did encounter a serious shortfall in other essential skills.

Military and civilian personnel with appropriate Southeast Asia training and language expertise were rare. Most were assigned to either the National Security Agency or the Defense Intelligence Agency's Stony Beach program. A good number had come over from the old resolution center and became the core of their linguists and analysts. But expanded operations required more personnel. Needham, insisting he wanted a completely overt "vanilla" operation, would have nothing to do with any intelligence personnel. Desperate to fill out the projected field teams, the joint task force turned to a problematic pool of earnest young military men. Irrespective of their current occupations and skills, the joint task force began to accept ethnic Lao, Vietnamese, and Cambodian U.S. military personnel. The task force was soon staffed with cooks, medical technicians, truck drivers, and the like—anyone who could pass the language test. All were enlisted personnel, most with high school educations, and many had difficulty with written English. The majority had never conducted any kind of interview, let alone questioning and interpreting under sensitive political conditions. The joint task force, intent on collecting enough Lao, Vietnamese, and Cambodian speakers, had overlooked the capacity of these young servicemen to construct and pose questions, write up the material in reports, and serve as translators at meetings and official functions. These were all skills taught in military and civilian courses, but not made available to these Southeast Asian-Americans; they would receive on-the-job training.

The majority had left Southeast Asia as children and had little understanding of their former homelands. History, geography, social conventions, and even significant changes in current language usage were often unknown to them. Like most Americans of their generation, they knew little about the war or the political and military structure of the Lao and Vietnamese communist governments. Such a background, of course, was key to meaningful interviewing and archival research.[52] More importantly, the joint task force had not considered the distaste Lao and Vietnamese cadre would frequently feel toward those who had chosen to flee communism. Senior officers at the joint task force also failed to recognize that while native speakers seemed to offer the U.S. advantages, persons who might easily blend into the population were anathema to the public security officials given the task of controlling American movements in Laos and Vietnam.

Not surprisingly, Vietnam and Laos both resisted the entry of these native speakers. This reduced the joint task force's capability to conduct field and archival work and for several years was a major point of contention, especially in Laos. One example provides some insight into this issue. On September 9, 1992, the joint task force hosted a delegation of Lao officials at Camp Smith, Hawaii. Several ethnic Lao sergeants had worked very hard to prepare for a meeting in which they would translate for Needham and provide a briefing for the Lao visitors. Within minutes of beginning his translation one of these sincere young men, under enormous pressure, found himself stumbling and unable to keep up. He was then humiliated by the senior Lao official, Done Somvorachit, who began to correct, in English, the young man's Lao. Needham seethed while his terrified officers tried to gain control of the situation. Done, quite amused, then proclaimed in English that he would translate for himself. In mere moments the Lao had gained enormous face and belittled the powerful American general and his staff.

Needham, however, had not learned his lesson. Making light of the sergeant's performance, he formally requested the Lao government's approval to permit ethnic Lao servicemen to participate in field operations. Done agreed to consider this only if the men would provide the Lao government with complete information on family members remaining in Laos and family residing in the United States. Without a moment's hesitation Needham agreed and ordered all of the Lao to comply. "I'll have the information to you before you leave," he announced. Unbelievably, the general had just directed a group of American citizens to surrender to a communist government personal family information which might then be used by the Lao to pressure any number of people. As the U.S. servicemen raced off to meet the general's demands and Needham departed the conference room, a longtime Indochina watcher quietly observed "That was the most shameful performance by a senior commander I have ever seen. In an effort to gain answers about our missing men Needham just trampled on the rights of his defenseless men."[53]

Even though Needham provided the detailed dossiers, the Lao government later declared the men were unacceptable and refused them visas. Needham's uncaring abuse of command came to nothing—except that the Lao security services had easily obtained a great deal of information on American citizens and their extended families.

Two months later, after determined intervention by the State Department, the Lao government approved a single Lao-American for a brief stay in Laos. Over time additional Lao-American servicemen have been permitted into Laos, but the joint task force continues this egregious practice of submitting detailed information on U.S. citizens.

In order that the POW-MIA families and the American public have faith in these important government efforts, the operation and standards of the joint task force should be judged by a rigorous scholarly analysis of their voluminous field investigations and archival research reporting.[54] The required examination is beyond the scope of this study, but there are several policies which are relevant to the eleven American missing from Site 85.

On June 28, 1995, former JCRC and the joint task force Vietnamese linguist/analyst Michael Janich testified before the U.S. House Subcommittee on Military Personnel. Janich, who served successfully as a field investigations team leader from 1992 until his resignation in 1994, provided specific examples of what he believed were sloppy investigations and disingenuous report writing. Of particular relevance to the Site 85 losses were Janich's comments about Needham's directive to place speed over accuracy. Janich recalled that in a large meeting in Bangkok the general outlined his policy by "criticizing JCRC's methods as being too slow and cumbersome. He then explained what he called his '80 percent rule.' His philosophy, and consequently that of his new command, was that completing a task quickly with an 80 percent standard of success was preferable to completing it perfectly but taking more time. He emphasized this rule was to be the guiding principle in all JTF operations." Janich also spoke on the issue of linguist/analyst qualifications.

> The rapid establishment of JTF-FA also led to the rather haphazard selection of junior military personnel to fill linguist and analyst billets. Native speakers . . . were recruited from military occupation specialities totally unrelated to the JTF-FA mission. Analysts were typically selected from the ranks of Order of Battle (OB) analysts, whose analytical skills and methods differed considerably from that required to successfully analyze information obtained during field operations.[55]

At the urging of the National League of Families of American Prisoners and Missing in Southeast Asia POW-MIA, U.S. Senator Sam Nunn (D., Georgia) asked CINCPAC to investigate Janich's charges. CINCPAC responded with a fifteen-page point-by-point letter, causing many observers to suspect the criticism had touched a raw nerve. Interestingly enough, the rebuttal confirmed many of Janich's statements. On the "80 percent rule" CINCPAC replied, "JCRC's methods were too slow and inefficient to meet the challenge of the expanding access afforded by Vietnam while guarding against the risk that political changes would end the access with little accomplished. JTF-FA's policy was to investigate each case thoroughly, yet quickly at least once and gather as much information as possible." On the subject of qualified personnel the letter stated, "The lack of trained linguist/analysts is not unique to the military services. JTF-FA could not delay its operations to locate suitable analyst/linguists." Nonetheless, CINCPAC assured Senator Nunn that despite an initial "significant amount of suspicion and hostility exhibited by our hosts, primarily in Vietnam and Laos" relations had improved over time."[56]

Because CINCPAC feared the Vietnamese and Lao might suddenly close down POW-MIA operations Needham was willing to carry out his mission in a less than professional manner. The message from above seemed clear: "something was better than nothing." While the joint task force has done excellent work on hundreds of cases, accomplished by dedicated men and women under extraordinarily difficult circumstances, the leadership has fallen short. Regrettably, the Vietnamese and Lao realized that some officials involved in the U.S. government POW-MIA issue wanted to demonstrate success at almost any

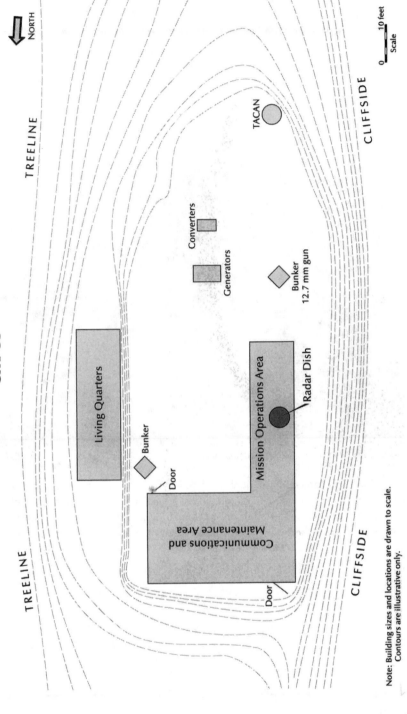

SITE 85

NORTH

TREELINE

TREELINE

Living Quarters

Bunker

Door

Communications and
Maintenance Area

Mission Operations Area

Radar Dish

Door

Converters

Generators

Bunker
12.7 mm gun

TACAN

CLIFFSIDE

CLIFFSIDE

0   10 feet
Scale

Note: Building sizes and locations are drawn to scale.
Contours are illustrative only.

This North Vietnamese photograph of the Heavy Green buildings was taken within days of the capture of Site 85. Found in 1981 by an American journalist in the photographic archives of the Lao Ministry of Information and Propaganda, it confirms the communists seized the facilities nearly intact and took steps to document their prize.

(NORTH VIETNAMESE PHOTO)

In March 1994, nearly twenty-six years to the day after the attack on Site 85, an NBC News team and members of the Pentagon's casualty resolution task force reached the former Heavy Green area. Looking toward the north, this was all that remained of the original 150 tons of equipment needed to operate the radar facility.

(AUTHOR'S COLLECTION)

March 1994 close-up view of the remaining pieces of the radar facility, looking to the west. (AUTHOR'S COLLECTION)

March 1994 close-up of the generators that once powered the radar facility.

Some Vietnamese communist officers claim to have seen American bodies in this ravine located just north and below the radar facility. A complete U.S. search of this area in December 1994 failed to locate any human remains.

In 1994 a Pentagon team, under the supervision of a trained forensic anthropologist, scoured Phou Pha Thi for any clues. They found nothing, suggesting the communists had removed the remains or that they had been obliterated by U.S. bombing.

(AUTHOR'S COLLECTION)

The NBC News team, Lao government officials, and local residents in March 1994 in front of a former wartime cave complex in Sam Neua, Laos. In addition to visiting Phou Pha Thi, NBC was provided unique access to many of the Lao government's most important wartime facilities.

(AUTHOR'S COLLECTION)

Twenty-six years after his dramatic rescue from Site 85, Jack Starling (L) meets with his former commander, Jerry Clayton. Starling, now a hospital facilities maintenance supervisor, was picked up by an Air Force helicopter following a night of playing dead in the midst of the North Vietnamese onslaught. (AUTHOR'S COLLECTION)

On March 11, 1968, in the midst of the North Vietnamese attack, John Daniel (L) and Stan Sliz sought safety on a narrow ledge just below the radar buildings. They endured hours of terror as the communist sappers tossed explosives and fired on them with automatic weapons. Both sustained serious wounds and, in October 1994, they met at an Air Force facility in Colorado named for the "Skyspot" radar bombing program. (AUTHOR'S COLLECTION)

The Vietnamese government has for years claimed to possess little information on the loss of Site 85. During a 1994 visit to the Vietnamese Air Force museum in Hanoi, the author found a prominent and detailed display of the January 1968 attack by AN-2 Colt biplanes. This photograph claims to show one of the victorious aircrews. The display underscores the Vietnamese penchant for keeping records and propagandizing wartime activities. (AUTHOR'S COLLECTION)

An AN-2 Colt biplane, similar to those used in the January 1968 aerial bombing of Site 85. This incident, the only communist air attack against U.S. forces during the entire war, underscores the importance Hanoi placed on destroying the facility.

(AUTHOR'S COLLECTION)

Captain Russ Cayler, commanding rescue helicopter "Jolly Green Giant 67," hovering just yards away from the radar buildings and hidden North Vietnamese soldiers, made the prudent decision not to fire on communist forces. Cayler recalls seeing American bodies near where Jack Starling was rescued. (COURTESY JOE PANZA)

Captain Joe Panza, co-pilot of "Jolly Green 67," assisted Cayler in maintaining the dangerous hover, monitored the radio, and scanned the cliffs and radar site for enemy forces. Panza would later participate with Cayler in a number of other rescues where their helicopter would be riddled with enemy gunfire.

(COURTESY JOE PANZA)

Rescue specialist "JJ" Rogers was lowered by cable onto the western cliffs of Phou Pha Thi and, while searching among a group of bodies, was startled to find a severely wounded Jack Starling. Two years later, Rogers would be part of the elite team that participated in the attempt to rescue Americans from the Son Tay prisoner of war camp located near Hanoi. (COURTESY JOE PANZA)

Radio specialist Melvin Holland was thirty-one years old when he joined the Heavy Green program. This photograph was taken for the tourist passport kept on file for his entry into Laos. Holland's wife, Ann, has spent nearly thirty years trying to learn his fate.

(COURTESY ANN HOLLAND)

Cryptographic specialist Willis Hall was forty years old when he accepted the Heavy Green assignment and went to Laos. Nearing retirement, he looked forward to returning to his family in Kansas. At the time of the attack, it is believed he was inside one of the radar buildings. Along with ten others, he remains unaccounted for.

(COURTESY MARY HALL)

The last photograph of Melvin Holland and his family taken just days before he departed for Laos. His two sons would follow in his footsteps and join the U.S. Air Force.　(COURTESY ANN HOLLAND)

Ann Holland and some of her many grandchildren.

In December 1968, in a closed Pentagon ceremony attended by a number of other stoic generals, General McConnell, Air Force Chief of Staff, presented Katherine Etchberger, widow of Heavy Green member Richard Etchberger, with the U.S. military's second highest decoration, the Air Force Cross. The award of this decoration was not officially recognized and publicized by the Air Force until 1998.

The Heavy Green facility as it appeared just hours after the communist assault. As the photograph shows, at this time the facility was relatively undamaged. Although eleven Americans were unaccounted for, photos like this convinced Air Force generals and the U.S. Ambassador to Laos to bomb the facility in order to destroy any evidence of a U.S. presence. (AUTHOR'S COLLECTION)

In the aftermath of the North Vietnamese raid, the site was extensively photographed in an effort to determine if any Americans had survived and the extent of the damage to the facility. This reconnaissance photograph was taken about twenty-four hours after the initial assault. When examined by specialists it appeared to show a number of bodies located along the cliffside. Over a period of days, the forms did not move and were presumed to be dead bodies. There was no certainty, however, that all were Americans or who they might be.

(AUTHOR'S COLLECTION)

Willie (Bill) Husband was the diesel mechanic responsible for maintaining the generators that powered the Heavy Green operations. As the Air America rescue helicopter was about to depart, Husband came running down the cliffside path and joined Richard Etchberger as they were pulled aboard. He is the only survivor known to have successfully hidden from the enemy among the rocks and brush near the radar facility. Although he was perhaps in the best position to have reported on enemy movements and the last known locations of his missing colleagues, he died in 1990 without ever having been interviewed officially.

(COURTESY HUSBAND FAMILY)

price. The consequences were evident in rushed and less than complete investigations. Despite documented cases of longstanding
sophistry, witness tampering, and financial misdeeds, the Lao and Vietnamese would be constantly lauded for their "superb cooperation."[57]
Accordingly, the joint task force began to carry out ambitious work
plans in Vietnam and Laos.

Faced with determined Lao opposition to archival research and
interviews with knowledgeable Pathet Lao wartime leaders, CINC-
PAC convinced Washington to concentrate on gaining permission for
increased surveys and remains-recovery operations. The Lao did begin
to expand the pace and number of these important efforts. The price
of their cooperation, however, was a tacit agreement that there would
be no meaningful archival work or oral history interviews in Laos. In
Vietnam these same investigative methods, albeit carried out under
close Vietnamese control and by well-intentioned but often poorly
qualified U.S. military personnel, were in routine use. Indeed, Hanoi's
astute orchestration of this circumscribed access to wartime records
and veterans would create the basis for normalization of U.S.-Viet-
namese relations.

Thoughtful observers understood that, absent additional information, the Lao field operations would end with hundreds of unresolved
cases. The likely alternative, if the U.S. insisted on greater cooperation,
was continued Lao stonewalling on any U.S. accounting activity. Thus,
the diplomatic price for remains recovery in Laos is an unspoken
understanding not to press the Lao government too hard on access to
written records and oral history interviews. Once the field work is
completed, hundreds of families will still be without answers. Meanwhile, the memories of the Pathet Lao veterans will have grown dim-
mer and their records (written reports, photographs, films, etc.) will
have further deteriorated due to time and poor storage conditions.
Again, the Lao strategy is simple—"slow roll" the issue. The real question is whether or not the American public and the families of the
unaccounted for, who with time dwindle in numbers and clout, will
continue to be heard by U.S. politicians and bureaucrats.

The outlook is not sanguine; the American people have accepted
the establishment of full diplomatic relations with Vietnam and mem-
bership and public financial contributions to POW-MIA organizations
continue to drop.[58] There is mistrust of the Vietnamese, but also a
good deal of apathy by generations of Americans who accept that their

government and elected representatives play fast and loose with the truth.

This examination would be incomplete, however, without a brief discussion of the Lao and Vietnamese view toward American military and civilian investigators tramping around their country and inspecting their wartime records.[59] As noted, the Vietnamese are very concerned about U.S. involvement in their domestic politics. Professor Goodman points out, "Dealing with the U.S. involves a level of scrutiny about human rights, religious freedom, and immigration policies . . . [which] could produce the reaction that once again a foreign power is intervening in Vietnam's internal affairs."[60]

The situation in Laos is similar. In a perceptive 1993 article for the *Asian Survey*, U.S. State Department analyst Stephen Johnson wrote: "The ruling Lao People's Revolutionary Party . . . is a child of Ho Chi Minh's Indochinese Communist Party and has been profoundly disturbed by what has happened to communism . . . and now faces a situation where the legitimacy of any one-party state is open to challenge." Johnson noted this "disquiet" in an October 5, 1992, Lao Politburo resolution:

> It is noteworthy that the imperialists have concentrated on carrying out a strategy of effecting change through peaceful means with the hope of doing away with our party's leadership and moving our country into their orbit. They carry out sabotage and subversive schemes through armed activities . . . [taking] advantage of economic difficulties, problems in daily life, and various negative phenomena to sabotage and change our country . . . as they have already done against the former Soviet Union and other socialist countries in Eastern Europe.[61]

The presence of Americans in Laos and Vietnam is viewed by many senior leaders in both nations as a major threat to their political and security sensibilities, and communist authorities are understandably very nervous about the ramifications of contact between their citizens and mostly young U.S. military and civilian personnel. Having stood off the Americans in a long and bloody war, these communist cadre must now play host to former enemies who routinely ask permission to travel throughout the countryside, peek in official buildings, and request all manner of documents. One can imagine the horrified reaction of U.S. agencies to requests from foreign nationals to rummage through their files. Likewise, the public response to a team of foreign-ers showing up at any American house, farm, ranch, or apartment building to ask personal questions and disrupt one's daily affairs would not be a favorable one. In remote areas, especially in Laos, the situa-tion can be even more obtrusive; helicopters full of strangers drop into villages that have infrequent contact with their own government, let alone Americans. Government officials must constantly be on guard against inappropriate contact, from romantic to political, and the obvi-ous trappings of wealth possessed by these young Americans raise many touchy issues for the communist regimes. In response, the U.S. teams are constantly reminded to avoid any unofficial contact or "frat-ernization" with the local population. This dictum also prevents locals from privately passing on information of possible relevance. For their part, the governments of Vietnam and Laos have stated their commit-ment to assist the United States and, therefore, ostensibly accept this activity as the price of improved bilateral relations. They also, of course, carefully control all American activity.

What of the U.S. perspective? Many Americans working in the POW-MIA accounting effort seem to forget, or choose to ignore, that Laos and Vietnam remain communist countries run by wartime veter-ans with considerable animosity toward the United States. There is today a great deal of pragmatism in Vietnam and Laos, and one often hears "the war is behind us." For those under thirty this is undoubt-edly true. The leadership in Hanoi and Vientiane, however, are not friends of America. The United States wreaked tremendous havoc on their countries and all have relatives killed by U.S. bombing attacks. If not for the collapse of the Soviet Union and their forced search for economic survival, the Lao and Vietnamese probably would not have been very receptive to U.S. POW-MIA initiatives.

American naivete in dealing with Lao and Vietnamese colleagues is primarily based on ignorance. Detachment commanders, those in the the joint task force who deal most directly and frequently with host nation officials, are selected for their proven ability to manage and direct military operations. None of these men are provided area or lan-guage training prior to assignment, although the U.S. Army has a well-regarded Foreign Area Officer (FAO) program. Placed in a exotic country where a misstep could cause immediate dismissal, these offi-cers quickly learn to depend upon the advice of civilian linguists assigned to their detachments. The power of these civil servants, all retired U.S. military sergeants, is considerable. The detachment commanders, lieutenant colonels destined for higher rank, understand their future career is based on achieving results. Smart and skilled in the local language and customs, the former sergeants become an essential element in the detachment's smooth operation. Compensated with special allowances and civil service rank normally reserved for college graduates, these men are not naive. Their job security is based on cordial relations with the host government and, therein, lies a serious problem. The detachment commanders are unschooled in the language, history, and customs of the country. They are under great pressure to perform a very difficult mission. In turn they must rely on people who, for their continued employment, must avoid confrontations with the local government. This creates an atmosphere in which both the commander and his linguist assistant are loath to become involved in untidy discussions with the local authorities. It is a situation that breeds a "get along" mentality and often prevents detachment commanders from speaking publicly and accurately about the true level of host nation POW-MIA cooperation.[62]

At higher levels in the U.S. POW-MIA accounting effort there are those who are not interested in the views of genuine area experts. They don't want to be conflicted by "negative" information, no matter if it clearly details obfuscation and deceit. Indeed, I have observed many senior officials refuse to read or consider relevant reporting because these details would hinder results. Consequently, during important negotiations they are often oblivious to the manipulations of their Lao and Vietnamese interlocutors . I would add, however, that many senior leaders do have specific knowledge of egregious efforts to tamper with witnesses and hide information from U.S. investigators. Although well informed, they simply ignore the facts. Results, or the perception of progress, are very important to the ambitious and career-minded bureaucrats—in and out of uniform—who supervise America's POW-MIA effort.

In an effort intended to improve oversight of the accounting effort, on July 16, 1993, the Department of Defense created the Defense Prisoner of War/Missing in Action Office (DPMO). Secretary of Defense Les Aspin announced that four separate offices were being combined to provide "an efficient management structure for pursuing our goals."[63] The new organization, headed by retired U.S. Air Force Brigadier General James W. Wold, expanded to more than

100.[64] Wold was appointed a Deputy Assistant Secretary of Defense and a number of longtime Defense Department employees received promotions. Similarly, there were promotion and hiring opportunities for others wishing to join the new office.[65]

The new agency, like the the joint task force, was formed at the recommendation of the U.S. Senate Select Committee on POW/MIA Affairs. Those who were sincerely dedicated to finding truthful answers believed DPMO and the joint task force represented the best means by which to accomplish "the highest national priority." Regrettably, there were managers in both organizations and at senior U.S. policy levels who saw an opportunity to close the issue once and for all—and as quickly as possible. Moreover, although there were analysts and operations personnel intent on undertaking sincere and thorough reviews of all the cases, both organizations included longtime employees who did not welcome any fresh analysis. Fearing an examination of their past methods and conclusions, many of which had been rounded criticized during earlier high-level DIA reviews and by members of the Senate Select Committee,[66] several of these civil servants were intent on deliberately impeding any analytical work that might have exposed their shortcomings.

Nevertheless, the establishment of DPMO and the joint task force created new hope for the families and an American public anxious to bring closure to one of the most troubling aspects of the Vietnam war. For the Heavy Green families it seemed especially timely. After several years of rebuffs, the Lao government had given approval for a survey of Site 85. The long-awaited return to the mountain was about to commence.

15

Return to the Mountain

*Given the Vietnamese penchant for recording the results of their wartime
activities, and particularly noting the fate of Americans involved,
[PAVN] records . . . and interviews . . . could confirm the fate of some, if
not all, of the unaccounted for men lost in this incident. It is very likely
that Vietnamese forces would have a detailed account of what took place.*
—JTF-FA Assessment, April 1994.[1]

*From the PAVN perspective . . . this attack . . . rated little more than one
or two brief handwritten entries [and] was a relatively small tactical
action in the overall campaign to oust Vang Pao's forces
from Houaphan Province.*
—DPMO Research and Analysis Assessment, February 13, 1997.[2]

*The sapper force attacked . . . with detailed preparations, and close coordi-
nation between the sappers and the infantry and artillery. This was a big
victory, not only militarily, but also politically.*
—PAVN Military History, May 11, 1997.[3]

On March 9, 1994, twenty-six years
to the day after the CIA reported
thousands of North Vietnamese troops arrayed around Site 85, the
joint task force began moving personnel and equipment to northeast
Laos. This was an assignment for which that organization is indeed

expert. These operations, called joint field activities, involve months of intergovernmental coordination and preparation, complicated logistics, weather and safety considerations, diplomatic wrangling with foreign governments, and last-minute changes to anything and everything. Inevitably, however, the joint task force and their host country counterparts bring these operations to fruition. The investigation of the losses (referred to as a Joint Field Activity, or JFA) at Phou Pha Thi, was referred to by the joint task force as case 2052.[4] In addition to 2052, there were requirements to investigate and recover remains, if possible, in twenty-eight other cases located in Houaphan and Xiengkhouang provinces. To accomplish this formidable work thirty-one Americans and nine Lao officials were deployed to a staging area in the city of Sam Neua. The group was then divided into several teams that moved around the provinces by vehicle and helicopter. Once in Sam Neua, however, the JFA commander, U.S. Army Colonel John M. Kendall, learned from his Lao counterpart that the visit to Phou Pha Thi was being temporarily delayed.[5] Management of these operations is always a complex, difficult, and costly process.[6]

While field teams modified their work plan and turned to other investigations, the Lao Foreign Ministry was finalizing a decision to permit media coverage of the Pha Thi operations. For several months John Wright, an independent producer working in conjunction with the NBC News television program *Now*, had lobbied the Lao embassy in Washington for permission to observe and film this field activity. He had also discussed his plans in detail with the joint task force's public affairs office, which posed no objections to his project. Wright specified that he also wished to visit and film areas of Laos that had suffered as a result of the American bombing—a story the Lao government felt had been very much neglected in U.S. media accounts of the war in Laos. The opportunity to have a sympathetic story on the effects of the U.S. bombing on Laos, presented on a prime time news magazine show, was very appealing to the Lao.[7]

During the negotiations with the Lao I was hired to act as a technical consultant for the project.[8] Jerry Clayton, the former Heavy Green commander, joined the team as an adviser. The hope was that the Lao would permit him to visit Pha Thi where he could provide his recollections of Site 85 and the men who served on the mountaintop. At my urging Deth Soulatha, a talented Lao-American, was also hired as a technical consultant. The decision proved to be very judicious; we were later told by a senior Lao official that the inclusion of an ethnic Lao in our group showed great respect and understanding of Lao culture.[9] Privately, Deth was told the Lao government would hold him personally accountable for maintaining the "proper perspective" during our visit.[10] Notwithstanding this pressure, his genial manner, creativity, and intellect would prove invaluable.

In early March the NBC team flew to Bangkok where we were to receive our visas from the Lao Embassy. Other members of the group now included veteran overseas correspondent Mike Boettcher, producer Geoff Stephens, and cameramen Bill Fellows and Ruel Kaplan.[11] One of Deth's first tasks was to complete the paperwork for the visas. In my case, he had to assure the Lao Embassy I was no longer associated with the U.S. government. Additionally, they wished to review a copy of my recent book on Laos. Because the latter was not an unusual request of academics requesting entry in Laos, I complied and reassured the Lao officials I was now a civilian teaching at a California college.[12]

On the anniversary of the attack on Site 85, Deth and I crossed by river ferry into Laos to begin coordinating with the Lao for our visit to Pha Thi. We quickly gained rare permission to visit Vieng Sai, the former Pathet Lao headquarters, along with the Plain of Jars and the former royal capital at Luang Prabang. The highlight of the trip, however, was actually to have reached the mountain to interview anyone who might have knowledge regarding the eleven missing men. The Lao Foreign Ministry had promised us this would not be a problem. Once airline space became available the rest of the news team arrived in Vientiane with several thousand pounds of movie camera equipment and supplies.

While awaiting final permission to join the JFA at Sam Neua City, Deth arranged a visit to the Lao National Film Archives. During my Stony Beach stint I had tried to elicit U.S. government interest in these materials. As discussed in chapter 13, in 1981 Roger Warner had gained extraordinary access to the Pathet Lao photo archives. He suspected that many of these images had been taken from North Vietnamese movie footage. After Wright discussed film preservation concerns with the Lao archival staff, and contributed some film supplies to their efforts, the Lao archival staff located a copy of a Pathet Lao propaganda movie called "Summer Victory." The film, a portion of which contains genuine footage of Phou Pha Thi, purports to show Pathet

Lao soldiers seizing the facility. A placard in the film, however, dates the attack as "3–1–69," some ten months after the actual event. This staged presentation was obviously developed for internal Lao propaganda consumption. In comparing the film with materials obtained by Warner from the Pathet Lao archives, it is clear many of the still photos came from "Summer Victory."

One portion of "Summer Victory" was especially noteworthy; it showed a single post-attack image of the relatively undamaged TSQ-81 radar facility. The film was irrefutable proof that the PAVN forces had ample opportunity to seize a wide range of materials in the radar vans. Moreover, the presence of at least one North Vietnamese photographer underscored that efforts had been made to document the battle. The Vietnamese would later claim, in a contradiction of their consistent wartime practice, that they removed nothing significant from Site 85. This issue is further examined later in this chapter.[13]

On March 17, our rented helicopter touched down in Sam Neua and we prepared for the much anticipated flight to Site 85.[14] We quickly learned from a brusk Colonel Kendall that his Lao counterparts were unaware of any media coverage and that we were not allowed to join the joint task force personnel.[15] Our Lao escorts from the Ministries of Foreign Affairs and Interior then launched into discussions on our behalf with the accompanying Lao officials. Ultimately, they requested additional instructions from Vientiane, and we were given permission to visit Phou Pha Thi.

In the interim, Deth arranged for two important appointments with Lao officials. On the morning of March 18 our group met with the local military commander who, after the presentation of gifts, was very amicable and affirmed that travel to Pha Thi would not be a problem. We then met with Khamphanh Phimmavong, the personable deputy provincial governor. After accepting our cash donations to a local charity, Mr. Khamphanh agreed to an on-camera interview. The following day he escorted us on a tour of his "personal cave" located several miles east of the city. Like most of the local Pathet Lao population, he lived underground during more than seven years of U.S. air strikes.

Throughout these discussions, we frequently queried the Lao about Site 85. While the officials were familiar with the basic details of the attack, they had no first-hand knowledge. They further explained Pha Thi was located in a special military area with soldiers still stationed near the peak. The deputy governor suggested that during our visit to the mountain the current commander of these forces might be more helpful.[16]

Later on March 18, after meeting with a chastened JFA commander, our team flew by MI-8 from Sam Neua to a small landing strip at Ban Houayma[17] located some three miles south of Phou Pha Thi. The MI-8 pilots transporting us were fearful of high winds, unexploded ordnance, and a small landing site, and would not land at Pha Thi. From Ban Houayma the JFA team moved to the mountain by helicopter.[18] When we arrived at the intermediate stop, however, we learned that the joint task force Lao escorts were placing limits on the number of people allowed on Pha Thi. It was decided Boettcher, Clayton, Stephens, Wright, and one of the cameramen would proceed. They were allowed less than an hour at Pha Thi before being told to depart.

That evening, in a very animated meeting, Boettcher and Stephens made clear to Colonel Kendall that NBC had invested a great deal of money and time in the project. This was a story which would showcase the joint task force as it performed a very high-profile and difficult operation. Nevertheless, as Boettcher and Stephens emphasized, despite approval from the Lao government at every level, it appeared the JFA team was actively thwarting NBC's efforts to film and investigate the loss of Site 85. The following day, however, the entire NBC group was allowed on the mountain.[19]

Once we climbed the path and reached the summit the cameramen and producers rushed to film Mike Boettcher's prepared remarks, Jerry Clayton's recollections, and the remnants of Site 85. One unexpected, but especially compelling, moment occurred when Colonel Clayton and Major Siphon, the current commander of the Lao military forces stationed at Phou Pha Thi, shook hands and exchanged pleasantries. Both declared for the camera, and to the great pleasure of the Lao officials standing nearby, that the war was in the past.

In a later conversation in Sam Neua, Siphon, an ethnic Hmong, said he had served with a local Pathet Lao proselytizing unit but did not participate in the actual attack. He confirmed that after the site's capture North Vietnamese units remained on the mountain and in the surrounding region.[20] According to Siphon the Vietnamese were stationed there until at least 1975 when the Pathet Lao were given responsibility for local security. When further questioned about the North

Vietnamese forces that he replaced, Siphon claimed none of the Vietnamese could speak Lao or Hmong and none of his soldiers spoke Vietnamese. Therefore, he had no idea of their personal or unit identities.[21]

For a Pathet Lao veteran to insist no one in the area spoke Vietnamese or that none of the Vietnamese could speak the local languages is preposterous. Under this construct one must believe that Vietnamese soldiers lived for years in northeastern Laos and never learned even the basics of the local languages. Moreover, it would also be necessary to concede that Pathet Lao soldiers closely allied with the North Vietnamese and living near the border had never learned any Vietnamese.[22]

Siphon was also questioned about his knowledge of any American remains. A June 1977 U.S. signals intelligence report had detailed the interception of a startling Lao government communication. According to the declassified document, "Laotian officials have been searching for American war dead somewhat earlier than originally thought, as recently available information reveals the search was on-going in April and May rather than early June. The remains of some American war dead had been taken to office 208."[23] While the publicly available copy is heavily censored, the intercept refers to Houaphan and Xiengkhouang provinces and "finding the remains of one American and having moved the body" and "Americans killed in the area of Phou Pha Thi."[24] Siphon, who was in command of the Lao military forces at Pha Thi in 1977, responded that neither he nor his men had ever seen any U.S. remains.[25]

While the other members of the NBC team went about their tasks, I walked slowly around the area and considered the terrain and what the Heavy Green technicians must have experienced. My emotions ran deep, as a historian and a former Air Force officer. I knew the details of the Heavy Green operation and the deadly attack. Moreover, I understood the institutional culture of the men who had volunteered to serve at such a dangerous and remote location. Observing the young U.S. military personnel at work on the site, I wished that there had been an opportunity to talk with them about the brave men they were trying to account for.

The cliffside, now delineated for safety reasons with colored tape staked to the ground, showed a great deal of erosion and probable bomb damage. More than a mile in elevation, the views from the former site were breathtaking. Lieutenant Colonel Seitzberg had been correct: this certainly was "the most beautiful RBS site in the world."[26] One could easily imagine the technicians looking out into the valleys and thinking about a strange war that had them wearing civilian clothes and working atop a mountain located on the brink of North Vietnam. Surely they also reflected on home, family, and friends, and a return to the Air Force when the assignment was over.

I examined the adjacent rusting frames which had once supported the Heavy Green operations. It was not difficult to contemplate the horror the men must have felt as the *Dac Cong* fired into the vans. Coming out of the darkness so unexpectedly, the gunfire and grenade attacks would have caused tremendous shock as the Americans scrambled to find safety. For those who reached the flat depression on the side of the mountain to the north of the vans, an area still visible, there was obviously no way down. There had been just the enemy above. This was the place where the Jolly Green rescue helicopter team had plucked the dazed Jack Starling out of his living hell. West and below the radar vans, on the cliffside where Monk Springsteadah and Hank Gish were killed in the presence of three American witnesses, the small ledge had long since disappeared, blasted away by American bombs and artillery. This was where Dick Etchberger held off the *Dac Cong*, saving the lives of John Daniel and Stan Sliz. Bill Husband had run down the ledge to grab onto the rescue cable which pulled him and Etchberger to safety. While rescuing the four technicians, the unprotected Air America helicopter had hovered just yards from the radar vans and communist soldiers. As pilot Ken Wood pulled the Huey away from the mountain, bullets ripped through the helicopter's floor and mortally wounded Etchberger.

To the east the stripped hulks of the site's generators rested among the weeds. I looked beyond them and down toward the helipad. There was the descending path to safety that had been so close, and impossibly far. The area of the living quarters, just below and east of the radar vans, was now little more than a rocky plot. Howard Freeman and a small Hmong patrol had bravely climbed the trail and searched all these areas. They saw none of the American bodies reported by Truong Muc. Finally, looking off into the thick brush north of the vans where Bill Husband had successfully hidden from the attackers, it seemed quite possible that a few other Americans might also have escaped the initial assault. But what then? If there were survivors, were they wounded? Did the *Dac Cong* or other North Vietnamese forces capture them? Were they executed, or sent elsewhere? There were no obvious answers.

Standing on Pha Thi's western cliffs was also a powerful experience for Jerry Clayton. At one point, asked by correspondent Boettcher to express his feelings about the missing men, he softly admitted "I can still hear some of them talking now."[27] Nonetheless, Clayton was given very little time to contemplate and consider what lay before him. This seemed especially irresponsible on the part of Colonel Kendall and his advisers. Clayton was one of only a few Americans who had first-hand knowledge of the physical layout of the former radar facility. Here was a rare opportunity for the JFA specialists to speak with the former commander on the site about the normal routines and movements of his men. After all, the majority of those missing from Site 85 were believed to have been at work inside the vans. Because there was reason to believe some of the men might not have been killed during the initial assault, it seemed only prudent to investigate where the men might have sought safety.

Despite his availability and unique knowledge, Clayton was ignored by Kendall and his staff, who seemed to be in a continual snit over our presence. Clayton, almost seventy and suffering from serious heart problems, had willed himself to make this final visit to Site 85 in an effort to resolve the fate of eleven of his men. It was an emotionally and physically draining experience for the former commander, as was starkly evident to those with him atop Pha Thi on that day. Still, the JFA commander, who wore the same eagles on his uniform collar that Jerry Clayton had earned, seemed quite unmoved by this former commander's pain. He was equally oblivious to the retired colonel's expertise.

Clayton, like all the NBC team, reached Pha Thi without the slightest degree of assistance from the joint task force, and for this he was privately very hurt.[28] Expending hundreds of thousands of dollars and placing many at physical risk, the task force could ill afford many visits to Pha Thi. Nonetheless, they had glibly squandered an important opportunity. This episode calls into question the leadership, professionalism, and judgment of an organization pledged to conduct the fullest possible accounting of America's missing. At Site 85 they failed the families, Clayton, and the American public.

As will be recounted below, this attitude toward a retired American colonel was in stark contrast to the treatment later accorded a retired communist officer who claimed to have led the attack on Site 85. When that man was brought to Pha Thi in December 1994 to recount the killing of the Heavy Green team, the task force treated him with great deference.[29]

Lieutenant Colonel Jeannie Schiff did spend about fifteen minutes with Colonel Clayton and together they surveyed the site's ruins and cliffside. There was no discussion of possible survivors. Away from the task force members, she conducted an interview with the colonel at her Sam Neua hotel.[30] Schiff may have been overwhelmed by her surroundings and the complexity of the case. She had no applicable area or language expertise and had a number of other assigned cases. Moreover, Schiff had not been the primary analyst on the Phou Pha Thi losses. Scheduling problems had precluded sending the most knowledgeable person, David Rosenau, a former U.S. Marine Corps officer, who over many years had developed an expert familiarity with the case.[31]

Despite the difficulties we encountered, while walking the rocky promontory that day I did learn much detail about the physical layout of the facility. It was clear, given the topography, distances involved, and lighting conditions, that neither Starling nor Sliz could have witnessed the attack on the radar vans. While Husband could have seen some of the missing men during the *Dac Cong* attack, apparently no U.S. official had ever questioned him on this critical point. I had gathered a great deal of new information, but came away with many unanswered questions.[32]

Back in Sam Neua the JFA commander remained silent on the official findings. Procedure dictated their reports be submitted to their headquarters for eventual dispatch to the families. As presented in an April 1994 official summary report, there were a number of important judgments.

Dr. Robert Mann, the JFA anthropologist, found "no human biological or obvious personnel related physical evidence." Mann, a highly respected professional with lengthy Southeast Asia field experience, stated "It is my opinion that the shallow, usually less than ten centimeter, soil layer present along the summit (that is, the operations building and surrounding area), would make it unsuitable for burying a human body."[33] With regard to the physical condition of the site the report noted: "In spite of reported efforts to destroy the site after the enemy forces take over, there is no evidence that the site was hit by high explosive ordnance. While conducting the surface search . . . no transistors or wires were evident, as would be expected if the electrical equipment . . . [had been] destroyed."[34]

The lack of any direct bomb blasts indicated, "that the bodies of the individuals [missing technicians] also would not have been destroyed or blown away by explosion or shock wave." The report then posited:

> Given this probability and the fact that Vietnamese forces were known to remain on the mountain after the take over, the disposition of the remains would include at least the following possibilities . . . bodies were thrown over the cliff, in which case remains could have been detected by the IE2 [JFA] search party . . . [or] the Vietnamese forces took the bodies out of the immediate area and disposed of them elsewhere.[35]

The conclusion of the task force was that:

> Based on . . . the fact that no evidence of remains or personnel effects were found, the fact that the Vietnamese were known to remain at the site after take over in 1975, the fact that Lima Site 85 was a very important military strategic objective, it is very likely that Vietnamese forces would have a detailed account of what took place.[36]

In her portion of the report, Schiff determined:

> The attackers, who probably sought refuge away from the site during the bombing, probably returned afterward and policed [gathered] up any existing remains. They could have thrown these over the edge as reported or taken them elsewhere for burial. Given the Vietnamese penchant for recording the results of their wartime activities, and particularly noting the fate of Americans involved, records review and interviews with members of the units involved in the attack could confirm the fate of some, if not all, of the unaccounted for men lost in this incident.[37]

A Stony Beach "Live Sighting" investigation in Houaphan province, conducted March 14–19, resulted in no useful information. The search of a crash site, believed to be the wreckage of Major Westbrook's aircraft, produced no personal effects or human remains.[38]

The comprehensive investigation had therefore concluded that it was likely that the answers to the fate of the Heavy Green losses were only to be found in Hanoi. This judgment was sound, but it would later be subverted and manipulated by a Vietnamese government and a few Americans anxious to avoid a full recounting of what really transpired during and after the North Vietnamese attack on Site 85.

On March 21, the NBC team flew to Vieng Sai where we were allowed unprecedented access to the former Pathet Lao headquarters. Never before had a western news team been allowed to film the interior of these caves, including the personal quarters of Pathet Lao icons Prince Souphanouvong and Kaysone Phomvihan. As I walked through these enormous caves, most with very small entrances, it was not hard for me to understand why U.S. bombers, lacking the technology to guide their munitions, inflicted such little damage. Nonetheless, there is no question the lengthy American bombing had been a phenomenal hardship for a civilian population that could venture out of these damp caves only at night to harvest crops and search for other food. Moreover, the resulting unexploded ordnance remains buried throughout the countryside and doubtless will kill and maim at least another generation of Laotians.

Although at every opportunity in Vieng Sai we asked about the attack on Site 85, located only 30 miles to the west of the mountain, none of the Lao officials were willing to admit to anything more than a passing knowledge of the events. All knew the Vietnamese had been involved, but they were conspicuously silent about their allies and any further details of the battle. Nearly forty years of communist control had taught them to be very guarded in their comments.

Nonetheless, our group was treated with great courtesy by many people who had every reason to hate Americans for the bombing and deprivations of those long years of war. Their dignity spoke volumes about the pride these people felt in their successful struggle against a far more powerful enemy. Lifting off the soccer field in Vieng Sai which served as a helipad, we looked out at the omnipresent bomb craters and wondered out loud how they had found the strength to persevere under such conditions. Despite the politics involved, everyone on our team left Vieng Sai with great respect for the people of Sam Neua.[39]

Hanoi

Physical access to Phou Pha Thi, and the lack of information available from Pathet Lao veterans, underscored the importance of Vietnamese sources. Our conclusion, supported by the joint task force's findings, was that numerous North Vietnamese soldiers and their superiors would have knowledge of the men, documents, and 150 tons of equipment missing from Site 85. Therefore, on March 29, the NBC team landed at Noi Bai airport outside Hanoi and began to seek answers in Vietnam.

Co-producer John Wright arranged meetings with various Vietnamese officials and we toured a number of Vietnamese military museums. Two leads immediately surfaced. Wright was told that Le Thuy, a retired major general, claimed to have commanded the forces that attacked the site. Several weeks later, after sorting out coordination and visa problems, Wright and Deth Soulatha succeeded in arranging a meeting with the general.[1] With the assistance of Vietnamese government interpreters, Le Thuy was questioned on film for several hours and affirmed he led the attack on Site 85. He further claimed to have inspected personally the facility after the attack. Later, after this interview was broadcast by NBC, it was discovered that the general had done nothing of the sort.[2]

A visit to the PAVN Air Force museum yielded more positive results. On a large wall extolling the virtues of Vietnamese aircrews was a prominent display of the January 12, 1968, attack on Site 85. Included in the exhibit were the purported photographs of one of the crews and aircraft, a gunpod, and a mock-up of Pha Thi complete with miniature aircraft attacking the radar site. A narrative explained that "Ngo Quang Ngoc" served as a "ground controller" for the attack.[3] While the presence of a ground controller is otherwise unconfirmed, given the deployment of North Vietnamese forces in the area around Site 85, the statement seems plausible. The joint task force, however, has never pursued this lead.

In any event, here was direct, convincing, and very accessible evidence of North Vietnamese involvement in long-term efforts to destroy the radar facility. The detailed display, for many years presented to foreign delegations, directly contradicts statements by some Americans in the U.S. government who claimed Pha Thi was an insignificant battle.[4] While the Vietnamese air force did not destroy Site 85, as claimed in the display, the unprecedented assault was an important point of pride. They had flown a long, difficult mission into Laos and successfully dropped "bombs" (actually mortar rounds) on the American site.[5] Logic dictates that when the *Dac Cong* ultimately silenced the facility those responsible for the feat would have been elated and justifiably boastful. The destruction of an installation that was directing bombs on a battered Vietnamese population should have been trumpeted with great vigor.

Nevertheless, there were good security and political reasons to maintain secrecy regarding the actual circumstances of the Vietnamese occupation. There were 150 tons of equipment missing and, with communist photos proving the vans were still intact, it is reasonable to speculate the communications and radar gear may have been removed to North Vietnam or elsewhere in the communist world. Fraternal intelligence agencies would have been very interested in learning about black boxes and electronics from an American radar facility. The issue of captured Americans is far more problematic. But, if true, this too is a subject that would have been closely held. In 1968 there was also the issue of conceding the North Vietnamese presence in neutral Laos, where like the United States, the North Vietnamese officially maintained the fiction that they had no forces. Publicly accepting credit for an action involving thousands of soldiers in Laos did not fit this picture of purity.

The chronology of the following events is very important. Since November 1992 the Vietnamese Office for Seeking Missing Persons (VNOSMP) and the Hanoi-based joint task force detachment have been reportedly scouring the country for witnesses and documents related to U.S. losses.[6] The task force had established a number of "archival research teams" (ART) to work with the Vietnamese in locating documents and relevant artifacts. Robert Destatte, a retired U.S. Army warrant officer, working at DPMO, was transferred to Hanoi to assist with this effort. A longtime fixture from the days of the DIA POW-MIA office, he was known for his anti-communist rhetoric and ability to translate written Vietnamese. Despite having no training in historical research, Destatte soon took the title "Research Historian."

This was standard procedure. Anxious to move quickly, without the delays involved in hiring college educated area and language specialists, the joint task force leadership simply bestowed a title upon a convenient and agreeable government employee.[7] The decision had a serious cascading impact on the appearance and quality of these archival investigations. For visiting congressional, family, veterans' groups, and the general public back home, it seemed the task force was conducting serious archival investigations. In fact, a middle-aged linguist with precarious health problems and no archival training was overseeing teams of mostly young enlisted men, however well-intentioned, with varying degrees of language proficiency.[8] All these Americans, of course, were under the tight restrictions of the Vietnamese. Moreover, like the retired sergeants hired to be detachment linguists, Destatte's continued service with the task force was contingent on his ability to get along with his communist counterparts. It is easy to see how learning to avoid asking the tough questions could lead to a mutual accommodation. In any case, the outcome of the ART process was left to the whim of the Vietnamese.

Despite being the largest single Air Force ground combat loss of the war, neither the Vietnamese missing persons office nor the Hanoi-based task force detachment seemed interested in working on the Site 85 losses. This is extraordinary considering that there were so many Americans missing at a known location that had been completely controlled by the North Vietnamese army. In contrast to the difficulty of locating aircraft crash sites and then trying to determine what communist forces might have been involved, archival research efforts on behalf of the lost technicians should have been relatively easy.

The Vietnamese, and Americans, have records on the forces who participated in the battle. With thousands of men involved in the attack, there would be no shortage of soldiers who could identify former commanders. Once these people were identified it would be a simple process of finding personnel who had taken charge of Pha Thi's summit. Undoubtedly, there were scores of Vietnamese troops who had personal knowledge of the facility. There were also the *Dac Cong* participants. Again, a records search and some inquiries should have quickly revealed the names of those involved. Indeed, as discussed below, this is exactly the process later used by the Vietnamese to locate the purported *Dac Cong* leader and another North Vietnamese officer who claimed to have been at Site 85. Additionally, because the Vietnamese took post-attack photographs, a check with wartime cameramen might also have developed other leads. But, in early 1994, there is no indication any of this was being seriously pursued. No one in Vietnam, including those involved in the multi-million-dollar task force operation, seemed to be interested in asking questions about Site 85.

This attitude seemed particularly curious in view of a recent visit to Hanoi by a fact-finding delegation from the National League of Families of American Prisoners and Missing in Southeast Asia. Led by Executive Director Ann Mills Griffiths, on March 23 the family members met with senior Vietnamese officials. During the session Griffiths provided a copy of a detailed Air Force report on Site 85 and noted great interest on the part of the Vietnamese in such a detailed study. She then declared that, given the importance of the battle, the Vietnamese should have their own records and the "League expects answers . . . and provision of documents."[9] Among those attending was Senior Colonel Tran Van Bien, Vietnamese missing persons office Deputy Director and a veteran intelligence officer. Although Hanoi task force detachment officials were present at the meeting and documented these discussions in a memo, they waited three months to ask the Vietnamese for information on the loss.[10]

On July 27, 1994, a working-level U.S.-Vietnamese POW-MIA meeting was held in Hanoi to review and discuss the status of accounting efforts. On the subject of Site 85, Senior Colonel Bien reported that one of his specialists had interviewed the author of the "official history of the PAVN sapper command," and "the author . . . did not find any documents related to the incident." The writer claimed to have relied only on the memories of the participants.[11] In this regard, Bien advised that his office was now attempting to locate a "member of the unit which carried out the main attack."[12]

A month later, the task force was nudged into action by the long-delayed NBC broadcast of "Mystery on the Mountain." The twenty-minute segment was shown on the *Now* news magazine program and included portions of the Le Thuy interview in which the general claimed to have commanded the Vietnamese forces and personally inspected the facility shortly after it was captured.[13] The task force queried the Hanoi detachment for any information on the wartime activities of Le Thuy, and this request apparently spurred the research historian and the Vietnamese into action. The detachment responded on September 14 that Le Thuy was a "logistics officer" and "played no direct role in the attack." Accordingly, the specialists in Hanoi told their headquarters there was "no need" to interview the retired general.[14]

The same communication, however, did contain some dramatic news. The Vietnamese had just located "the retired PAVN officer who led the attack on Phou Pha Thi." A Vietnamese government interview of the man, identified as Truong Muc, advised, "The PAVN sappers found the bodies of ten or more Americans who had been killed in the action. Mr. Muc stayed on the site for two days to collect weapons and other materials. He said he sent this material to Headquarters NWMR [Northwest Military Region]."[15] The detachment added "PAVN writings on the incident are very limited and based on oral history."[16]

The detachment further advised its headquarters and DPMO that Destatte and the Vietnamese specialists were scheduled to conduct soon an in-depth interview of Truong Muc and solicited questions, diagrams, and photography of the site. It was noted, however, that the detachment already possessed the detailed Air Force report on Site 85.[17] The task force made no mention of the copy passed six months earlier by Mrs. Griffiths to Senior Colonel Bien.

Lientenant Colonel Schiff quickly notified me of this promising development and asked that I provide drawings and questions for use in the interview. Since my return from Site 85 I had become engaged in nearly full-time research on project Heavy Green. As a result, I had interviewed survivors Jack Starling and John Daniel, and conducted extensive document research in U.S. government archives. Together with information received from Jerry Clayton, I had amassed a great deal of data on Site 85. In the process of uncovering this material I had maintained contact with Schiff and often shared my findings with her. I was pleased with the opportunity to assist with the interview preparation and, with relatively little time to prepare a response to the task force, she was appreciative of my help. DPMO sent the task force a detailed set of interview questions on September 27, "with the understanding that this is to be a preliminary interview and further questions may arise as a result of the information."[18] This was a well-established practice, allowing U.S.-based analysts with greater resources to review a field interview and then, if necessary, propose additional questions for a follow-up session.[19] In the case of the critical questioning of Truong Muc, however, this standard procedure would be seriously violated.

The details of the March 11 attack in chapters 9 and 10 include information derived from the Truong Muc interview. This material covered the serious inconsistencies between what Howard Freeman observed on his search of the area and Truong Muc's claim of having complete control of the site. The *Dac Cong* leader also said his men killed Americans around the vans, but Freeman saw no bodies and little damage to the vans.

We now turn to a careful review of several other assertions made by Truong Muc, a comparison with other available information, and some judgments as to the plausibility of his account. While I do not necessarily accept the task force conclusion that Truong Muc was the leader of the assault, his evident knowledge of the site and *Dac Cong* background supports his probable participation in the attack. In any case, it is often very difficult to question the bona fides of Vietnamese-supplied witnesses. The Vietnamese could certainly school an old soldier in a number of facts, which the person would then divulge to U.S. interviewers, thereby creating the appearance of being a true participant. Ferreting out these fakes is possible only when language qualified and highly skilled interviewers well briefed on the historical circumstances are permitted to ask tough questions and challenge dubious claims. As noted below, this was hardly the case in the investigation of Truong Muc's account of the attack on Phou Pha Thi.

Like all task force interviews in Vietnam, the Vietnamese Office of Missing Persons was deeply involved in the pre-interview preparation and questioning of Truong Muc.[20] Having reviewed the attack with him in their earlier unilateral interview, in which the Vietnamese officials most certainly used information from the U.S. Air Force report,[21] it came as no surprise that Truong Muc's responses were all favorable to the Vietnamese. For example, his version confirmed what the Vietnamese believed to be, from U.S. written sources, the correct number of American bodies at Site 85. Further, the Vietnamese effectively closed off any further investigation by proclaiming that Truong Muc was the only known member of the *Dac Cong* unit and that, since he had written no report, there were no records of the attack. Advancing this story, the Vietnamese government presumed they could satisfy the American desire to account for the eleven missing men and this information would preclude any further investigation into this politically sensitive case. In an atmosphere driven by a JTF-FA anxious to quickly account for as many Americans as possible, despite flimsy evidence, there were numerous opportunities for the Vietnamese to concoct all manner of explanations.[22] They were assisted in this process by a U.S. interviewer, Robert Destatte, who remained submissive throughout the questioning and never challenged a profusion of inconsistent and implausible statements.[23]

Truong Muc maintains that he received verbal orders for the mission and departed with his team from the Northwest Military Region headquarters at Son La, North Vietnam.[24] He claims to have arrived at Pha Thi at least a month before the attack, but "did not use local guides . . . and no Lao or other PAVN unit took part in the ground attack." If so, he managed to escape the notice of frequent U.S.-directed Hmong reconnaissance patrols and thousands of communist soldiers converging on the site. Moreover, although Truong Muc stated that "the attack was timed so that the artillery unit would stop firing before his team reached the summit," he insisted the *Dac Cong* had no contact with any PAVN units. For the PAVN supporting forces to have carried out the shelling at just the exact time, on orders presumably provided more than a month earlier, is quite remarkable. Interestingly enough, although there were more than seven battalions of North Vietnamese soldiers in the immediate vicinity of Pha Thi, neither Truong Muc nor the Vietnamese missing persons office could provide specific designations for any of these units.

After twenty-six years Truong Muc could recall few details about the site which were not available in the Air Force report. Nonetheless, he was certain his team counted the bodies "of more than 10" Americans—a crucial assertion considering that the U.S. study does not mention the circumstances involving the deaths of Springsteadah and Gish. As detailed in chapter 9, Springsteadah was killed on the path in the presence of his teammates and Gish was hit by a grenade blast which blew his body off the narrow ledge. Truong Muc, however, says "neither he nor any of his men inspected the ledge during or after the attack." While in the dark, in the midst of heavy artillery, rocket, and mortar fire, Truong Muc and his men had successfully climbed the rugged western cliffs of Pha Thi. Is it likely that, in victory, they failed to walk down a path[25] located a few yards from the radar vans to check for bodies or weapons?

Truong Muc recounted how, at about 5:00 A.M., his men had evacuated their five dead and wounded down the 3,000-foot cliffs to the base of the mountain. Considering the number of casualties involved this effort would have required the efforts of nearly all the healthy *Dac Cong*. Truong Muc claims that this dangerous round-trip, undertaken in darkness, took little more than an hour. Upon the return of his team to the summit Truong Muc says his men told him they had "killed more than 10" Americans. He then made a "personal survey of the site" but could not remember the "exact number of bodies he saw." Nevertheless, "the numbers of bodies and the locations of the bodies he saw were consistent with the information his men reported." In their quest to come up with eleven confirmed remains, the number mentioned in the Air Force report, the Vietnamese were caught in an obvious lie. Although there were eleven missing airmen, the bodies of Springsteadah and Gish lay somewhere on the side of the cliff—an area Truong Muc says was never searched.

Late on March 11, Truong Muc says he and his men "began collecting weapons, equipment, and documents and buried the dead Americans." By this time, however, U.S. bombing had "destroyed every structure . . . and all of the equipment at the site." These same bombs also "destroyed or flung away from the site some of the American bodies he had seen before the air strikes began." Truong Muc and his men then placed the remaining corpses "in a depression in the ground, in a bunker, or in a trench nearest to where they found the body." He reported that they dug no graves, but "simply piled six-to-twelve inches of earth and stone or a layer of sandbags on each body." The *Dac Cong* leader then helpfully "speculated that the method of burial would have given little protection from foraging animals." They took no "identification media from any of the Americans" and "did not mark any of the graves."[26]

North Vietnamese photography located in the Pathet Lao archives shows a mostly undamaged facility.[27] This is consistent with CIA officer Freeman's post-attack observations and subsequent U.S. aerial photography.[28] Because Truong Muc denied anyone on his team had a camera, the communist photos must have been taken by photographers assigned to the infantry forces who surrounded the mountain and probably reached the summit late on March 11. In order to manufacture a plausible explanation for the lack of accountable bodies, Truong Muc invoked U.S. bombing as an excuse for the missing remains.[29] As to the equipment, the task force found little evidence of the 150 tons of material once located on Pha Thi's summit. Truong Muc and his men could not have carried much away, but their North Vietnamese Army colleagues and fraternal communist friends certainly had an opportunity over the following months to dismantle and remove this potentially valuable equipment.

Truong Muc's final statements, as related by Destatte, are equally telling.

> Muc and his team departed the TACAN/TSQ site on the morning of 12 March 1968 and returned directly to the NWMR [Northwest Military Region] headquarters. Mr. Muc made a verbal report on the action in person to the NWMR commander, Senior Colonel Vu Lap. Mr. Muc said he did not prepare a written report and he was not aware that any written report was prepared. During the last 26 years he had lost contact with the men who participated in the attack . . . he no longer remembers the names of any of the men . . . [and] did not know anyone else who might know the names.[30]

Once the U.S. rescue operations were completed on the afternoon of March 11, there was little friendly Hmong resistance. U.S. air strikes were intermittent, but this would not have prevented communist soldiers from ascending the western slopes of the mountain and reaching the summit. It is therefore reasonable to conclude Truong Muc had contact with these forces prior to leaving Pha Thi. Why, indeed, would he then need to rush back to the headquarters? The North Vietnamese had excellent communications and, doubtless, senior commanders with the infantry and artillery units had already reported this considerable victory. All military personnel relish describing success to their superiors, and surely these senior officers did not wait for Truong Muc to complete a thirty day trek back to Son La so he could personally divulge the results of the attack. And why would a first lieutenant be making a verbal report only to a major regional commander? Moreover, it was a consistent North Vietnamese practice to document battles. Where were the reports received from the battalion commanders, intelligence specialists, and political officers who took part in this major campaign? What of the senior Vietnamese and Pathet Lao officials headquartered at Vieng Sai a few dozen miles away? They certainly knew what had occurred. Destatte did not ask any of these key questions and the Vietnamese missing persons office certainly offered no further views.

Truong Muc by his own account served forty-three years in the same area. Is it likely, then, that while he could not recall the names of fellow soldiers he had known for decades he was somehow able to recall the number of Americans who were killed at Site 85? He claimed twenty-six years had clouded his memory on the physical details of the site and the names of all involved. Yet, after the Site 85 attack he served with the North Vietnamese army for another fifteen years, until 1983, retiring as a sapper regiment commander. Yet, eleven years later he could not provide a single lead.[31]

From the Vietnamese perspective the interview of Truong Muc was intended to answer all the key U.S. questions about bodies and equipment and to dismiss the possibility there were additional witnesses. Although the Vietnamese provided implausible answers about the missing bodies and equipment, and a lone soldier who insisted there were no other sources of information, the task force accepted the report as fact. In spite of DPMO's cautionary view that this was to be "a preliminary interview," Destatte declared "it is unlikely additional interviews will produce better data about the location of remains unless the interviews are conducted on location."[32] There would be no discussion of follow-up questions on Truong Muc's obvious prevarications. It was a pitiful display of interviewing and a shameful toadying to the Vietnamese. Now there was just one last bit of unfinished business.

The Truong Muc interview allowed the task force and the Vietnamese the strong possibility they could close another case. Eleven names could be added to their "results" list. Although JFA teams had carefully examined the mountain for any remains in March and found nothing, a decision was made to move a recovery team to Phou Pha Thi for a full excavation, a type of work in which the task force excelled: bringing a Vietnamese witness to Laos provided an opportunity to showcase the cooperation of Hanoi and Vientiane. While it might seem harsh to suggest the task force would conduct another risky and expensive operation at Site 85 for the sake of public relations, the findings of the earlier JFA and Truong Muc's own recollections suggested it was highly unlikely remains would be recovered.

I choose to believe the recovery team was sent because there was the slim possibility that, with Truong Muc's assistance, they might find some remains. Nonetheless, this was a typical JTF-FA response. Instead of hiring highly qualified linguists, analysts, and real historians to conduct tough investigative work, the joint task force chose to concentrate on field work. As important as this is, it surely comes at the expense of hundreds of cases that can only be resolved with the true cooperation of the Lao and Vietnamese governments.

Whereas Clayton was given less than ninety minutes to look over the former radar site, Truong Muc was squired around the site with an interesting entourage. Robert Destatte was there along with a twenty-man task-force team and three Lao POW-MIA officials, all of whom were dutifully listed on the official report as having participated in the search at Site 85. One man whose name did not appear on the report was Lieutenant Colonel Pham Teo, a Vietnamese intelligence officer assigned to the Vietnamese missing persons office. As Truong Muc was walked around the site, Pham Teo coached and directed portions of the interview. The presence of a high-level Vietnamese official underscores the importance Hanoi placed on ensuring Truong Muc got the facts right.[33] Not surprisingly, no human remains were found on this second U.S. visit to Phou Pha Thi.[34]

The high-profile nature of this effort, and the sense it was futile, is indicated by the involvement and comments of the task force commander, U.S. Army Brigadier General Charles Viale. Viale, who had succeeded Major General Needham,[35] arrived at Site 85 on December 15 for a personal inspection. In a message sent to the National Security Council in the White House, Viale provided his personal assessment of the difficult task and concluded "I have little hope that Phou Pha Thi will yield human remains and even less hope that we will find identifiable remains. Nevertheless, the recovery team will continue to thoroughly excavate the burial locations as identified by LTC [Lieutenant Colonel] Muc." The General then included a statement that suggests he was not well-versed on North Vietnamese wartime policies or the facts of the case, a decidedly odd and unfortunate weakness for someone in his position. Addressing the possibility that the remains might have been moved he posited this theory, "There are no reports or evidence this occurred, but if an infantry unit did occupy the site, they would likely have disposed of the remains. The most expedient method of doing so would have been to throw them off the cliff."[36]

Viale was wrong on several counts. American remains, particularly those associated with an illegal U.S. military facility, would not have been carelessly discarded. As discussed earlier, there was strong evidence that remains from Site 85 might have been removed. There was also intelligence information available to the task force commander which, had he elected to consider it, would have tempered such declarations. Once again, the emphasis was on digging in the ground as opposed to digging in the archives.

Following the negative findings at Phou Pha Thi, the Heavy Green losses were placed in the "pending" category and the anthropologist officially recommended "no further recovery" operations at the site. Because the task force had accepted Truong Muc's recollections that all the men had been killed and buried on Pha Thi, and clearly there were no longer any remains at the site, further investigation was deemed unnecessary. Case 2052 seemed destined to join a long list of Southeast Asia losses that would never be explained.

Nevertheless Dave Rosenau and I, with the support of Warren Gray, then DPMO current operations branch chief, continued to work at developing leads from Americans who had worked at Site 85 or been involved in the rescue. We managed to locate important witnesses and documents that cast even greater doubt on Truong Muc's version of events.[37] However, the joint task force showed no interest in pursuing the case. Destatte had returned from Hanoi and was absolutely opposed to any further investigative work. Schiff, who had earlier documented her belief that the Vietnamese could account for the losses, began to defer to Destatte and our new information and suggestions were curtly dismissed. For more than a year critical investigative work on Site 85 came to a near standstill. Soon thereafter I was promoted to Chief, Southeast Asia Archival Research at DPMO and began the development and management of research programs in Cambodia and Laos. Although I was no longer responsible for specific cases, I continued to monitor case 2052. Vietnam, oddly enough, was not part of my new research portfolio. The formulation of research strategies in Vietnam was left to Destatte and another analyst, neither one trained in archival reviews.

In November 1996, Schiff attempted to submit the cases of the eleven men missing from Pha Thi to a "fate determined" review board. Under this procedure DPMO convened a group of impartial military officers, provided them with the circumstances of the loss, and asked that they certify that there was good reason to believe the person was dead. This board action had nothing to do with legal status, since all of the missing Americans had been officially declared dead by their services. The purpose of this board, in my view, is to provide justification for cases to be given a nonactive status. While officially any future leads would always be pursued, practically speaking, once a case is classified as "fate determined" there is no further investigatory action.

Rosenau and I immediately objected. As detailed in chapter 12, U.S. witnesses had confirmed the deaths of only Springsteadah and Gish. In a meeting called to resolve our differences over the case, Schiff insisted that Starling had witnessed several people being killed. Rosenau pointed out that he had interviewed Starling but, based on subsequent compelling information, did not now believe he was a credible witness. Rosenau, who at the time worked for Schiff, then said if it was necessary he would write a formal memorandum affirming his view. Schiff was incensed and later counseled Rosenau on his "attitude."[38]

Ultimately, based on information presented by Rosenau and me, Deputy Assistant Secretary of Defense James Wold ordered the case removed from board consideration. Wold had taken a personal interest in the case. During a recent visit to Southeast Asia I had escorted him to see the Pha Thi display at the North Vietnamese Air Force museum and explained the complexity of the Site 85 losses. Wold, a strong supporter of credible archival research, seemed concerned with the obvious inconsistencies in the Vietnamese version of the loss.[39]

Following his decision to remove the Heavy Green losses from the proposed board action, Wold asked me to provide him with recommendations for a further pursuit of the case.[40] On January 14, 1997, I submitted a lengthy memorandum that included wartime CIA reports and other materials that called into question Truong Muc's version of events. DPMO Chief of Staff Joe Harvey, then decided the policy directorate would review the Site 85 losses and attempt to establish an official position on the case. All involved parties were to write up their views and provide them to a policy officer for consideration. Rosenau and I complied and were told Schiff and Destatte would also submit material.

On February 13, without approval and in violation of established policies forbidding direct communications between DPMO and task force detachments, Destatte faxed the Hanoi detachment a lengthy memorandum on the case. Writing directly to two sergeant linguists and not the detachment commander, he declared "We have sufficient knowledge to conclude that 10 bodies were lying on top of the mountain and one on the face of the cliff on the west side of the mountain when Truong Muc and his team departed."[41] Thus, despite Wold's decision that there was insufficient information to support a declaration that all eleven men were known to have been killed, Destatte was telling the task force detachment just the opposite.

In a section called "Next Step" Destatte's facsimile outlined what actions the task force should now undertake. It was an incredible display of arrogance, which completely subverted all established procedures for coordinating case work through the task force headquarters. Moreover, Destatte had been explicitly told by the chief of staff to provide his views to a policy officer for consideration in a coordinated DPMO judgment.

His facsimile to Hanoi also advised, "I have reviewed nearly 400 PAVN historical books and documents searching for information about the 11 March 1968 attack on Lima Site 85. Only a few contained any mention of the attack." Destatte concluded:

> From the PAVN perspective (reflected in both historical writings and interviews), this attack was comparable to the hundreds of actions by U.S. forces that rated little more than one or two brief handwritten entries in the daily journal in the tactical operations center of some battalion, brigade, or divisions. Our review of Vietnamese documents and publications indicate that, from the PAVN perspective, the attack on Lima Site 85 was a relatively small tactical action in the overall campaign to oust Vang Pao's forces from Houaphan Province.[42]

Despite Destatte's unauthorized actions, he received no sanctions and continued to be involved in the Site 85 case.

On April 28, after returning from a lengthy archival research-related visit to Laos and Cambodia, I submitted a detailed memorandum on the Site 85 losses to a lieutenant colonel in the DPMO policy directorate. In this internal document, written at the request of the DPMO chief of staff, I provided my very frank views on the case and the actions of Schiff and Destatte. Within days the document was somehow leaked, circulated throughout the POW-MIA activist community, and placed on a number of web sites.[43] It became a very high interest item with several members of Congress and on May 22, Wold and I were summoned to meet with Congressman Benjamin A. Gilman (R, N.Y.). In his capacity as Chairman of the House International Relations Committee, Gilman has been a close observer of DPMO and task force operations. Gilman had read my memorandum and in our meeting asked if it was accurate. I assured him that although it was very direct and noncomplimentary about the research skills and ethics of people assigned to DPMO, and not written for public release, to the best of my knowledge it was very accurate. Questioned by Gilman, Wold said there were "differences in the office," but he assured the Congressman the case would be "vigorously pursued."[44]

The memorandum created some anxiety in DPMO, mostly among several old-time former DIA employees. Doubtless they felt my criticism of weak analytical and archival research skills was also directed at their years of POW-MIA employment. For the many professional and hard-working people at DPMO, however, the memorandum was no threat and not much of a surprise. Nonetheless, there was at least one very positive outcome from all this unsolicited attention.

On May 12, Wold was suddenly notified of a remarkable North Vietnamese document that provided new information on the Site 85 attack. Despite his longstanding claims that there was no other information, Destatte now advised that he had translated a chapter from a North Vietnamese military history that detailed the Site 85 attack. The chapter, "A Military Region Sapper Team's Surprise Attack on the 'TACAN' Site on Pha-Thi Mountain on March 11, 1968," had been published by the PAVN Publishing House in 1996.[45] It was unexplained how long Destatte had possession of the material and why the Vietnamese government had not provided the document to the task force through established channels. The speculation was that Destatte had received the document in Hanoi and, for reasons presumably known only to himself, had finally decided to reveal its existence.

This new material made clear that, far from being a "small tactical action," the attack had been carefully planned and included, from the very outset, close coordination with Communist Party officials and North Vietnamese infantry units. Under a subheading, "Combat Mission and Objectives," the article stated that "when preparations were complete the team [*Dac Cong*] would join the infantry and conduct a surprise attack, eliminate the enemy, and liberate the entire Pha-Thi area." Specifically, the *Dac Cong* were ordered to "destroy and seize the American communications center . . . attack and seize the TACAN . . . kill all the Americans . . . and defend in place and wait for the infantry to arrive and takeover."[46] The assault was carried out by three officers, fifteen noncommissioned officers, and fifteen soldiers of which "11 men were Party members, 20 were youth group members, and 2 were ordinary soldiers." The team comprised ethnic Vietnamese and four different tribal nationalities . . . equipped with three B-40s [grenade launchers], twenty-three AKs [assault rifles], four carbines, and two K54s [pistols]."[47] Of note, Truong Muc's basic team was "reinforced by one 9-man sapper squad from an infantry battalion." This unit served as the "reserve element."[48]

According to the document, the *Dac Cong* team was given the mission by the "Military Region"[49] on December 2, 1967. On December 7, "the operation moved to the base [Muang Kao][50] and briefed the [Party] executive committee, Party chapter and team on the intentions, missions, objectives, and significance of the battle." Eleven days later, an eight-man group led by Truong Muc reconnoitered the area, noting defensive positions and possible routes to the radar facility. This was followed a month later by a team led by Political Officer " Tap" who, according to the article, "crawled up next to the TACAN site" and confirmed the location of the helipad and all the U.S. buildings. On March 7, "the Party Committee held its final meeting" and it was "agreed that the attack would begin between 0400 and 0500 on the morning of March 11."[51]

In a discussion of the attack itself, the document provides specific details on how the radar facility was encircled and assaulted. "Comrade Phong immediately sent the B-40 gunner up to fire directly into the building that had many antennas. After only 15 minutes . . . [the team] had attacked and occupied the American communication center killing one officer and wounding several others." Other attacks were launched on the rest of the facility and "The Americans were taken by surprise, and ran outside and scattered. Only a few stubborn ones resisted." The *Dac Cong* consolidated their forces and at "0430, after killing all remaining stubborn enemy resistance, the team seized the TACAN."[52] In other parts of the attack narrative it is clear the author is recounting fighting between the *Dac Cong* and defenders other than the technicians. Therefore, from this account it is not possible to determine with any precision the number of Americans killed or wounded. There is no mention of capturing prisoners.

Following the helicopter rescue of the technicians from the western cliffs and the evacuation of the U.S. and support personnel from the helipad, the history reports, "Our men hid our wounded and dead in the rock crevices and avoided enemy bombs and aerial attacks, while defending the TACAN site." The report says the *Dac Cong* suffered one killed and two wounded. On March 14, "the entire unit withdrew to the assembly point."[53]

The report then notes that other troops captured a large quantity of weapons along with "a lot of equipment, military goods, and provisions. Later, our infantry went up and took control of everything."[54] The North Vietnamese were clearly very pleased with the achievements of the *Dac Cong* and its successful integration with other units.

> Based on the sapper forces team's attack on the TACAN, we can conclude that sapper forces can be used not only independently and separately against a single target . . . but also that sapper forces can very effectively join infantry, artillery, and other branches to accomplish missions (assuming there is specific tasking and coordination of targets, missions, and scope of responsibility for each branch).[55]

The chapter concluded, "The Military Region sapper force attacked the TACAN . . . with a high level of determination, detailed preparations, and close coordination between the sappers and the infantry and artillery. This was a big victory, not only militarily, but also politically."[56]

This document confirmed what had long been suspected by those who had carefully studied the Vietnamese attack on Site 85: the operation was carefully planned, involved other PAVN ground forces, the *Dac Cong* had contact with other units, and an important part of their mission was to hold the summit for the infantry forces. It exposes the Truong Muc interview and the statements of Senior Colonel Bien as a fraud and substantiates the premise that the Vietnamese have detailed records on the Site 85 attack.

There is far too much detail in this Vietnamese history for this to have been written from verbal reports. Moreover, there is the pervasive involvement of military intelligence and the Vietnamese Communist Party. The intelligence units would have been involved in the terrain analysis necessary for the successful *Dac Cong* movements and the accurate artillery, rocket, and mortar attacks. Additionally, they would have been very interested in capturing Americans and examining the American electronic gear at Site 85. Party influence is present throughout the planning and execution of the attack. The Party Executive Committee was well briefed on the preparation and intent of the operation and the Party Committee approved the date and time of the final assault.[57] A political officer is said to have led a reconnaissance team onto the top of the mountain. Finally, as indicated in the chapter's concluding comments, the North Vietnamese were very proud of this attack. They had successfully demonstrated that the *Dac Cong* could safely travel in hostile territory, successfully operate with infantry units, and hold a fixed position until the arrival of these larger forces. This successful campaign, both militarily and politically, was most certainly a point of great pride in Hanoi and dutifully recorded in both military intelligence and Party records. Consequently, the other shoe was about to drop.

In May 1997, a delegation from the National League of Families of American Prisoners and Missing in Southeast Asia flew to Hanoi for a first-hand evaluation of the new U.S.-Vietnamese relationship. Promised by the White House that full diplomatic relations would increase the level of POW-MIA cooperation, the League's Executive Director, Ann Mills Griffiths, carried a lengthy list of questions. In a meeting with the Vietnamese missing persons office at the Joint Documentation Center[58] she reminded them of her March 1994 comments on the Site 85 losses and reiterated her belief the Vietnamese could provide additional information on this case. Bien responded that his men had located several participants of the attack and he intended to interview these men personally.[59]

Bien, well aware of the League's ability to marshal support from senior U.S. political leaders, had suddenly developed more information. During a mid-July consultation visit to DPMO, Bien advised that he had recently met with the "commanders of Military Regions 1 and 2, the former political commissar of the PAVN 927th Volunteer Battalion, and the author of an official PAVN account of the attack." His discussions with the military commanders resulted in the identification of a Senior Colonel Luu Quang Dinh, "who was the Political Commissar of the PAVN 927th Volunteer Battalion" which participated in the Pha Thi campaign. Dinh confirmed his presence with the 927th and recalled that the 923rd Volunteer Battalion also took part in the battle. He further acknowledged that Truong Muc had led the *Dac Cong* assault.[60] Bien then related that Dinh said he had visited the radar facility between 5:00 and 7:00 A.M., possibly on the day the site was overrun. Dinh claimed he made the trek up the mountain "for the purpose of scavenging electronic components from the American radios and radar equipment." Dinh intended to use the pieces to "build a radio receiver." In this regard he had shown Bien a small electronic component he allegedly removed from the site. Dinh said when he reached the summit the *Dac Cong* were no longer on the mountain. The most important information, however, was Dinh's claim that he had seen "the bodies of about 10 Americans in a ravine on the edge of the site. He recalled that one or more of the dead Americans appeared to be Black." Dinh did not know who placed the bodies in the ravine. He suggested that veterans of the 923rd Battalion, who were "responsible for holding and defending the mountain," might be a good source of information on these U.S. losses.

Bien had also spoken with the author of the 1996 history of the North Vietnamese army, which had recently been translated. The writer explained that he compiled the chapter from oral interviews and a June 11, 1968, reference document, "Report by the Northwest Military Region General Staff Department, preliminary summation of the sapper attack on the American TACAN site on Pha-Thi mountain." Bien insisted the history and the June document were "nearly identical."[61]

Faced with pressure from Griffiths, the Vietnamese decided to offer additional information they had either long possessed or could easily have obtained. The pattern is well known; the Vietnamese claimed for years they possessed no U.S. remains and then, when the situation suited them, remains would suddenly be located.[62] For this reason, their motivation and evidence must closely examined.

In 1994, the Vietnamese and the task force supposedly began a careful examination of all relevant Vietnamese records for information on U.S. losses. On their own initiative they located nothing relevant to the Site 85 losses. After receiving the detailed Air Force report on Site 85 from Griffiths the Vietnamese, amazingly enough, located Truong Muc, who claimed there were no written reports of the attack. This extraordinary lack of documentation was substantiated, claimed Bien, by a historical account developed exclusively from an interview with Truong Muc. Based on this assurance, Truong Muc's interview was accorded great credence and the task force launched a major remains investigation at Site 85. No remains or equipment were found and, at the urging of DPMO's senior Vietnamese analyst, the investigation of the Heavy Green losses appeared headed for oblivion.

Three years later, after credible investigative work with U.S. sources and the dissemination of my memo, the detailed history suddenly appeared. This was quickly followed by Bien's now greatly revised version of the facts. Despite years of claiming that they had no other witnesses and no further documentation, and that the *Dac Cong* were never in contact with any other forces, the Vietnamese now acknowledged there were other witnesses and documentation. The combined infantry and sapper assault on Pha Thi was the subject of senior political and military attention and doubtless well documented. Moreover, a review of the history chapter showed more than a score of names, many who were Communist Party members.

Of course, all of this revisionism was done in the spirit of cooperation. No U.S. government official raised publicly the obvious point that these revelations made a mockery of Vietnam's promises to assist the families of Americans unaccounted for in Southeast Asia. Notwithstanding clear leads pointing to other sapper personnel involved in the assault, at this writing DPMO, the task force, and the Vietnamese missing persons office are focused on the recollections of Senior Colonel Dinh. Indeed, in a February 20, 1998 evaluation, the task force praised Bien and his officers for being "so thorough."[63] Because this political officer says he saw American bodies stacked in a ravine, perhaps the task force will have to launch another major operation to Phou Pha Thi. This is what they do best.

Clearly, a review of Vietnamese efforts related to Site 85 shows a consistent pattern of stalling, distortion, manipulation, and equivocation. These delays and lies, all in Vietnam's national interest, will continue as long as the U.S. government allows this highest national priority to be controlled by politics and dishonorable people.

The breach of trust continues. U.S. government officials on March 12, 1968, decided to declare all the men dead and destroy Site 85. They did so to prevent the exposure of a major American violation of the Geneva agreements which, in turn, would have caused serious political damage to the U.S. Southeast Asia war effort. Ironically, the fullest accounting for these eleven Air Force men is now being blocked by U.S. officials intent on bringing their own closure to the Vietnam war. Hanoi knows what happened at Site 85 and, although the facts on this score are myriad, senior American bureaucrats now impede a thorough U.S. review and have acquiesced to a sham Vietnamese investigation.

In order to avoid a derailment of improved U.S.—Vietnam relations, the long-suffering families of eleven decent men and the American public are left to ponder if they will ever know the truth. This is a shameful episode in U.S. history which all Americans, particularly but not exclusively those who have worn the uniform or watched their loved ones go off to fight our wars, should find especially appalling.

17

Conclusions

"The higher up the chain of command, the greater is the need for boldness to be supported by a reflective mind, so that boldness does not degenerate into purposeless bursts of blind passion."
—CARL VON CLAUSEWITZ, PRUSSIAN MILITARY THEORIST.

"Do not demand accomplishment of those who have no talent."
—TU MU, NINTH-CENTURY CHINESE COMMENTATOR AND POET.

Heavy Green was an audacious plan, the sort of initiative the U.S. military strives to inculcate in its officer professional military education programs. Nonetheless, as Von Clausewitz suggests, to avoid failure boldness must be tempered with careful thought. The United States Air Force, ordered by the President in 1965 to begin the Rolling Thunder bombing campaign against North Vietnam, could not conduct all-weather, night operations. The only capable aircraft, B-52 strategic bombers, were considered by the administration to be politically unacceptable. In place of these heavy bombers the Air Force used F-105 and F-4 fighter-bombers. For two years, amidst growing White House pressure, the Air Force flew these "phony B-52s" in an effort to inflict pain on the Hanoi government. Regular periods of bad weather and the inability of the fighter-bombers to operate at night provided the enemy important respites from the bombing. America's vaunted air power appeared woefully inept against a marginal communist military power.

The success in South Vietnam of B-52s using the MSQ-77 ground-directed radar bombing system, "Combat Skyspot," inspired U.S. military leaders to consider using the radar against North Vietnamese targets. This technology, used in various versions since World War II, seemed to provide a solution. If placed within 200 nautical miles of a target, the radar would allow fighter-bombers to attack round-the-clock in any type of weather. Reaching important targets in and around Hanoi, however, required the establishment of a radar site in northeastern Laos.

Ambassador William Sullivan, intent on preserving the facade of Lao neutrality, rejected out of hand a proposal to place the radar in Laos. Nonetheless, the Pentagon was desperate to improve its bombing capability against North Vietnam and, in February 1967, Admiral Sharp, CINCPAC, recommended that the Joint Chiefs of Staff seek political support for the placement of a modified MSQ-77 at Site 85. Despite Sullivan's strong opposition, the Johnson White House approved the Pentagon's request. Following assurances from the Ambassador that the program would be deniable, thereby allowing Prime Minister Souvanna Phouma to claim ignorance of this serious violation of the 1962 Accords, the Lao government granted approval for the installation.

The leadership of the U.S. Air Force, and particularly those at 7th AF responsible for managing Rolling Thunder, faced a dilemma. Tasked with a politically driven air campaign against North Vietnam and, therefore, unable to use the bombers most suited for such an operation, the Air Force attempted to carry out the mission by using a jury-rigged ground-directed bombing system flown by F-105 fighter-bombers. This need to demonstrate a war-fighting competence compelled the Air Force to embark on a bold initiative that quickly developed into a meaningless exercise, in which bombs would fall on targets of questionable value. Nevertheless, confronted with an embarrassing lapse in capability, the Air Force had "done something."

Operational needs immediately clashed with secrecy concerns—dooming Heavy Green from its very inception. Phou Pha Thi was a technically ideal locale from which to direct U.S. airplanes to downtown Hanoi, but the mountaintop was well known to local communist forces. News of the dynamite blasting, the sudden appearance of more than a dozen Americans, and the constant shuttle of aircraft hauling supplies to the site doubtless reached the North Vietnamese leadership quickly. It was the height of American arrogance to presume that a heavily manned radar facility located in neutral Laos on the edge of North Vietnam could remain a secret. Within weeks far more Lao and Vietnamese knew about Site 85 than did Americans. Moreover, no State Department or CIA official familiar with the North Vietnamese and their pattern of warfare in northeastern Laos believed the site could safely remain in operation for more than a few months. Political and security perils notwithstanding, the Air Force determined that a temporary capability was better than none at all.

After final approval was obtained the program was divided between two distinct military worlds, the U.S. Air Force Special Plans office and the ground-directed bombing specialists of the Strategic Air Command. There was little common ground between the two groups. Special Plans was the conduit to the black world of secret technologies and support to foreign operations, while SAC's primary mission was to train and test aircrews for missions involving nuclear weapons. SAC provided the men and equipment, and the Special Plans office acted as the project facilitator. Once deployed to southeast Asia, neither of these organizations had any operational control over Heavy Green. The program was created and promptly placed in the hands of others. This lack of institutional responsibility during the operational phase may explain, but certainly does not excuse, the post-attack actions of the Special Plans office.

In 1967 most senior and mid-level Air Force officers were veterans of the Korean war, and many had also served in World War II. SAC, especially, was filled with experienced men confident of their ability to undertake successfully any task. It is, therefore, ironic that the command that flew the politically unacceptable B-52s would be called upon to develop and man a radar facility to direct the F-105s. Indeed, the Heavy Green program was built around the Vietnam service of Combat Skyspot specialists. These men believed in their technology, had witnessed its effectiveness with B-52s in South Vietnam, and wished to see an end to the frustrating Vietnam war.

While conventional wisdom says no one in the military should ever volunteer, it is nonetheless a truism that talented and dedicated men and women have always stepped forward. In the case of Heavy Green this meant not only the honor of being asked to participate in a top secret mission with the very finest technicians in the command, but also joining an operation that was going to end the war. At least that is what the men were told. In spite of the extraordinary requirement to separate from the Air Force, relocate their families, and serve at an unknown location in Southeast Asia, there was no shortage of volunteers.

In this regard, the Air Force was again conflicted by the politics of the Vietnam war. Following rules established for other U.S. military personnel serving in Laos, Ambassador Sullivan demanded that the team wear civilian clothes while working at the site. While there was no reluctance to violate the Geneva Accords, in order to protect their Geneva Convention rights General McConnell decided that the men would have to be separated from the Air Force. The act of becoming civilians, however, was technically nullified by the top-secret memorandum that the men signed, which assured they would eventually be restored to military status without loss of service time. In effect, they never left the Air Force.

This pretense within a facade mandated a double life, which many of the Heavy Green team members found difficult to maintain. They had one foot in the black world and another in the U.S. military. Moreover, recruited in haste without benefit of psychological testing or background checks to determine suitability for such a stressful, isolated, and dangerous assignment, several of the men would later demonstrate they lacked the proper temperament and judgment for this work. The late addition of the TACAN responsibilities compounded these problems by combining two different missions and including a group of young, marginally qualified personnel to an already complex operation. Ultimately, these deficiencies required a great deal more supervisory attention than was possible from an overworked Lieutenant Colonel Jerry Clayton.

Ambiguity plagued security arrangements for Site 85. William Sullivan, always uncomfortable with U.S. military personnel in Laos, decided the CIA's Hmong and Thai soldiers were capable of defending the site. He consistently rejected as unnecessary the presence of U.S. combat forces and firearms for the technicians. Experience supported Sullivan's decision and, if the Ambassador had followed the advice of the agency's paramilitary officers, there would have been no need for U.S. ground forces to protect Site 85. The CIA, always candid about the inability of the Hmong to defend fixed locations against heavy North Vietnamese pressure, presumed the radar site would be abandoned prior to any imminent assault. Ceding territory in the face of North Vietnamese pressure was a well-established practice. When in the CIA's judgment this threshold was reached, however, Sullivan instead deferred to the wishes of General Momyer and the site was not evacuated. This unexpected development left the CIA and their defensive forces in a severely compromised position

There is no equivocation, but considerable controversy, about Heavy Green's effectiveness as a bombing system. Colonel John C. Giraudo insisted from the outset of the Heavy Green program, and subsequent results confirmed, that ground-directed bombing was dangerous for the F-105 pilots and would not produce an improved strike capability against key North Vietnamese targets. General Momyer, his 7th AF staff, and certainly many in the U.S. military knew that the TSQ-81 system was not performing as it had been touted to the White House. The records are explicit: Heavy Green was unable to direct accurate air strikes on key targets in and around Hanoi. Following a brief and deadly experience in November, the system was relegated to area targets where precision was not so important and pilots would be less likely to perform evasive actions against surface-to-air missile and antiaircraft artillery sites that affected accuracy.

These facts raise many issues of integrity. In their zeal to do something the Air Force leaders continued with a program that, as Momyer would later admit, was ineffective. Heavy Green was not going to help end the Vietnam war; it was simply a stopgap measure to save the Air Force from an embarrassing conundrum. While there is no doubt of Momyer's cognizance, it is uncertain William Sullivan knew Site 85's primary targets were quickly reassigned from the Hanoi area to northwestern North Vietnam and northeastern Laos. Sullivan certainly knew the site was increasingly involved in self-defense missions against ever greater numbers of enemy forces enveloping Phou Pha Thi. Nonetheless, the Ambassador says, Momyer assured him the site's continued operation was critical to the Rolling Thunder program. Contemporaneous messages and actions support the view that regardless of the CIA warnings the Air Force wanted the site kept open. Indeed, in the wake of the increased threat Momyer actually ordered an increase in manning, and more technicians were placed at risk. Only in the final days, says Sullivan, did he go over the head of the military and request from Washington formal instructions. The Ambassador says he was then directed by the highest authority to keep the site in operation.

When Ambassador Sullivan finally ordered the site evacuated, in spite of Air Force wishes, it was too late. While the January 12, 1968, air attack heightened security concerns, the focus was always on a conventional enemy encirclement and bombardment of the mountain. There was precedent for this tactic, and this is exactly what the North Vietnamese seemed to be planning as they built roads and moved battalion after battalion into the area. At no time was there any indication the Vietnamese were planning a commando raid. Even without the *Dac Cong* assault, given the presence of such an overwhelming force armed with heavy weapons, it was criminal to leave the technicians and the other Americans and their security forces stranded at Phou Pha Thi. American civilian and military veterans of the Lao war are unequivocal in their belief that once the enemy placed Pha Thi within range of their artillery and mortars, an air evacuation was problematic at best. After more than four years in Laos William Sullivan well understood the threat, and records show senior military officers were so advised. Nonetheless, General Momyer judged the bombing operation too important to be shut down.

Ambassador Sullivan faced a dilemma on March 11. Somehow, in the aftermath of the attack, the diplomat had to salvage the Lao facade of neutrality and maintain plausible deniability concerning U.S. military operations in Laos. During these crucial hours U.S. foreign policy interests were no doubt foremost in his mind. Presented with Prime Minister Souvanna's admonition to destroy the evidence at Site 85, and reports from a rushed, incomplete, and speculative investigation, Sullivan declared all the technicians dead. At the Ambassador's direction the Air Force undertook immediate actions, albeit mostly ineffectual, to bomb all the American facilities at Phou Pha Thi. These efforts, had they been successful, necessarily meant the probable destruction of the American bodies and any persons caught in the attacks. Giving the order for these missions could not have been easy. Based on what he was told at the time, William Sullivan stands by his decision.

Nonetheless, it is now painfully obvious that the Ambassador did not possess the facts, and the actions and movements of the technicians could not have occurred in the manner described by Captain Sliz. What is more, to then attempt to ascribe primary blame for the tragedy to the technicians because of a perceived failure to follow questionable evacuation procedures is plainly reprehensible. Sullivan's statements on this issue are baffling and uncharacteristic of such a careful and thoughtful diplomat.

Within days of the Site 85 attack Momyer and Sullivan were trading not so subtle charges over who should be held responsible for the tragic loss of life. It is far from reassuring that both men seem to have been more intent on placing the blame elsewhere than learning the facts. There is no doubt the general misrepresented his knowledge of the threat in a bid at self-serving revisionism. Less clear, as described earlier, is Sullivan's culpability. The Ambassador, by his own determination, was the final authority for directing the closure of Site 85. Based on Momyer's recommendations, and despite proven CIA warnings, Sullivan failed to order a prudent evacuation. Both certainly share responsibility for the loss of the technicians. Further, Momyer's later actions in writing a false history of these events, and seeking to maintain a top-secret classification of important source documents, reveals an overriding desire to see the entire incident forgotten and hidden from the public.

My exhaustive review of the known information shows the U.S. government did not know at the time, and still does not know, what happened to nine of the eleven men missing from Site 85. We know what happened to Donald Springsteadah and Henry Gish; they perished on the ledge in the presence of their team members. Without the cooperation of the Vietnamese or Lao, however, there is probably no way to learn the fate of Clarence Blanton, James Calfee, Patrick Shannon, Donald Worley, David Price, Herb Kirk, James Davis, Willis Hall, and Melvin Holland. While compelling photographic evidence and the accounts of rescue personnel suggest that many of the men were killed during the attack, there were no credible U.S. witnesses who could explicitly place names, or even nationalities, on those presumed bodies. Moreover, there is strong evidence to suggest some of the technicians could have hidden themselves in the darkness and survived the attack.

Intelligence reporting and General Singkapo's unguarded comments fuel informed speculation that the North Vietnamese may have captured men at Site 85. While there is no confirming evidence of this, it is difficult to imagine any ulterior motive on Singkapo's part that would motivate him to falsely claim that prisoners were taken and subsequently turned over to the North Vietnamese. Conversely, if American prisoners were, in fact, captured, most analysts familiar with the Pathet Lao-North Vietnamese relationship would have expected the general to make no mention of prisoners. Certainly, the Laotian government's reaction to Singkapo's surprising statements suggests a great sensitivity on their part. We are unlikely to find a more credible source than Singkapo, and the Lao government's decision to silence him is very troubling. Be that as it may, the possibility that any American captured at Site 85 survived long-term communist imprisonment is even more unlikely. The known facts and logic dictates that the men were either killed at Pha Thi or later died in custody. Nevertheless, there can be no question that senior Vietnamese and Lao officials know, with some accuracy, what happened to each of these men.

Hanoi and Vientiane's well-documented deceit and obfuscation regarding the battle at Phou Pha Thi raise obvious questions: what happened to the remains of the missing men and where are the documents, equipment, and personal effects known to have been under North Vietnamese control after the site was lost? Out of 150 tons of material on that mountain the Vietnamese and Lao have turned over not as much as a button—yet their museums are filled with U.S. equipment recovered from hundreds of other engagements. If all the technicians were killed on March 11, why have these governments lied and continued to block a full investigation of the incident? The easy answer is that the Vietnamese and Lao may be hiding some atrocity, or that at least one or more of the men was captured. A parallel and complementary conclusion is the Vietnamese and Lao are simply maintaining the longstanding communist myth that North Vietnam did not direct and dominate the communist ground war in Laos. For political reasons, the Vietnamese do not want to embarrass their Lao allies and disclose fully the extent of their wartime activities in the neutral kingdom. More simply, what benefit would they derive from a full disclosure? From their perspective, absolutely nothing.

Communist dissembling is understandable. It is far more difficult to make sense of the post-attack actions of many U.S. officials. The U.S. Air Force Special Plans office, chartered to develop deniable U.S. activities, appears to have been incapable of telling the truth even in classified interagency memorandums. Perhaps the only government office with access to all the U.S. facts, Special Plans nonetheless initiated and continued a campaign of lies and misrepresentations that stretched over a period of at least fifteen years. The activities of this office have probably ensured there will never be an accounting for some of the Heavy Green families. The most critical information, exactly what the Site 85 survivors said to investigators at Udorn, has never been made available to POW-MIA investigators. These reports were certainly known, and probably stored, in the Special Plans office.

Equally troubling is the well-documented response of the Air Force and the Special Plans office to Ann Holland's lawsuit. Given the known information available to the Air Force and the subsequent government answers to the interrogatories, one can only conclude gross legal misconduct. Among the many inaccuracies presented by the Air Force, the most egregious is the declaration that the loss of Site 85 was due to a surprise attack. It seems inconceivable that a fully informed U.S. Attorney's Office would have supported such falsehoods. In any case, the treatment accorded Ann Holland by the very office assigned to counsel the Heavy Green families stands as a monumentally cynical and shameful betrayal of trust.

Having failed to receive justice from the Air Force, Holland turned to the State Department and Congress. Although it appears the offices she contacted received their information and guidance from officers at Special Plans, there seems to have been little enthusiasm for assisting in a review of what was surely a very questionable situation. The State Department, which did have knowledge of the entire case, provided a purely bureaucratic response. While it is difficult to know for certain, there is no indication that the country officer attempted to develop any further information by checking with former U.S. embassy officials who had served in Vientiane. Instead, the replies were in line with the Air Force version. This was also the case with Representative Hansen's office, which merely conveyed the military's answers rather than investigating the truthfulness of the assertions. The same cannot be said for Senator Stuart Symington. During his October 1969 hearings on Laos the Senator was told a great deal about Site 85 and, after his conversation with Stan Sliz, there can be no question that he knew Holland was being misled. Symington provided no help whatsoever.

All of these U.S. government responses raise another important question: how much did the executive and judicial branches know about Site 85? The publicly available facts are spotty. Approval for Heavy Green most certainly came from the White House. Ambassador Sullivan has said that he informed the White House of his concerns about the safety of Site 85 and was told to delay an evacuation. State Department and military cables show the White House was informed of the site's loss and the immediate post-attack actions. Beyond this, the paper trail ends. Despite a comprehensive investigation and a review of many thousands of documents, there are no known executive branch communications on Site 85. Following President Nixon's March 1970 misstatements on Laos, there was an acknowledgment of the losses, but nothing more. Later, during the Holland lawsuit, there is evidence of discussions between the Justice Department and the Air Force. Once again, curiously enough, there are no other confirming documents. Still, given the political, military, and foreign policy ramifications of this entire affair, it seems highly improbable Site 85 did not receive high-level government attention. Perhaps someday these files will be publicly released.

To recapitulate, the Air Force response to its inability to conduct all-weather bombing over North Vietnam was to construct a project that very soon proved ineffective. Nevertheless, the Heavy Green program continued. This strategy, to do something no matter how phony, has also been followed in the Laos and Vietnam-based investigations of the Site 85 losses. The current U.S. administration is intent on bringing its own version of closure to the Vietnam war. While there are important regional and international trade and security concerns that dictate normalization of relations with Indochina, these issues should not take precedence over the longstanding presidential promises of the fullest accounting for those missing in Southeast Asia. As carefully documented, the Joint Task Force-Full Accounting and the Defense Prisoner of War Missing in Action Office have acquiesced to sloppy work and shockingly loose ethical standards and the Site 85 case is thus indicative of a broader problem. The Vietnamese and Lao governments have consistently lied about their knowledge of Site 85 and these blatant falsehoods have been accepted and, in some cases, encouraged by U.S. government employees. There is much more to be learned about the fate of the missing Heavy Green technicians. Moreover, the appalling conduct of the Site 85 investigation necessarily calls into question the quality and professionalism accorded hundreds of other cases. The truth will surface only when qualified men and women, with the full support of honorable senior government officials, undertake true archival investigative work and demand answers from Hanoi and Vientiane. Only then will this commendable effort gain the credibility it deserves and bring a final conclusion for so many hurting families.

There is no pleasure in recounting the story of Site 85. From the beginning of the Heavy Green program until the present, there is an unseemly pattern of U.S. government duplicity. It is understating the obvious to say this is a case where the American public has not been well served by its government. The ultimate betrayal, of course, is the long-term and continuing breach of trust between the government and the families of Americans who proudly left home intent on helping to end a terrible war from a faraway Lao mountaintop. Perhaps an understanding of this ugly chapter of U.S. history will encourage greater accountability and responsibility from those who are involved in sending our most precious resource into harm's way.

![NOTES]

NOTES

Introduction

1. *Phou*, or *Phu*, as it is often spelled, is the Lao word for mountain, making the literal translation "mountain Pha Thi." In order to avoid confusion I will use "Phou," the spelling used most often in U.S. official documents.

2. According to an Air America publication, LS 85 was located at map grid coordinates 48Q UH 6860, at an elevation of 4,500 feet. "Air Facilities Data. Laos. Flight Information Center Vientiane. May 1970." Air America was a secretly owned CIA proprietary. See Castle, *At War in the Shadow of Vietnam*, 2, and 29–30. See chapter 1 for details on the establishment of the "Lima Sites."

3. In addition to this 600-foot runway, there was a smaller dirt strip located just below the summit at Phou Pha Thi. In 1967 and 1968 this strip, used mostly by helicopters, would prove critical to Site 85 operations.

4. The Air Force would not normally consider officers assigned to Heavy Green to be technicians; however, since these officers performed technical functions side-by-side with their enlisted men, for simplicity I will refer to all of the Heavy Green personnel who served at Site 85 as technicians.

5. Vietnam specialist Douglas Pike has called these sapper forces "the darlings of PAVN. They are surrounded by a special aura that the High Command always has sought to enhance." Pike, *PAVN: People's Army of Vietnam*, 108.

6. Following the Lao communist takeover in December 1975, Vieng Sai became the location of numerous reeducation camps. Many members of the Lao royal family, as well as thousands of government and military officials, were sent to the camps. Stuart-Fox, *Laos: Politics, Economics, and Society*, 161–62. See also electrical message, FBIS, "Laos' Phomvihan Confirms King's Death," FBIS Vienna AU, 141912Z December 1989. According to a Thai newspaper account, the King died a prisoner on December 9, 1980. Brown and Zasloff, *Apprentice Revolutionaries: The Communist Movement in Laos, 1930–1985*, 153.

7. Vallentiny, "The Fall of Site 85." Project CHECO report. CHECO is an Air Force acronym for Contemporary Historical Examination of Current Operations. The Project CHECO program began in 1962 as an effort to "compile, document, analyze, and report on a timely basis the new forces, new tactics and techniques, new materials, and new methods being employed in aerial operations in Southeast Asia." "Research Guide to Contemporary Historical Examination of Current Operations (CHECO) Reports of Southeast Asia," iii. Air Force Historical Research Agency (AFHRA), Maxwell AFB, Alabama, 1992. The program produced several hundred reports, mostly written as classified documents. While they are uneven in quality and many contain contradictory information and factual errors, the majority are well written and researched and often provide otherwise unavailable primary material on the war in Southeast Asia. The AFHRA provides excellent facilities and a talented and dedicated staff always willing to assist military and civilian researchers.

8. Van Staaveren, *The United States Air Force in Southeast Asia. Interdiction in Southern Laos, 1960–1968*, (hereafter *Interdiction in Southern Laos*), 289. My previous writings on Lima Site 85, where I followed the official accounts, have also on some points been faulty. Despite the inaccuracies concerning Site 85, Van Staaveren has written an excellent book with extraordinary and unprecedented detail on U.S. activities in Laos. It is truly regrettable that nearly two decades passed before the Office of Air Force History was allowed to publish this important research.

9. See Corn, *Blond Ghost*; Secord with Wurts, *Honored and Betrayed*; Robbins, *The Ravens*; and Hamilton-Merritt, *Tragic Mountains*. Hamilton-Merritt has produced the most implausible and defective account.

1. Sustained Reprisal

1. Herring, ed., *The Pentagon Papers: Abridged Edition*, 107. For an excellent in-depth examination of the military and political events leading up to this time see Clodfelter, *The Limits of Air Power*, 39–59, and Sharp, *Strategy for Defeat: Vietnam in Retrospect*, 27–62.

2. Italics in original.

3. Sheehan, et al., *The Pentagon Papers as Published by the New York Times*, 433.

4. Clodfelter, *Limits of Air Power*, 63. See also Sharp, *Strategy for Defeat*, 63, who says Johnson had mandated that the South Vietnamese air force take part in the bombing. Sharp believes the coup-related problems would have prevented the South Vietnamese from participating in the attacks as originally scheduled.

5. Sharp, *Strategy for Defeat*, 64.

6. Ibid.

7. Westmoreland, *A Soldier Reports*, 152–53. See also Broughton, *Going Downtown*, xv-xvi.

8. Momyer, *Air Power in Three Wars*, 15.

9. Tilford, Jr., *Setup*, 109 and Clodfelter, *Limits of Air Power*, 85. The original group of four, Johnson, McNamara, Rusk, and Bundy, were referred to in Washington as the "awesome foursome." Bundy would resign in early 1966 and be replaced by Walt W. Rostow. See Herring, *LBJ and Vietnam*, 6–9.

10. Schlight, *The War in South Vietnam: The Years of the Offensive 1965–1968*, 16.

11. Laotian Prime Minister Souvanna Phouma agreed to these air strikes, as long as there was no public acknowledgment by either the Lao or U.S. governments. See Castle, *At War in the Shadow of Vietnam*, 88.

12. Schlight, *War in South Vietnam*, 18.

13. Marolda and Fitzgerald, *The United States Navy and the Vietnam Conflict. Volume II. From Military Assistance to Combat, 1959–1965*, 515.

14. This first mission tragically began with the loss of two B-52s in a pre-attack mid-air collision over the South China Sea. Of the twelve crewman aboard the two aircraft, only four survived. Schlight, *War in South Vietnam*, 51–52. The remaining seven are formally listed in military records as "killed-in-action, body not recovered." A post-attack photo of the target appears in the photo insert.

15. B-52's first dropped bombs on Laos in December 1965 and on North Vietnam in April 1966. Ibid., 150.

16. Clodfelter notes, "the Air Force headquarters with direct control over fighter wings . . . received guidance not only from PACOM [CINCPAC] and PACAF, but also from 13th Air Force (13th AF) in the Philippines. Meanwhile, the Navy's Carrier Task Force (CTF) 77 in the Tonkin Gulf received supervision from PACOM and PACFLT," *Limits of Air Power*, 128.

17. Ibid, 129.

18. Schlight, *War in South Vietnam*, 119.

19. On the issue of body counts see Lewy, *America in Vietnam*, 78–82.

20. Schlight, *War in South Vietnam*, 119.

21. Clodfelter, *Limits of Air Power*, 130.

22. Sharp, *Strategy for Defeat*, 78.

23. The Route Packages, known as RPs, were divided this way: RPI operations were conducted by Seventh Air Force (7th AF) aircraft under the control of the Commander, United States Military Assistance Command, Vietnam (COMUSMACV). The Commander-in-Chief, Pacific Fleet (CINCPACFLT) was responsible for RPs II, III, IV, and VIB. Operations in these RPs were conducted by the U.S. Naval Commander, Carrier Task Force 77 (CTF-77), operating in the Gulf of Tonkin. The Commander-in-Chief, Pacific Air Forces (CINCPACAF) was responsible for Route Packages V and VI-A, which included Hanoi. Clodfelter, *Limits of Air Power*, 129, and Overton, "Rolling Thunder, January 1967-November 1968," 2. Project CHECO report.

24. Momyer, *Air Power in Three Wars*, 177. See also Tilford, *Setup*, 113, and Clodfelter, *Limits of Air Power*, 131.

25. Tilford, *Setup*, 113.

26. Clodfelter, *Limits of Air Power*, 133. See also, Broughton, *Going Downtown*, 48–51. As to the F-105's incredible weight, it was also sometimes called the "25-ton canary."

27. Clodfelter, *Limits of Air Power*, 133. For an excellent resource on aircraft involved in the "30-year air war" in Southeast Asia, see Francillon, *Vietnam Air Wars*.

28. Clodfelter, *Limits of Air Power*, 118–19.

29. Harrison, "Impact of Darkness and Weather on Air Operations in SEA," 120. Project CHECO report.

30. Developed from the SCR-584 gun-laying radar, the system was first used by U.S. forces in Europe and later during the Korean War. Momyer, *Air Power in Three Wars*, 178.

31. John G. Daniel, interview, September 2, 1994, Gerald H. Clayton, interview, July 27, 1996, "History of 1 CEVG 1961- 1981," Headquarters 1st Combat Evaluation Group, February 25, 1982, Barksdale Air Force Base, Louisiana, and Durkee, "Combat Skyspot," 2 and 4. Project CHECO report, and Jerry E. Beck, "Combat Skyspot—A Study of a Ground Directed Radar Bombing System in a Limited Warfare Environment," Air Command and Staff College, May 1970. I am indebted to retired Technical Sergeant Daniel, a survivor of the attack on Site 85, for providing me with a copy of the 1 CEVG history.

32. U.S. Air Force background paper, "Combat Skyspot," February 6, 1969, HQ USAFE, APO New York 09633, Durkee, "Combat Skyspot," 3–4, and Schlight, *War in South Vietnam*, 135.

33. Two earlier nicknames for the system were "Skyspot" and "Combat Proof."

34. Clayton, interview, July 16, 1994, and 1 CEVG history. Clayton, then a lieutenant colonel, commanded the initial 1 CEVG Southeast Asia deployment to install and activate the MSQ-77 sites. He was present at Dong Ha just hours before the ambush and was recalled to the site to assist in the identification of the bodies. Those killed; Technical Sergeant Antone P. Marks, Staff Sergeant John P. Guerin, Staff Sergeant Bruce E. Mansfield, Sergeant Jerry D. Olds, Sergeant Ephraim Vasquez, and Airman First Class Rufus L. James.

35. Van Staaveren, *Interdiction in Southern Laos*, 178–79.

36. Since North Vietnam was also bordered by the Gulf of Tonkin one might logically ask why an MSQ-77 was not placed aboard the relative safety of a ship operating in international waters. In fact, beginning in late 1967 the 1st CEVG began tests, code-named "Combat Keel," using an MSQ-77 on board the USS *Thomas J. Gary*, a radar picket escort ship. The system was tested in the Gulf of Mexico with simulated missions flown against the Matagorda, Texas bombing range. Durkee, "Combat Skyspot," 25–26, and 1 CEVG documents in my possession. According to Colonel Clayton, this ship-borne system never reached the operational stage because of the difficulties involved in maintain-

ing and returning to an exact location, an imperative for the system to successfully operate. Clayton, interview, October 27, 1994.

37. Dommen, *Conflict in Laos*, 224.

38. Blaufarb, "Organizing and Managing Unconventional War in Laos," 19–20.

39. For an excellent U.S. Air Force overview of the skill and ingenuity shown by the North Vietnamese as they moved people and supplies down the Ho Chi Minh Trail see Vallentiny, "USAF Operations from Thailand, 1 January 1967 to 1 July 1968," 39–42. Project CHECO report.

40. The Lao People's Party was founded on March 22, 1955 in Sam Neua. See Brown and Zasloff, *Apprentice Revolutionaries*, 54–59.

41. Stuart-Fox and Kooyman, *Historical Dictionary of Laos*, 86 and 114. I first visited the plain and examined the jars in 1990. In 1994 my colleagues and I were lodged in a series of very comfortable cabins on a hillside overlooking the town of Phon Savan. A flower garden at the entrance of the establishment had once been a very large bomb crater and guest room keys were attached to a small caliber shell casing. Unhappily, by this time someone, presumably a Lao government official, had decided to inventory these antiquities by painting large white numbers on the outside of the jars. During my most recent visit to the plain in November 1996, I saw that some of the numbers had been covered by white paint and new markings placed inside the jars. Needless to say, the effect is aesthetically devastating.

42. Castle, *At War in the Shadow of Vietnam*, 4 and 106. According to a comprehensive U.S. study of the air war, from 1965 through 1971 more than 1.6 million tons of bombs were dropped on Laos. *The Pentagon Papers* 5: 280–81. An official USAF history notes that on the very first B-52 bombing raid against the Plain of Jars, February 17–18, 1970, thirty-six aircraft dropped 1,078 tons of munitions on communist positions. Berger, ed., rev. ed., *The United States Air Force in Southeast Asia*, 131. Although no one can be sure of the exact tonnage, various Lao government officials have told me the figure is more than 3 million tons dropped on Laos. "A ton for every Laotian," they say. For a unique and impassioned perspective with drawings and essays by civilians who suffered through the bombing, see Branfman, *Voices from the Plain of Jars*. The United States military is currently involved in several humanitarian projects aimed at improving the quality of rural Lao life. Of special relevance, the U.S. is training Laotians to deal with the extraordinary problem of unexploded bombs and other explosives. Decades after the war, many Lao are still being killed and maimed.

43. Castle, *At War in the Shadow of Vietnam*, 31. See also Blaufarb, "Unconventional War in Laos," 75–77, for an excellent review of the Lao political, social, and economic factors that often dictated the role of the U.S. in Laos.

44. Although accounts of this period invariably refer to the Hmong as "Meo," this term is now known to westerners as a pejorative. For a brief history of Hmong

migration into Laos and thoughts on the use of the word "Meo" see Yang Dao, *Hmong at the Turning Point*, xi-xvi. Yang Dao is a highly respected Hmong scholar who was forced to flee Laos in 1975 and now teaches and writes in Minnesota.

45. Major General Vang Pao, interview, February 6, 1979.

46. John E. "Jack" Shirley, interview, August 17, 1990. Shirley was one of the original CIA paramilitary officers assigned to Laos.

47. Castle, *At War in the Shadow of Vietnam*, 35 and 59. Under the system airfields located at the major Lao towns were designated "Lima" followed by a numeral. For example, Vientiane, L 08 and Savannakhet, L 39.

48. Ibid, 37–40.

49. Ibid, 111–12. Some of Thailand's most senior military and police officers, including a former prime minister, General Chavalit Yongchaiyut, are veterans of the HQ 333 program.

50. Interviews with Shirley, James W. "Bill" Lair, and Lloyd "Pat" Landry, August 17, 1990. Landry was also a career CIA officer who served as Lair's deputy and inherited the program in 1968 when Lair was reassigned. For a lengthy and engaging account of the CIA's early contact with Vang Pao see Warner, *Shooting at the Moon*, 20–34. Warner had earlier published a slightly different version of this book under the title *Backfire*. For details on the "White Star" teams see Castle, *At War in the Shadow of Vietnam*, 32.

51. Bowers, *Tactical Airlift*, 442.

52. Dommen, *Conflict in Laos*, 197. The 1954 Geneva agreements on Laos stated that "All foreign powers except France were prohibited from establishing or maintaining bases on Lao soil." The United States was not a signatory, however, and the State Department took the position that the U.S. had no legal obligation to refrain from providing military assistance and advisors to the Royal Lao government. Ibid., 53. For a comprehensive study of the 1954 Geneva Conference see Randle, *Geneva 1954: The Settlement of the Indochinese War*.

53. Shirley, interview, August 1, 1990. Shirley still possessed a vivid recollection of the communist shelling and the hectic evacuation over remote mountain trails to safety.

54. Goldstein, *American Policy Toward Laos*, 247—72, esp. p. 249.

55. For a detailed review of this period see Dommen, *Conflict in Laos*, 200–22, and Mirsky and Stonefield, "The Nam Tha Crisis: Kennedy and the New Frontier on the Brink," in Adams and McCoy, eds., *Laos: War and Revolution*, 163–75.

56. Sam Thong was designated LS20. Long Tieng, LS20A. It was also sometimes referred to as LS 98.

57. In 1994 I regularly overflew Long Tieng as I helicoptered back and forth between Vientiane and Phon Savan on the Plain of Jars. Although the area is

now sparsely populated and generally off-limits to outsiders, the runway and aircraft parking areas are still clearly visible. Small helicopters owned by a private company, Lao West Coast, occasionally land at the field. This is quite a contrast from the last years of the war when Long Tieng was one of the busiest airports in southeast Asia with a population in the surrounding area of nearly 50,000 men, women, and children.

58. Dommen, 224, and Paul, "Laos: Anatomy of an American Involvement," 533.

59. Castle, *At War in the Shadow of Vietnam*, 49–50.

60. Colby, *Lost Victory*, 195. For another account of the CIA officers who remained in Laos see Warner, *Shooting at the Moon*, 85. Warner reports that one hundred of the PARU remained as well. I have not seen this documented elsewhere, but respect the credibility of his sources.

61. The Royal Lao government, of course, had never made any such request of the North Vietnamese. Dommen, *Conflict in Laos*, 240.

62. Colby, *Honorable Men*, 192.

63. For a more detailed account of this period see Castle, *At War in the Shadow of Vietnam*, 52–61.

64. Electrical message, Amembassy Vientiane to SECSTATE, 140210Z May 1965. Presumably, the deleted portion contained a reference to the CIA.

65. This policy was "reiterated and clarified" by the White House in March 1966. In a cable to senior U.S. military officials, Sullivan used the opportunity to remind them of his unique authority over their operations. Electrical message, Amembassy Vientiane, 110723Z March 1966, Project Corona Harvest. For a detailed explanation of the presidential directive and Sullivan's military role see Castle, *At War in the Shadow of Vietnam*, 77–9.

66. Sullivan, *Obbligato*, 211.

67. Sharp, interview, March 6, 1990.

68. Westmoreland letter, March 3, 1990, and interview, April 13, 1990.

69. For specifics see Westmoreland, *Soldier Reports*, 96–97, 256, 449, and Van Staaveren, *Interdiction in Southern Laos*, 138.

70. Electrical message, Amembassy Vientiane to CINCPAC, 240550Z July 1967. See also Foreign Relations of the United States (hereafter FRUS) 1964–1968, Volume 28, Laos, document 301, and the follow-on cable, document 302.

71. Blaufarb, "Unconventional War in Laos," 67.

72. Castle, *At War in the Shadow of Vietnam*, 88–90.

73. Blaufarb, "Unconventional War in Laos," 59.

2. "I Wonder If It Is Worth It"

1. Stevenson, *The End of Nowhere: American Policy Toward Laos Since 1954*, 217.

2. Van Staaveren, *Interdiction in Southern Laos*, 54.

3. Barrel Roll was defined as an area in Laos north of a line of coordinates 18 degrees 21 minutes North by 103 degrees 57 minutes East to 18 degrees 27 min-

utes North by 105 degrees 6 minutes East. Steel Tiger was located along the entire eastern side of Laos south of the above coordinates.

4. Van Staaveren, *Interdiction in Southern Laos,* 55–56.

5. Ibid, 56.

6. Van Staaveren, *Interdiction in Southern Laos* 58–61. A complete review of early Steel Tiger operations can be found on pp. 53–74.

7. For details see Castle, *At War in the Shadow of Vietnam,* 69–71.

8. Bowers, *Tactical Airlift,* 161. For a detailed, albeit dated, explanation of the TACAN system see Bauss, ed., *Radio Navigation Systems for Aviation and Maritime Use,* 59–70.

9. U.S. Air Force study, "USAF Communications and Air Traffic Control Operations in Southeast Asia, 1960–1973," 40–42. As an example of the weight and size involved, a ground transfer of the equipment at one site required the use of three 2.5 ton trucks.

10. Ibid., 39–40.

11. This was the official designation used in radio communications.

12. The personnel were from the USAF 1973d Communications Squadron, Udorn Royal Thai Air Force Base. A discrepancy exists in the USAF records regarding the actual dates involved. Van Staaveren, *Interdiction in Southern Laos,* 129, cites sources that report movement of the equipment from Ubon air base, Thailand to Phou Kate on January 9, 1966. However, he later states, p. 288, that the site was installed in April. According to "USAF Communications and Air Traffic Control Operations in Southeast Asia, 1960–1973," 40, the equipment was installed in April and became operational in June 1966.

13. As noted earlier, Long Tieng was also known as Lima Site 20A/Lima Site 98.

14. "USAF Communications and Air Traffic Control Operations in Southeast Asia, 1960–1973," 40–41. The radios were being monitored by CIA and PARU personnel operating from the site.

15. Sullivan insisted that civilians maintain and operate the Laos-based TACANs. In February 1966 the Federal Electric Company (FECO) received a year's contract for two navigational aids. Upon renegotiation in the spring of 1967, a third TACAN was added and FECO accepted a six month contract worth nearly a million dollars. All was not well with the program, however. The Air Force experienced a number of recurring problems with the contract, often having to "bail the contractor out." According to the report, "FECO experienced difficulties in recruiting cleared technicians and ground power mechanics." Thus, in addition to paying a premium for the contract, the Air Force was often having to send its own personnel into Laos to assist the FECO technicians. Faced with a totally unsatisfactory situation, in mid-1967 Headquarters Pacific Air Forces (HQ PACAF) directed the FECO contract not be renewed. Responsibility for the TACANs was to be transferred to a new, highly classi-

fied project, called Heavy Green. See "USAF Communications and Air Traffic Control Operations in Southeast Asia, 1960–1973," 43–44.

16. "USAF Communications and Air Traffic Control Operations in Southeast Asia, 1960–1973," 41–42. The town of Muang Phalane was located along Route 9, the principal roadway connecting the Lao Mekong river town of Savannakhet and the South Vietnamese border at Lao Bao. Khe Sanh was located just a few miles beyond the boundary. In 1991 and 1992 I traveled extensively along Route 9. The subject of extensive U.S. bombing in the late 1960s and early 1970s, most of the original population abandoned the area and all of the buildings were destroyed.

17. Van Staaveren, *Interdiction in Southern Laos*, 288–89.

18. For example, on November 24, senior leaders at PACAF were being told they "must get MSQ in N. Laos." Rockly Triantafellu, letter, April 21, 1998. From 1966–69, Brigadier General Triantafellu was the Director of Intelligence at Headquarters PACAF. The general has graciously reviewed contemporaneous notes of the period and provided me with relevant excerpts.

19. William H. Sullivan, interview, January 16,1995, and U.S. Joint Chiefs of Staff Memorandum for the Secretary of Defense, JCSM-231-67, "Installation of MSQ-77 in Northern Laos," April 25, 1967, 3. This key document, formerly classified Top Secret, was first brought to my attention by Vietnam war author/researcher George "Jay" Veith.

20. Electrical message, Admiral U.S.G. Sharp to General Wheeler, "Installation of MSQ 77 in Northern Laos," 250152Z February 1967. Copies were also sent to General Westmoreland, COMUSMACV, and General Ryan, CINCPACAF. Ryan had recently replaced General Harris.

21. "Installation of MSQ-77 in Northern Laos," 3.

22. Most of these CIA and Air Force operations were launched from LS 36, Na Khang. Site 85's often poor weather conditions made it too unreliable for planned missions. Freeman, interview, January 10, 1997. For details on Air Force rescue work from Na Khang see Tilford, *Setup*, 82–83.

23. Confidential interviews, May 2, 1988. Air force rescue helicopters and an extraordinarily brave pararescue specialist would return to Pha Thi on March 11, 1968, for a very different purpose. See chapter 10. My confidential sources were active duty USAF pararescue specialists who occasionally landed at Site 85. Although these events had occurred twenty years earlier, they were reluctant to have their names disclosed in conjunction with U.S. activities in Laos.

24. Theodore G. Shackley, interview, December 17, 1996.

25. Lair, interview, March 6, 1994. Lair affirmed that he was repeatedly assured by Air Force officers that the radar would make flying against heavily defended targets safer for the aircrews. "Lives would be saved," he was told . See also Warner, *Shooting at the Moon*, 205–7.

26. Installation of MSQ-77 in Northern Laos," 1.

27. Ibid., 2. Although Nakhon Phanom is mentioned as the support base, the location was later changed to Udorn. While Nakhon Phanom was smaller and more isolated, easing concerns about security leaks, Udorn was the headquarters for 7/13th AF. As noted previously, Udorn was also the home of Air America and the operations center for the CIA's paramilitary program in northeastern Laos.

28. "Installation of MSQ-77 in Northern Laos," 3.

29. Ibid.

30. Ibid.

31. Ibid. In another response to the difficulties of all-weather bombing over North Vietnam, in April 1967 the U.S. Air Force began a program code-named "Commando Nail," using F-105F and F-4D aircraft, specially trained two-pilot crews, and enhanced ground maintenance support. The aircraft's internal radar and a bombing computer were used to determine location and bomb release point. Later, the F-111A was also used in a Commando Nail role. The original idea came from General John D. Ryan, CINCPACAF. See "Summary of Commando Nail Operations, 26 April–31 October 1967." Operations Analysis, Headquarters, USAF, November 22, 1967. Corona Harvest Report.

32. U.S. State Department memorandum from William Sullivan to William Bundy, "Limitations on Military Actions in Laos," May 1, 1967, 5. Sullivan went on to say, "for limited operational advantages on the Ho Chi Minh Trail (none of which I am convinced would succeed) we would probably lose the entire Mekong Valley. To quote President Kennedy, this would be like trading an apple for an orchard." DDRS, 1995, document 3489.

33. "Limitations on Military Actions in Laos," 4.

34. Sullivan, interview, January 16, 1995.

3. Heavy Green

1. Official USAF statement, Heavy Green project officer, Lieutenant Colonel Robert A. Cornetti, AF Office of Special Plans, September 16, 1975. The statement was written eight years after the events discussed and in direct response to a lawsuit filed against the Air Force by Ann Holland, wife of Melvin A. Holland, a Heavy Green participant who did not return from Site 85. See endnote 12. The lawsuit is discussed in chapter 13.

2. Sullivan, testimony before U.S. Senate Subcommittee on U.S. Security Agreements and Commitments Abroad, October 21, 1969, 489. At the time Sullivan was Deputy Assistant Secretary, Bureau of East Asian and Pacific Affairs, U.S. State Department. I am indebted to the staff of Senator Claiborne Pell, Senate Foreign Relations Committee, who upon my request provided declassified copies of this heretofore unavailable material. A State Department cable to Sullivan declared "We appreciate your skillful handling of this delicate problem with Souvanna and are of course pleased that he agreed." Electrical mes-

sage, State Department to Amembassy Vientiane, "MSQ-77," July 8, 1967. Little else, however, has been publicly released regarding Souvanna's agreement to place the bombing radar in Laos. When asked about his efforts to gain Souvanna's approval for the radar, Sullivan has said that he no longer has a clear recollection of these discussions. He did comment, however, that "there was extensive cable traffic on this issue." Sullivan, interview, January 16, 1995. Perhaps one day the State Department will declassify the entire series of cables dealing with these events. Sullivan's CIA Chief of Station, Theodore G. Shackley, at the Ambassador's order, had little contact with Souvanna. Although Shackley was involved from the very beginning with the Heavy Green project, he did not participate in any discussions with the Lao regarding permission to place the radar at Site 85. Shackley, interview.

3. Narration by Donald Staeger of movie film taken of the arrival and assembly of prototype radar at Bryan, Texas, airfield. Staeger was a civilian contracting officer assigned to the USAF Sacramento Air Material Area, McClellan AFB, California. He served as the liaison between the Reeves Corporation and the Air Force. The contract number was 04606–67-C-1442. A video tape copy of the film was provided to me by Colonel Clayton.

4. Bryan airfield video tape. Of note, during the narration of the tape Staeger expresses doubt that all the identification markings could have been removed before the equipment was shipped to Southeast Asia.

5. Letter (ca. 1988) written by Robert C. Seitzberg to Gerald H. Clayton, and Seitzberg, interview, November 20, 1994. Clayton has graciously made the letter available to me. While switching to the helicopter at LS 107 Seitzberg briefly spoke to several USAF search and rescue helicopter pilots on alert duty at the remote site. As fate would have it, Seitzberg knew one of the pilots who, doubtless, was startled to see a 7th AF staff officer in northeastern Laos.

6. This strip was located at an elevation of about 5,300 feet. Mostly used by helicopters, a few very talented pilots landed Short-Takeoff-and-Landing (STOL) airplanes on the short and narrow tract.

7. In December 1967 Seitzberg was transferred from Saigon to South Korea. He remained with the Skyspot program, however, and was informed of the subsequent attack and loss of life. In addition to knowing most of those who served at Site 85, Seitzberg had enjoyed a close friendship with Lieutenant Colonel Clarence F. Blanton, the on-duty Heavy Green commander. Seitzberg, interview.

8. Ibid.

9. Ibid. Seitzberg recalled that the explosives expert was on board a ship returning to the U.S. when he was contacted and asked to take on the project. He was flown from the Philippines back to South Vietnam where "he was put up in at a hotel in downtown Saigon and wined and dined."

10. Clayton, interview, August 26, 1994.

11. Interview with a senior enlisted man formerly assigned to the 1 CEVG.

12. Cornetti, statement. The AF attorneys concluded that the men would be conducting a clandestine mission in Laos disguised as civilians. They were, therefore, not entitled to POW or "protected person" status as defined under the Geneva Convention.

13. Ibid. In U.S. Air Force lexicon the Special Plans office was designated AFXP-DRC.

14. Lockheed Aircraft Service was a division of the Lockheed Aircraft Corporation.

15. Dettloff [Holland] v. United States of America and Lockheed Aircraft Corporation, Civil Action C76–131s, U.S. District Court, Western District of Washington, "Interrogatories," July 13, 1978, attachment A, 1. This document is one of many unique records made available to me by Ann Holland. In 1975, on behalf of herself and her five minor children, she filed suit for $1.6 million against Lockheed and the U.S. government for "Wrongful Death and Damages for Mental Suffering." I am greatly indebted to Ann Holland and her attorney Howard A. Pruzan, since much of the declassified information on Site 85 is available only in these lawsuit-related materials. Mrs. Holland's legal odyssey is detailed in chapter 13.

16. The contract number was F33601–68-C-0221. Interrogatories, July 13, 1978, A1–2.

17. Since 1966 the Air Force had been sending combat-seasoned forward air controllers to Laos, best known by their nickname, "Ravens." These men never wore uniforms and carried USAID identification. If captured, they were told to claim civilian status. See Castle, *At War in the Shadow of Vietnam*, 86–87.

18. Alan C. Randle, interview, December 14, 1994 and A.J. Born, interview, December 10, 1994.

19. Randle, interview. For details on the relationship between the Deputy Commander, 7/13th AF and the U.S. Embassy and CIA in Laos see Castle, *At War in the Shadow of Vietnam*, 88–90.

20. Randle and Born, interviews.

21. Born, interview.

22. Ibid. Born says that he allowed the men to visit Udorn every two or three weeks, but personally remained on the mountain throughout the entire operation.

23. Ibid. The TACAN at Site 85 required periodic maintenance and Born recalled seeing at least two technicians working on the navigation aid during his time on the mountain. Later, while aboard a military aircraft en route from Thailand to the United States, Born had a chance encounter with one of these men. "He seemed quite surprised to see me in uniform. We did not speak to each other." Born, interview. Despite Born's inability to recall any specific meetings with CIA personnel at Pha Thi, CIA officers are known to have occa-

sionally visited the site during the installation phase. Lair, interview, March 6, 1994.

24. The installation crew communicated with Randle at Udorn via a single side band radio. Personal mail, which Born says was censored, was forwarded to the site on supply helicopters. Born, interview.

25. One of the CH-3 "Jolly Green" helicopter pilots from the 20th Helicopter Squadron, then Air Force Major Howard D. Armstrong, recalls that his first impression of Pha Thi was that it was "a fortress nobody could take." Howard D. Armstrong, interview, December 6, 1994.

26. Randle and Born, interviews. More than two decades after the events, the former Air Force pilot was effusive in his praise of the U.S. Army CH-47 helicopter support. "Absolutely professional," declared Randle.

27. Chief Warrant Officer 5 Dennis X. McCormack, U.S. Army retired, interview, December 5, 1996. McCormack spent more than twenty-five years flying army helicopters, including several tours in South Vietnam and duty in Iraq during the Persian Gulf war.

28. Bowers, *Tactical Airlift*, 455.

29. Electrical message, 7/13th AF to 7th AF and Headquarters PACAF, "Summary Status Report 2 as of 0200Z, 26 Aug 67." The term "Operating Location" was a Strategic Air Command term for the ground-directed bombing radar sites.

30. Using a satellite-based global positioning system (GPS), in 1994 U.S. government investigators determined the radar site had been located at grid coordinate 48Q UH 6623561101.

31. I am indebted to Chief Master Sergeant Born for providing me with detailed sketches of these buildings and the associated equipment. Likewise, Ann Holland has given me a video copy of a U.S. Air Force film made at the conclusion of the site's construction and Colonel Clayton has provided photos of the site. I have, therefore, based this description on Born's sketches, the USAF film, discussions with the participants, and my own visit to Phou Pha Thi.

32. Ibid.

33. Ibid.

34. At this time the Pha Thi TACAN was located on the western edge of the helipad several hundred yards below the radar facility. During their maintenance checks the contractors did have limited contact with the installation crew but were not allowed up the path to the facility. As noted in chapter 2, Air Force records reveal financial and maintenance issues as major concerns for a switch to Heavy Green. Clayton recalls being told to keep the new TACAN duties very closely held, so as not to alert the contractor that the military was taking back the project. Clayton, interview, October 27, 1994. The decision was likely a result of all three issues: security, money, and maintenance problems. The

Air Force, to its dismay, would soon experience the very high cost of proper security and maintenance.

35. Clayton, interviews, October 27, 1994, and December 9, 1996.

36. Ibid.

37. Cornetti, statement.

38. Interrogatories, Case C-76–131S, U.S. District Court, Seattle, Washington, May 16, 1978, Exhibit A. Paragraph two is dated Sept 12, 1967 and signed by Melvin A. Holland. Paragraph three is dated Sept 7, 1967 and signed R. H. Ellis, indicating that General Ellis had signed blank copies in preparation for the Barksdale briefing. Of note, Ellis later became a four-star general and USAF vice chief of staff.

39. Clayton, interview, December 9, 1996.

40. As an example, before taxes and other deductions, Lockheed would pay a former staff sergeant about $343 a week.

41. Interrogatories, April 5, 1976, 2–3.

42. Permanent Change of Station orders, Melvin A. Holland, HQ 1 Combat Evaluation Group, special order A-458, September 14, 1967. Holland moved his family from Mississippi to Washington State and on October 7, his eldest son's eight birthday, left for Bolling AFB. Ann Holland, interview, December 18, 1994.

43. Francis A. Roura, interview, November 27, 1994.

44. Cornetti, statement.

45. Mary C. Hall, interview, December 10,1996. Mrs. Hall's husband did not return from Site 85.

46. NBC News, interview, Ann Holland and Stanley J. Sliz, April 28, 1994.

47. Gerald H. Clayton, Deposition, Case C-76–131S, U.S. District Court, Seattle, Washington, November 14, 1978, 21. Clayton was deposed in conjunction with the Holland lawsuit.

48. Hall, interview.

49. Holland, letter, January 18, 1997.

50. Cornetti, statement. One wife vigorously objected to the loss of her military dependent status. However, because her husband was so deeply involved in the program and wanted very much to participate, the refusal was ignored and he was allowed to proceed with the assignment. Clayton, interview, November 21, 1997. It is unclear if she was allowed to retain her dependent identification card. Her husband was not at Site 85 during the attack and "returned" to the Air Force in mid-1968.

51. Holland, letter, January 18, 1997. During her efforts to convince her husband to turn down the assignment, Holland remembers asking her husband to think about the fate of U-2 reconnaissance pilot Francis Gary Powers. He replied "this isn't the same thing." Powers, who had also resigned from the Air Force in order to be hired by Lockheed, was shot down over the Soviet

Union in May 1960. His intelligence collection mission and capture were first revealed not by the U.S., but by Soviet Premier Nikita Khrushchev. Ann Holland's point was that if there were some sort of calamity her husband and the others might find themselves disavowed by their government. Holland, letter, January 18, 1997. For details on the Powers shoot down, see Prouty, *The Secret Team*, 419–22.

52. Holland, interview, December 18, 1994, and Clayton, deposition, 22.

53. Jack C. Starling, interview, September 17, 1994.

54. Klaus R. Kirk v. United States of America, U.S. District Court, Western District of Washington, Judgment, August 12, 1983, 3–4.

55. Peter Lewis, "Laos Death Unsettled Case," *The Seattle Times*, April 14, 1983, sec. C1–2.

56. Ibid. For a less specific version of these events see Klaus R. Kirk v. Lockheed Aircraft Corporation and United States of America, U.S. District Court, Western District of Washington, No. C76–247s, Deposition Upon Oral Examination of Klaus Ruediger Kirk, December 2, 1981, 11–2.

57. Herbert Kirk, although a longtime serviceman, was a staff sergeant. His rank, E-5, on a scale of E-1 to E-9, would have made him a rather compliant subject for a senior officer. While I have no doubt Kirk wanted this assignment, I am also certain his loyalty should have been rewarded. If the Air Force had reason to reject Kirk's wife for a security clearance, which I believe they did, it is difficult to understand why they did not find another repairman.

58. Roura, interview, November 27, 1994. Roura eventually retired from the Air Force as a Chief Master Sergeant, the highest enlisted grade.

59. Interrogatories, July 13, 1978, A2. The effective date of employment was listed as October 16, 1967, the same date the men were officially released from the Air Force. One of the men, whose identity is known to me, initially refused to purchase the life insurance offered by Lockheed. Complaining, he was finally cajoled by his fellow airmen into signing the paperwork. He did not return from Site 85. The life insurance was underwritten by Lloyd's of London, $25,000 per man, and the Traveler's Insurance Company, $35,000 per man.

60. Ibid. In place of their uniforms, the men went to a Sears store and bought dark blue two-piece civilian work clothes. During the Lockheed processing Melvin Holland managed to get away for a few days for a final visit with his family in Woodland, Washington. Holland, interview, January 19, 1997. A number of the other men took the opportunity to visit the nearby casinos at Las Vegas. Harold D. Summers, interview, January 14, 1995. Master Sergeant Summers was a radar technician and one of the Heavy Green participants. He was on leave in the United States at the time Site 85 was lost.

61. Clayton, interview, October 27, 1994.

62. Ibid.

63. Clodfelter, *Limits of Air Power*, 142.

64. On October 10, the men were placed on U.S. Air Force temporary duty (TDY) orders for Udorn, Thailand. Using their correct names and military ranks, the orders were issued by the same organization that processed them, on the same day, out of the Air Force. Special Order number TB-928, 10 October 1967. Purpose of the TDY was, "To Provide Radar Scope/Tape Evaluation for Hqs 7th and 13th Air Forces." Length of the temporary duty was listed as approximately 248 days. Although assigned on their permanent change of station orders to "Detachment 1, 1043 Radar Evaluation Group," the TDY orders specified Detachment 1 as a squadron.

65. Clayton, interview, October 27, 1994.

66. Roura, interview, November 27, 1994.

67. Ibid., and Daniel, interview, September 2, 1994.

68. A surveyor's mark made on a stationary object of previously determined position and elevation and used as a reference point in tidal observations and surveys.

69. Randle, December 14, 1994 and Armstrong interviews. Armstrong was the French-speaking pilot.

70. Born, interview.

71. There were two Thai-based F-105 wings, the 355th, and the 388th located at Korat Royal Thai Air Force Base.

72. John C. Giraudo, U.S. Air Force Oral History, January 8–12, 1985, 275. After a long and distinguished career, Giraudo would retire at the rank of major general. For background on Momyer's accusations see Broughton, *Going Downtown*, especially chapters 11 and 12. Broughton was the 355th Vice Wing Commander prior to Giraudo's arrival. He was court martialed and relieved of command after the controversial bombing by 355th pilots of the *Turkestan*, a Russian freighter anchored at a North Vietnamese port.

73. Giraudo, oral history, 283.

74. While Momyer allowed the 355th to fly without the IFF engaged, the 388th continued to employ it.

75. Giraudo, oral history, 307.

76. Giraudo, oral history, 324, and Gordon F. Blood, interview, October 26, 1994. General Blood recalled his own experience in Korea with ground-directed radar bombing and admitted that "pilots didn't like it very much." Nonetheless, Blood pointed out that "with the weather conditions that existed in North Vietnam there were few other options."

77. Giraudo, oral history, 324. Lieutenant Colonel Randle, the controller for this mission, recalls no such request for the IFF to be turned on. According to Randle, "IFF should not have been a problem, we were using the beacon on the aircraft. We couldn't use the IFF to track the aircraft. I don't recall the subject of the IFF ever being raised." Randle, interview, January 17, 1997.

78. Giraudo, oral history, 325.

79. Giraudo, letter, October 12, 1994.

80. Rockly Triantafellu, interview, February 24, 1998.

81. There is no doubt, however, that Blood was gravely concerned by Rolling Thunder's mounting losses in men and equipment. "There was a great deal of frustration. Momyer said the bombing restrictions were 'dumb flying,' but we were under civilian control." Blood, interview.

82. An incendiary mixture of fine aluminum powder and iron.

83. Born, interview. Master Sergeant Donnell W. Hill, who served with the Heavy Green operations crew, recalled that the thermite was wired to a switch located near the door to the radar operations area. In the event of an emergency destruction order, the switch was supposed to activate ignition caps embedded in the thermite. Donnell W. Hill, interview, February 16, 1995. Prior to the turnover camouflage netting was draped on the equipment and buildings in an attempt to conceal the Heavy Green activities. Sometime thereafter U.S. Air Force photographers filmed the entire area, including aerial views from a helicopter.

84. Master Sergeant Norman D. Mooty, interview, January 7, 1995. Mooty was the radioman assigned to the Layman crew.

85. Born, interview. Part of his briefing involved the procedures for emergency destruction using the thermite.

4. "Commando Club"

1. Hereafter, air strikes flown under the control of the TSQ-81 would be referred to as "Commando Club" missions. Depending on level of security clearance and organization involved, there were now seven different designations assigned to the operations at Phou Pha Thi: Site 85, Commando Club, Heavy Green, radio call-sign "Wager," Channel 97 (also known as Clara) for the TACAN operations, OL (Operating Location) 28 within the Strategic Air Command, and "North Station," an unofficial name used in some USAF communications. See also Major General Gordon F. Blood, USAF, End of Tour Report, August 1967–January 1969, part E, 11.

2. After the North Vietnamese rejected Johnson's peace initiative, known as the "San Antonio Formula," the President approved air attacks on targets within ten miles of Hanoi and Haiphong. Berman, *Lyndon Johnson's War*, 83–84, and Sharp, *Strategy for Defeat*, 202. For a lengthy discussion on President Johnson's efforts to negotiate with the North Vietnamese see Herring, *LBJ and Vietnam*, chapter 4.

3. Overton, "Rolling Thunder," 8.

4. U.S. Air Force Working Paper for Corona Harvest Report. *Out-Country Air Operations, Southeast Asia, 1 January 1965–31 March 1968*, 135.

5. Blood, interview. From January to the end of November, air strikes in RP V and VI-A claimed more than 100 USAF aircraft. During the same period, 78

U.S. Navy planes were downed while flying against targets in RP VI-B. Ground fire claimed most of these aircraft. "Air Operations Southeast Asia." (Headquarters PACAF: Directorate of Tactical Evaluation), 40: 3 and 5–24. (Hereafter cited as AOSEA.)

6. For a detailed discussion of Site 36 and the role of U.S. Air Force close air support see Porter, *The Defense of Lima Site 36*, May 25, 1966, and Porter, *The Second Defense of Lima Site 36*, April 28, 1967. Both project CHECO reports.

7. John W. Spence, interview, September 9, 1994, Terry Quill, interview, June 8, 1995, Colonel Chalong Nakpong, interview, March 6, 1994, and USDAO/PW-MIA, Bangkok, report "Survivor Account of Loss of Lima Site 85," August 30, 1994. Chalong, a sergeant in the Royal Thai army at the time of the March attack, was assigned to the mountain as part of the CIA-controlled Thai government program known as "Headquarters 333." See chapter 1. The source of the USDAO/PW-MIA report was the Zulu-16 team leader, currently a Thai police lieutenant colonel.

8. Spence, interview, September 9, 1994. Another CIA officer, Howard J. Freeman, recalled that the enterprising Hmong in the village of Pha Thi soon "tapped into" the generator's electrical output and "lit up the whole place." Freeman was one of two CIA officers at Site 85 during the final attack. Freeman, interview, May 11, 1995. Controlled American Sources or CAS, was the wartime euphemism for the CIA. The term is commonly found in U.S. military documents of this period and was the expression normally used by the military when referring to the CIA or its personnel.

9. Spence, interview, September 9, 1994, and Vallentiny, "The Fall of Site 85," 4.

10. Clayton, interview, October 27, 1994.

11. Spence, interview, September 9, 1994, and Freeman, interview, May 11, 1995.

12. Electrical message, American Embassy Vientiane, March 1, 1968.

13. Daniel, interview, September 2, 1994.

14. For political and security reasons 7th AF assigned a specially equipped U.S. Air Force C-135 aircraft, flying over the Gulf of Tonkin near the 19th parallel, to operate in conjunction with the Commando Club missions. Under the system the TSQ controller's bomb run instructions were sent encrypted to the C-135, where they were instantly decoded and relayed in plain voice by a radio operator to the strike aircraft. This procedure effectively cloaked from the North Vietnamese and their allies the actual source of the air strike commands. See Momyer, *Air Power in Three Wars*, 179.

15. Clayton, letter, January 11, 1997, and Randle, interview, January 17, 1997.

16. Although the TACAN technician was assigned to Heavy Green, he had no role in the TSQ-81 operations.

17. This was not the first strike at Phuc Yen. For years CINCPAC and JCS had requested permission to attack the airfield. Secretary of Defense Robert McNamara, who feared the bombing of Phuc Yen would cause the People's

Republic of China to deploy fighters in an air defense role over North Vietnam, steadfastly refused. President Johnson, dissatisfied with the pace of peace talks, decided to turn up the pressure and Phuc Yen was struck on October 25, 1967. Momyer, *Air Power in Three Wars*, 22, and Clodfelter, *Limits of Air Power*, 110.

18. AOSEA 40: 5A-12. The Vietnamese later reported that Colonel Burdett, commander of the 388th TFW, had died in captivity and in March 1974 his remains were repatriated to the U.S.

19. Giraudo, oral history, 306 and 325. The counter argument, of course, was that the Air Force was already losing significant numbers of pilots and aircraft over North Vietnam and there was no proof that Colonel Burdett had been lost as a result of flying under radar control. Very few wing commanders, senior colonels, were lost during the war to enemy action. Undoubtedly, Burdett's position added visibility to the ground-directed bombing debate.

20. U.S. Air Force Working Paper for Corona Harvest Report. *Out-Country Air Operations, Southeast Asia, 1 January 1965–31 March 1968*, 137 (hereafter cited as CHWP).

21. Ibid., 137–38. Colonel Clayton recalls that one of changes allowed the fighter-bombers to perform defensive maneuvers, called "jinking," until the final thirty seconds of the bomb run. While the jinking created problems for the Heavy Green team in tracking the aircraft and providing directions to maintain proper course and speed, and probably reduced the accuracy of the bombing, the maneuvering afforded the pilots an additional defense against communist SAMs and AAA.

22. Major General William C. Lindley, USAF, End of Tour Report, June 1967–June 1968, 3.

23. CHWP, 138.

24. As of August 1967 there were 427 fixed targets on the combined JCS-CINCPAC "Operating Target List." Clodfelter, *Limits of Air Power*, 109. Interestingly enough, a detailed history of wartime weather forecasting suggests that during Rolling Thunder operations Momyer had little patience for weathermen. See Bates and Fuller, *America's Weather Warriors: 1814–1985*, 209.

25. Overton, "Rolling Thunder," 17.

26. Ibid, 18.

27. Ibid, 17. The undercast was a significant concern since it prevented a post-strike reconnaissance evaluation of bombing accuracy and damage. See also DDRS, 1996, document 0622, for a detailed CIA appraisal of the bombing of North Vietnam, 1 January—31 March 1968.

28. The barracks was located at Kim Lang and the storage facilities were located at Son La and Coc Bang. AOSEA 40: 1–12. This recently declassified U.S. Air Force series provides the most detailed information yet available on Commando Club. It is, however, often at odds with other Air Force documents.

Moreover, the monthly summaries are inconsistent (and sometimes contradictory) in the presentation of data. Among other obvious problems, this
makes it very difficult to draw month-by-month comparisons. Nonetheless,
after years of research I believe these materials offer the best available evidence
on the Heavy Green missions.

29. Targets included Hoa Loc and Kep airfields, railroad yards at Mo Trang, Thai
Nguyen, Tien Cuong, and Yen Bai. Army barracks were attacked at Kim Lang,
Thai Nguyen, Tuyen Quang, and Xom Bai. AOSEA 41: 7A2–7A4.

30. 42: 1–13, 2, 2–6, 7A1–7A2.

31. Hoa Loc airfield was hit, but other North Vietnamese targets are unspecified.
AOSEA 43: 1–9, 1–12, 2–6, 2–7. During this period Commando Club began
directing beacon-equipped A1E and A—26 aircraft against Lao targets. Of
note, the A1s flew fourteen bomb runs, while the A-26s participated in six
attacks. AOSEA 43: 2–7.

32. AOSEA44: 1, 1–12. A Pacific Air Forces study provides limited data on the
mathematical probabilities of bombing miss distances and addresses eleven
Heavy Green targets. However, there is no information on actual target damage. See Headquarters Pacific Air Forces, Assistant for Operations Analysis,
"Bias Errors in Commando Club Operations." April 16, 1968.

33. For discerning remarks on the significance of Rolling Thunder see Clodfelter,
Limits of Air Power, 134–146, and Tilford, *Setup*, 282–299.

34. Momyer commanded the 7th AF from July 1966 to August 1968 and was
deeply involved in the establishment and operation of Site 85.

35. Established by the chief of staff of the Air Force in mid-1968, the purpose of
Corona Harvest was to evaluate the effectiveness of American air power in
Southeast Asia. Under the plan, the Air Force sent hundreds of thousands of
pages of reports and raw data to Air University at Maxwell AFB, Alabama, to
be studied by military students and specialists under the direction of a panel of
senior Air Force officers. See *Journal of the Armed Forces*, June 22, 1968. In
1973 General Momyer, recently retired, was hired by the Air Force as a consultant to oversee the conclusion of the Corona Harvest project.

36. The message errs in referring to the Pha Thi system as an "MSQ." While the
systems being used in South Vietnam and Thailand were indeed designated
"MSQ," as discussed in chapter 1, Heavy Green was using a specially developed TSQ-81.

37. Momyer, *Air Power in Three Wars*, 179.

38. Momyer has searched his own memory and was kind enough to query other
officers who served with him in Vietnam, but none could provide specifics on
the Heavy Green program. William W. Momyer, letter, November 11, 1997.

39. North Vietnamese efforts to propagandize the air and ground attacks against
Site 85 are reviewed in chapter 14.

40. U.S. Air Force study, Corona Harvest, "Out-Country Air Operations, South-

east Asia, 1 January 1965–31 March 1968," Memorandum for General Ellis from General Momyer, July 23, 1974. Maxwell AFB, Alabama. Momyer was specifically referring to military students who possessed the "need to know" and the appropriate security clearances. While some of Momyer's source documents remain classified, the materials under discussion here were declassified in 1995.

41. Berger, *USAF in Southeast Asia*, 126.

42. These issues are discussed in later chapters.

43. Berger, *USAF in Southeast Asia*, 126.

44. That is, if Hanoi concluded the site was responsible for directing bombing strikes. Evidence suggests the North Vietnamese did know there was a TACAN at Pha Thi, but there is no clear indication they knew there was a separate radar bombing system, which would, for them, have been a difference without a distinction. The site had to be destroyed because it was involved in the bombing of their country. See chapter 8.

45. "USAF Communications and Air Traffic Control Operations in Southeast Asia, 1960–1973," 42.

5. Sowing the Wind, Reaping the Whirlwind

1. Clayton, interview, October 27, 1994.

2. In Washington an Air Force special programs officer provided Clayton the station chief's name. Clayton was told Shackley would be his first point of contact, "I was told not to talk to anyone else." Clayton, interview, October 27, 1994.

3. Shackley, interview.

4. Sullivan, interview, and Clayton, interview, October 27, 1994.

5. Clayton, interview, October 27, 1994.

6. Shackley, interview.

7. Sullivan, interview.

8. Clayton, interview, October 27, 1994.

9. Jerry Clayton is just as adamant that Shackley was informed of the visit. Clayton carried with him to Vientiane all of the Heavy Green team member passports. He recalls that when he presented the documents to Shackley, and began to discuss entry and exit procedures, the station chief closed the conversation and called for Colonel Pettigrew. Clayton, interview, August 9, 1997. The Heavy Green team would be entering and departing Laos via Air Force and Air America aircraft without the formal approval of either the Thai or Lao governments. It was important, however, that the passports be available in the event the men had to use more traditional transportation to and from Thailand.

10. Shackley, interview. Warner, *Shooting at the Moon*, 208, says Shackley refused to meet with Clayton, a point Shackley strongly denied. Colonel Pettigrew had no recollection of the meeting. Pettigrew, interview.

11. For additional information on Air America's unique operations in Laos see Castle, *At War in the Shadow of Vietnam.*

12. Clayton, interviews, October 27, 1994, and December 9, 1996.

13. See chapter 2 for details on the earlier TACAN operations.

14. Ibid and Starling, interview, October 28, 1994. Starling was one of those who attended the TACAN course at Clark air base.

15. Vallentiny, "The Fall of Site 85," 7.

16. See chapter 2.

17. Vallentiny, "The Fall of Site 85," 8, and Warner, *Shooting at the Moon,* 225.

18. My interviews in Sam Neua with former Pathet Lao personnel, March 1994.

19. Spence, interview, September 12, 1994, and Vallentiny, "The Fall of Site 85," 9–10.

20. My interviews in Sam Neua with former Pathet Lao personnel, March 1994, and Chalong, interview.

21. Some Hmong have suggested there was dissension at the Pha Thi village. See Castle, *At War in the Shadow of Vietnam,* 170, n86.

22. CIA briefing to CINCPACAF, as cited in Vallentiny, "The Fall of Site 85," 7. The citation provides no exact date for the briefing.

23. Electrical message, Gen Lindley to Gen Momyer, November 24, 1967. Lindley reported that 42 trucks had been sighted the day earlier on Route 68. In his request, Lindley noted current 7AF policy which prohibited Barrel Roll sorties during specified unfavorable weather conditions, and asked that this restriction be waived.

24. According to the plan the LADC was Gia Tou, a Hmong captain. In practice, the defense was supervised by the senior CIA officer at Pha Thi.

25. Vallentiny, "The Fall of Site 85," 5–6.

26. Conboy, *Shadow War: The CIA's Secret War in Laos,* 178, electrical message, AMEMBASSY Vientiane to SECSTATE, 251511Z Dec 67, and Roura, interview, November 27, 1994. The Filipino was released by the Pathet Lao in April 1968. Conboy, 181.

27. Conboy, *Shadow War,* 178. Although a December 25 U.S. Embassy Vientiane message reported there were three Americans aboard the downed helicopter, based on his research and sources I believe Conboy to be more accurate.

28. Electrical message, Walt Rostow to President, December 26, 1967.

29. Clayton, interviews, October 27, 1994, and December 9, 1996. On December 28 the U.S. Embassy reported that villagers in the Muang Phalane area were claiming the attack was carried out by Pathet Lao, not North Vietnamese, forces. Electrical message, AMEMBASSY Vientiane to SECSTATE, 281106Z Dec 67. The embassy made no comment and, given the normally incidental combat role of the Pathet Lao and the known presence of North Vietnamese regulars, it is highly unlikely the attack was a Pathet Lao affair.

30. At the time of the incident Ambassador Sullivan was temporarily out of the country. Hurwitch was closely following the events.

31. Electrical message, AMEMBASSY Vientiane to SECSTATE, 280828Z Dec 67.

32. "USAF Communications and Air Traffic Control Operations in Southeast Asia, 1960–1973," 45–46. See also, Van Staaveren, *Interdiction in Southern Laos*, 289. However, Van Staaveren is in error when he reports on the same page a January 12, 1968 "NVA/PL" ground attack on Site 85. It is difficult to understand such an obvious error in this otherwise well-written and exceptionally well-researched official history. Coincidentally, while flying with the 21st Special Operations Squadron in 1972, I landed on the small helicopter pad used to support Channel "99." While it was certainly an isolated location, this Thai site was infinitely more secure than anywhere in south central Laos.

33. Clayton, interviews, October 27, 1994, and December 9, 1996, and Roura, interview, November 27, 1994. Roura recalled Morris, aged 25, as an especially hard worker with a large family. Scott, 22, was single. The issue of receiving dual benefits, civilian and military, is discussed in chapter 12.

34. "USAF Communications and Air Traffic Control Operations in Southeast Asia, 1960–1973," 45.

35. Electrical message, AMEMBASSY Vientiane to CINCPAC, as cited in Vallentiny, "The Fall of Site 85," 10. Unfortunately a complete, unclassified version of this message, which might explicate the evacuation plans, is still not available.

36. Ibid.

37. CIA field report, January 15, 1968, as cited in Vallentiny, "The Fall of Site 85," 11.

38. Theodore H. Moore letters, June 17 and July 12, 1988, and interview, June 27, 1988. Captain Moore kindly provided me with copies of his flight logs.

39. Located 25 miles NNE of Hanoi.

40. CIA Intelligence Information Cable, "Aircraft Involved in the Attack on Phou Pha Thi (Site 85)," 131338Z Jan 68.

41. Public display entitled "The 'P' Battle," in the Vietnamese Air Force museum, Hanoi. I originally viewed the exhibit on March 1994 and it was still in place during a subsequent visit in November 1996. The model and my visit to Hanoi are further discussed in chapter 15.

42. "Aircraft Involved in the Attack on Phou Pha Thi (Site 85)."

43. Public display entitled "The 'P' Battle," in the Vietnamese Air Force museum, Hanoi.

44. The involvement of a ground controller in this unique attack reinforces the contention that this attempt, and the successful assault on Site 85 in March, was well planned and coordinated. This issue is further discussed in chapter 14.

45. Daniel interview, September 2, 1994.

46. Starling, interview, October 28, 1994.

---

47. Clayton, interview, October 27, 1994.
48. Starling, interview, October 28, 1994, and "Aircraft Involved in the Attack on Phou Pha Thi (Site 85)."
49. Had the Vietnamese pilots departed directly to the north or northwest after the attack they might have reached the relative safety of North Vietnam. There is, however, a mountain directly to the north of Pha Thi and in having to turn northwest the pilots flew directly toward a mountain range that divides the two countries.
50. "Aircraft Involved in the Attack on Phou Pha Thi (Site 85)," and Moore letter, July 12, 1988. During the chase Captain Moore was assisted by Captain Walt Darran, a Continental Air Services (CASI) pilot who had just completed a rice drop to friendly forces from his Pilatus Porter transport. Darran relayed Moore's requests for U.S. Navy carrier-based aircraft in the Gulf of Tonkin. The Navy planes did not arrive. Moore letter, July 12, 1988, and Walt Darran letter, June 20, 1988.
51. The display in Hanoi erroneously proclaimed the site was destroyed.
52. Electrical message, AMEMBASSY Vientiane to SECSTATE, 120740Z Jan 68.
53. Ibid., 121120Z Jan 68.
54. "Aircraft Involved in the Attack on Phou Pha Thi (Site 85)."
55. Vallentiny, "The Fall of Site 85," 12. I have a photograph showing the bombing apparatus.
56. Moore letter, July 12, 1988.
57. Electrical message, AMEMBASSY Vientiane to SECSTATE, January 13, 1968, as cited in Vallentiny, "The Fall of Site 85," 13. It is worth noting that even in this highly classified message Hurwitch continues to refer to the Site 85 equipment as a "navigational facility."
58. Ibid.
59. It must be noted that there may well have been State Department and CIA cables on the issue of "who" ordered the aerial attack. To date none of these materials has been made public. Vietnamese wartime records would surely answer this fundamental question.
60. Located four miles southeast of Phou Pha Thi.
61. United Press International, Vientiane, Laos, January 15, 1968.
62. Goldstein, *American Policy Toward Laos*, 310. A photograph of the aircraft can be found in Berger, *USAF in Southeast Asia*, 128. Numerous Air America and Heavy Green personnel have told me that many "souvenirs" were removed from the aircraft and passed out among them. Woods is said to have recovered the yoke. He was later killed in a crash at Long Tieng. L.M. Irons, interview, September 16, 1994. Irons was a fellow flight mechanic who was a close friend of Woods. In March, Irons would play a significant role in the rescue of Heavy Green personnel from Site 85.

6. Folly at Nam Bac

1. CIA Intelligence Information Cable, "Appraisal of the Lao Armed Forces Defeat at Nam Bac and Repercussions from this Defeat as of 30 January 1968."
2. Conboy, *Shadow War*, 183–84.
3. Ibid., 184–6. Conboy provides a very useful Vietnamese drawing of the attack
4. "Appraisal of the Lao Armed Forces Defeat at Nam Bac and Repercussions from this Defeat as of 30 January 1968,." For a similar Lao army performance, six years earlier, see Goldstein, *American Policy Toward Laos*, 256.
5. Conboy, *Shadow War*, 187.
6. Corn, *Blond Ghost*, 156.
7. Warner, *Shooting at the Moon*, 227.
8. Ibid, 183. Warner's sources include Richard V. Secord, a U.S. Air Force officer assigned to the CIA, and Bill Lair, CIA Chief of Base at Udorn. In my own interviews, Sullivan and Shackley told me Warner has misinterpreted the events and unfairly placed blame. Shackley, interview, and Sullivan, interview, January 16, 1995. Conboy, who has written the most complete analysis of the Lao ground war, has observed that 1967 was a major "turning point" in the war. Conboy, *Shadow War*, 163.
9. On the alleged remark, Shackley told me "It is not something I am likely to have said." Shackley, in the process of writing a book, intends to include an explanation of his role in the Nam Bac disaster. Shackley, interview.
10. Located some 85 miles northwest of Nam Bac near the tri-border area with Burma and China.
11. Located about 35 miles west of Nam Bac.
12. Blaufarb, "Organizing and Managing Unconventional War in Laos, 1962–1970," 37–38. This unique document, written for the Rand company and originally classified secret, is mandatory reading for anyone interested in Laos and/or unconventional warfare.
13. Corn, *Blond Ghost*, 153.
14. Warner, *Shooting at the Moon*, 410.
15. Sullivan, testimony, 496–97.
16. Corn, *Blond Ghost*, 154.
17. Ibid, 136.
18. See chapter 1.
19. Teams, including Americans, South Vietnamese, and indigenous tribesmen, sent into enemy areas to select likely targets for air strikes and to conduct post strike bomb damage assessment.
20. Van Staaveren, *Interdiction in Southern Laos*, 231. For a more detailed discussion of U.S. activities during this period in southern Laos see pp. 229–237.
21. Castle, *At War in the Shadow of Vietnam*, 92–93.

7. The Heights of Abraham

1. *Wolfe at Quebec*, 122, and 133. My interest in the similarities between Phou Pha Thi and the Heights of Abraham was piqued during a 1996 conversation in Vientiane with Dr. James R. Chamberlain, a gifted scholar of linguistics and valued friend.

2. As cited in Liddell Hart, *When Britain Goes to War*, 107. For a detailed analysis of deception see Whaley, *Stratagem: Deception and Surprise in War*.

3. "Installation of MSQ-77 in Northern Laos," 3.

4. Ibid.

5. Vallentiny, "The Fall of Site 85," 5–6. See chapter 5.

6. The North Vietnamese Air Force was becoming increasingly bold in flying operations northeast of Sam Neua province. On January 7, 1968, two MIG-21 fighters fired air-to-air missiles at two A1Es operating near the border. Eleven days later, A1Es were approached by MIGs in the same area. No weapons were fired. During the first week of February, A1Es were twice scrambled to Site 85 to counter a "possible" AN-2 Colt attack. No Colts were sighted in Laos. "56th Air Commando Wing History, 1 January 1968 to 31 March 1968," 32–34.

7. Spence, interview, September 9, 1994.

8. Ibid., and my discussions with several other CIA officers familiar with the defense of Pha Thi.

9. See chapter 5.

10. Colonel Soua Yang, interview, conducted by Brigadier General Soutchay Vongsavanh, August 29, 1995. Soua Yang is now living in Nîmes, France. The decision was not popular with the local Hmong, who felt that the arrival of Soua Yang reflected a lack of confidence in Captain Gia Tou and caused him to "lose face." Gary E. Smith, letter, August 23, 1993. Smith was a Stony Beach Lao linguist who obtained the information from Colonel Lee Lao, a former senior Hmong commander. I heard much the same story in an October 27, 1979, interview with a senior Hmong leader living in California. See Castle, *At War in the Shadow of Vietnam*, 170, note 86.

11. Vallentiny, "The Fall of Site 85," 15.

12. Chalong, interview. Located at Udorn, the Thais covertly provided the CIA with Royal Thai army troops who were "sanitized" and sent into Laos to support the Royal Lao government. See Castle, *At War in the Shadow of Vietnam*, 61, and 111–12.

13. See Warner, *Shooting at the Moon*, 229, for comments on the use of U.S. ground forces to defend Pha Thi.

14. Mooty, interview, and Hill, interview.

15. Spence, letter, September 9, 1994, and Daniel, interview, September 13, 1994. Vallentiny, "The Fall of Site 85," 15, and 23, mentions the introduction of these weapons, but reports the delivery of two 105mm howitzer, two 12.7mm guns,

and two 4.2-inch mortars. Spence is sure there was only one 105mm gun. Spence, letter, September 12, 1994. John Daniel, who along with other teammates fired the 12.7mm, recalls just the one weapon. Daniel interview, September 13, 1994. It is, of course, possible that some of these weapons were deployed with Hmong forces in other areas.

16. The Technical Services Division (TSD) was responsible for developing innovative responses to difficult problems. Excelling in electronic wizardry, the TSD has enjoyed countless unpublicized intelligence collection successes.

17. Spence, letter, September 12, 1994. During a March 1994 investigation at the Site 85 helipad, Joint Task Force Full Accounting (JTF-FA) explosive ordnance disposal (EOD) specialists discovered numerous 2.75 rockets strewn around the area.

18. Spence, interview, September 9, 1994.

19. Houei Houk, which had an adjacent airstrip designated Lima Site 198, was receiving Air America-delivered food and supplies. Quill, interview, and Spence, interview, September 9, 1994.

20. Summers, interview.

21. Daniel, interview, September 2, 1994, and Starling, interview, October 28, 1994.

22. This was for the period up until the actual March attack.

23. Or longer if the aircraft was delayed by weather or maintenance problems.

24. Daniel, interview, September 2, 1994, Starling, interview, October 28, 1994, and Hill, interview. Hill was a radar operator.

25. Because the men were no longer in the military they could not receive government food supplies; none seemed to mind. The cake took more than five hours to properly bake. Summers, interview. One technician claims the men were allowed a case of beer each, but no hard liquor during their duty cycle at Site 85. Clayton had a policy against any alcohol at the mountain and was unaware of any violation. Clayton, interview, October 27, 1994.

26. Daniel, interview, September 2, 1994, and Summers, interview. The exchange of audio tapes with loved ones was a common practice with many American military personnel.

27. Roura, interview, November 27, 1994.

28. No psychological testing was conducted to determine the ability of the men to cope with the isolation of Pha Thi and the pressure to maintain their cover story. While such screening is routine in many military specialities, apparently the Air Force planners concluded the process would be too time-consuming and posed a security risk. Clayton, interview, October 27, 1994.

29. Vallentiny, "The Fall of Site 85," 16–7. Vallentiny has said this reference to a failed test was much stronger in his original draft. When submitted for approval by 7th AF, however, a general "didn't like the tone" and the narrative was "toned down." According to Vallentiny, this was the only passage

deemed controversial in the entire report. Vallentiny, interview, January 27, 1998.

30. 7th and 7/13th AF, OPREP-4 reporting, as cited in Vallentiny, "The Fall of Site 85," 17.
31. See chapter 2.
32. FRUS, 1964-1968, Volume 28, Laos, document 330.

8. Imminent Threat

1. CIA report, Vientiane, February 25, 1968, as cited in Vallentiny, "The Fall of Site 85," 24.
2. Electrical message, CIA Intelligence Information Cable, "Appraisal of Enemy's Dry Season Offensive and His Objectives in Laos as of 5 March 1968," March 4, 1968.
3. CIA report, Vientiane, February 25, 1968, as cited in Vallentiny, "The Fall of Site 85," 22, and electrical message, 7/13th AF to Headquarters PACAF, May 6, 1968. The possession of this information, down to the level of a small reconnaissance patrol, confirms the widespread North Vietnamese knowledge of this campaign and its specific objectives.
4. Upon his arrival at Site 85, Gary was nearing his 35th birthday and had been a combat controller for over ten years. James Gary, interview, June 6, 1995.
5. 7th and 7/13th AF, OPREP-4 reporting, as cited in Vallentiny, "The Fall of Site 85," 2, 3, and 17.
6. AOSEA 43: 1–9, 1–12, 2–6, 2–7. Vallentiny, "The Fall of Site 85," 2, reports twenty-seven missions flown during February over North Vietnam. As stated earlier, it is unlikely there will ever be definitive numbers for these air operations.
7. Electrical message, CINCPACAF to CINCPAC, "Site 85," February 13, 1968.
8. Shackley, interview.
9. CIA report, Vientiane, February 25, 1968, as cited in Vallentiny, "The Fall of Site 85," 24.
10. As cited in Ibid., pp. 24–25.
11. This cable appears to have caught the attention of Secretary of State Dean Rusk. On February 28, the State Department Director of Intelligence and Research forwarded a two-page Top Secret memo to Rusk, "in response to your request for information on the significance of Phou Pha Thi." While mostly very accurate in discussing the equipment and manning at Site 85, the document declares "Prime Minister Souvanna Phouma has authorized the stationing of US personnel at the TACAN sites, but he has not been told about the TSQ-81 at Phou Pha Thi." DDRS, 1995, document 3482. See also FRUS, document 336. This statement is, of course, inconsistent with other official records discussed earlier which detail Souvanna's knowledge of the Heavy Green project. See chapter 3. When asked to comment on this memo, Ambas-

sador Sullivan responded "I can only assume that INR [Intelligence and Research] was not in the loop. Some of the message traffic on that matter was very tightly held." Sullivan, letter, February 5, 1996. The memo also noted that "the enemy has been completing elaborate preparations, including the building of roads," and repeated the judgment that the site would be attacked "within two weeks." While defending the U.S. government in a lawsuit brought by Ann Holland, in 1976 the U.S. Attorney's Office would claim the attack on Pha Thi "was a matter of complete surprise." See chapter 13.

12. Electrical message, Ambassador Sullivan to General McConnell, February 26, 1968, as cited in Vallentiny, "The Fall of Site 85," 25.

13. This critical point is detailed below.

14. More commonly known as Lima Site 20A or Long Tieng, but designated LS-98 in this series of communications.

15. CIA memo, "Emergency Evacuation Plan for Site 85," February 24, 1968, to DO 7/13th AF, as cited in Vallentiny, "The Fall of Site 85," 26–27. It is unclear if the memo was written by CIA personnel at Udorn or Vientiane. The Vallentiny report misstates an important fact regarding the planned evacuation. The reader is told that Site 98 was "nearby" Site 85; in fact, Site 98, or 20A, was located some 120 miles to the south. With regard to a night rescue attempt, numerous senior CIA case officers and Air America and U.S. Air Force helicopter pilots who worked in northern Laos have told me that a night rescue operation at Site 85 would have been a foolhardy and probably impossible undertaking.

16. Electrical message, Air Attaché, Vientiane, to 7/13th AF, March 4, 1968, as cited in Vallentiny, "The Fall of Site 85," 26.

17. Vallentiny, "The Fall of Site 85," 28.

18. Clayton, interview, October 27, 1994. The augmented crew was organized in the following manner. Radar team one: Clarence "Bill" Blanton, Controller; James Calfee, Crew Chief; Patrick Shannon, Board Operator; Donald Worley, Radar Technician; and David Price, Radar Technician. Radar team two: Stanley Sliz, Controller; Richard "Dick" Etchberger, Crew Chief; John Daniel, Board Operator; Donald "Monk" Springsteadah, Radar Technician; and Henry "Hank" Gish, Radar Technician. Non-radar positions were as follows: Mel Holland, Radio Repairman; Jack Starling, TACAN Technician; Willis Hall, Cryptographic Technician; Willie "Bill" Husband, Generator Repairman, Herbert Kirk, Teletype Repairman; and James Davis, Data Computer Operator. Clayton, interview, October 27, 1994, Roura, interview, January 8, 1995, and AF Form 626, Temporary Duty Order, TB-928, October 10, 1967. This is the military order which sent the men to Southeast Asia. Concurrently, the men were covered under Lockheed Aircraft Services civilian documentation.

19. Melvin Holland to Ann Holland, letter, March 3, 1968, and Mooty, interview.

In his letter Holland mentioned the delays in leaving Udorn and said that they would try again the next morning. From the beginning of the Heavy Green assignment Ann Holland retained all of her husband's letters and was kind enough to share a number of the letters with me. Master Sergeant Mooty was assigned to the Layman crew as a radio maintenance technician.

20. See chapter 4.

21. Hill, interview.

22. Clayton, interview, October 26, 1994.

23. Confidential interviews with several Heavy Green team members.

24. Clayton, interview, October 26, 1994.

25. Howard J. Freeman, letter, August 19, 1996.

26. While I understand Freeman's point, the men could have expressed to Lieutenant Colonel Clayton the security rationale for their visit. They did not, but instead chose to hide from their Udorn supervisors this prohibited behavior. Moreover, while Freeman was in a much better position than Sullivan to judge how to interact with the local villagers, the Ambassador had decreed that there be no contact. Had Sullivan known of this fraternization, there seems little doubt that the offenders and Heavy Green would have received some sort of ambassadorial sanction.

27. Roura, interview, January 8, 1995.

28. Melvin Holland to Ann Holland, letter, January 7, 1968.

29. Roura, interview, January 8, 1995. In his last letter to his wife, dated March 8, 1968, Lieutenant Colonel Blanton referred to his recent efforts to increase the number of Heavy Green personnel. Norma K. Blanton, letter, March 7, 1998.

30. Hill, interview.

31. Ibid.

32. Roura, interview, November 27, 1994. The individual is known to me, but there is no compelling reason to reveal his name and add to the grief of his survivors.

33. Gary, interview, Roger D. Huffman, interview, August 22, 1995. Some sources have suggested that Technical Sergeant Gary had a family emergency and this was why he was removed at such a critical moment. According to Gary, however, he left Site 85 as part of his normal rotation and went on to Vientiane, where he was debriefed on the situation at Pha Thi. Gary, interview. Prior to his assignment to Pha Thi, Roger Huffman had participated in nearly fifty combat missions with the 56th Air Commando Wing located at Nakhon Phanom, Thailand. Huffman, interview. Why, as enemy units were closing on Pha Thi, the Air Force would replace a veteran combat controller who had been on the mountain for nearly a month with someone completely unfamiliar with the local threat situation remains unexplained. I have been unable to determine precisely when Huffman arrived on the mountain and when Gary

departed, but feel confident that the switch took place between March 4 and March 8, 1968.

34. Electrical message, American Embassy Vientiane, March 1, 1968. The cable also provides a glimpse of the humor Sullivan often attached to his requests to 7th AF for increased air support in Laos. One of Sullivan's proposed agenda items was "Need for programmed air support in Lao counter-insurgency program, and Vientiane proposal for 'dedication' 56 ACW (accompanying soul music to be provided by Spike Momyer and his singing strings)." Sullivan was intent on gaining a measure of control, or "dedication," over the 56 Air Commando Wing (ACW) at Nakhon Phanom Royal Thai Air Base, Thailand. The Ambassador's efforts to lay claim to these resources was opposed by the 7th AF commander, General Momyer. For additional details on the Sullivan request for a "dedicated" Air Force see electrical message, American Embassy Vientiane, February 20, 1968. The SEACOORD meetings, which alternated between sites in South Vietnam and Udorn, Thailand, permitted senior U.S. military officers and the U.S. ambassadors to Laos, Thailand, and South Vietnam a face-to-face opportunity to exchange views. For Ambassador Sullivan's views on the SEACOORD process see U.S. Air Force Project Corona Harvest Oral History Interview #258, Interview of Ambassador William H. Sullivan, April 15, 1970, 1–5. I am indebted to Colonel Richard S. Rauschkolb, USAF, a dedicated intelligence officer and historian, for bringing this document to my attention.

35. Sullivan, interview, January 16, 1995.

36. Electrical message, 7th AF to Air Attaché, Vientiane, March 2, 1968, as cited in Vallentiny, "The Fall of Site 85," 27–28.

37. I have, however, found no information which suggests that the Lao or Vietnamese communists did intercept Heavy Green transmissions. Someday, perhaps, communist records will answer this question.

38. Freeman, interview, August 27, 1996, and Freeman, letter, August 19, 1996. CIA station chief Ted Shackley confirmed that his case officers had repeatedly requested that the technicians be armed, but that Ambassador Sullivan had always been opposed to what he considered such a conspicuous violation of the accords. Shackley, interview.

39. According to John Daniel, the men who "were neither encouraged, nor discouraged" from target practice. Daniel could not recall the exact number of M-16's at the site, but believed everyone was provided one of the rifles. Daniel interview, September 2, 1994.

40. John Daniel believes more than one person carried a pistol. Daniel interview, September 2, 1994. At some point early in the program, Clayton became aware that one of his men was carrying a handgun at Pha Thi and ordered the man to get rid of the weapon. Clayton, interview, October 27, 1994. It is unknown if the order was followed; the individual is among the eleven men missing from Site 85.

41. Electrical message, *CIA*, March 4, 1968. See also White House Situation Room report to President Johnson, "Heavy Fighting Reported in Southern Laos," February 23, 1968, LBJ Library, NSF CF Laos, Box 272, and Bureau of East Asian and Pacific Affairs, "The Military Situation in Laos," February 27, 1968, LBJ Library, NSF CF Laos, Box 272. The White House Situation Room report was prepared in Washington and transmitted to Johnson at his Texas ranch.

42. Electrical message, *CIA*, March 4, 1968.

43. CIA Intelligence Information Cable, "Appraisal of the Security of the Guerrilla Base at Phou Pha Thi, Site 85, as of 9 March 1968," March 9, 1968.

44. Sullivan, interview, January 16, 1995.

45. Electrical message, CIA Intelligence Information Cable, "Appraisal of the Security of the Guerrilla Base at Phou Pha Thi, Site 85, as of 9 March 1968," March 9, 1968.

46. Although the interview transcript shows TSQ-77, Sullivan was referring to the TSQ-81.

47. Sullivan, oral history, 75–76.

48. During this same period an additional one hundred non-TSQ directed sorties were flown against targets in the area of Pha Thi. 7th and 7/13th AF, OPREP-4 reporting, as cited in Vallentiny, "The Fall of Site 85," 3, and 29. Another Air Force source reports 153 Commando Club missions hit Lao-based targets from March 1–10, but provides no sortie totals. See AOSEA 44, 1: 1–12.

49. In March 1968, the A-6 Intruder, flown by the U.S. Navy and Marine Corps, was the only tactical bomber in Southeast Asia with a true all-weather bombing capability. See chapter 1.

50. Sullivan, interview, January 16, 1995. See also Sullivan, oral history, 76.

51. Although the original document has the abbreviation NVA, which is normally associated with the North Vietnamese Army, based on the context I believe the reference was to North Vietnam.

52. Electrical message, 7th AF to CINCPACAF, March 5, 1968, as cited in Vallentiny, "The Fall of Site 85," 28. This message becomes a critical "smoking gun" when the Air Force later claims the March 11 attack was a "surprise." See chapter 13.

53. Electrical message, CINCPACAF to 7/13th AF, March 5, 1968, as cited in Vallentiny, "The Fall of Site 85," 29. As with many of the documents cited in this report, I have been unable to locate a complete, unclassified copy of OPLAN 439–68. It is, therefore, impossible to judge the soundness of the USAF evacuation plan. In fairness, however, only the CIA would have possessed the most complete knowledge necessary for such an operation. Without the full cooperation and confidence of the CIA, which 7/13th AF did not enjoy, any plan would have been suspect.

54. Electrical message, 7/13th AF to Headquarters PACAF, May 6, 1968. Major

General William C. Lindley, in 1998, did not have a clear recollection of send-ing the message. Upon reviewing a declassified copy he declared he had "never seen it before." Lindley, interview, May 5, 1998. While General Lindley has a good recollection of other details from this period (which are supported in available written accounts), given the strict Air Force procedures for dispatch of such a high-level communication, there can be little doubt he approved the message.

55. Sullivan, interview, January 15, 1995.

56. Sullivan's power and propensity to display it earned him the nickname "Field Marshall." See Castle, *At War in the Shadow of Vietnam*, 77–79.

57. Vallentiny, "The Fall of Site 85," 26.

58. Clayton, interview, October 26, 1994, and Sullivan, interview, January 15, 1995.

59. Sullivan, oral history, 77–78. In our discussions and correspondence, Sullivan did not have a clear recollection of the oral history interview.

60. Discussed in chapter 9.

61. See chapter 11.

62. Sullivan did, however, proudly and emphatically make the point that in more than four years as U.S. Ambassador to Laos Washington had sent him only a handful of directives. Except for these very rare occasions, Sullivan says he per-sonally developed and implemented U.S. policy in Laos. Sullivan, interview, January 17, 1995.

63. Quill, interview, September 20, 1995, Spence, interview, September 12, 1995, and Freeman, interview, August 25, 1996. Freeman had served as a noncom-missioned officer with the 77th Special Forces Group (ABN) and was gradu-ated from Johns Hopkins University. At the time of the attack he had been a CIA adviser to the Hmong for three years.

64. CIA Vientiane report, March 9, 1968, as cited in Vallentiny, "The Fall of Site 85," 29.

65. Electrical message, CIA Intelligence Information Cable, "Appraisal of the Security of the Guerilla Base at Phou Pha Thi, Site 85, as of 9 March 1968," March 9, 1968.

66. Electrical messages, CIA Intelligence Information Cables, "Large-Scale Enemy Move in Direction of Phou Pha Thi, Site 85," and "Enemy Attack Preparations Against Phou Pha Thi, Site 85," March 9, 1968. The reports were transmitted within minutes of each other.

67. Spence, interview, September 12, 1994, and Freeman, interview, August 27, 1996.

68. Spence, letter, September 12, 1994.

69. Lair, interview, March 6, 1994. See also chapter 2.

70. Spence, letter, September 12, 1994.

71. Clayton, interview, October 27, 1994.

72. Following discussions with language and military affairs specialists who have

interviewed hundreds of Vietnamese wartime veterans, I have decided to use the complete name. Because there is a near certainty this is an alias, the individual is a member of a Vietnamese ethnic minority group, and false names were a standard practice, it seems prudent to use both the family and given name.

73. Electrical message, JTF-FA, "Interview of LTC Truong Muc, Leader of Attack on Lima Site 85—Case 2052," October 25, 1994. Later it would become obvious that much of what Truong Muc said in the interview was untrue. Nonetheless, verifiable evidence does suggest he participated in the attack. See chapter 15.

74. See chapter 7.

75. Griffith, ed., *Sun Tzu: The Art of War*, 66, and 69.

9. "Everything to Defeat the U.S. Aggressors"

1. As quoted in Ford, *Tet 1968: Understanding the Surprise*, 208. A North Vietnamese slogan exhorting the people to prepare for what became known as the 1968 Tet offensive.

2. Spence, interviews, September 9 and 12, 1994.

3. Ibid and Spence letter, September 12, 1994. The USAF study on Site 85, citing a February 25, 1968, CIA report, says "another 105 mm howitzer" was recently sent to Pha Thi. Vallentiny, "The Fall of Site 85," 23. Spence does not recall the presence of two 105's, but says that a captured 85mm field gun was sent up to the mountain and placed just north of the CIA living quarters on the opposite side of the helipad.

4. According to CIA reporting the North Vietnamese and Pathet Lao units surrounding Pha Thi were equipped with 105mm howitzers, 81mm mortars, 82mm mortars, 60mm mortars, and various recoilless rifles. Based on the accuracy of the first rounds to hit the mountain on March 10, it seems probable they were fired from a 105mm howitzer. Electrical message, CIA, January 30, 1968. When asked in 1970 for his recollections of the attack, Ambassador William H. Sullivan stated that the initial rounds came from a 105mm gun. Sullivan, oral history, 74.

5. Huffman, interview.

6. Spence also believes that the North Vietnamese may have used the odd-shaped and clearly visible tree as an aiming point for their initial mortar round. Spence, interview, September 12, 1994.

7. Kuhn, letter, March 8, 1994. The combat controller, Roger Huffman, has no recollection of talking with Kuhn. Huffman, interview. Nevertheless, based on Kuhn's detailed notes of the incident, I believe that there was radio contact between the two men.

8. Secord would gain international notoriety in 1988 as a principal figure in the "Iran-Contra" scandal.

Secord and Wurts, *Honored and Betrayed*, 82–84. Lair was far more familiar with Site 85 than either Secord or Clines. Unfortunately, Lair had been called to a meeting in Bangkok.

10. Confidential interviews with two Air Force general officers. I have been unable to locate any record of an Air Force general officer named Arnold C. Craig.

11. Ballard, *Development and Employment of Fixed-Wing Gunships, 1962–1972*, 90, and 105.

12. Ibid., 47, 59, and 62.

13. The AC-130 prototype had a crew of ten and contained state-of-the-art equipment; invaluable prizes if the aircraft had been downed by the North Vietnamese or Pathet Lao. While AC-130 gun ships would later perform extraordinary missions in Laos, in March 1968 they were not candidates for use in any rescue operation at Pha Thi. For details on the AC-47 and AC-130 see Ballard, *Fixed-Wing Gunships*, 262.

14. Senior CIA official, letter, December 10, 1994. Given Secord's normal deportment, it is not difficult to believe he could berate senior officers over the telephone. In this instance, however, a careful review of the facts show that Secord's recollections are incorrect.

15. Daniel, interview, September 2, 1994. Sliz , interview , October 21, 1994, and Starling, interview, October 28, 1994, provided similar accounts. See also Sliz testimony, in Report of U.S. Senate Subcommittee on U.S. Security Agreements and Commitments Abroad of the Committee on Foreign Relations, May 8, 1970, Washington, D.C., 3.

16. Daniel, interview, September 2, 1994.

17. Starling, interview, October 28, 1994.

18. Ibid. Daniel, interview, October 21, 1994, and Sliz, interview, October 21, 1994, reported much the same information.

19. The Heavy Green radio call-sign.

20. Electrical message, AFSSO Udorn, to AFSSO 7th AF, entry in Udorn TACC log, and post-attack survivor debriefing, all as cited in Vallentiny, "The Fall of Site 85," 31–32.

21. Sliz, interview, October 21, 1994.

22. Sliz, testimony.

23. This was the consensus of Daniel, Sliz, and Starling. Daniel, interview, September 2, 1994, Sliz interview, October 21, 1994, and Starling, interview, October 28, 1994.

24. This is a pseudonym; the officer is still on active duty.

25. Spence, interview, September 12, 1994.

26. Log entry, March 10, 1968, Rescue Coordination Center, Udorn air base, Thailand.

27. Rostow memorandum to the president, March 10, 1968. This memo, written at 8:00 P.M. in Washington, D.C., begins by noting that the President had

been "informed this morning" of the situation at Site 85. See below for further details on the Rostow memo.

28. As cited in Vallentiny, "The Fall of Site 85," 32.

29. Entry in TACC Udorn log, as cited in Vallentiny, "The Fall of Site 85," 32, and Spence interviews, September 9 and 12, 1994, and Spence letter, September 12, 1994. Later in the war, the C-130 flare ships would be called "Blindbat" and the "Lamplighter" nickname dropped.

30. Daniel, interview, September 2, 1994, Sliz, interview, October 21, 1994, and Starling, interview, October 28, 1994. The TACAN antenna sustained minor shrapnel damage. Vallentiny, "The Fall of Site 85," 32.

31. Electrical message, CIA, March 10, 1968. Although the dates are different, 17 vice 18 February, this may be a reference to similar information recovered in a Vietnamese notebook with the words "TACAN." See chapter 8, note three.

32. Daniel, interview, September 2, 1994.

33. Clayton, interview, October 27, 1994.

34. Electrical message, Air Attaché, Vientiane, to DIA, March 10, 1968. Under the U.S. Defense Attaché system Colonel Paul Pettigrew worked for the Defense Intelligence Agency (DIA). When queried in 1994, the Colonel did not have a precise recollection of these events, recalling only that "things were very busy that night." Paul Pettigrew, letter, November 29, 1994.

35. Electrical message, CIA , "Initial Results of Enemy Attack on Phou Pha Thi, Site 85," March 10, 1968.

36. Electrical message, JANAF, Vientiane to JCS, March 10, 1968, as cited in Vallentiny, "The Fall of Site 85," 32.

37. Spence, interview, January 11, 1995.

38. Freeman, interview, September 3, 1996, and Freeman's comments as cited in Vallentiny, "The Fall of Site 85," 34.

39. See Whaley, *Stratagem: Deception and Surprise in War*, 128–30, for a discussion on the concept of alternative objectives. This theory comes from the thoughts of Pierre Joseph Bourcet. See chapter 7.

40. Log entry, March 10, 1968, Rescue Coordination Center, Udorn air base, Thailand.

41. TACC Udorn log entry, March 10, 1968, as cited in Vallentiny, "The Fall of Site 85," 33.

42. Electrical message, 7th AF to CINCPACAF, March 5, 1968, as cited in Vallentiny, "The Fall of Site 85," 28.

43. Electrical message, JANAF, Vientiane, to JCS, March 10, 1968, as cited in Vallentiny, "The Fall of Site 85," 33. The discrepancy between the number of men to be evacuated, nine vice eight, is unexplained. To my knowledge there was never a firm list of those to be evacuated at first light.

44. When the first HH-3 rescue helicopters were deployed to Southeast Asia, painted a deep green camouflage color, they soon earned the nickname "Jolly

Green Giant." Their radio call-sign became "Jolly." Later, the much larger HH-53's were called "Super Jolly Green Giants."

45. Log entry, March 10, 1968, Rescue Coordination Center, Udorn air base, Thailand.

46. On March 18, 1968, Detachment 2 was redesignated the 40th Aerospace Rescue and Recovery Squadron (ARRS). As a result, the rescue reports dealing with LS-85 are included in the history of the 40th ARRS. History of 40th Aerospace Rescue and Recovery Squadron, 1 January 1968—31 March 1968. Maxwell AFB, Alabama. For the most comprehensive study of U.S. combat rescue operations in Southeast Asia see Tilford, *Search and Rescue in Southeast Asia, 1961–1975*. Tilford's book is part of the official U.S. Air Force history series on the Vietnam war. Ostensibly for security reasons, the rescue at LS-85 was not included. For an excellent pictorial representation of wartime air rescue in Southeast Asia see *National Geographic* (September 1968): 346–369.

47. As the alert pilots, they would be the primary crew to respond to any rescue mission.

48. Interviews with other Jolly Green pilots and crew members has failed to determine the name of Captain Montrem's co-pilot. Alfred Montrem passed away in 1994, before I was able to conduct an interview. His widow, Helen J. Montrem, was kind enough to share with me some of her husband's personal papers, including his citation to accompany the award of the Silver Star Medal for his rescue work at Site 85. Montrem, interview and letter, February 7, 1995.

49. "Sandy" was the radio call sign for these propeller-driven aircraft. Originally designed for carrier duty with the U.S. Navy, these aging aircraft were slow enough to work very effectively with rescue helicopters, carried significant amounts of ordnance to suppress enemy fire, and had considerable fuel endurance. Francillon, *Vietnam Air Wars*, 70.

50. Russell L. Cayler, interview, February 5, 1995, and Joseph A. Panza, interview, February 10, 1995.

51. Sliz, testimony.

52. Sliz, interview, October 21, 1994, and Daniel, interview, October 21, 1994.

53. Daniel, interview, September 2, 1994.

54. Sliz, testimony.

55. The numerical designator for the Pha Thi TACAN.

56. Starling, interview, October 28, 1994, Cayler, interview, February 5, 1995, and James J. Rogers, interview, February 28, 1995. Starling was unable to recall with any precision his exact location on the side of the mountain. I have, therefore, relied on Cayler and Rogers' recollections of the rescue point. Rogers was the pararescueman. See chapter 10 for specific details on the rescue.

57. Clayton, interview, July 16, 1994. The teletype was "secure," meaning that it produced encrypted messages that could only be decoded by the receiving machine at Udorn air base.

58. "Durax" was the call sign used by Air America to denote any company aircraft involved in a rescue operation. This entry indicates that there were two Air America Helio Super Courier airplanes on the ground at Na Khang awaiting orders.

59. Log entry, March 11, 1968, Rescue Coordination Center, Udorn air base, Thailand.

60. JTF-FA, "Interview of LTC Truong Muc, Leader of Attack on Lima Site 85—Case 2052," October 25, 1994. In his interview, Muc stated the time as 2:30–3:30 A.M. However, at the time of the incident the North Vietnamese recognized a different time zone. In order to maintain a consistent and clear chronology I will use the time as observed by U.S. and Royal Lao forces.

61. Clayton, interview, July 16, 1994. None of these support personnel were required to be in the radar/operations buildings during bombing missions. Adding to the uncertainty of where the men might have been located, records and survivor accounts are inexact in determining whether or not the radar operators were controlling aircraft at the time of the ground attack.

62. Vallentiny, "The Fall of Site 85," 34.

63. JTF-FA, "Interview of LTC Truong Muc, Leader of Attack on Lima Site 85—Case 2052," October 25, 1994.

64. Starling, interviews, September 17, 1994, and October 28, 1994, and NBC News interview May 5, 1994.

65. Starling has provided official and unofficial investigators with varying versions of the North Vietnamese assault. I have carefully reviewed all available interviews and questioned Starling at length on several occasions. The above account, while probably imprecise, represents my best reconstruction of his statements. The inconsistencies are further examined in later chapters.

66. Sliz, testimony and Sliz, NBC News interview.

67. Sliz, testimony. Over the years, Sliz has recounted somewhat different versions of the events of that terrifying morning. I have, therefore, relied mostly on testimony he provided just two years after the fact and the recollections of the other survivors. With regard to the death of Gish, Sliz has recently said that he placed Gish's body, and then his own, over the grenade. Sliz, NBC News interview. John Daniel, who says he was between Gish and Sliz, and is the only other living witness to these events, agrees that Gish was killed almost immediately. "He was shot in the upper and lower body." Daniel says it was he, however, who pushed the corpse onto the grenade. He then "saw Gish blown off the mountain." Daniel, interview, September 2, 1994. Oddly, in recent interviews, Sliz has said little about Dick Etchberger's actions. Hours after their rescue, and the death of Etchberger, Sliz and Daniel described the sergeant's heroic efforts to save his comrades. As a result, Etchberger received a posthumous Air Force Cross Medal. See chapter 11. Sliz has also displayed some bitterness about the level of post-attack recognition, telling an inter-

viewer "And all I got out of it was a Purple Heart [medal] and a pat on the back." Sliz, NBC News, interview.

68. Daniel, interview, September 2, 1994. Sliz has testified that Monk Spring-steadah "died in my arms." Sliz, testimony. Neither Sliz nor Daniel could recall if Springsteadah's body remained on the ledge, or was blown or fell down the cliff side. Sliz, interview, October 21, 1994, and Daniel, interview, October 21, 1994.

10. "One Day Too Long"

1. Electrical message, American Embassy Vientiane, Ambassador Sullivan to SECSTATE, March 11, 1968.
2. Log entry, March 11, 1968, Rescue Control Center, Udorn air base, Thailand, and Cayler, interview, February 5, 1995.
3. JTF-FA, "Interview of LTC Truong Muc, Leader of Attack on Lima Site 85—Case 2052," October 25, 1994.
4. Starling, interview, October 28, 1994, and Daniel interview, September 2, 1994.
5. The veracity of this purported feat has been questioned by special forces-qual-ified personnel from several countries. All have told me that, given the time, distance, and darkness involved, the events described by Truong Muc are highly improbable.
6. JTF-FA, "Interview of LTC Truong Muc, Leader of Attack on Lima Site 85—Case 2052," October 25, 1994.
7. Freeman interviews, May 18, and 30, 1995. Freeman also provided me detailed sketches of his route of travel.
8. Huffman, interview. Years after the loss of Site 85 a hoax was perpetuated on several of the Heavy Green family members and, to some degree, on U.S. gov-ernment investigators. A self-described movie producer claimed that he had interviewed the Site 85 combat controller and the sergeant had reported see-ing at least one American cross his position near the helipad. Clayton, inter-view, October 27, 1994. Later, a Pathet Lao film would be located that showed a body near a 105mm gun located on the lower helipad. This would lead to speculation that an American had been killed on the helipad. As evidenced by the known facts and Huffman's recollections, it is clear none of the Heavy Green technicians escaped during the battle to the helipad.
9. Freeman, interview, May 30, 1995.
10. The "Sandy" call-sign designated a rescue role, while the "Firefly" call-sign identified the aircraft in a strike function.
11. Ibid.
12. Spence, interview, September 12, 1994.
13. Starling, interview, October 28, 1994, and Daniel interview, September 2, 1994.

14. This was the radio frequency assigned to downed airmen. Throughout the war Air America pilots and crews routinely monitored this frequency and, as a result, were often the first on the scene of downed aviators.

15. Despite the rescue plan described in chapter 7, Wood and Irons insist they were not part of any pre-organized rescue. Kenneth E. Wood interviews, September 16, and October 24, 1994, and Loy M. Irons, interview, September 16, 1994.

16. Ibid.

17. This was a metal canister with fold-down seats that allowed the survivor to sit down and grasp the canister while being hoisted up. It was commonly referred to as a jungle penetrator.

18. Irons, interview.

19. Wood, interview, October 25, 1994.

20. Daniel, interview, September 2, 1994.

21. Wood and Irons interviews, September 16, 1994. Understandably, after so many years, it has been difficult for these men to recall precisely when and how certain events transpired.

22. Starling, interview, September 17, 1994.

23. Irons, interview, and Starling interview, September 17, 1994.

24. In praise of his pilot, Rusty Irons had a simple but powerful comment, "Ken Wood did an outstanding job." Irons, interview.

25. Log entry, March 12, 1968, Rescue Control Center, Udorn air base, Thailand.

26. Freeman, interview, October 27, 1995.

27. Rostow memorandum to the President, March 10, 1968. In this early message the number of Americans was erroneously reported, the number was actually nineteen.

28. This does not, of course, exclude the possibility that such material did exist at one time. As with the CIA and USAF records, it is unknown whether these materials still exist, are classified and/or are buried in some unknown archive.

29. Walt W. Rostow interview, October 27, 1994.

30. For an excellent examination of this defining engagement see John Prados and Ray W. Stubbe, *Valley of Decision: The Siege of Khe Sanh.*

31. Spence, interview, September 12, 1994, and log entry, March 12, 1968, Rescue Coordination Center, Udorn air base.

32. Spence, interview, September 12, 1994. Spence believes that Captain Phil Goddard was the Air America pilot who rescued him. In an interview with the author, Goddard confirmed that he performed a rescue at Pha Thi but was unsure if it involved Spence or the earlier pick-up of Freeman. Freeman cannot recall who piloted his aircraft. Phil Goddard, interview, September 14, 1994, and Freeman, interview, May 18, 1995. There is also confusion as to whether or not Huffman departed on the same aircraft as Spence. The Rescue Control Center log records the departure of "two people." In the context of

the log, this indicated two Americans. However, Huffman cannot be certain if he departed with Spence and Spence insists that Huffman did not leave with him. Huffman, interview, and Spence, interview, September 12, 1994. On December 27, 1968, in a ceremony at CIA headquarters, Woody Spence was presented with the CIA's "Certificate of Distinction." In part, the certificate read, "As an assistant adviser to friendly forces, Mr. Spence assumed responsibility for maintaining radio contact with other outposts and defensive positions despite the enemy presence and the hazard of enemy fire." As a result of the enemy barrage, Spence sustained a significant and permanent hearing loss. Upon his retirement from the CIA, Spence received a government disability rating for this injury. Unclassified CIA documents provided to me by Spence.

33. Spence, interview, September 12, 1994. A retired senior CIA official has observed that the Thai were extremely nervous about losing men at Site 85. According to this source, the Thai Headquarters "333" unit at Udorn, which supported CIA operations in Laos, had not received "official" permission from Bangkok to assign Thai forces to Pha Thi. Once it became obvious the Thais were in danger and, perhaps more importantly, at risk of being captured by the Vietnamese and used for propaganda, senior Thai military officers at Udorn were frantic to get their men out. Retired CIA official, interview, March 5, 1994. There were no Thais killed or captured during this attack on Pha Thi. Chalong, interview.

34. Often referred to as "PJs," for para-jumpers, these highly trained medics routinely rode the rescue hoists down to the ground to recover injured airmen.

35. Cayler, interviews, February 5, and 10, 1995, and log entry, March 11, 1968, Rescue Coordination Center, Udorn air base. Co-pilot Panza recalls that as he and Cayler fought to hold the aircraft in a hover the "radio was going nuts" as the C-130 "King" command aircraft was trying to coordinate the mini armada of aircraft swirling about the mountain. Panza, interview.

36. James J. Rogers, interview, February 28, 1995.

37. Cayler, interviews, February 5, and 10, 1995. Rogers made the comment to his crewmates after the rescue.

38. Rogers, interview, and log entry, March 11, 1968, Rescue Coordination Center, Udorn air base. In November 1970, Al Montrem and "JJ" Rogers would serve as members of the elite American team sent into North Vietnam to rescue American prisoners of war at a camp located at Son Tay. See Schemmer, *The Raid.* In November 1978, Major Cayler would lead a U.S. Air Force humanitarian mission to another isolated outpost in the jungle—Jonestown, Guyana, where his unit was responsible for recovering hundreds of dead cult members and returning their remains to the United States. Cayler, interviews, February 5, and 10, 1995.

39. Cayler, interviews, February 5, and 10, 1995, log entry, March 11, 1968, Rescue Coordination Center, Udorn air base, and Panza, letter, June 8, 1996. For

their efforts that day Captains Cayler and Montrem were awarded the Silver Star Medal. Although submitted for a Silver Star, Captain Panza was awarded the lesser Distinguished Flying Cross Medal. In keeping with a squadron policy which dictated that the enlisted members would not be submitted for the same level decoration as the officers, Jim Rogers received a Distinguished Flying Cross Medal.

40. See chapter 15. Berl King subsequently perished in a flying accident. Frank C. Bonansinga, interview, September 16, 1994, and letter, September 22, 1994. Captain Bonansinga was one of the principal pilots involved in this little known, but highly regarded intelligence collection. Although Bonansinga did not fly on the day Site 85 was overrun, he did take photographs of the mountain on March 18, and April 14, and 15, 1968. He has graciously allowed me to read parts of his unpublished manuscript.

41. Quill, notified of the attack while on leave in Thailand, had immediately reported to Udorn and was flown to LS 36 where he joined up with Daniels. It was Quill, of course, who was normally assigned to Pha Thi.

42. Quill, interview, September 20, 1995.

43. Freeman, interview, September 3, 1996.

44. Clayton, interview, October 27, 1994. See chapter 11 for further details.

45. Edward Vallentiny, who authored the project CHECO report on Site 85, has said that a sergeant assigned to his office had a tape recorder and was present when the technicians were returned to Udorn. Vallentiny, interview. These voice recordings, which have been reported by others, have never been located by POW/MIA investigators.

46. Freeman, interview, September 3, 1996. Udorn CIA deputy Pat Landry was also present at the debriefing, but no longer has a clear recollection of what was said. For his actions during the attack on Site 85 Howard Freeman was awarded the CIA's Intelligence Star and the Exceptional Service Medallion.

47. As noted throughout this book, however, Freeman has provided me detailed recollections of his involvement in the attack.

48. Highest possible sending priority.

49. Electrical message, American Embassy Vientiane, Ambassador Sullivan to SECSTATE, March 11, 1968. See also FRUS, 1964–1968, vol 28, Laos, document 341, where the reference to "Lockheed" has been excised.

11. Deniability

1. U.S. Air Force Oral History Program, Interview of General Richard H. Ellis, August 17–21, 1987, 135. Ellis was referring to his tenure as Director of Plans, 1967–69. For Ellis's involvement with Heavy Green see chapters 3 and 4.

2. ''56th Air Commando Wing History, 1 January 1968 to 31 March 1968," 36.

3. Electrical message, AMEMBASSY Vientiane (5073) to SECSTATE, March 12, 1968, and Conboy, 193.

4. Electrical message, AMEMBASSY Vientiane (5073) to SECSTATE, March 12, 1968. It is likely Sullivan was also aware that Captain Cayler and Sergeant Rogers had reported seeing bodies at the site. Sullivan told me that he was presented with "compelling evidence" that none of the Heavy Green personnel had survived. Sullivan, interview, January 16, 1995.

5. Electrical message, AMEMBASSY Vientiane (5103) to SECSTATE, March 12, 1968.

6. Electrical message, AMEMBASSY Vientiane (5119) to SECSTATE, March 13, 1968.

7. Sullivan, interview, January 16, 1995.

8. Sullivan, interview, January 17, 1995, and electrical message, AMEMBASSY Vientiane (5119) to SECSTATE, March 13, 1968.

9. Sullivan, testimony before U.S. Senate Subcommittee on U.S. Security Agreements and Commitments Abroad, October 21, 1969, 489. See chapter 3.

10. Logic dictates that Sullivan understood that effective air strikes would destroy any bodies along with the equipment and other materials. I do not believe, as some have suggested, that he was trying to kill any remaining technicians. He judged the men were already dead.

11. "56th Air Commando Wing History, 1 January 1968 to 31 March 1968," 36, and AOSEA 44: 5-A-6. The pilot of "Sandy 1" was Major Donald E. Westbrook. This loss is further discussed in chapter 15.

12. Electrical message, SECSTATE (129109) to AMEMBASSY Vientiane, March 13, 1968.

13. Electrical message, AMEMBASSY Vientiane (5118) to SECSTATE, March 13, 1968. See below for further details on these documents.

14. Electrical message, SECSTATE (129954) to AMEMBASSY Vientiane, March 14, 1968.

15. Sullivan, interview, January 17, 1995.

16. This procedure is described in chapter 3. The Special Plans office was also in immediate contact with Lockheed.

17. Holland, interview, December 17, 1994. Only ten of the families were contacted by the Special Plans office. Kirk, who had been excluded from the top-secret briefing, was informed by Lockheed and not told of her husband's true status.

18. Interrogatories, June 30, 1977, 24.

19. Western Union Telegram, March 13, 1968. Copy provided by Ann Holland.

20. Holland, interview, December 17, 1994.

21. Electrical message, HQ 7th AF to AMEMBASSY Vientiane, March 14, 1968, as cited in Vallentiny, "The Fall of Site 85," 46.

22. On March 5, 7th AF told Headquarters PACAF the site would probably not be evacuated "until capture appeared imminent." It is certain Momyer knew of this message and probably approved its release. See chapter 8.

23. Electrical message, AMEMBASSY Vientiane (5181), to HQ 7th AF, March 16, 1968, as cited in Vallentiny, "The Fall of Site 85," 46.

24. Ibid, 47. See also FRUS, document 351. In the distribution instructions Sullivan requested the cable "be given absolute minimum distribution."

25. Electrical message, AMEMBASSY Vientiane (5181), to HQ 7th AF, March 16, 1968, as cited in Vallentiny, "The Fall of Site 85," 46–47.

26. TACC Udorn log entry, March 10, 1968, as cited in Vallentiny, "The Fall of Site 85," 33. See earlier discussion chapter 9.

27. Sullivan, oral history, 74–75. This document was originally classified Top Secret.

28. Hill, Mooty, and Summers, interviews.

29. Sliz, NBC interview.

30. See chapter 9.

31. I have interviewed survivors John Daniel, Stan Sliz, and Jack Starling and reviewed public statements by Sliz and Starling. The remaining survivor, Bill Husband, passed away in February 1990, and to my knowledge was never interviewed on the loss of Site 85.

32. Roura, interview, November 19, 1997.

33. Clayton, interview, October 27, 1994. I have been unsuccessful in locating any records related to the 7/13th AF interview of Sliz and Daniel. Like the CIA debriefing of Howard Freeman, they have been misplaced or destroyed. The only available direct references are found in Vallentiny, "The Fall of Site 85." Howard Freeman, who was also aboard the evacuation aircraft, recalls the technicians were questioned by Air Force officials shortly after arriving at the air base hospital. Freeman, interview, September 3, 1996. John Daniel, who believes he was given a morphine shot for the pain, has no recollection of any interview at Udorn. Daniel, interview, September 2, 1994.

34. Vallentiny, "The Fall of Site 85," 34 and 36.

35. Daniel, interview, September 2, 1994. Based on CIA photography and the recollections of the Air Force crew which rescued Starling, it is more likely the technicians fled to the north of the TSQ building and the cliffside area where Starling was eventually rescued. See chapter 10.

36. Sliz, interview, November 21, 1994, and NBC interview.

37. Roura, interview, November 19, 1997.

38. Starling, interview, September 17, 1994

39. Daniel, interview, September 2, 1994. John Daniel has provided me with pertinent copies of his medical records.

40. Husband's wife, Barbara, first learned of her spouse's injuries when she received a letter from the Clark hospital saying, "Hi Honey, suppose you know that I've been wounded and I'm on my way home." She immediately called the Special Plans office for an explanation and was told she hadn't been notified "because the wounds were not important enough." Bill Husband was

also awarded the Purple Heart Medal, but told "not to publicize it." Barbara M. Husband, interview, October 30, 1994, and Chandler D. Husband, October 30, 1994. I am greatly indebted to Mrs. Husband and her son for providing me with details on Bill Husband's wounds and his post-attack activities.

41. According to Starling his injuries were treated at Udorn and after a few days he was driven to Korat to see Sliz. During his hospital recovery Starling says he was urged by a supervisor "to get well soon" so he could return to "repairing TACAN equipment." Starling told them he wanted to depart as soon as possible and was transferred to Bergstrom AFB, Texas, near his home. Despite the tragedy at Site 85, the Air Force had a TACAN program to maintain. Starling, interview, October 28, 1994, and Sliz, NBC interview.

42. Sliz, NBC interview.

43. None of the Heavy Green survivors were trained to respond to the shock and uncertainty of combat. Their observations therefore must be regarded with considerably more caution and skepticism than, for example, combat veterans like CIA officer Howard Freeman and helicopter pilot Russell Cayler. Although air-dropped flares may have occasionally provided some lighting, witnesses and my own March 1994 observations at Phou Pha Thi confirm there was virtually no ambient light. Rocks, trees, buildings, and the mountain's physical features also precluded any clear observations. These physical factors also call into question the purported actions of the *Dac Cong* attackers. See chapters 9 and 15.

44. Cayler, interviews, February 5, 1995, and Rogers, interview, February 28, 1995.

45. Quill, interview, September 20, 1995.

46. Clayton, interview, October 27, 1994, and Roura, interview, November 19, 1997. As described in chapter 10, the agency used a modified Beechcraft turboprop to conduct these reconnaissance missions.

47. Clayton, interview, October 27, 1994.

48. Interview, Udorn-based CIA imagery specialist who examined the photos, March 17, 1995. His name is omitted because he remains in government service.

49. Clayton, interview, October 27, 1994, and Roura, interview, November 19, 1997.

50. Sullivan, interview, January 17, 1995.

51. Electrical message, SECSTATE (132391) to AMEMBASSY Vientiane, March 19, 1968. For a summary of the Pathet Lao broadcast see BBC: Summary of World Broadcasts, March 19, 1968, FE/2724/A3/8.

52. Electrical message, AMEMBASSY Vientiane (5230), to SECSTATE, March 19, 1968.

53. As discussed in chapter 10, in 1994 Rostow said he could not even recall the project.

54. Schulzinger, *A Time for War: The United States and Vietnam, 1941–1975,*

265–66. For an excellent in-depth review of this period see Herring, *LBJ and Vietnam: A Different Kind of War*, 151–77.

55. Richard H. Immerman, " 'A Time in the Tide of Men's Affairs': Lyndon Johnson and Vietnam," in *Lyndon Johnson Confronts the World: American Foreign Policy, 1963–1968*, ed. Warren H. Cohen and Nancy Bernkopf Tucker, 76-79.

56. Johnson, *The Vantage Point*, 435.

57. *The Pentagon Papers: Senator Gravel Edition* 4: 597.

58. Ibid. 5: 275. In 1979 I raised the issue of a connection between the March 31 bombing halt and the loss of Site 85. Castle, M.A. Thesis, "Alliance in a Secret War: The United States and the Hmong of Northeastern Laos," 1979, San Diego State University. Subsequently, my research has revealed errors and serious limitations in these earlier sources. I am now convinced there was no connection between the loss of Site 85 and the subsequent bombing halt.

59. Clayton, interview, October 27, 1994. Following a July 2, discussion in Vientiane with Momyer the Ambassador reported "We both feel that, in current circumstances, there is no justifiable requirement for MSQ [TSQ] installation in Laos." Electrical message, AMEMBASSY Vientiane to SECSTATE, July 3, 1968, as cited in Vallentiny, "The Fall of Site 85," 48. Jerry Clayton recalls, however, that within a month of the site's loss Major Layman was sent to survey a possible new locale. While trying to land the helicopter was taken under gunfire and the survey party barely escaped. Clayton, interview, October 27, 1994.

60. AOSEA 44: 1–11. The F-111 program was also known under the codename "Combat Lancer." See also chapter 2.

61. Roura, interview, November 19, 1997.

62. Ibid.

63. Ibid. As the commander, Clayton signed the recommendation.

64. Robert L. Etchberger, interview, February 25, 1998. Etchberger, Dick's brother, had also been present when Clayton and the Pentagon team briefed the Etchberger family in March 1970. Steven Wilson, Etchberger's twenty-year-old stepson, was then an Air Force sergeant serving in California. He recalls arriving in Washington and being greeted by a military car and driver which took him and the rest of the family to the Pentagon ceremony and a tour of the city. Steven Wilson, interview, February 25, 1998. The other Etchberger children, Richard and Cory, were, respectively, aged eleven and nine at the time of the ceremony.

65. Citation to accompany the award of the Air Force Cross Medal, Richard L. Etchberger. The decoration was authorized by U.S. Air Force Special Order GB-645, December 13, 1968, signed by General J. P. McConnell. I am indebted to the Etchberger family for providing me with a copy of the official order. See below.

66. The decoration was listed without comment in the February 12, 1969, edition of *The Air Force Times*.

67. John Daniel, who shared a copy of his decoration with me, received his Purple Heart from the commander of the Fitzsimons Army Hospital in Denver, Colorado. Daniel was hospitalized for thirteen months and his thigh wound caused a 1.5 inch shortening in his right leg. He was returned to full duty status and in 1975, astonishingly enough, was sent on temporary assignment to the ground-directed bombing program at Nakhon Phanom, Thailand. Daniel had earlier been told that for security reasons none of the Heavy Green personnel could ever return to Southeast Asia. Nonetheless, his name came up for the temporary duty and he went. Daniel, interview, September 3, 1994.

68. Chief Master Sergeant Gary R. Akin, interview, November 25, 1997. Akin is Director, Air Force Enlisted Heritage Research Institute, Air Force Senior Noncommissioned Officers Academy, Maxwell-Gunter Air Force Base, Alabama. My presumption is that in 1968 the incident was considered so sensitive that even unclassified documentation was withheld from Etchberger's personnel file. Until my inquiries, no one had ever raised the issue.

69. Because of privacy considerations, the Air Force was unable to assist in this effort.

70. I am indebted to Steven Wilson, Dick's stepson and an Air Force veteran, and Cory and Richard Etchberger. Although they knew their father was a hero, like most Americans they had no knowledge of Site 85 and project Heavy Green.

71. Akin, interview, February 24, 1998.

72. Wendy Alexis Peddrick, "Crosses and Stripes," *Air Force Magazine*, (April 1998): 61. The inclusion of Etchberger in this article came about through the efforts of Akin.

73. Although the State Department informed Vientiane "USAF investigation now completed," there is no available official record of any official review. Electrical message, SECSTATE (174325) to AMEMBASSY Vientiane , May 31, 1968. Nonetheless, lawsuit materials, declassified materials, and the recollections of the participants permit a helpful reconstruction of these events.

74. Electrical message, SECSTATE (179255) to AMEMBASSY Vientiane , June 7, 1968.

75. Ann Holland has kindly provided me copies of the relevant State Department documents. Although there was no mention of Lockheed in the referenced statement, the form shows "disposition of effects" to "Mr. D. Layman, Lockheed Representative," Udorn Air Base, Thailand, and Lockheed is listed as the employer. Place of death is given as Houa Phan Province, Laos.

76. Hoskinson replaced Cornetti as the Special Plans Office liaison to the Heavy Green wives. The families were located in Arkansas, Kentucky, Louisiana, Missouri, Nebraska, Oklahoma, Oregon, Pennsylvania, and Utah. As noted earlier, Lockheed and not the U.S. Air Force, contacted the Kirk family.

77. "Briefing to Widows," presented by Major Thomas Hoskinson, USAF. In

fact, as discussed above, there had been at least one Pathet Lao media report. Additionally, by this time, detailed articles on the loss at Site 85 had appeared in many U.S. newspapers. See chapter 12.

78. "Briefing to Widows." Ann Holland was visited by Hoskinson on June 13, and verified the contents of the script and memorandum. She provided me with a copy of the briefing. Details of the visit are also covered in "Deposition, Thomas M. Hoskinson, November 14, 1978," Dettloff vs United States of America, No. C-76-131S, 109–120.

79. For an insightful review of the U.S. prisoner situation in Laos during this period see George J. Veith, *Code-Name Brightlight: The Untold Story of U.S. POW Rescue Efforts During the Vietnam War*, 57–78.

80. "Briefing to Widows." The Lockheed insurance policies were held by two separate companies, Traveler's in the amount of $35,000, and Lloyd's of London for $25,000. Holland, interview, December 19, 1994, and Lockheed Aircraft Service Company correspondence to Ann Holland, July 17, 1968 and January 27, 1969.

81. "Briefing to Widows." As an example, Holland's military pay had been $390 a month. His survivors received approximately $200 a month in California Workmen's Compensation and another $250 in Social Security payments.

82. "Plaintiff's Brief in Opposition to Government's Motion to Dismiss or for Summary Judgment," February 4, 1982," Kirk vs Lockheed Aircraft Corporation and United States of America, No. C-76–247R, 5–6. See also *The Seattle Times*, "Laos Death Unsettled Case," April 14, 1983.

83. "Air Support of Counterinsurgency in Laos. July 1968—November 1969," 124–26, November 10, 1969, Headquarters PACAF, Project CHECO report.

84. According to the report "An effective strike in strength on the Sam Neua military complex would destroy or render ineffective the 16 battalions inside the area and a large number of weapons, vehicles, equipment, and supplies." "Air Support of Counterinsurgency in Laos," 127. This is the same area where hundreds of large caves served as safe havens for the communist forces and the local civilian population. U.S. pilots were also held prisoner in this area. In March 1994 I traveled extensively throughout this region as a technical adviser to an NBC News team. See chapter 15.

85. "Air Support of Counterinsurgency in Laos," 127–8. Four AC-130 gun ships had recently arrived at Ubon Air Base, Thailand. See Ballard, *Fixed-Wing Gunships*, 105–7.

86. Ibid, 130.

87. Ibid, 131. There was no further clarification on the presence of Chinese advisers. Extensive research and interviews in the People's Republic of China by Qiang Zhai, however, confirms that Chinese military advisers did serve from 1964–68 in the Sam Neua area. Zhai, "A Secret War: China's Involvement in Laos, 1963–1975," 12–18, unpublished paper.

88. "Air Support of Counterinsurgency in Laos. July 1968–November 1969," 132 and 134. The 927th was one of three battalions assigned to PAVN Group 766. The 148th belonged to the 316th PAVN Division.
89. "Air Support of Counterinsurgency in Laos," 132–33.
90. Ibid.

12. Oath of Secrecy

1. *Public Papers of the Presidents of the United States, Richard M. Nixon, 1970*, 248. See also Kissinger, *White House Years*, 453–56.
2. Holland, interview, December 19, 1994.
3. Ibid.
4. Ibid. According to sworn testimony, Hoskinson says he contacted the U.S. State Department about the news article and was told "it was not associated with our location out there where these people were at." Hoskinson, Deposition, November 14, 1978, 118–19.
5. *The Baltimore Sun*, May 2, 1968, and Holland, interview, December 19, 1994.
6. While senior officers in the Special Plans office were certainly culpable, they were most certainly reporting their actions up the chain of command. Given the high-level interest in Heavy Green, it seems likely that the office of the Air Force Chief of Staff was receiving updates on these developments.
7. Holland, interview, December 19, 1994.
8. Ibid. During his November 14, 1978 deposition Hoskinson did not dispute this conversation with Mrs. Holland, but said he could not recall any specifics. Hoskinson, Deposition, 30.
9. United Press International, "Reds to Bar POW Mail," circa December 1968.
10. Connors, letter to Mrs. Myrtle A. Holland, February 17, 1969, Murphy, letter to Mrs. Myrtle A. Holland, March 12, 1969, and Barnes, letter to Myrtle A. Holland, March 25, 1969.
11. The senior State Department official tasked with POW/MIA issues.
12. Thomas J. Barnes, letter to Mrs. Melvin A. Holland, April 14, 1969.
13. As previously discussed, Herbert Kirk was excluded because his family was never told about the Heavy Green project.
14. I am indebted to Ann Holland for providing me with copies of the above mentioned documents. Life insurance in the amount of $10,000 was paid to the designated beneficiaries.
15. U.S. Air Force Congressional Inquiry Division, Office of Legislative Liaison, letters to Congresswoman Hansen, March 16, 1969, and April 16, 1969. The State Department and U.S. Embassy in Vientiane discussed a March 17, 1968, Pathet Lao broadcast which claimed clearly exaggerated numbers of killed "including some American advisors." See chapter 11. I have been unable to locate any other official mention of these March 21, communist statements.
16. John Hart Ely, "The American War in Indochina, Part II: The Unconstitu-

tionality of the War They Didn't Tell Us About," *Stanford Law Review* 42:1093–94 and 1124–25. Ely's extraordinarily well-researched and documented article is highly recommended for anyone interested in America's secret war in Laos.

17. Prados, *Presidents' Secret Wars*, 284, Colby, *Honorable Men*, 201–2, and Ely, "American War," 1118. Prados recounts a detailed October 1967 CIA briefing to Senator Symington and others on the Senate Armed Services Committee. Some members of Congress later claimed they had been misled about the true nature of the involvement.

18. A bombing pause in North Vietnam was already in effect.

19. As cited in Hammond, *Public Affairs: The Military and the Media, 1968–1973*, 261–62.

20. Ibid, 262–63.

21. See Stevenson, *The End of Nowhere*, 226–27.

22. Hammond, *Public Affairs*, 262–63.

23. Castle, *At War in the Shadow of Vietnam*, 99–100.

24. Hammond, *Public Affairs*, 265. After nearly five years as ambassador, Sullivan departed Vientiane in March 1969.

25. James E. Carty, letter to Senator Warren Magnuson, October 21, 1969, and Magnuson, letter to Carty, October 28, 1969.

26. Prados, *Presidents' Secret Wars*, 284.

27. Symington, Hearings, 365.

28. Ibid, 470. It may well be that Blackburn and Tyrrell were told to dodge the question. Having personal experience in organizing myself and others for congressional testimony, I find it difficult to believe the officers were unprepared for the Pha Thi question. The only other explanation would be that the Air Force had decided not to highlight the subject.

29. Symington, Hearings, 470. In the original transcripts made public in March 1970, the number and USAF were deleted for security reasons. In 1991, through the office of Senator Claiborne Pell, Chairman, Foreign Relations Committee, I was able to obtain the redacted information.

30. Symington, Hearings, 489. This was the phrase placed on the death certificates issued to the Heavy Green families.

31. Symington, Hearings, 490.

32. Ibid, 499.

33. This was operation "Pig Fat," as discussed in chapter 11.

34. At least there has never been a public release of any other discussions about the radar site.

35. Stuart Symington, letter to James E. Carty, October 30, 1969.

36. With regard to the Lao hearings Henry Kissinger has written, "Symington had behaved honorably. In those far-off years, secrets conveyed were still sacrosanct in many Congressional committees; Symington would not release clas-

sified material without the consent of the Administration." Kissinger, *White House Years*, 454.

37. In December 1969, President Nixon had acknowledged the U.S. was conducting a bombing campaign in southern Laos, but refused to comment any further, explaining "I do not think the public interest would be served by any further discussions." Hammond, *Public Affairs*, 266. On February 19, 1970, the *New York Times* reported B-52 air strikes against communist positions in northern Laos. There was an immediate uproar in Congress and on February 25, Senator Symington demanded a public release of the October secret testimony. Symington also wanted the U.S. Ambassador to Laos, G. McMurtrie Godley, flown in from Vientiane to answer his subcommittee's questions. A March 2, editorial in the *Washington Post*, "Laos: The Same Old Shell Game," made clear the administration needed some damage control. Kissinger provides a detailed account of these events, *White House Years*, 452–55. See also Hammond, *Public Affairs*, 269–72.

38. *Public Papers of the Presidents of the United States, Richard M. Nixon, 1970*, 244.

39. Ibid, 248.

40. *The Pentagon Papers: Gravel Edition* 5: 278.

41. *Public Papers of the Presidents of the United States, Richard M. Nixon, 1970*, 248.

42. Kissinger, who approved the initial statement, has said, "Subsequent inquiry into who was responsible for the errors produced the unstartling conclusion that it was the result of a series of misunderstandings and a failure of communication." Kissinger, *White House Years*, 456. On this point, Winston Lord, Kissinger's special assistant and the person responsible for preparing the statement, has said "I was never told of the Site 85 losses." Recalling this as "a very painful time," Lord says "the White House was shocked. It would have been far better, had we known about these losses, for the administration to have admitted to this relatively small number of deaths. At the time we were being accused of far greater involvement in Laos." Lord, interview, January 21, 1998.

43. Prados, *Valley of Decision*, 291. See also Symington, Hearings, 380. Hammond, *Public Affairs*, 273, incorrectly reports 300 casualties.

44. At the same time, all U.S. military personnel in Laos were receiving combat pay. *The Pentagon Papers: Gravel Edition* 5: 277 and 291.

45. Testimony of Ann Holland, Congress, U.S. House of Representatives, "Subcommittee Hearings on the Presidential Determination of 'Full Faith Cooperation' by Vietnam," June 19, 1996, 4.

46. The most detailed story on Site 85 attack appeared in the *Washington Post*, March 16, 1970. Written from Vientiane by longtime Lao watcher T. D. Allman, the article opened, "More than a dozen Americans were killed in Laos two years ago in defense of a secret American installation which assisted U.S. bombings of North Vietnam."

47. Hammond, *Public Affairs*, 274.

48. Etchberger's family was included, even though his body had been returned. Kirk's family, never briefed on the Lockheed cover, continued to be excluded.

49. U.S. Air Force, Special Plans Office, "Trip Report," n.d. (ca late March 1970), 1. The report was signed by Clayton, Zielezienski, and Jackson. Clayton has said he had no part in the preparation of the trip report or the statements contained therein. Dettloff v. United States of America, Clayton Deposition, November 14, 1978, 74.

50. By 1970 Clayton had been promoted from lieutenant colonel to colonel and was working in the Pentagon as a personnel officer.

51. "Trip Report," 1. See also Clayton Deposition, 57–58. The Air Force considered the visits such a top priority that an aircraft and crew were provided the team to transport them around the country.

52. "Trip Report," 1.

53. This same claim was contained in the original April 1967 Joint Chiefs of Staff memo to Secretary of Defense McNamara.

54. See chapter 8.

55. "Trip Report," 2–3.

56. These issues are detailed in chapter 10.

57. Apparently a reference to the March 21, 1968 Pathet Lao propaganda broadcast which claimed "nearly 20 Americans killed."

58. A similar claim, equally lacking in credibility, would later be proffered by the Vietnamese government.

59. See chapter 11.

60. "Trip Report," 3.

61. Ibid, 4. With regard to Clayton's comment on the "President's remarks," it is worth noting that the Special Plans office would later deny there was any connection between Nixon's Laos announcement and their decision to visit the families. See chapter 13.

62. In fact, the Special Plans office questioned each of the families to determine if they had talked to anyone about the project.

63. Both women had remarried.

64. "Trip Report," 4 and 12.

65. Ibid, 5.

66. Ibid, 6–7.

67. Starling, interview, September 17, 1994.

68. "Trip Report," 14.

69. She was remarried.

70. Ibid, 4.

71. Ibid, 6.

72. Ibid, 10–11.

73. Blanton has said her husband was "very committed to the program and really wanted to be there." Although she continues to have questions about how Blanton died, she has come to terms with her loss. Blanton, interview, January 14, 1998.

74. "Trip Report," 7 and 11.

75. Ibid, 9–10.

76. Holland, interview, January 8, 1998.

77. "Trip Report," 9.

78. Holland, interview, January 8, 1998.

79. "Trip Report," 13.

80. See chapter 11. Given the darkness and Starling's hiding place on the mountainside, it would have been impossible for him to have seen the vans.

81. See chapter 9.

82. Ibid.

83. Symington, Sliz testimony, 11.

84. Holland, interview, January 8, 1998.

13. An End and a Beginning

1. From February 12 to April 1, 1973, 591 American prisoners of war, 566 military and 25 civilians, were returned to the United States. North Vietnam released 457, Laos, 9 (via Hanoi), China, 3, and 122 were turned over in South Vietnam. Congress, Senate, Select Committee on POW/MIA Affairs, *POW/MIAs*, Report of the Select Committee on POW/MIA Affairs, 103d Congress., 1st sess., January 13, 1993, p. 247.

2. Herring, *America's Longest War*, 267. The Khmer Rouge took control of Phnom Penh on April 17, the Vietnamese seized Saigon on April 30, and the Royal Lao government was replaced by the Lao People's Democratic Republic on December 2, 1975.

3. Holland, interview and notes provided by her, November 14, 1994. The notes indicate her source of information had either spoken to one of the Heavy Green participants (not necessarily a survivor of the attack) or had gained access to some of the highly classified cable messages on the loss. She did not reveal the man's name.

4. Holland, interview, December 19, 1994, and Holland, testimony, 6–7. "Channel 79" was actually the designation for the TACAN at Long Tieng, Laos. The TACAN at Site 85 was "97." See chapter 2. The very mention of these numbers, however, set off security concerns in the Special Plans office. Clayton retired from the U.S. Air Force February 1, 1973.

5. Dettloff v. Lockheed Aircraft Corporation, Summons, July 22, 1975, 5. This legal document, and others I cite related to this lawsuit, were provided by Holland. I have also profited from a discussion with her attorney, Howard P.

Pruzan. See also "AF Man's Kin Files Suit for $1.6 Million," *Seattle-Post Intelligencer* , July 24, 1975, and "Widow sues Lockheed over husband's death in Laos," *The Seattle Times,* July 24, 1975.

6. Standard Form 95, "Claim for Damage or Injury," July 21, 1975.

7. Dettloff v. Lockheed Aircraft Corporation, "Answer to Complaint for Wrongful Death and Damages for Mental Suffering, No. 799374, August 22, 1975.

8. Dettloff v. Lockheed Aircraft Corporation, "Plaintiff's First Interrogatories to Defendant," No. 799374, December 10, 1975. There were forty multi-part questions.

9. Dettloff v. United States of America and Lockheed Aircraft Corporation, "Plaintiff's First Interrogatories to Defendant United States of America," No. C-76–131, April 1, 1976. There were thirty-seven multi-part questions.

10. I have been unable to locate any White House or Justice Department documents on this issue. Indeed, with the exception of the initial notifications to President Johnson on the loss of the site, there are no known Executive-level documents on the subject of Heavy Green. Nonetheless, *prima facie,* it seems likely the White House would have been advised of such a potentially sensitive and embarrassing lawsuit.

11. Department of the Air Force, Special Plans Office, Memorandum for the Record, "Declassification of Project Heavy Green," May 3, 1976. The Under Secretary's name is omitted in the memo, but official references for 1976 describe James W. Plummer in this position. On April 14, 1976, the United States Attorney for the Western District of Washington wrote Dettloff's attorney, "I have been informed that there is a push on in the Air Force to declassify the information you seek so the interrogatories may be answered in detail but that the decision to do so must go through all chains of command, civil as well as military." Thomas B. Russell, Assistant United States Attorney, Western District of Washington, Letter, to Howard P. Pruzan, April 14, 1976.

12. Only four survivors returned from Laos.

13. Dettloff v. United States of America and Lockheed Aircraft Corporation, First Interrogatories, August 27, 1976, 6a.

14. Ibid, 7–8.

15. Electrical message, 7th AF to CINCPACAF, March 5, 1968, as cited in Vallentiny, "The Fall of Site 85," 28. See chapter 8 for initial discussion of this message.

16. Electrical message, 7th AF to AMEMBASSY Vientiane, March 14, 1968, as cited in Vallentiny, "The Fall of Site 85," 46. See chapter 11.

17. Ibid, 47. See chapter 8.

18. Dettloff v. United States of America and Lockheed Aircraft Corporation, First Interrogatories, August 27, 1976, 9, 10, and 18.

19. See chapter 11.

20. Dettloff v. United States of America and Lockheed Aircraft Corporation,

"Plaintiff's Second Interrogatories to Defendants," No. C-76-131s, September 23, 1976. There were thirty-nine, multi-part, questions.

21. Dettloff v. United States of America and Lockheed Aircraft Corporation, "Plaintiff's Second Interrogatories to Defendants," June 30, 1977, 7.

22. Ibid, 9. Among the errors, Master Sergeant Calfee's name was spelled "Cakfeem," and Staff Sergeant Davis's last name was given as "McKinney." Davis's wife had remarried and this was her new name. It is difficult to believe a serious investigation, carried out by competent attorneys, could have made these errors. Obviously, as evidenced by the other more serious errors in fact, the Air Force was not engaged in an honest effort.

23. Dettloff v. United States of America and Lockheed Aircraft Corporation, "Plaintiff's Second Interrogatories to Defendants," June 30, 1977, 16.

24. See chapter 12.

25. Dettloff v. United States of America and Lockheed Aircraft Corporation, "Plaintiff's Second Interrogatories to Defendants," June 30, 1977, 10.

26. Ibid, 17

27. "Air Support of Counterinsurgency in Laos," 124. It is unclear why the photos were included in this study. The text refers only to Site 85's loss "earlier in the year" and the photos then appear as figure 17. Moreover, photos experts who studied the original film were unable to make any certain judgment on the presence of dead or alive Americans on the side of the mountain. See chapter 11.

28. Dettloff v. United States of America and Lockheed Aircraft Corporation, "Plaintiff's Second Interrogatories to Defendants," June 30, 1977, 19, and Dettloff v. United States of America and Lockheed Aircraft Corporation, First Interrogatories, August 27, 1976, 17.

29. The Air Force did not intend to voluntarily offer Sliz as a witness, however. Citing his right to privacy, they refused to provide the plaintiff's attorney with Sliz's address or phone number. Dettloff v. United States of America and Lockheed Aircraft Corporation, "Plaintiff's Second Interrogatories to Defendants," June 30, 1977, 19.

30. Dettloff v. United States of America, "Judgment," September 28, 1979, 3.

31. Dettloff v. United States of America, "Memorandum," No. 79-4732, June 1, 1981, 4.

32. In 1980 her second marriage was annulled and she reverted to the Holland name.

33. Dettloff v. Lockheed Aircraft Corporation, "Order Granting Defendant Lockheed Aircraft Corporation's Motion for Summary Judgment," March 30, 1982, 3-4.

34. For details on Kirk's entry into the Heavy Green program see chapter 3.

35. The Seattle Times, April 14, 1983. See also Klaus R. Kirk v. Lockheed Aircraft Corporation and United States of America, U.S. District Court, Western Dis-

trict of Washington, "Plaintiff's Brief in Opposition to Government's Motion to Dismiss or for Summary Judgment," C-76–247R, February 4, 1982.

36. Department of the Air Force, Special Plans Office, Memorandum for the Record, "Heavy Green," May 20, 1982, 2.

37. Momyer, *Air Power in Three Wars*, 178–79. At least one Heavy Green target was as close as five nautical miles from Hanoi. See chapter 4.

38. Berger, *USAF in Southeast Asia*, 126.

39. As a senior CIA official once said in a training situation, "Stick to the truth, it's easier to remember."

40. I say "reluctantly," because prior to Judge Rothstein's prodding there is no indication the Air Force ever intended to return Kirk to military status.

41. Klaus R. Kirk v. United States of America, U.S. District Court, Western District of Washington, "Findings of Fact and Conclusions of Law," C-76–247R, April 5, 1983, 5. The benefits had to be used prior to his 25th birthday.

42. *The Seattle Times*, April 14, 1983. After learning from Lockheed in 1968 of her husband's death, Kirk suffered a nervous breakdown and returned to Germany with her other son. The insurance payment did not occur until June 1983, apparently because she was still residing in Germany.

43. See chapter 3.

44. *The Seattle Times*, April 14, 1983

45. The delay in the decision seems to have been caused by the fact that Judge Thomas was based in Mobile, Alabama, and was presiding over a number of other cases. On July 22, 1983, Howard Pruzan wrote the judge about the delay saying "We have heard nothing further regarding the case." This letter was also communicated to the U.S. Attorney's office in Seattle, Washington. Howard P. Pruzan, letter, to Daniel H. Thomas, July 22, 1983.

46. The Judge began his ruling by saying, "When Sgt. Kirk undertook to serve his country in Laos under cover provided by Lockheed, he was for all intensive [sic] purposes a member of the armed services. The military had assumed a duty to provide information to the families of servicemen and women concerning their condition while in the service of their country. This duty was evidenced by the fact that every family other than that of Sgt. Kirk was notified when the men . . . were killed. A further duty arose . . . to reinstate Sgt. Kirk after his death." Klaus R. Kirk v. United States of America, U.S. District Court, Western District of Washington, "Judgment," C-76–247R, August 12, 1983, 10.

47. Ibid, 14.

48. Ibid.

49. *The Columbian*, March 30, 1994. The Holland daughters are Doreen, Carolyn, and Debbie.

50. Whenever the U.S. government receives information about a supposedly unaccounted for person, the name is checked initially against this list. If the

name is not present, a report can still go forward, but often this information is presumed to be false and not pursued.

51. Over the years the JCRC and the Defense Intelligence Agency have received thousands of false names. It is, therefore, quite possible that information could have been initially reported on any of the eleven men, but never processed into the accounting system because—according to the system—none of these men were missing.

52. For a detailed account on the JCRC's predecessor organization, the Joint Personnel Recovery Center (JPRC), see Veith, *Codename: Brightlight*.

53. Mather, *MIA: Accounting for the Missing in Southeast Asia*, 11. Mather, an engineer by training, joined the JCRC at its inception. His people skills are legendary and, amazingly, he served more than half of a 31-year Air Force career in the U.S. Embassy in Bangkok, Thailand. Following his military retirement in 1990 he was hired by the Department of Defense as a civilian POW/MIA analyst, where he still labors at casualty resolution. For a more detailed perspective of JCRC's first two years of operation, see U.S. Air Force, "Joint Personnel Recovery in Southeast Asia," September 1, 1976, Headquarters PACAF, Hawaii. This Project CHECO report, originally classified Secret, contains many excellent primary sources. Unlike Mather's monograph, which was held up for years until officials were confident it presented the correct government facts, this contemporaneous account was written without oversight.

54. The U.S. was never able to gain permission from either the Lao or North Vietnamese governments to conduct missions from Nakhon Phanom into their countries. As a young Air Force sergeant, I was stationed at Nakhon Phanom when the JCRC arrived to establish its headquarters.

55. Mather, *MIA*, 39.

56. Ibid, 39, and 74.

57. Electrical message, JCRC to DIA, "Request for Information (Melvin A. Holland)," July 31, 1980.

58. Joe B. Harvey, interview, October 3, 1997. Like Paul Mather, and many other JCRC and CIL military personnel, Harvey retired from the military and made a near seamless transition from uniform to a government civilian accounting position. Unlike most of them, Harvey is a school-trained Foreign Area Officer (FAO) who did relevant Southeast Asian graduate work and had experience as a mid-level intelligence analyst. At the time of my interview he was the Chief of Staff for the Defense POW-MIA Office.

59. In February 1978, the DIA POW-MIA office evaluated an intelligence report alleging a male Caucasian prisoner had been captured in March or April 1968, near Phou Pha Thi. The intelligence report and the wording of the evaluation makes clear the analyst and her supervisor had some knowledge of the North Vietnamese attack. Intelligence Information Report, "Prisoner of War Report—Capture of a Reported Male Caucasian at Phou Pha Thi," Novem-

ber 17, 1972, and Defense Information Report Evaluation, 2 237 0203 72, February 22, 1978. See later in this chapter for a detailed discussion of these reports.

60. Finding Melvin Holland's name on the Air Force list gave credence to the newspaper report and, to their credit, JCRC analysts then researched the time frame and location of the incident. They discovered a reference to the loss in an unclassified U.S. Army history that described "the North Vietnamese 1968 dry season offensive as the elimination of USAF bombing control facilities in Sam Neua Province, Laos." The source went on to say "in February 1968 the NVA 316th Division seized the control facility at Phou Pha Thi . . . killing all but one of the Americans." JCRC, Memorandum for Record, "Information Received on 17 Nov 1981," November 20, 1981. The unclassified reference was written by a former Royal Lao army general. See Oudone Sananikone, *The Royal Lao Army and U.S. Army Advice and Support*, 142. The monograph also stated, "They [Vietnamese] even employed their air force in a bombing raid against the site manned by USAF officers and men at Phou Pha Thi and two of their old airplanes were shot down" (p. 119). Albeit somewhat incorrectly, once again an official history had discussed Site 85.

61. JCRC, Memorandum for Record, November 20, 1981.

62. In spite of numerous DIA and DPMO archival searches and requests to all U.S. government agencies for any information of possible POW-MIA accounting value, including classified materials, these documents have never been located.

63. My interviews with Freeman, including his invaluable sketches of his search route, were all provided to the other DPMO analysts assigned to REFNO 2052, the Heavy Green case. As indicated in earlier chapters, Freeman's willingness to provide me his recollections has added an otherwise unavailable dimension to this study and, hopefully, will assist in a meaningful resolution of these losses.

64. In 1981, Roger Warner, author and photographer, was perhaps the first westerner to examine the Pathet Lao photographic archives in the Lao Ministry of Information and Propaganda. He obtained extraordinary access to hundreds of wartime photos, including those of crashed airplanes and the corpses and personal property of American personnel. Many of these images are seen in Warner, *Out of Laos—A Story of War and Exodus, Told in Photographs*. Although Warner quickly made his information available to JCRC and DIA, little came of his efforts. Roger Warner, letter and memorandum, June 23, 1981. Many of these same photos are seen in a collage in W. Randall Ireson and Carol J. Ireson, "Laos," in Allen and Ngo Vinh Long, eds., *Coming to Terms: Indochina, the United States, and the War*, 139. One photo shows the mostly undamaged TSQ-81 radar. See also chapter 15.

65. Wartime Pathet Lao propaganda film, "Summer Victory," undated.

Aside from Monk Springsteadah and Hank Gish, killed on the side of the mountain in the presence of multiple U.S. witnesses, there is no conclusive evidence on the purported deaths of the other nine men.

67. For a discussion of these groups and their impact on the POW/MIA issue see Mather, *MIA*, especially 95–100. For another perspective, written by an anti-war activist who believes the POW/MIA issue has been used for political purposes, see Franklin, *M.I.A. or Mythmaking in America*, especially 49–57. The zenith of U.S. official support for the POW/MIA issue came on January 28, 1983 when President Ronald Reagan addressed the National League of Families of American Prisoners and Missing in Southeast Asia at their annual meeting in Crystal City, Virginia.

68. Holland, interview, December 17, 1994.

69. Intelligence Information Report, "Prisoner of War Report—Capture of a Reported Male Caucasian at Phou Pha Thi," November 17, 1972. According to Ann Holland, her husband Melvin is the only missing technician who wore glasses. Moreover, his glasses had light-colored frames. Holland, interview, December 17, 1994.

70. See chapter 10 for the circumstances of the loss.

71. Intelligence Information Report, "Prisoner of War Report—Capture of a Reported Male Caucasian at Phou Pha Thi," November 17, 1972.

72. Although the 1978 evaluation reflects an earlier analysis of the report, this document is no longer available.

73. Some DIA personnel may have known there were serious problems with the "everyone was killed" story. If so, clearly no one was willing to step forward and challenge the Air Force version.

74. See Mather, *MIA*, 71–83. In 1992–93 I supervised screening programs in Hmong and Lowland Lao refugee camps in Thailand. By this time, however, the U.S. was regularly sending teams into Laos. In some cases refugees told me about locations in Laos that I had visited personally. The knowledge gained from in-country investigations allowed more detailed questioning of refugees and reduced the number of spurious reports.

75. A process whereby government personnel excise or black out classified or personal information prior to its public release.

76. It is important to note the declassified copy was not sanitized in any manner. References to foreign governments, CIA operations, and the names of nearly everyone involved were left intact. Similar information contained in other Air Force documents is routinely excised during declassification.

77. Vallentiny, interview.

78. *The Sunday Oklahoman*, "Report Describes Loss of Secret Base," and "Survivor Details Bloody Attack," October 5, 1986. Blanton and Shannon were Oklahoma residents.

79. *The Sunday Oklahoman*, "Atrocity May Have Led to Cover-Up," November

23, 1986, and DIA Intelligence Report, "NVA Participation in the War for Northern Laos: 1955–1973," May 1, 1974.

14. "The Highest National Priority"

1. During his January 28, 1983, speech to the National League of Families of American Prisoners and Missing in Southeast Asia, President Reagan discussed his administration's commitment to gaining the release of any prisoners, achieving the fullest possible accounting of the missing, and repatriating the remains of those killed in the Southeast Asia war. He assured the families and the American public, "The government bureaucracy now understands that these goals are the highest national priority." Mather, *MIA*, 93

2. According to U.S. government records, as of June 1998 there were 2,089 Americans unaccounted for from the Vietnam war. Vietnam, 1,559; Laos, 447; Cambodia, 75; and the territorial waters of the People's Republic of China, 8.

3. Full diplomatic relations with Vietnam were restored on July 11, 1995. Although operating at a reduced level of representation, the U.S. and Laos never severed diplomatic contact. Charles B. Salmon, Jr., a gifted career diplomat, became the first postwar U.S. Ambassador to Laos in 1992. On May 23, 1996, President Clinton nominated ex-Congressman and former Vietnam prisoner of war Pete Peterson to become U.S. Ambassador to Vietnam. Following some procedural wrangling, Peterson assumed the post in early 1997. There are, of course, other important security, economic, and political considerations involved in the U.S.—Vietnamese rapprochement. For a thoughtful discussion of the period leading up to the decision to normalize relations see Keith Richburg, "Back to Vietnam," *Foreign Affairs*, (Fall 1991): 111–31, and Ann Mills Griffiths, "Should we lift embargo against Vietnam?," *USA Today*, February 3, 1994.

4. Allen E. Goodman, "Vietnam's Post-Cold War Diplomacy and the U.S. Response," *Asian Survey* 33 (8) (August 1993): 837. This is an excellent overview which includes many thoughtful viewpoints. The quote, "callousness and deceit," is taken from 1993 remarks to the U.S. Senate Committee on Foreign Relations by Assistant Secretary of State for East Asian and Pacific Affairs (Designate) Winston Lord. The Lao and Vietnamese view is further discussed below.

5. Stern, *Imprisoned or Missing in Vietnam*, 1. Stern, a longtime government employee with an earned doctorate, has traveled extensively to Hanoi with high-level U.S. delegations. Using his own recollections and Vietnamese and English-language sources, he has compiled the most comprehensive study of U.S.—Vietnamese POW-MIA negotiations currently available.

6. Ibid, 129.

7. See chapters 1 and 6.

8. U.S. Department of Defense, "POW-MIA Fact Book," July 1991, 6.

9. For more than two years I worked in the Defense POW-MIA office developing and initiating strategies to bring about access to Lao wartime archival materials. Lao intransigence and a U.S. political decision not to pressure the Lao government on this critical issue has resulted in no meaningful progress. For explicit examples of Lao archival materials see Nordic Institute of Asian Studies, "Libraries in Laos and Vietnam: A Report from a Consultant Mission on the Library Sector in Laos and Vietnam," 1991.

10. I was the first U.S. military researcher allowed into Laos since the Vietnam war. This visit was made possible through the efforts of a valued mentor, Lieutenant General Richard G. Trefry, U.S. Army, retired, then military assistant to President George Bush. I was also greatly assisted in Laos by Charles B. Salmon, then U.S. Chargé d'Affaires, and his talented staff.

11. See Castle, "At War in the Shadow of Vietnam: U.S. Military Aid to the Royal Lao Government, 1955–1975," doctoral dissertation, University of Hawaii, 1991.

12. As of this writing, Khamouan Bhoupa is the Minister of Justice, while Singkapo Sikhotchounamaly is the President of the Lao Peace Committee and the Lao Olympic Committee. Sisana Sisane is semi-retired and is affiliated with the Kaysone Phomvihan museum, dedicated to the former president and secretary general of the Lao Communist Party. Wycoff continues a distinguished career in the U.S. Foreign Service.

13. Singkapo Sikhotchounamaly, interview, August 21, 1990.

14. Singkapo has otherwise shown a willingness to speak his mind. In a February 11, 1994 article in the Lao Communist Party official newspaper, *Pasason*, the general asked, "Who is really selling out their country?" and then went on to suggest it was the country's elite. Apparently the government was not amused, as copies of the newspaper were quickly rounded up and destroyed. Singkapo, a national hero, was not arrested but soon adopted a lower public profile. *Pasason*, February 11, 1994, and interview with informed Laotian official. Interestingly enough, during this same period, Singkapo told an expatriate writer in Vientiane that he was "ready to be interviewed for the record" by western scholars. This information was passed along to Douglas Pike, Indochina Archives, University of California, Berkeley. Pike provided me a copy of the correspondence. While there have been rumors Singkapo has been interviewed by nongovernment affiliated westerners, no information has been made publicly available.

15. Stony Beach, established by DIA in May 1987, was staffed with trained intelligence personnel fluent in Thai, Vietnamese, and Lao. The operation, quite separate from JCRC, had a much more flexible charter for information collection and investigations than the casualty resolution office.

16. D. Warren Gray, interview, August 15, 1991.

17. For background on Singkapo see Wilfred Burchett, "Pawns and Patriots: The

U.S. Fight for Laos," in Adams and McCoy, eds., *Laos: War and Revolution*, 292–93. For a 1950 photograph of Singkapo and the Lao resistance government see Brown and Zasloff, *Apprentice Revolutionaries*, 140. As an indication of his vanity, when I showed Singkapo the photograph he took out his pen and corrected the spelling of his name in the photo's caption.

18. Veith, *Codename: Brightlight*, 32–33. For additional details on the search and rescue efforts for Klusmann, which were mostly carried out by Air America, see Castle, *At War in the Shadow of Vietnam*, 70–71.

19. Electrical message, CIA, February 12, 1965. During the declassification process this message was heavily redacted, to include the subject line and the timing of the Singkapo comments. The intelligence community, of course, has an unedited copy. Soth Phetrasy was the Pathet Lao spokesman in Vientiane who occasionally met with his senior leadership at their Vieng Sai headquarters and elsewhere and then delivered their messages to the press. To accomplish this he traveled via North Vietnam.

20. Electrical message, CIA, "Two American Pilots Held Captive in Khang Khay, Xiengkhouang Province, in May 1965," April 13, 1967.

21. Electrical message, U.S. Embassy Vientiane (2176), March 23, 1973.

22. Electrical message, Defense Intelligence Agency, "Proposed Follow-up on Singkapo Interviews," October 25, 1990.

23. Electrical message, Defense Intelligence Agency, "Contact with LPDR Official Knowledgeable of PW Issue," April 29, 1991.

24. *The Washington Times*, June 3, 1991.

25. Electrical message, U.S. Embassy Vientiane, June 20, 1991. The Soubanh-Wycoff meeting took place the day before.

26. The Singkapo "interview" occurred on August 9, 1991. Gray, interview, August 15, 1991. Curiously, the Lao granted permission for the meeting just after Gray checked in at the airport and completed customs formalities. Gadoury, who the Lao knew to be easygoing and malleable, asked no tough questions and merely carried out the charade of an interview.

27. A U.S. intelligence report of October 19, 1973, stated the Pathet Lao "policy toward foreign prisoners was to treat all prisoners humanely during their temporary incarceration at provincial jails pending turn over to the North Vietnamese." The document did state, however, that this was a post-1968 policy. "U.S. personnel captured prior to 1969 by the NVA were kept by the NVA and any U.S. personnel captured by the PL were kept by the PL." Electrical message, USDAO Vientiane, "IR 2 237 0435 73 (Project 5310–03-E)," October 19, 1973.

28. My 1994 visit to Vieng Sai is discussed in chapter 15.

29. According to the 1991 Department of Defense POW-MIA Fact Book, the precise number was 523.

30. Mather, *MIA*, 141–42.

31. Ibid, 142–43.

32. The collapse of the Soviet Union has also raised the possibility that documents and officials formerly working in Laos and Vietnam might provide details on American POWs and MIAs. Moreover, there have also been reports of American POWs transferred to the former Soviet Union. See "The Cold War in Asia," *Cold War International History Project Bulletin* (5–6) (Winter 1995/1996). With regard to Site 85 there was a stunning find. The Russian Internal Affairs Ministry, working with U.S. government POW-MIA officials, compared the list of American MIAs with persons in the Soviet penal system. On May 14, 1992, the Russians responded with a group of forty-one names, including "Arnold Mikhalevich Holland." Although the name was eerily similar to Melvin A. Holland, the Russians explained Holland was an Estonian born in 1914 who had been convicted by a military tribunal in 1945 for "counter-revolutionary activities." There was no further information. The coincidence was almost too much for Ann Holland who was not officially informed of the document until early 1994. Memorandum, Russian Internal Affairs Ministry, Main Information Center, February 14, 1992, and Holland, interview, December 18, 1994. In 1993, Stephen J. Morris, a Soviet scholar associated with Harvard University, revealed a document purportedly prepared by the former Soviet military intelligence directorate. According to the material, in December 1972 the Hanoi government listed a total of 1,205 Americans captured in all theaters of the war. If true, it meant the Vietnamese had withheld the return of more than 600 American POWs. Dubbed the "1205" document it hit Washington and Hanoi, in the midst of normalization talks, like a bombshell. It remains a highly controversial subject among those who follow the POW-MIA issue. See McConnell, *Inside Hanoi's Secret Archives*, 341–56, Stern, *Imprisoned or Missing*, 100–102, and Stephen J. Morris, "The 1205 Document," *The National Interest* (Fall 1993): 28–42.

33. Stuart-Fox, *Buddhist Kingdom, Marxist State: The Making of Modern Laos*, 204–5.

34. Pike, *Vietnam and the Soviet Union: Anatomy of an Alliance*, 196. See also 191–200 for a very valuable discussion on the Vietnamese-Soviet military alliance.

35. Stuart-Fox, *Laos: Politics, Economics, and Society*, 176, and 182.

36. Mather, *MIA*, 169.

37. For a useful chronology of U.S. diplomatic activity on the POW-MIA issue with Vietnam and Laos up to 1991, see U.S. Senate Report, "POW/MIA's," 370–79.

38. Vessey's efforts, which continued until 1994, are well documented by Department of Defense analyst Lew Stern who took part in much of this dialogue. See Stern, *Imprisoned or Missing*, especially chapters 3–6. Ironically, from 1972–73, Vessey had traveled throughout Laos as the chief of the covert U.S.

military assistance group, Deputy Chief, JUSMAGTHAI. The general knew the Lao quite well. See Castle, *At War in the Shadow of Vietnam*, 103–4. Vessey's concentration on negotiations with the Vietnamese was a concession to their predominant role in POW-MIA accounting and a belief that most of the Lao losses would be explained through Hanoi's assistance.

39. Franklin, xi, and 140. See also McConnell, *Inside Hanoi's Secret Archives*, 170, and Gaylyn Studlar and David Desser, "Rambo's Rewriting of the Vietnam War," in Allen and Ngo Vinh Long, eds., *Coming to Terms: Indochina, the United States, and the War*, 275–88.

40. This subject is reviewed in chapter 15.

41. For a summary of the committee's work see U.S. Senate Report, "POW/MIA's," 1–14.

42. Library of Congress. Congressional Research Service, "POWs and MIAs: Status and Accounting Issues," August 5, 1996. This is a very helpful document, while the massive Senate report is often uneven in quality. Rushed into print, the Senate material suffers from the lack of a good editor.

43. JTF-FA included personnel from all the military services.

44. Mather, *MIA*, 183. Harvey, who had commanded JCRC for eleven years, retired and was immediately hired at CINCPAC headquarters as a senior civilian policy adviser for POW-MIA matters. Repeatedly passed over for promotion to colonel, Harvey now had the equivalent civilian rank. Later, U.S. Army Lieutenant Colonel Johnnie Webb, Harvey's longtime colleague at the Central Identification Laboratory (CIL), would retire and immediately be hired as a civilian deputy at CIL.

45. At this writing JTF-FA continues operations.

46. McConnell, *Inside Hanoi's Secret Archives*, 149.

47. For political and economic reasons hundreds of thousands of refugees were flowing out of Indochina. While a great deal has been written about the boat people, land refugees streaming into Thailand were a significant political and security problem for Bangkok. See SarDesai, *Vietnam*, 135–39. From 1992–93, while assigned to Stony Beach, I interviewed refugees throughout Thailand. I must add, however, that there were several Stony Beach "debriefers" whose language skills were far from fluent—including myself. With pressure from the Senate Committee to increase operations there was little opportunity for lengthy language training or even refresher courses for those of us with prior experience in the language. In my case, in June 1992, I left a position at the Air Force Academy teaching history and within a month was deployed on a field operation. My language refresher training occurred on the ground in southern Laos.

48. George E. Scearce, interview, February 7, 1998, and McConnell, *Inside Hanoi's Secret Archives*, 171–73. I was present in Bangkok for the latter stages of the investigation. Scearce is a retired U.S. Navy intelligence officer, fluent

in Thai and Vietnamese, who would later head Stony Beach. An exceptional manager, gifted with people and computers, he epitomized the talent offered by the Stony Beach operation. He is one of the unsung heros of the POW-MIA accounting efforts.

49. Shorthand for maintaining on-going field operations and archival research, hollow or not, as a demonstration of Lao and Vietnamese cooperation. This, in turn, validates the decision to normalize relations and open the region to economic opportunities.

50. I was assigned to Stony Beach during part of Needham's tenure. During our very first conversation in the U.S. Embassy in Bangkok he told me not to brief him on any classified material—the exact purpose of my visit. Later, I was periodically present in meetings with him in Hawaii, Thailand, and Laos.

51. Two civilian Vietnamese linguists who did complain, Garnett "Bill" Bell and Michael Janich, ultimately resigned from JTF-FA over their differences with Needham. A U.S. Army linguist/analyst who retired as a senior noncommissioned officer with the JCRC and then became a civilian, Bell is generally considered to be an expert on U.S. losses in Vietnam. For a summary of Bell's career and concerns see McConnell, *Inside Hanoi's Secret Archives*, 146–51. Janich's criticisms are detailed later in this chapter.

52. I wish to be explicit that these men all met the posted requirements for their jobs. My point is that they were not trained intelligence debriefers, a skill not all native English speakers could master. I had numerous opportunities to observe their work and never saw anyone who did not try to do his best. Their assignment to these critical jobs without proper training was ill-conceived and, in some cases, produced marginal work. See later in this chapter similar thoughts by a longtime Vietnamese linguist/analyst.

53. I was present in the room for this entire episode. It is worth noting that none of the Lao-Americans publicly protested the order. Apart from being afraid to question the general, they all wanted the opportunity to visit Laos. This was another indication of their naivete regarding the Lao government's intelligence collection efforts.

54. Needham, in an effort to provide the families with as much information as possible, decreed that virtually all reporting would be unclassified. While this caused some difficulties in the protection of intelligence sources and methods, it did result in the creation of thousands of unclassified reports. Although much of JTF-FA's internal communications are conducted via e-mail, and unlikely to be available for review, serious researchers will find much to consider in these materials.

55. Michael Janich, testimony, U.S. House Subcommittee on Military Personnel, June 28, 1995.

56. U.S. Senator Sam Nunn, letter, to National League of Families of American Prisoners and Missing in Southeast Asia, January 2, 1996. The CINCPAC response is an enclosure to this letter.

57. Janich recounts many examples of Vietnamese interference with JTF-FA operations, including the brandishing of weapons at his team. Janich, testimony. My own experiences are that it was routine for the Lao to "pre-interview" witnesses. In the field, where the government officials were always present for any discussions, witnesses were often halted and taken away if they began to recount events unknown to the government. While this does not necessarily mean the person was about to divulge POW-MIA information, it demonstrates a strong government policy—no Lao was to speak to an American without first discussing the information with a Lao official.

58. The oldest and largest organization, the National League of Families of American Prisoners and Missing in Southeast Asia, has struggled for years with financial problems. Nonetheless, their board of directors and executive director, Ann Mills Griffiths, continue to speak out and lobby U.S. and foreign officials for continued and appropriate accounting work. Another strong voice for government action, the National Alliance of Families for the Return of America's Missing Servicemen, carries out their work with volunteers using the Internet, fax machines, and phone networking.

59. I have excluded Cambodia because it is not specifically germane to the losses at Site 85. However, Khmer Rouge veterans and their meticulous records could be vital in resolving American losses in Laos and Vietnam. From 1996–97, I managed the development and operation of a very useful research program in Phnom Penh. A major factor in the success of the project was the hiring on contract of some of the finest Cambodian specialists, including David Chandler and Stephen Heder. Working with Richard Arant, the premier Khmer linguist/analyst in the Department of Defense, these academics uncovered heretofore unavailable information related to U.S. losses in Cambodia. Internal Cambodian political problems and a lack of official U.S. interest have precluded further progress. Nonetheless, this project demonstrated that serious scholars and military specialists can develop significant information from communist records.

60. Goodman, "Vietnam's Post-Cold War Diplomacy," 844. For a thoughtful essay on this subject, carefully framed within the official view of the Democratic Republic of Vietnam, see Luu Doan Huynh, "The American War in Vietnamese Memory," in Jayne S. Werner and Luu Doan Huynh, eds., *The Vietnam War: Vietnamese and American Perspectives*, 243–7.

61. Stephen T. Johnson, "Laos in 1992: Succession and Consolidation," *Asian Survey* 33 (1) (January 1993): 75. The reference to "armed activities" is a reference to Lao rebel factions that the Vientiane government believes, and the facts support, are being subsidized by anti-communist groups outside of Laos.

62. I witnessed this in Laos with four different commanders. They all had their way of coping; one of the best retreated to his room and played the guitar all night. In fairness to the detachment commanders, most decent men working

very long hours, what else could they do? If the officers called into question the integrity of the linguist, or the host government, cooperation would suffer. The commanders were always focused on field operations and remains recoveries. For this important task the linguists were essential. For a candid view by a Hanoi detachment commander on the true level of Vietnamese cooperation see McConnell, *Inside Hanoi's Secret Archives*, 337.

63. Department of Defense, News Release, "Department of Defense announces consolidation of POW/MIA offices," July 16, 1993.

64. Although it was envisioned that DPMO would provide policy and analytical oversight to the JTF-FA, CINCPAC has never been comfortable with such a relationship. As a result, while there is a good deal of coordination between the two organizations, JTF-FA sees itself as beyond DPMO control.

65. I was hired by DPMO in February 1995 as a senior Laotian analyst.

66. See U.S. Senate Report, "POW/MIA's," 172–77.

15. Return to the Mountain

1. Electrical message, JTF-FA, "Detailed Report of Investigation: Priority Case 2052," April 16, 1994. U.S. Air Force Lieutenant Colonel Jeannie Schiff coauthored this section of the report. See following note for a startling change in her perspective. The most comprehensive, nongovernment, study of the North Vietnamese documentation of U.S. wartime losses is McConnell, *Inside Hanoi's Secret Archives*. As indicated by earlier references to this work, I have found it quite compelling with solid, indeed overwhelming, evidence of Vietnamese deceit on this issue. See also, *U.S. News & World Report*, "A treasure trove of Vietnamese horrors: Does Hanoi know more about POW/MIAs?," February 20, 1995. For the Vietnamese reaction to these revelations see Stern, *Imprisoned or Missing*, 85–86.

2. DPMO, Research and Analysis, "Position Paper on SEA Archival Research Proposal, REFNO 2052," February 13, 1997. This paper, which completely ignored extensive contemporaneous CIA reporting, was written by Schiff and GS-15 civil service employee Robert Destatte. At the time, Schiff was the Acting Current Operations Branch Chief and Destatte was the senior Vietnamese analyst. These incredible statements, totally at odds with the facts and Schiff's own findings during her visit to Pha Thi, are further discussed in this chapter. In January 1968 the CIA station reported, "The enemy's operation against Phou Pha Thi appears to be one of his most carefully planned offensives in northern Laos during the war." CIA Intelligence Information Cable, "Enemy Encirclement of Phou Pha Thi, Site 85, in Houa Phan Province and Indications that an Attack on Phou Pha Thi is Imminent," January 30, 1968.

3. PAVN History, "A Military Region Sapper Team's Surprise Attack on the 'TACAN' Site on Pha-Thi Mountain on March 11, 1968," in *Military Region 2, Several Battles During the War of Liberation 1945–1975*. This book was pub-

lished in 1996, but was not translated and provided to the DPMO leadership by Destatte until May 1997. In discussing this Vietnamese language material I have relied on the translation of a skilled U.S. government specialist with more than twenty-five years of experience in this area. The page reference numbers I will cite come from this translation and not Destatte's.

4. The case is part of Joint Field Activity (JFA) 94–4L. The designation consists of the fiscal year, followed by the operation number and country. In this instance, the fourth Lao field activity in fiscal year 1994.

5. Electrical message, JTF-FA, "Summary Report of Joint U.S.-Lao Joint Field Activity 94–4L, 9 Mar—4 Apr 1994."

6. These costs have always been a sensitive subject. While it is widely reported the U.S. government spends more than $100 million a year on POW-MIA efforts, generally little is said about the actual cost breakdown. In Laos the practice has been to pay the Lao government in two checks, one to the Ministry of Foreign Affairs (MFA) and the other to the Ministry of National Defense (MND). In a month-long Lao field activity in early 1995 the Lao government submitted an MND bill for $308,000 in helicopter fees and another for $98,000 in MFA-related expenses. A year later, a similar field activity resulted in a $413,000 MND bill and MFA charges of $113,000. In 1998 the costs had grown to $767,000 for the MND and $112,000 for the MFA. While the helicopter fees are high ($2,800 an hour, flying or not, plus night charges), the Lao government finds other creative financial opportunities during these operations. In 1995–96 any Laotian who supported this work was paid $18 a day. By 1998 the rate was set at $24.50 a day. At jungle sites the U.S. government regularly pays for the services of four people to serve as "cooks and maids for Lao officials" for the period of the field activity. From January 9 to February 12, 1998, these servants cost the U.S. $2,842. The maids and cooks, apparently, also required help. U.S. taxpayers paid another $180 for the construction of a "kitchen area and latrines." These are significant sums in a country where a senior government official receives a salary of less than $125 a month. Because these payments are made in Vientiane it remains unspoken how a villager in remote Laos would then receive these extraordinary wages. The answer is that they do not. There are many other egregious and suspicious fees, but all these expenses are viewed as the cost of doing business. Further, the U.S. government also pays hundreds of thousands of dollars for additional helicopter support from private companies. None of these expenditures, of course, include any U.S. military and civilian costs for salaries, meals, or transportation and housing to and from the provinces. Electrical messages, JTF-FA, "Payment to Lao government for JFA 95–3L," "Payment to Lao government for JFA 96–2L," and "Payment to Lao government for JFA 98–2L." While participating in JFAs I personally watched the exchange of monies and preparation of these payments to the Lao government. The POW-MIA

accounting effort has been, and continues to be, a very lucrative occupation for many Lao officials. The situation may be far worse in Vietnam. For a scathing review of Vietnamese corruption and JTF-FA spending practices see *Honolulu Advertiser*, "Vietnam Skims MIA Search Funds," April 28, 1996.

7. John J. Wright, interview, January 16, 1994.

8. At the time I had retired from the U.S. Air Force and was teaching at the University of San Diego.

9. Meeting in Vientiane with Hiem Phommachanh, Lao Ambassador to the United States, March 12, 1994. Hiem was on home leave attending a funeral.

10. Deth Soulatha, interview, March 12, 1994.

11. Boettcher's brother, Thomas, was a 1967 graduate of the Air Force Academy and had served in Vietnam and later wrote an engaging popular history of the war.

12. I was also privately told that I would not be allowed any contact with Singkapo. Although NBC was very anxious to get the general on film, I demurred. It was clear that such a meeting would have resulted in our immediate departure from Laos.

13. The film also showed footage of a body located near a 105mm howitzer. Because there was such a gun located near the lower helipad at Site 85 the JTF-FA would examine this area for possible remains. However, as detailed in chapter 10, it appears certain none of the Heavy Green personnel escaped during the battle to the helipad.

14. We were lodged at a two-story government guest house our hosts told us was one of only a few structures in Sam Neua not destroyed during the American bombing. The reason, we noted, was its close proximity to a Buddhist shrine. Over a period of more than thirty years, Soviet, Chinese, Eastern European, Vietnamese, and other friends of the Pathet Lao had shared these Spartan, but history-filled, quarters. The JTF-FA personnel were living in a local hotel.

15. I was told by Kendall, whom I had worked with when assigned to Stony Beach, that it had taken him nearly a year of difficult negotiations to gain access to Pha Thi. He did not believe we could gain permission in a few days. Kendall was a competent officer, but he did not know the Lao very well. He depended upon William Gadoury, who had recently traded his sergeant stripes for a civilian position, and Gadoury seemed particularly upset by our presence. When we prevailed, both men seemed chagrined by our success.

16. Khamphanh Phimmavong, interviews, March 17–18, 1994.

17. Formerly Lima Site 107, it was now a small Lao military outpost with an adjacent Hmong village.

18. They were flown aboard small French-built helicopters belonging to the Lao West Coast charter company and flown by mostly New Zealander pilots. The charter company is routinely hired by the JTF-FA to move personnel into areas not accessible by other means. Having flown with them through-

out northern and southern Laos, I can testify to their extraordinary airmanship.

19. Deth Soulatha, not keen on riding in small helicopters, voluntarily remained behind.

20. Siphon, interview, March 18, 1994. This was the same officer mentioned by the deputy governor.

21. JTF-FA, "Detailed Report of Investigation: Priority Case 2052," April 16, 1994.

22. Even if the North Vietnamese forces were frequently rotated out of the area, it strains credibility to believe they all lived in total isolation from the Lao. How did the exchange of security responsibilities take place, where, and how, did the North Vietnamese purchase their food supplies and other necessities? Siphon's claim that the two groups could not communicate is simply ridiculous. For a detailed discussion of the Vietnamese-Pathet Lao relationship see Edwin T. McKeithen, "The Role of North Vietnamese Cadres in the Pathet Lao Administration of Xieng Khouang Province." McKeithen, a gifted Lao-speaker, served in Laos for several years.

23. In addition to eleven men missing from Site 85, Major Donald Westbrook was lost in a March 13, 1968, A1E/H crash on the slopes of Phou Pha Thi. See chapter 11. Moreover, there are a number of other U.S. losses in Houaphan that might have been the subject of the Lao communication.

24. Electrical message, National Security Agency, "Remains of American War Dead," June 7, 1977. The censoring of more than half the text of this message makes it very difficult to analyze.

25. JTF-FA, "Detailed Report of Investigation: Priority Case 2052," April 16, 1994.

26. See chapter 3.

27. Clayton, interview, March 19, 1994.

28. Ibid. Clayton could not understand why he was being treated so shabbily, but remained silent lest the JFA further restrict his activities.

29. Schiff and I, acquaintances from my Stony Beach assignment, also discussed the case.

30. Clayton, interview, March 19, 1994.

31. Rosenau had been assigned to work on a high priority task force supporting U.S. operations in Somalia and could not make the trip to Laos. I have known him professionally for nearly ten years. He had interviewed many of the principals, including Jerry Clayton and Jack Starling, and doubtless would have been much more aggressive in investigating the possibility of captured Americans. In contrast to Schiff's limited field experience, Rosenau had spent years in Okinawa leading Marines in jungle warfare training scenarios, was accomplished in land navigation, and felt at ease in remote and physically challenging surroundings. He had an infantryman's perspective which, coupled with

his in-depth knowledge of the case, would have been invaluable on the mountain. Two years later, his unwillingness to compromise his integrity and knowledge of the case would bring about a serious confrontation with Schiff and her views on the Site 85 losses.

32. See chapter 11.

33. JTF-FA, "Detailed Report of Investigation: Priority Case 2052," April 16, 1994. While some bones were found near the former radar building, they were determined to be nonhuman. It was my privilege to have earlier worked with Bob Mann on a number of other investigations, mostly in southern Laos.

34. Ibid.

35. Ibid.

36. Ibid.

37. Ibid.

38. Electrical message, Department of Defense, USDAO Bangkok, "Report of Live Sighting Investigation, LA-004, Phou Pha Thi, Laos," May 2, 1994. An evaluation of this report is found in electrical message, DIA, "IIR Evaluation, Report of Live Sighting Investigation, LA-004, Phou Pha Thi, Laos," July 26, 1994.

39. Obviously, as one who had studied Laos for more than twenty years, the visit to Vieng Sai was a very exciting and special time. The others, including Deth, who had never been in Houaphan province, were also most impressed with the people and environs. Our NBC team remained in Laos for another ten days filming JFA activities in Xiengkhouang and touring the Plain of Jars and the royal capital at Luang Prabang. Returning to Vientiane, John Wright continued to donate his expertise and photo supplies at the Lao film archives and Geoff Stephens busied himself with a myriad of production concerns. Mike Boettcher departed for another story in Vietnam, but we arranged to join him in Hanoi.

16. Hanoi

1. The rest of the NBC team, having other commitments, had since returned to the United States.

2. Deth Soulatha, Interview, April 14, 1994, and JTF-FA , FAX message "Witness to Phou Pha Thi Incident–Case 2052," September 14, 1994. NBC, unaware of the hoax, aired footage of the Le Thuy interview on the August 3, 1994. See below.

3. I was allowed to take extensive photos and video of the museum displays. The staff, which collected our entrance fee, quickly wandered off. They seemed pleased to have a few dollars on a day where there were no other visitors.

4. DPMO Research and Analysis, "Position Paper on SEA Archival Research Proposal, REFNO 2052," February 20, 1997.

5. There was minimum damage to the site and two aircraft were lost. See chapter 5

6. Stern, *Imprisoned or Missing*, 87–88.
7. As I have discussed earlier, there were competent area and language qualified military officers who had the intellectual curiosity and breadth to undertake this important work. Academically trained government civilians were also available. Lewis Stern, a DOD analyst and expert on the Vietnamese, would have been an outstanding candidate for a serious research position.
8. While in Hanoi John Wright invited Destatte to join us for dinner. Destatte, who I knew slightly from my Stony Beach tour, complained of his medical problems. He had nothing but praise, however, for the Vietnamese. He explained that they were now doing their very best and should not be criticized. I was not the only person who noted this drastic change in his former vitriolic attitude toward the Vietnamese.
9. Ann Mills Griffiths, letter, April 14, 1998.
10. JTF-FA Memo, "National League of Families Questions Regarding Phou Pha Thi," March 23, 1994, and JTF-FA , "Witness to Phou Pha Thi Incident— Case 2052," September 14, 1994.
11. This would later prove to be quite false.
12. Electrical message, JTF-FA, "Summary of POW-MIA Technical Meeting, Hanoi 27," July 28, 1994.
13. The program was broadcast on August 3, 1994, after having been preempted several times by high-priority domestic news events. NBC was unaware of Le Thuy's apparent hoax. The show did feature interviews and photography of the bomb damage in Laos, prompting Lao Ambassador Hiem Phommachanh to write Deth Soulatha a letter of appreciation. Deth Soulatha, interview, September 30, 1994.
14. JTF-FA , "Witness to Phou Pha Thi Incident– Case 2052," September 14, 1994.
15. In a later interview, discussed below, these initial statements would be significantly revised.
16. Ibid.
17. Ibid.
18. Electrical message, DPMO, "Proposed interview with witness to Phou Pha Thi incident," September 27, 1994.
19. The responsibility of the field collector is to obtain information for analytical review. While field comments can be an important part of this process, finished analysis is conducted with the benefit of all-source materials unavailable to field personnel. This is standard procedure in all reputable intelligence collection activities.
20. Interview, George E. Scearce, February 2, 1998. Scearce served as the deputy and then team chief for the DIA Stony Beach program. In this capacity he frequently interacted with the Vietnamese. A number of other linguists who have worked with the VNOSMP have affirmed the pervasive presence of these trained intelligence officers.

21. The VNOSMP had also received specific information from the JTF-FA about the Pha Thi case. This information sharing is risky, but unavoidable. The Indochina governments must be provided with the details of each loss in order to conduct witness and document searches. The danger, of course, is that these data will be used to construct false but plausible explanations for the American losses. U.S. investigators must be on guard for this duplicity and, in this case, it seems clear that material in the Air Force CHECO report on Site 85 made the scam more believable. This is precisely why a field collector cannot conduct proper analysis. All-source information must be factored into any final determinations. The very worst situations, however, involve the U.S. passing these governments the names of people believed to have POW information. In Laos, this has sometimes resulted in terse responses claiming that the individual is dead, retired, or cannot be located. One is left to speculate on what happens to those people with information considered "unhelpful" to their communist government.

22. See chapter 14.

23. In late 1995, in a DPMO meeting convened to discuss the possibility of a re-interview, Destatte vehemently objected. He exclaimed that he was certain Truong Muc was "telling the truth" because "he cried in front of me." Destatte then added that another interview would be "inconvenient" for Truong Muc. In more than twenty years of academic and military interviewing I had never found tears to be an infallible sign of veracity. It also seemed odd that Destatte would be more concerned about impinging on the time of a retired North Vietnamese soldier, well paid by the U.S. for his trouble, than gaining the fullest accounting.

24. JTF-FA, "Interview of LTC Truong Muc, Leader of Attack on Lima Site 85—Case 2052," October 25, 1994.

25. The ledge was mostly undamaged at the time; Bill Husband had run down this same path to jump on the rescue hoist.

26. Ibid.

27. See chapter 13.

28. See chapter 10 for discussion of photo reconnaissance flights. One photograph, dubbed the "wing" photo because the aircraft's wing is so obvious, shows very little damage to Site 85. While it is has been impossible to fix an exact time and date, CIA personnel associated with the program believe it was taken on March 11, 1968.

29. This is the same excuse used by the Lao government which claims the remains of two Americans known to be held prisoner near Vieng Sai, whom the Lao say died of illness, were destroyed by U.S. air strikes. Veith, *Codename Brightlight*, 62–70, and 365.

30. JTF-FA, "Interview of LTC Truong Muc, Leader of Attack on Lima Site 85—Case 2052," October 25, 1994.

31. Ibid.
32. Ibid.
33. During more than three years association with the JTF-FA, this was the only instance where I saw an attempt to conceal the travel and presence of a foreign government official. The normal practice was to list them in the reporting message, and this was especially true for Vietnamese and Lao officials traveling to other countries. For one thing, the travel had to be documented so they could be paid their special allowances. More importantly, however, case analysts needed to know who was present during witness interviews. In this instance, no one reading the report would know that a senior Vietnamese intelligence officer had controlled Truong Muc's interview. When I first asked Destatte about the coaching at Pha Thi he denied any irregularities. Later, when advised there was a video tape of the interview (taken by a U.S. team member), he admitted it was Lieutenant Colonel Pham Teo standing between him and Truong Muc. No one could explain why Pham Teo's name does not appear in the official report. A U.S. Embassy Vientiane report of the Truong Muc visit also omits any mention of the intelligence officer. This message describes how Truong Muc "carefully examined" the mountaintop before describing what happened. An analyst, or anyone else reading this, would have no idea the interview was being carefully monitored and sometimes coached by Pham Teo. While the message came from the U.S. Embassy, the practice was for the JTF-FA representative to author MIA-POW reports. Electrical message, U.S. Embassy Vientiane, "Vietnamese Witness at Phou Pha Thi," December 15, 1994.
34. Electrical message, JTF-FA, "Detailed Search and Recovery of Case 2052," January 13, 1995. Pham Teo, Truong Muc, and Destatte remained for only a brief time. The recovery team spent nearly a month on Pha Thi, departing each afternoon for their quarters in Sam Neua, in some of the most difficult and dangerous recovery work in Laos. Their extraordinary work is often forgotten when, through no fault of their own, it produces no answers.
35. Needham had been promoted during his JTF-FA tour.
36. Electrical message, JTF-FA, "Commander's Observations of Recovery Operations Concerning REFNO 2052—Interim Report," December 29, 1994. This message was a bit unusual in that the National Security Council (NSC) was the "principal" addressee, as opposed to the more normal "information" addressee on the message routing. One probable explanation for the NSC interest is that the Clinton administration was about to announce steps to normalize diplomatic relations with Vietnam. A successful remains recovery from Pha Thi would have been a nice show of Vietnamese and Lao cooperation.
37. Specifically, we interviewed the rescue pilots, pararescueman, combat controller, all three case officers who worked at Site 85, and located a rescue log

that established a critical time-line. Information gained from these contacts has been included in earlier chapters.

38. This was, understandably, a very difficult situation for Rosenau. Nevertheless, he handled it with great integrity. As noted in earlier chapters, I had interviewed Starling on several occasions and also concluded he was not a dependable witness.

39. Wold fully supported my efforts to establish archival research programs in Laos and Cambodia and we often discussed how DPMO might improve JTF-FA research in Vietnam. Nonetheless, Vietnam remained off-limits to my research strategies.

40. DPMO internal memorandum, DASD Wold to Dr. Castle, December 11, 1996.

41. DPMO, Facsimile from Robert Destatte to Gary Flanagan and Master Sergeant Ron Ward, JTF-FA, Hanoi, February 13, 1997. Flanagan and Ward are Vietnamese linguists. Flanagan, a retired sergeant, is a civil servant who works for the detachment commander. Like his contemporary William Gadoury in Laos, his well-paid job depends on maintaining good relations with his communist counterparts.

42. Ibid.

43. It is an unfortunate fact of life in DPMO, where many employees are upset with office and administration policies regarding POW-MIA work, that documents were often shared with outsiders. In this case, I believe the memorandum was circulated in an effort to embarrass the office.

44. This meeting was also attended by two congressional staffers. A week after the Gilman meeting I resigned from DPMO and accepted a faculty position at the Air Command and Staff College, Maxwell Air Force Base, Alabama. Although the timing may have suggested otherwise, my departure from DPMO had been planned for many months. I departed the office with very mixed feelings. My work with Cambodian archival materials had been very promising and I continued to hold out some hope we could convince the Lao government to approve meaningful archival research and oral history programs. Nonetheless, there were frustrations with these projects and a realization that the DPMO leadership was unable or unwilling to address serious deficiencies within the office. After more than two years I was ready for a change and the prospects of spending more time with my family and returning to the classroom and my own research interests were the final determining factors.

45. PAVN History, "A Military Region Sapper Team's Surprise Attack on the 'TACAN' Site on Pha-Thi Mountain on March 11, 1968," in *Military Region 2, Several Battles During the War of Liberation 1945–1975*.

46. Ibid, 11–12.

47. Ibid, 9. Elsewhere in the article the team is reported to have also carried hand grenades and satchel charges.

48. Ibid, 12, and 14.
49. A regional military/political committee.
50. Identified elsewhere in the document as located some 25 miles northwest of Pha Thi.
51. Ibid, 14, 15, 18.
52. Ibid, 20. In the context of the narrative it is clear the author is recounting fighting between the *Dac Cong*, the technicians, and other defenders. Therefore, it is not possible to determine with any precision the number of Americans killed or wounded.
53. Ibid, 22–3.
54. Ibid, 23.
55. Ibid, 25.
56. Ibid, 27.
57. According to George "Jay" Veith, an author and researcher specializing in Vietnamese wartime documents, this PAVN history of Phou Pha Thi represents "textbook Party and military intelligence operations." Veith, interview, February 19, 1998. For a useful explanation of the NVA Party apparatus, complete with diagrams, see also U.S. Army, Republic of Vietnam, Combined Military Interrogation Center, "NVA Political Structure," Report no. 427–66/1100, November 15, 1966.
58. This small building, housing a limited number of documents and photographs, is a wonderful public relations venue. The VNOSMP and JTF-FA relish showing visiting Americans this "visible sign of cooperation." There is much more symbolism than substance, but most people on one- or two-day sojourns to Hanoi have no way of knowing the hollowness of Vietnamese assistance. Griffiths, who has dealt with the Vietnamese for years, does not fall into this category.
59. Griffiths, interview, February 10, 1998, and letter, April 14, 1998.
60. It was unexplained how he would have known this fact.
61. DPMO, Memorandum, "Update on Status of Investigation of Case 2052," July 27, 1997. Vietnamese specialists believe otherwise, pointing out that the Northwest Military Region General Staff Department document would normally contain detailed political, military, and intelligence information. Obviously, this would include the names of additional units and participants in the attack. Veith, interview, February 20, 1998, and Scearce, interview, February 17, 1998.
62. Stern, *Imprisoned or Missing*, 24—2-5.
63. Electrical message, JTF-FA, "Translation and Evaluation of Vietnamese Document: VNOSMP Unilateral Investigation Report of Case 2052," February 20, 1998.

SELECT BIBLIOGRAPHY

Books and Articles

Ballard, Jack S. *Development and Employment of Fixed-Wing Gunships, 1962–1972.* Washington, D.C.: Office of Air Force History, 1982.

Bates, Charles C., and John F. Fuller. *America's Weather Warriors.* College Station: Texas A&M University Press, 1986.

Bauss, W. ed., *Radio Navigation Systems for Aviation and Maritime Use.* New York: Pergamon Press, 1963.

Berger, Carl., ed. *The United States Air Force in Southeast Asia. An Illustrated Account.* 2d ed. Washington D.C.: Office of Air Force History, 1984.

Berman, Larry. *Lyndon Johnson's War.* New York: W.W. Norton, 1989.

Blaufarb, Douglas S. "Organizing and Managing Unconventional War in Laos." Rand Corp. 1972. Reprinted by Dalley Book Service, Christiansburg, Virginia.

Bowers, Ray L. *Tactical Airlift.* Washington, D.C.: Office of Air Force History, 1983.

Branfman, Fredric C. *Voices From the Plain of Jars. Life under an Air War.* New York: Harper & Row, 1972.

Broughton, Jack. *Going Downtown: The War Against Hanoi and Washington.* New York: Simon & Schuster,1988.

Brown, MacAlister, and Joseph J. Zasloff. *Apprentice Revolutionaries: The Communist Movement in Laos, 1930–1985.* Stanford: Hoover Institution Press, 1986.

Burchett, Wilfred. "Pawns and Patriots: The U.S. Fight for Laos." In Nina S. Adams and Alfred W. McCoy, eds. *Laos: War and Revolution.* New York: Harper & Row, 1970.

Castle, Timothy N. *At War in the Shadow of Vietnam: U.S. Military Aid to the Royal Lao Government, 1955–1975.* New York: Columbia University Press, 1993.

Clodfelter, Mark. *The Limits of Air Power: The American Bombing of North Vietnam.* New York: The Free Press, 1989.

Colby, William E. *Honorable Men.* New York: Simon & Schuster, 1978.

Colby, William E. with James McCargar. *Lost Victory.* Chicago: Contemporary Books, 1989.

Conboy, Kenneth. *Shadow War: The CIA's Secret War in Laos.* Boulder, Colorado:Paladin Press, 1995.

Corn, David. *Blond Ghost. Ted Shackley and the CIA's Crusades.* New York: Simon & Schuster, 1994.

Dommen, Arthur J. *Conflict in Laos: The Politics of Neutralization.* 2d ed. New York: Praeger, 1971.

Ely, John Hart. "The American War in Indochina, Part II: The Unconstitutionality of the War They Didn't Tell Us About." *Stanford Law Review* 42: 1093–1125.

Ford, Ronnie. *Tet 1968: Understanding the Surprise.* London: Frank Cass & Company, 1995.

Francillon, René J. *Vietnam Air Wars.* London: Aerospace Publishing, 1987.

Franklin, H. Bruce. *M.I.A. or Mythmaking in America.* New Brunswick, New Jersey: Rutgers University Press, 1992.

Goldstein, Martin E. *American Policy Toward Laos.* Teaneck, N.J.: Farleigh Dickinson University Press, 1973.

Goodman, Allen E. "Vietnam's Post-Cold War Diplomacy and the U.S. Response." *Asian Survey* 33 (8), (August 1993): 832–47.

Hamilton-Merritt, Jane. *Tragic Mountains. The Hmong, the Americans, and the Secret Wars for Laos, 1942–1992.* Bloomington: Indiana University Press, 1993.

Hammond, William M. *Public Affairs: The Military and the Media, 1968–1973.* Washington, D.C.: Center of Military History, 1996.

Herring, George C. *LBJ and Vietnam: A Different Kind of War.* Austin: University of Texas Press, 1994.

—— *America's Longest War: The United States and Vietnam, 1950–1975.* New York: McGraw-Hill, 1996.

Herring, George C. ed., *The Pentagon Papers: Abridged Edition.* New York: McGraw-Hill, 1993.

Hibbert, Christopher. *Wolfe at Quebec.* Cleveland: World Publishers, 1959.

Immerman, Richard H. "A Time in the Tide of Men's Affairs': Lyndon Johnson and Vietnam." In *Lyndon Johnson Confronts the World: American Foreign Policy, 1963–1968,* eds. Warren I. Cohen and Nancy Bernkopf Tucker, 57–97. New York: Cambridge University Press, 1994.

Ireson, W. Randall, and Carol J. Ireson. "Laos." In Douglas Allen and Ngo Vinh Long, eds. *Coming to Terms: Indochina, the United States, and the War.* Boulder: Westview, 1991.

Johnson, Stephen T. "Laos in 1992: Succession and Consolidation." *Asian Survey* 33 (1) (January 1993)75–82.

Kissinger, Henry. *White House Years.* Boston: Little, Brown and Company, 1979.

Lewy, Guenther. *America in Vietnam.* New York: Oxford University Press, 1978.

Liddell Hart, B. H. *When Britain Goes to War.* London: Faber and Faber, 1935.

Luu Doan Huynh, "The American War in Vietnamese Memory." In Jayne S. Werner and Luu Doan Huynh, eds. *The Vietnam War: Vietnamese and American Perspectives.* New York: M. E. Sharpe, 1993.

Marolda, Edward J., and Oscar P. Fitzgerald. *The United States Navy and the Vietnam Conflict. Volume II. From Military Assistance to Combat, 1959–1965.* Washington, D.C.: Naval Historical Center, 1986.

Mather, Paul D. *MIA: Accounting for the Missing in Southeast Asia.* Washington, D.C.: National Defense University Press, 1994.

McConnell, Malcolm. *Inside Hanoi's Secret Archives. Solving The MIA Mystery.* New York: Simon & Schuster, 1995.

McKeithen, Edwin T. "The Role of North Vietnamese Cadres in the Pathet Lao Administration of Xieng Khouang Province." Vientiane, Laos. American Embassy, April 1970. Unpublished paper.

Mirsky, Jonathan and Stephen E. Stonefield, "The Nam Tha Crisis: Kennedy and the New Frontier on the Brink." In Nina S. Adams and Alfred W. McCoy, eds. *Laos: War and Revolution.* New York: Harper & Row, 1970.

Momyer, William W. *Air Power in Three Wars.* Washington, D.C.: Office of Air Force History, 1978.

Morris, Stephen J. "The 1205 Document." *The National Interest* (Fall 1993): 28–42.

Oudone Sananikone. *The Royal Lao Army and U.S. Army Advice and Support.* Washington, D.C.: Center of Military History, 1978.

Paul, Roland A. "Laos: Anatomy of an American Involvement." *Foreign Affairs* (April 1971), 49: 533–47.

The Pentagon Papers: The Senator Gravel Edition. 5 vols. Boston: Beacon Press, 1973.

Pike, Douglas. *PAVN: People's Army of Vietnam.* Novato, California: Presidio, 1986.

—— *Vietnam and the Soviet Union: Anatomy of an Alliance.* Boulder: Westview, 1987.

"POW-MIA Fact Book." Washington D.C.: Defense Department, 1991.

Prados, John. *Presidents' Secret Wars. CIA and Pentagon Covert Operations From World War II Through Iranscam.* New York: Quill, 1986.

Prados, John, and Ray Stubbe. *Valley of Decision: The Siege of Khe Sanh.* Boston: Houghton Mifflin, 1991.

Prouty, Fletcher L. *The Secret Team: The CIA and its Allies in Control of the World.* New York: Ballantine, 1973.

Public Papers of the Presidents of the United States, Richard M. Nixon, 1970. Washington, D.C.: Government Printing Office, 1971.

Randle, Robert. *Geneva 1954: The Settlement of the Indochinese War.* Princeton, N.J.: Princeton University Press, 1969.

Richburg, Keith. "Back to Vietnam." *Foreign Affairs* (Fall 1991): 111–31.

Robbins, Christopher. *The Ravens: The Men Who Flew in America's Secret War in Laos.* New York: Crown, 1987.

SarDesai, D.R. *Vietnam. The Struggle for National Identity.* 2 ed. Boulder: Westview, 1992.

Schemmer, Benjamin F. *The Raid.* New York: Harper, 1976.

Schlight, John. *The War In South Vietnam. The Years of the Offensive, 1965–1968.* Washington, D.C.: Office of Air Force History, 1988.

Schulzinger, Robert. *A Time for War: The United States and Vietnam, 1941–1975.* New York: Oxford University Press, 1997.

Secord, Richard V., with Jay Wurts. *Honored and Betrayed: Irangate, Covert Affairs, and the Secret War in Laos.* New York: Wiley, 1992

Sharp, U.S. G. *Strategy for Defeat.* San Rafael, California: Presidio, 1978.

Sheehan, Neil, et al. *The Pentagon Papers as Published by the New York Times.* New York: Quadrangle Books, 1971.

Stern, Lewis M. *Imprisoned or Missing in Vietnam: Policies of the Vietnamese Government Concerning Captured and Unaccounted for United States Soldiers, 1969–1994.* Jefferson, N.C.: McFarland & Company, 1995.

Stevenson, Charles A. *The End of Nowhere: American Policy Toward Laos Since 1954.* Boston: Beacon, 1972.

Stuart-Fox, Martin. *Laos: Politics, Economics, and Society.* London: Frances Pinter Publishers, 1986.

—— *Buddhist Kingdom, Marxist State: The Making of Modern Laos.* Bangkok: White Lotus, 1996

Stuart-Fox, Martin, and Mary Kooyman. *Historical Dictionary of Laos.* London: The Scarecrow Press, 1992.

Studlar, Gaylyn, and David Desser, "Rambo's Rewriting of the Vietnam War. In Douglas Allen and Ngo Vinh Long, eds. *Coming to Terms: Indochina, the United States, and the War.* Boulder: Westview, 1991.

Sullivan, William H. *Obbligato: Notes on a Foreign Service Career.* New York: Norton, 1984.

Tilford, Earl H. Jr. *Search and Rescue in Southeast Asia, 1961–1975.* Washington, D.C.: Office of Air Force History, 1980.

—— *Setup - What the Air Force Did in Vietnam and Why.* Maxwell AFB, Alabama: 1991.

Van Staaveren, Jacob. *Interdiction in Southern Laos, 1960–1968.* Washington, D.C.: Center for Air Force History, 1993.

Veith, George J. *Code-Name Brightlight: The Untold Story of U.S. POW Rescue Efforts During the Vietnam War.* New York: The Free Press, 1998.

Warner, Roger. *Shooting at the Moon: The Story of America's Clandestine War in Laos.* South Royalton, Vermont: Steerforth Press, 1996.

—— *Out of Laos: A Story of War and Exodus, Told in Photographs.* Rancho Cordova, California: Southeast Asia Community Resource Center, 1996.

Westmoreland, William C. *A Soldier Reports.* New York: Dell, 1976.

Whaley, Barton. *Stratagem: Deception and Surprise in War.* Cambridge, Mass.: Massachusetts Institute of Technology, 1969.

Yang Dao. *Hmong at the Turning Point.* Minneapolis: WorldBridge Associates, 1993.

Interviews

Akin, Gary R. November 25, 1997, February 24, 1998.

Armstrong, Harold D. December 6, 1994.

Blood, Gordon F. October 26, 1994.

Bonansinga, Frank C. September 16, 1994.

Born, A.J. December 10, 1994.

Cayler, Russell L. February 5, 1995, February 10, 1995.

Chalong Nakpong. March 6, 1994.

Clayton, Gerald H. , July 16, 1994, August 26, 1994, October 26, 1994, October 27, 1994, July 27, 1996, December 9, 1996, August 9, 1997, November 21, 1997.

Daniel, John G., September 2, 1994, September 13, 1994, October 21, 1994.

Deth Soulatha. March 12, 1994, April 14, 1994.

Etchberger, Robert L. February 25, 1998.

Freeman, Howard J. May 11, 1995, May 18, 1995, May 30, 1995, October 27, 1995, August 25, 1996, August 27, 1996, September 3, 1996.

Gary, James. June 6, 1995.

Goddard, Phil. September 14, 1994.

Gray, D. Warren. August 15, 1991.

Hall, Mary C. December 10, 1996.

Harvey, Joe B. October 3, 1997.

Hill, Donnell C. February 16, 1995.

Holland, Ann. November 14, 1994, December 17–19, 1994, January 19, 1997, January 8, 1998.

Huffman, Roger D. August 22, 1995.

Husband, Barbara M. October 20, 1994.

Husband, Chandler D. October 20, 1994.

Irons, Loy M. September 16, 1994.

Khamphanh Phimmavong. March 17–18, 1994

Lair, James W. August 17, 1990, March 6, 1994.

Landry, Lloyd. August 17, 1990.

Lindley, William C. May 5, 1998.

McCormack, Dennis X. December 5, 1996.

Montrem, Helen J. February 7, 1995

Moore, Theodore H. June 27, 1988.

Mooty, Norman D. January 7, 1995.

Panza, Joseph A. February 10, 1995.

Quill, Terry. June 8, 1995, September 20, 1995.

Randle, Alan C. December 14, 1994, January 17, 1997.

Rogers, James J. February 28, 1995.

Rostow, Walt W. October 27, 1994.

Roura, Francis A. November 27, 1994, January 8, 1995, November 19, 1997.

Scearce, George E. February 2, 1998, February 7, 1998.

Seitzberg, Robert C. November 20, 1994.

Shackley, Theodore G. December 17, 1996.

Sharp, U.S.G. March 6, 1990.

Shirley, John E. August 1, and 17, 1990.

Singkapo Sikhotchounamaly. August 21, 1990.

Siphon. March 18, 1994.

Sliz, Stanley J. October 21, 1994.

Spence, John W. September 9, 1994, September 12, 1994, January 11, 1995.

Starling, Jack C. September 17, 1994, October 28, 1994.

Sullivan, William H. January 15, 1995, January 16, 1995, January 17, 1995.

Summers, Harold D. January 14, 1995.

Triantafellu, Rockly. February 24, 1998.

Vallentiny, Edward. January 27, 1998.

Vang Pao. February 6, 1979.

Westmoreland, William C. April 13, 1990.

Wilson, Steven. February 25, 1998.

Wood, Kenneth E. September 16, 1994, October 24, 1994, October 25, 1994.

Wright, John J. January 16, 1994.

Correspondence

Blanton, Norma K. March 7, 1998.

Bonansinga, Frank C. September 22, 1994.

Clayton, Gerald H. January 11, 1997.

Darran, Walt. June 20, 1988.

Freeman, Howard J. August 19, 1996.

Giraudo, John C. October 12, 1994.

Holland, Ann January 18, 1997.

Kuhn, Ernie. March 8, 1994.

Momyer, William W. November 11, 1997.

Montrem, Helen J. February 7, 1995.

Moore, Theodore H. June 17, 1988, July 12, 1988.

Panza, Joseph A. June 8, 1996.

Pettigrew, Paul. November 29, 1994.

Smith, Gary E. August 23, 1993.

Spence, John W. September 12, 1994, June 14, 1995.

Triantafellu, Rockly. April 21, 1998.

Westmoreland, William C. March 3, 1990.

INDEX

Ford, Gerald, 178
Foreign Area Officer program (U.S. Army), 211
France, 20, 262*n*52, 325*n*18; *see also* French forces
Franklin, H. Bruce, 315*n*67
Freedom of Information Act, 191, 193
Free French forces, 18
Freeman, Howard ("Howie"), 301*n*43; air strikes ordered by, 127–28, 171; arrival of, 107; background of, 289*n*63; bombing coordinates from, 116; debriefing of, 136, 138, 145, 189–90, 300*n*33; decoration of, 298*n*46; DPMO and, 314*n*63; foray by, 148; on Hmong forces, 117; on hospital interviews, 300*n*33; reconnaissance by, 125–26, 170, 171, 220, 230, 232; rescue of, 130, 135, 296*n*32; rocket fire by, 111, 114; Rodman and, 115; threat assessment briefing by, 108; on villagers, 274*n*8, 286*n*26
French and Indian War, 86, 90
French forces, 18, 90, 131

Gadoury, William, 199, 318*n*26, 325*n*15, 331*n*41
Gary, James: arrival of, 94, 284*n*4; departure of, 101, 286–87*n*33; Huffman and, 100, 101; visual control by, 95
Geneva Accords (1954), 19, 262*n*52
Geneva Accords (1962), 16, 102, 104; "armed reconnaissance" flights and, 164; CIA and, 23; communist violation of, 17, 21; LBJ and, 33; MSQ-77 proposal and, 247; protection issue and, 37, 249; site destruction and, 244; Sullivan and, 22, 27, 101, 287*n*38; terms of, 20

Geneva Conference (1954), 9
Geneva Conference (1961), 19–20, 21, 22
Geneva Convention (1949), 37, 38, 47, 249, 268*n*12
Gia Tou, 88, 278*n*24, 282*n*10
Gilman, Benjamin A., 239, 331*n*44
Giraudo, John C., 52–54, 55, 59–60, 250, 272*n*72
Gish, Henry ("Hank"): death of, 123, 146, 231; final witnesses of, 171, 176, 237, 252, 315*n*66; hiding position of, 120, 220; remains of, 156, 232; responsibilities of, 285*n*18; Sliz on, 177, 294*n*67; Special Plans team on, 172; unaccounted for, 136
Gish, Mrs. Henry ("Hank"), 172
Goddard, Phil, 296*n*32
Godley, G. McMurtrie, 307*n*37
Goodman, Allen E., 194, 210
Gray, D. Warren, 199, 236, 318*n*26
Great Britain, 9, 19, 20, 86, 160
Griffiths, Ann Mills, 322*n*58, 332*n*58; report copy of, 228, 229, 243; VNOSMP and, 242
Guerin, John P., 260*n*34
Gulf of Mexico, 260*n*36
Gulf of Tonkin, 102, 259*nn*16, 23, 260*n*36, 274*n*14, 280*n*50
Gulf War (1991), 269*n*27

Ha Dong boat yard, 62
Haiphong, 16, 273*n*2
Hall, Mary, 48, 172, 191
Hall, Willis: alleged death of, 172, 176; ambush of, 122; responsibilities of, 285*n*18; unaccounted for, 136, 252, 270*n*45
Hamilton-Merritt, Jane, 258*n*9
Hammond, William M., 307*n*43